Reshaping the
American Workforce
in a Changing Economy

Edited by
Harry J. Holzer and Demetra Smith Nightingale

Reshaping the
American Workforce
in a Changing Economy

Edited by Harry J. Holzer and Demetra Smith Nightingale

THE URBAN INSTITUTE PRESS
2100 M Street, N.W.
Washington, D.C. 20037

Library of Congress Cataloging-in-Publication Data

Reshaping the American workforce in a changing economy / edited by Harry J. Holzer and Demetra Smith Nightingale.
    p. cm.
    Conference papers.
    Includes bibliographical references and index.
    ISBN 0-87766-735-7 (alk. paper)
    1. Labor market--United States--Congresses.   2. Labor supply--United States--Congresses.   3. Manpower policy--United States--Congresses.   I. Holzer, Harry J., 1957–   II. Nightingale, Demetra S.
    HD5724.R444 2006
    331.10973--dc22   2006039474

Printed in the United States of America

10   09   08   07   1   2   3   4   5

THE URBAN INSTITUTE is a nonprofit, nonpartisan policy research and educational organization established in Washington, D.C., in 1968. Its staff investigates the social, economic, and governance problems confronting the nation and evaluates the public and private means to alleviate them. The Institute disseminates its research findings through publications, its web site, the media, seminars, and forums.

Through work that ranges from broad conceptual studies to administrative and technical assistance, Institute researchers contribute to the stock of knowledge available to guide decisionmaking in the public interest.

Conclusions or opinions expressed in Institute publications are those of the authors and do not necessarily reflect the views of officers or trustees of the Institute, advisory groups, or any organizations that provide financial support to the Institute.

CONTENTS

ACKNOWLEDGMENTS

We want to thank the Joyce Foundation, and especially Whitney Smith and Jennifer Phillips, for their generous financial support for the project on which this book is based.

We held our conference at the Urban Institute in Washington D.C., on November 11, 2005, with the support of both the Urban Institute and the Johns Hopkins University Institute for Policy Studies. We thank the following individuals who participated in the conference that day as either session chairs or discussants: Robert Atkinson, Jared Bernstein, Betsy Brand, Susan Dynarski, Nada Eissa, Ron Haskins, Edward Montgomery, Marion Pines, Alice Rivlin, Howard Rolston, Steven Savner, Isabel Sawhill, Ray Uhalde, Andy Van Kluenen, and Wayne Vroman. Mason Bishop of the U.S. Department of Labor provided stimulating comments in a lunchtime talk, as did Tony Carnevale of the National Center for Education and the Economy as the conference "rapporteur."

We also benefited from the hard work and dedication of many staff members of the Urban Institute and Johns Hopkins, including Mildred Woodhouse, Latasha Holloway, Anne DeCesaro, Edward McGaffigan, Emily Gallagher, Fredrica Kramer, and John Trutko. We appreciate the comments and assistance of Kathleen Courrier, and several members of the staff of Urban Institute Press, as this manuscript went to press. Finally, we thank two anonymous referees for helpful suggestions.

INTRODUCTION

Labor markets in the United States have been buffeted by a range of forces over the past few decades. Business demand for workers at various skill levels has changed, due to large-scale technological changes, workplace reorganizations, and growing trade. Some businesses report that they continue to have difficulty finding and retaining highly skilled workers. At the same time, some less-skilled workers find it harder to maintain regular, stable employment. Also, the institutions (such as unions and minimum wage laws) that have traditionally protected low-wage workers have weakened. As a result, employment outcomes have changed quite dramatically, with growing wage and employment gaps between more- and less-skilled workers. The relative wages of less-educated workers have declined, and inequality in the labor market has grown.

Both the supply and demand sides of the labor market will continue to change in major ways over the next decade and beyond, though in ways that cannot be predicted with complete accuracy. On the supply side of the market, the retirements of baby boomers and continuing immigration (as well as the relative youth of the immigrant population already here) will generate some major changes in the demographic makeup of the workforce. For instance, the Bureau of Labor Statistics (BLS) and the Census Bureau project that

- the labor force will grow more slowly over the period 2004–14—at a rate of just 1.0 percent a year—than it has in the preceding decade (1.2 percent) and in the one before that (1.4 percent);

- there will be virtually no net growth in the number of young workers (i.e., those age 16–24 and those age 25–44) in the labor force in this decade, while the number of workers age 55 and above will grow by over 40 percent; and
- minorities will account for over one-third of the labor force by 2014 and just about half the nation's population by 2050—with Hispanics accounting for 15 percent and 24 percent, respectively.[1]

Important changes will no doubt occur on the demand side of the labor market as well. For instance, BLS projects that

- manufacturing jobs will continue to decline (by 0.6 percent each year) and those in construction and wholesale trade will grow more slowly than average, while jobs in professional and business, educational, and health care services will grow rapidly (at 2.5 percent a year or more); and
- production jobs will continue declining (at 0.9 percent each year) while those in the high-paid professional categories and low-paid service categories will grow most rapidly (at roughly 2 percent a year—see Saunders 2005).

The demand-side projections suggest continuing growth at the top and bottom ends of the job distribution relative to the middle, though some occupational and industrial growth in the latter will certainly continue.[2] These projections are also somewhat more uncertain than those on the supply side of the labor market, as demand-side developments will reflect changes in technologies and trade patterns that are somewhat harder to predict from those in the past. The demand-side changes will also reflect the growing "offshoring" of work by U.S. firms, particularly to China, India, and other newly emerging industrial economies, that are not captured in the BLS projections to date (Saunders 2005).

What kinds of impacts will all these developments have on the U.S. labor market? Baby boomer retirements will likely generate a slowdown in the growth of the U.S. supply of labor, while growing offshoring will likely generate a decline for U.S. workers on the demand side. All else equal, the slowdown in labor-force growth should result in tighter labor markets, generating better employment opportunities and perhaps higher wages for U.S. workers, while offshoring implies the opposite.

Will these two developments simply offset one another, or will one outweigh the other? Given that the exact future magnitudes of baby boomer retirements and especially of offshoring remain unclear, it is somewhat difficult to predict in advance which will dominate.[3] Technological changes and immigration are most likely to compound the effects of offshoring and generate further reductions in demand for less-skilled workers, though even here future trends remain uncertain.

But, along one dimension, the effects of baby boomer retirements and growing offshoring are likely to be similar: both should generate a growing demand in the United States for worker education and skills, relative to the current supply of educated and skilled workers. The baby boomers will be replaced by younger workers, including many immigrants in the labor market, whose average educational attainment is considerably lower than the current workforce's. Thus, the demand for skills in the labor market will likely grow at or near its recent trend, while the supply of skills may fail to grow proportionately (Aspen Institute 2003).

The impacts of offshoring on demand for skills are somewhat harder to predict, as it may involve occupations that require a fairly wide range of skills (Bardhan and Krol 2003; Mann 2003). But, even if offshoring (and other technological changes) completely dominates the demographic shifts described above, the importance of education and skills in the workforce is likely to grow. For instance, maintaining our nation's "comparative advantage" in the development of new technologies will likely require improved levels and quality of math and science education throughout the workforce. In the absence of the tight labor markets that baby boomer retirements might otherwise generate, improving the skills of less-educated workers might become even more critical to narrowing the huge earnings gaps that have emerged between them and more educated workers.[4] And higher levels of education and broad skill levels will likely cushion the blow and improve the labor market prospects of those displaced by offshoring (Kletzer 1998), suggesting another reason higher education and skills might become even more valuable to workers over time.

If a growing demand for skilled labor is not matched by a comparable trend in supply, then labor market inequality will likely continue to grow in the United States. And, while labor markets will respond to these developments with a variety of adjustments (such as further substitution of capital and technology for labor, relative wage adjustments, workers investments in education and skills, and the like), output and productivity growth might be constrained by a relative dearth of skilled workers, at least in some sectors and in some places or periods.

Thus, both *equity* and *efficiency* considerations suggest that policies to further promote education and skill development among U.S. workers would be important responses to the shocks that will likely buffet our labor markets in the coming years. Exactly how to do so, particularly for less-educated workers, in a cost-effective manner is not always clear. And, at the federal level, the retirement of baby boomers is likely to strain public budgets for many years to come, especially since the costs of meeting Social Security and Medicare obligations will be growing dramatically. This means that new, very large federal outlays for education and training are fairly unlikely.

A number of questions become clear in this context. What are the various ways to encourage education and training, especially options that might require less expenditure of public resources and do more to leverage private-sector investments? How can public policy help meet employer needs for different types of workers? How can we make sure that new education and training opportunities are equitable and reach the populations at the lower end of the workforce, who might need special support to access these opportunities? Could other approaches beyond public policies related to training and education—perhaps involving immigration, retirement policy, and the like—effectively raise the supply of appropriately educated and skilled workers? And what kinds of policies will deal with other dimensions of worker needs in these changing labor market environments—including the growing need for insurance against labor market displacements (from new technologies and global forces), and the increasingly difficult task of balancing work with family responsibilities for working parents?

In this volume, we hope to shed some light on these issues. The chapters here, which were presented at a conference at the Urban Institute in Washington, D.C., in November 2005, are written by a distinguished group of researchers who are at the forefront of analysis on each issue considered here. The chapters provide broad overviews of what we know (and don't know) from research to date on these workforce issues and on potential policy responses. In particular, each author reviews empirical evidence on labor force trends and various policy options that suggest important directions for workforce policy over the next few decades and beyond.

The chapters are grouped into five topic areas. The first section lays out the likely labor market and policy contexts in which workforce policies will be devised over the next few decades. Richard B. Freeman focuses on likely trends in the labor market, particularly the effects of retirements and offshoring. Burt S. Barnow and Demetra Smith Nightingale present a broad overview of current workforce policies at the federal and state levels and of the factors that will influence their use over time.

The next two sections deal with education and training policies. The first of these, focusing mostly on formal schooling and especially younger individuals, features chapters by Robert I. Lerman on career training for youth in high school and beyond and by Sarah E. Turner on the access of lower-income youth and young adults to higher education. The section that follows features two chapters on training for adults: one by Paul Osterman on training for less-educated workers defined fairly broadly, and the other by Dan Bloom and David Butler on "hard-to-employ" adults with poor skills and labor market prospects.

The last two sections of the book address issues and policies beyond the realm of education and training. One focuses on efforts to increase the supply of skilled workers in the labor force, either through immigration policy or retirement policy; these chapters are written by George J. Borjas and Alicia H. Munnell, respectively. The last section of the book then highlights some remaining issues and problems that will increasingly concern workers in the future—namely, efforts to insure workers against the effects of job displacement, reviewed by Gary Burtless; and efforts to ensure a balance between work and family responsibilities for working parents of children, reviewed by Jane Waldfogel.

Together, these chapters address some of the more controversial issues in workforce policy, including these six:

- the extent to which secondary education should focus purely on academics and general skills as opposed to more specific occupational training;
- whether postsecondary financial aid for less affluent students should take the form of means-tested scholarships and loans, universally available "merit" scholarships, or broad-based tuition reductions at state colleges and universities;
- whether funding for the Workforce Investment Act can or should be increased substantially, whether the public funds can more effectively leverage private investment in training, and whether funding and "pathways" for skills training more broadly can be made less fragmented and more coherent;
- whether the least-skilled workers—including the disabled and those with criminal records—should be expected to work in much greater numbers, and how we should encourage and assist them to do so;
- whether we should change our national policies to encourage relatively greater immigration among those with more education (perhaps at the expense of less-educated immigrants), how to improve support to older workers, and whether to encourage later retirement ages in ways that might place new burdens on older workers; and
- how we can provide such benefits as unemployment insurance, health insurance, and parental leave to more workers without

hurting the incentives of employees to work and employers to hire them.

Below we summarize the key themes in these chapters. We conclude by synthesizing the main policy prescriptions that emerge from these chapters.

THE LABOR MARKET AND POLICY CONTEXTS

In "Is a Great Labor Shortage Coming? Replacement Demand in the Global Economy," Richard B. Freeman analyzes the likely effects of baby boomer retirements on the labor market, especially in light of growing competition from workers overseas. Freeman notes that many analysts predict shortages of labor when the boomers retire, especially in key occupations; but he also emphasizes several reasons these predictions might be overblown. These reasons include that the predicted magnitudes of these retirements may not be as large as is often assumed (especially if boomers work longer and retire only partially between the ages of 60 and 70); BLS projections of future occupational demand are often incorrect and only weakly correlated with actual occupational growth; retirements in the 1990s were concentrated in declining sectors of the economy, so retirements did not induce sector-specific shortages of workers; and the employment outcomes of the baby boomers themselves were only modestly affected by the size of their cohort, while the diminished size of the "baby bust" cohort generated little recovery in terms of labor market outcomes.

These findings can be attributed to the fact that workers often face demand shocks in the labor market—associated with shifting demand over time for goods and services produced domestically and shifting modes of production—that are hard to predict in advance but are often large enough to overcome the more modest labor supply shifts caused by cohort size changes. In Freeman's view, demographically based supply shocks might be easier to predict but are not powerful enough to overcome large demand shocks. And the latter might well predominate over the next several decades, given the doubling of the effective global workforce associated with the entry of Indian, Chinese, and Eastern European workers into the world economy and the resulting increasing competition that U.S. workers will face through offshoring and immigration.

Freeman makes a powerful case for the argument that predictions of worker shortages in light of impending baby boomer retirements have been overblown. Labor markets have many ways of responding to such supply shifts, including rising wages that draw marginal workers into the labor market; substitution of capital and technology for workers; slower retirements; replacement of retiring workers with other groups, including those from other cohorts and immigrants; and offshoring. Freeman clearly believes that the last of these factors will be very important and on net will generate slack labor markets with declining wages rather than tight ones with rising wages for less-skilled workers.

Nonetheless, the boomer retirements constitute a moderately large supply shift that can be predicted with reasonable certainty, unlike other adjustments and demand shifts that are considerably more uncertain. Even if the boomer retirements have no effects on the overall U.S. labor market, they are likely to matter in some sectors of the economy, such as health care, elder care, and personal services, where demand is likely to be very strong and where wages may not be able to rise sufficiently to "equilibrate" (or balance) supply with demand.[5] Short supplies of semiskilled labor (in the installation, maintenance, and repair occupations, for example) may also materialize from time to time—especially in states and regions where immigration is limited and in sectors (like construction) that cannot easily be offshored. The limited mobility of workers across industries, regions, and skill groups in the short term often compounds these problems.

Thus, the net effects of retirements, offshoring, immigration, and other factors may vary considerably across sectors and areas in the coming years. This will create a need for policies that help educate and train workers to meet business demand for labor in at least some important sectors and areas and for a broader set of policies that help improve worker mobility across occupations, industries, and regions to adjust as needed to the changing economy. And, as noted above, the importance of raising the supply of skills in the workforce will likely grow, not diminish, if Freeman's predictions are accurate.

In "An Overview of U.S. Workforce Development Policy in 2005," Burt S. Barnow and Demetra Smith Nightingale review a set of policy goals for the labor market, as well as a set of "levers" that are used to pursue these goals. The goals include meeting employer demand, achieving worker skills and security, enhancing opportunity, and strengthening work incentives; the levers include social insurance, regulations and mandates, tax credits, direct financing of human capital formation, labor exchange services, and other support services.

Worker training in the United States is primarily done by businesses and employers. Federally funded training of workers is mainly funded through grants and loans for postsecondary education for a large share of the population and through the Workforce Investment Act (WIA), which focuses mainly on dislocated workers, the unemployed, and workers having difficulty finding jobs. The funding provided through WIA is relatively modest compared with other public funding sources that can support education and education-based occupational training, such as the Higher Education Act. Tax credits for higher education— through HOPE scholarships and lifelong learning credits—have expanded over time. Tax-based incentives to expand employment— including the earned income tax credit for low-income workers and various education and hiring tax incentives for employers—have also grown increasingly important in recent years. Universally available labor exchange services funded by the Department of Labor and provided through local one-stop career centers and over the Internet have been further developed. Attention to the needs of employers and workers has grown as well, and the importance of matching labor demand with the appropriate supply has increased with time.

State and local governments, which combine funding from multiple federal sources and use their own policy levers in somewhat different modes and proportions, will also grow increasingly important over the next several years, although the ability of states to fund training depends heavily on the business cycle and its effects on their fiscal situations. The role of states will become more important, in part because of federal budget constraints that limit direct funding of training, and in part because of the broader tendency for the federal government to devolve more responsibilities down to state and local levels.

In this context, public policy responses to major labor market shifts will vary greatly across states and local areas, with much experimentation and adaptation occurring in response to varied regional labor market conditions and more limited federal activity and funding. Meanwhile, national policy options that emphasize creative strategies for using federal funds to leverage private and state funds may receive more attention.

SCHOOL-BASED EDUCATION AND TRAINING FOR YOUTH

Robert I. Lerman analyzes employment and training options for youth, mostly those who are not bound for four-year colleges, in his chapter, "Career-Focused Education and Training for Youth." Lerman challenges the notion that secondary school education should focus exclusively on academic achievement and the expectation of "college for all." These efforts do little to diminish high rates of dropping out of high school, especially among students who lack motivation to pursue serious academics. They also do little to prepare high school graduates who do not obtain any postsecondary education for the labor market.

Lerman reviews efforts that fall under the rubric of "career and technical education," including career academies, Tech-Prep programs, apprenticeships, and other activities funded in the 1990s by the School to Work Opportunities Act. In general, career education is associated with moderate gains in labor force outcomes for high school students after graduation; rigorous evaluation indicates much stronger gains for career academies, in which at-risk young men experience gains in earnings of nearly 20 percent four years after leaving school, without suffering any declines in their postsecondary enrollments. The strong potential of apprenticeships and other sources of private training is noted as well. On the other hand, Lerman notes that further improvements are needed in the academic quality and workplace relevance of many career education programs, and that more evaluation evidence in this area is sorely needed.

Lerman also reviews evidence on "second-chance" programs for out-of-school youth, noting the successful shorter-term impacts of the Job Corps and the promising new National Guard Youth ChalleNGe program, among other efforts.[6] He argues for a good deal more experimentation with and expansion of career-focused educational efforts, along with some second-chance programs for out-of-school youth. He thinks these can help link more disadvantaged youth to the labor market and provide them with general and occupation-specific skills, for a labor market that increasingly rewards such skills.

The labor market returns to higher education in the United States have grown consistently over the past three decades and will likely remain high in the future. Sarah E. Turner, in her chapter on "Higher Education Policies Generating the 21st Century Workforce," notes two important developments in terms of higher education outcomes: there are growing gaps across students from different family income backgrounds in rates of college attendance, and even more so in college completion; and the time needed for completion of four-year college degrees is growing, as is the presence of adults in college more broadly. Gaps across family background in college attendance and completion likely reflect some combination of differences in academic preparation, financial abilities to meet costs, and information/supports for college. The growing time needed to complete degrees and the rising presence of adults on campus could reflect changing student preferences and a desire for more flexible schooling arrangements, as well as rising costs; but the trend seems more concentrated among students at "non-flagship" state colleges and universities, where students from less affluent families are most heavily concentrated.

Turner notes that rising tuition costs at state universities likely impede the ability of students from less affluent homes to attend or complete college, and she cites evidence showing that at least some students face credit constraints that limit their ability to borrow against their future earnings for college tuition. Of course, the actual monetary costs of college attendance are often significantly lower than official tuition levels suggest, due to a variety of grant programs (such as Pell grants for low-income students) and loans (such as Stafford loans) offered by the federal government, as well as scholarship and loan assistance based on state or private funds. The evidence that Pell grants help low-income young people attend college is fairly limited, though they seem more helpful for older (nontraditional) students. Somewhat stronger evidence appears in favor of the merit scholarships at state universities that reward students with financial assistance if they meet certain academic achievement levels (usually in the form of minimum grade point averages).

Thus, while tuitions at state universities will likely continue to grow more rapidly than inflation (especially as state funding of universities faces growing competition from Medicaid and other expenditures), various forms of more targeted aid within more universally available funding opportunities like the merit programs create the best hope of helping students from less affluent families have access to higher education. Turner would also explore some restructuring of the federal grant and loan programs for lower-income students, and especially try to improve their transparency and visibility in low-income communities. And, as Turner and others have noted, equalizing access to higher education across more- and less-affluent students will require closing gaps in academic preparation and achievement in the pre-K and K–12 years, in addition to efforts to limit costs and provide greater financial assistance.

TRAINING FOR LESS-EDUCATED ADULTS

Paul Osterman reviews the state of training in the United States for less-educated adults, and considers some new approaches, in his chapter, "Employment and Training Policies: New Directions for Less-Skilled Adults." Osterman notes that most on-the-job training for adults in the United States is privately provided and financed, and it is heavily skewed toward more-educated workers. Training for the less-educated is financed through various public sources, including funds from the Workforce Investment Act and other resources at the federal and state levels. Based on evaluation evidence, he notes some clear success stories—including adult training funded by the Job Training Partnership Act (now WIA), certain welfare-to-work programs (such as that in

Portland, Oregon, in the 1990s), and programs that involve employers as well as employees (such as Project QUEST in San Antonio).[7]

Yet Osterman also notes some major weaknesses in the public employment and training system as a whole. In general, funding levels for less-educated workers fall far short of need. The system is highly fragmented and somewhat disconnected from private employers; few workers or employers use the public employment service, and few pathways or "ladders" provide access to private employment opportunities for those getting training from community colleges or other service providers.

In Osterman's view, the most promising models for overcoming these gaps in the workforce system rely heavily on private labor-market intermediaries that work with employers and workers to improve the latter's employment opportunities. Some of these efforts involve sectoral approaches, which target important sectors of local economies for training. The intermediaries often work with employers to build career ladders with training, increasingly provided by community colleges, while preparing less-educated workers for training and jobs in these sectors.

Given WIA's limited scope and funding, Osterman argues that the program should be used primarily as a tool to encourage innovations in the workforce training system. State and local workforce boards would support these efforts and fund evaluations and replications of successful models. WIA performance standards would also have to be substantially modified to provide the incentives for state and local boards to play this innovative role.

Of course, some potential workers face particular barriers and have specific limits on their abilities to participate at all in the labor force. These groups include those with very poor skills or English language abilities, those with physical disabilities and other physical or mental health problems, and those with criminal records. Employers are often reluctant to hire these individuals (especially ex-offenders), even after accounting for their weak skills and work experience, while the workers themselves exhibit very limited labor force attachment in many cases.

In their chapter, "Overcoming Employment Barriers: Strategies to Help the 'Hard to Employ,'" Dan Bloom and David Butler review approaches to improve employment opportunities for individuals who can work but have special issues that must be addressed in order for them to be most productive. Bloom and Butler find that a mix of treatments (for workers with health issues or disabilities, substance abuse problems, and so on), employment and training services, and efforts to improve work incentives hold promise for increasing the employment and earnings of these populations. But little solid evidence exists on the cost-effectiveness of various approaches. Further, the multiple public systems that serve these individuals—including transfer programs like Supplemental Security Income and Social Security Disability Insurance as well as the criminal justice and parole systems—often do not emphasize encouraging labor market participation. But Bloom and Butler also note that some systems can change dramatically over time: in particular, the nation's welfare system changed its mission and its emphasis to one of encouraging employment in the wake of welfare reform in the late 1990s.

In light of this situation, Bloom and Butler call for a multi-pronged effort to improve employment outcomes for the hard-to-employ. They argue for major efforts to change the missions of the systems that serve (or incarcerate) these groups to put greater emphasis on employment; this would require major changes in system policies, practices, accountability, and incentives for staff. Bloom and Butler argue for improved work supports and services, including child care and training, to be provided in these systems; they also call for improved work incentives, such as expansions of the earned income tax credit, to encourage more employment. Finally, they call for much greater efforts to evaluate existing models to improve our knowledge base in this area.

INCREASING THE SUPPLY OF SKILLED LABOR: IMMIGRANTS AND THE ELDERLY

Beyond efforts to increase education and training for less-skilled workers, potential policy reforms might be implemented to increase the presence of skilled workers or to more fully use available human capital, especially among such populations as immigrants and the elderly.

In "Immigration Policy and Human Capital," George J. Borjas notes that the federal law controlling immigration since 1965 emphasizes family unification rather than personal skills in determining which foreigners can reside in the United States. As a result, immigrants in the past few decades have increasingly been concentrated among the least-educated and lowest-paid workers in the labor market. Indeed, immigration in this period has raised the supply of high school dropouts in the U.S. labor market by nearly 40 percent, while it has raised the supply of more-skilled groups by much smaller amounts. In addition, Borjas provides evidence that the concentration of immigrants among the less-skilled has significantly reduced earnings levels among native-born high school dropouts.[8] He also notes the drain on public resources created by the relatively greater reliance on transfer payments among lower-income immigrant groups.

According to Borjas, the United States would be better served by immigration policies that place greater relative weight on the education and skills of those seeking admission—as is done in many other English-speaking countries (including Australia, Canada, and New Zealand)—to encourage the immigration of more highly educated instead of less-educated workers. Of course, such a policy would involve some clear trade-offs. For instance, the costs of some categories of consumer goods—including food, housing, and health care—would likely rise a bit, especially in regions of the country where most immigrants now reside; and, if the overall flow of immigrants slows while its composition changes, the future solvency of our retirement programs might be affected. Whether and what kinds of policies would effectively reduce the flow of illegal as well as legal immigrants also remain open to question, as do the potential effects of various "guest worker" programs. The diplomatic and humanitarian impacts of these changes in immigration policy would need to be weighed as well. Still, Borjas makes a compelling case for at least considering these trade-offs in immigration policy.

Alicia H. Munnell's chapter, "Policies to Promote Labor Force Participation of Older People," notes that both employers and workers will face growing incentives to increase the rates of labor force activity among older Americans over the coming decades. Employers will face a need to retain skilled workers in the face of baby boomer retirements (subject to the caveats noted by Freeman), while older workers will face increasing financial strains as their savings and retirement benefits increasingly fall short of their income needs during their older years, especially as their life expectancy continues to increase.

Of course, these incentives imply that private-market forces will generate reduced rates of early retirement and longer working lives among the elderly. But Munnell also notes several barriers that could limit these adjustments, including the high costs of older labor to employers (due to both high salaries and medical and pension costs), health problems among older workers, the fixed costs of part-time work for employers, and discrimination against the elderly. In addition, labor force participation rates among the elderly have been fairly flat in recent years and so far show little sign of adapting on their own to the new realities facing older workers. Even the phasing out of defined-benefit pensions and the elimination of mandatory retirement and declines in benefits received for early retirees (at age 62) that have already been implemented have done little to increase participation of this group so far.

Munnell thus calls for considering additional policies that might actively promote more labor force activity among older workers. These include delays in the age of eligibility for early retirement benefits (beyond age 62), allowing Medicare to become the primary payer on health benefits for working older Americans, or exempting older workers from payroll taxes. But the first proposal could be costly to workers with poor health and lower life expectancies (and would face significant political opposition), while the latter two proposals would impose extra financial costs on a retirement system that already faces large future solvency problems. Thus, smaller changes to improve skills among the elderly, further decrease discrimination, or modestly reduce the costs older workers impose on employers are more feasible at this time.

INSURING WORKERS AND PROMOTING WORK-FAMILY BALANCE

In addition to efforts to increase the supply of skills in the workforce, policymakers might need to address some concerns and pressures that already affect workers and will do so increasingly over time. One is the growing insecurity felt by many workers as they face growing rates of job displacements and shorter periods of tenure with particular employers. Another is the growing tension felt by many parents who struggle to balance their family responsibilities with their jobs and careers—especially in a world where most mothers as well as fathers work.

Gary Burtless's chapter, "Income Supports for Workers and Their Families: Earnings Supplements and Health Insurance," addresses the first of these issues. Burtless notes that average tenure on the job is declining, while there is at least some evidence of secular increases in the rates of job displacement. Workers increasingly need some protection against income declines associated with job loss, owing to both their lack of employment between jobs and the earnings declines that most suffer when they regain employment. The loss of health insurance is a further consequence of permanent job loss for many workers, though this problem increasingly plagues many of those working as well.

Unemployment insurance (UI), a program regulated by the federal government but financed and administered mostly at the state level, represents the country's primary effort to protect workers from the effects of involuntary job loss. According to Burtless, UI in the United States replaces less of the lost earnings of the unemployed (on average, roughly half) and for shorter periods (usually up to six months) than is true in most other industrial countries. The fractions of unemployed workers covered by UI have also fallen over time: partly because the fraction of the unemployed experiencing long spells of joblessness (i.e., six months or longer) has risen, and partly because of changes in the demographics of unemployed workers and lost jobs (i.e., more low-income women and part-time workers, more service jobs, and so on). While Burtless is open to some modest fixes that might improve eligibility or take-up rates for marginal groups in the workforce, he cautions against simply increasing replacement rates or durations of coverage, as these actions would reduce incentives of unemployed workers to actively seek new jobs.

Burtless is more enthusiastic about implementing a new form of earnings insurance, in which displaced workers might be insured for a substantial period (e.g., up to two years) after they regain employment for any losses in wages or earnings between their old and new jobs. Such a policy would not only help workers who have suffered earnings declines from involuntary job losses, it would also increase labor market efficiency by encouraging displaced workers to seek and accept new employment more quickly than they might under current circumstances.

Burtless also reviews health insurance coverage among U.S. workers. The U.S. health system is the most expensive in the world, yet it provides more limited coverage (as well as worse health outcomes, along some dimensions) than occurs in almost any other industrial country. At least part of the problem with health insurance coverage here, according to Burtless, lies in the concept and features of employer-sponsored coverage that provides most private insurance in the United States. Because employer spending on insurance is not taxed (under a system implemented during World War II for firms looking to raise worker compensation in ways that would not violate wage and price controls), the U.S. government heavily subsidizes such insurance coverage. But, because of rising costs, increasing numbers of employers are choosing to forgo providing coverage, especially for lower-wage workers and their dependents. In addition, such a system encourages employers to discriminate in hiring against employees with potentially large health costs (such as the elderly, sick, and disabled), and it discourages job mobility among workers who fear the loss of coverage if they change jobs.

Accordingly, Burtless argues that efforts to expand health insurance coverage among U.S. workers should seek to sever the link between coverage and employer provision, phasing out tax deductions for employer provision and instead focusing on expanding individual coverage through public subsidies. Of course, the transition from the current system to a new one would be both costly and very uncertain, especially given the highly charged political environment around health care. But the new health care plan adopted by the state of

Massachusetts (which mandates individual coverage and some employer contribution to health care) indicates that dramatic new approaches to expanding coverage are certainly possible.

In "Work–Family Policies," Jane Waldfogel reviews the evidence on a range of family-friendly work practices, including sick leave and parental leave, child care and early childhood development programs, and flexible work schedules for parents. Overall, she finds clear evidence of the benefits these practices provide for the health and well-being of children and for their parents. But lower-income workers are much less likely to enjoy paid leave, and they spend proportionately more on child care, than do higher-income workers. The passage of the Family and Medical Leave Act in 1993 has had limited impact because it covers only unpaid leave (which most low-income families cannot afford) and is limited to larger employers. Various expansions of subsidized child care for low-income workers in the 1990s certainly helped, but they still leave the vast majority of eligible families without any subsidy.

But Waldfogel, like Burtless, does not endorse mandates on employers to provide paid leave or child care. Such mandates would likely result in lower employment or earnings for low-income families, leaving them no better (and perhaps worse) off on average. Instead, she proposes financing expanded coverage of parental leaves and child care through payroll taxes (in the UI system) or some other revenue source, as California and some other states have recently done. She also praises a new system in the United Kingdom in which employers are required to consider (but not necessarily to grant) employee requests for flexible work schedules. As a result of such a flexible, voluntary system, large percentages of employers granted requests that do not appear costly to them but that workers would not have requested in the absence of the new policy.

CONCLUSIONS AND IMPLICATIONS FOR FUTURE POLICY DIRECTIONS

Despite considerable uncertainty about the magnitudes and net impacts of future labor market shocks such as baby boomer retirements and continuing globalization, there is some consensus on the need for policies that will continue to improve the skills of U.S. workers in the presence of these shocks. Other needs of American workers, such as insuring them against earnings declines and loss of health insurance when they lose jobs and helping them balance the needs of their jobs and their families, will be critical as well. On the other hand, a review of the policy context suggests that, while a range of policy levers will be available, the fiscal pressure generated by funding retirement programs for baby boomers render large increases in federal funding unlikely, at least in some areas.

While the specific policy recommendations of individual chapter authors are discussed above, the following broad conclusions seem warranted:

- **A wide range of skills must be encouraged among workers to meet future labor market needs, and a wide range of high-quality education and training options should be available to help meet these needs.** Strong basic and analytical skills are essential to ensure students' access to higher education—and to high-quality career options that do not require four-year college degrees. To fully meet future needs, it is important to increase the readiness of low-income students to access higher-level skills training and education. Thus, there is no controversy over the need to reduce "achievement gaps" between lower-income and other students in the K–8th grade years (and earlier). But there is also no clear trade-off between the provision of career education and academic achievement in high school; indeed, expanding the provision of high-quality career and technical education does not limit access to higher education, and likely complements it. Various second-chance programs for youth, and other education and training options for less-educated adults and the hard-to-employ, could also contribute significantly to a broad skill-building effort.

- **Funding for training and higher education should be targeted to low-income individuals more than in the past, but not limited to them exclusively.** To improve the overall skill level of the nation's workforce, future public efforts should focus on increasing education and training for those who will otherwise be among the least-educated. The chapters by Lerman, Osterman, and Bloom and Butler all emphasize efforts to improve training for various groups of individuals who will likely not achieve four-year college degrees. But improving access to higher education for lower-income youth and adults is critical as well. Sarah Turner notes that tuition at state universities will rise over time as universities receive less generous funding from states than in the past. Pell grants and loans for low-income students can perhaps be made more transparent and more visible to low-income youth, while they remain fairly effective for nontraditional student populations. Other approaches—such as merit scholarships—might have more potential to reach lower-income students, while providing at least some benefits to those from a wide range of backgrounds.

- **Education and training should be at least somewhat targeted to private-sector employment opportunities, and, where possible, should directly involve employers.** As Robert Lerman and Paul Osterman emphasize in their chapters, publicly financed training efforts must be linked to available jobs, and they should involve private employers—who should provide some of the training as well as the jobs. Of course, workers benefit from having both general and more specific labor-market skills, and the willingness of employers to help pay depends on the mix of the two skill sets (Becker 1975).[9] Still, linking training to available jobs improves the quality of the matches between the two, strengthens worker motivation, and seems to improve the resulting payoff for workers.

- **States should continue to experiment with a range of programs that fund education and training options, as well as those providing health insurance, family leave, and child care coverage.** Lerman, Turner, and Osterman all advocate a range of state efforts to improve worker access to education and training, with appropriate federal financial support. Waldfogel also notes the promising efforts in California and elsewhere to fund parental leave and other family-friendly work practices, while Burtless notes the recent steps taken by Massachusetts to expand health insurance coverage.

- **Efforts to improve the skill levels of workers through immigration reform or policies to encourage employment among the elderly are feasible but involve some major costs and difficult trade-offs.** George Borjas advocates immigration reforms to increase the skill levels of immigrants, and Alicia Munnell considers efforts to increase labor force participation among the elderly. But both acknowledge potential costs (including economic, fiscal, diplomatic, and humanitarian costs) as well as political opposition. These reforms should be considered, but only with a careful weighing of potential benefits and costs in each case.

- **In designing new policies and approaches, federal and state governments must pay careful attention to the incentives facing both employers and workers.** Dan Bloom and David Butler note the critical role played by work incentives for welfare recipients and other hard-to-employ individuals, and how lack of attention to these incentives still plagues the systems that treat them. Gary Burtless and Jane Waldfogel also note that mandates on employers to provide health insurance or supports for working parents might distort their incentives to hire these workers, though they support efforts to expand health coverage and other family supports through direct public subsidies. Unemployment insurance reforms and new earnings insurance efforts must also pay attention to work incentives of recipients, but without ignoring the business context facing employers.

- **More research and evaluation evidence is critical for the design of cost-effective policies in all these areas**. Much research and hundreds of program evaluations have been conducted on employment policies and programs over the past several decades. Yet, in virtually all the chapters focusing on education and training—and those focusing on insurance and work–family balance—many approaches were discussed that look promising but lack rigorous evaluation evidence. Increasing the stock of knowledge on cost-effective approaches to education and training for both employers and workers, including lower-income Americans, remains a high priority.

Finally, it is important to note some issues and concerns that were not a central focus of the chapters in this volume but that remain critical nonetheless. Most important, the growth of labor market *inequality*, and the need for policies that will directly raise or supplement the earnings of less-educated workers, will need to be addressed in future years. Policies that directly raise the earnings available in low-wage jobs, such as minimum wage increases and efforts to make it easier for workers to choose collective bargaining, deserve serious consideration.

Certain policies that directly target the demand side of the labor market should be considered as well. For instance, while some are skeptical of economic development policies that target particular sectors or industries for support (at either the national or state level), public supports and assistance for firms that provide higher wages, benefits, or advancement opportunities for low-wage workers should be seriously considered (Holzer 2004).[10] Such policies might help reduce the further erosion of the middle of the wage distribution, increase the number of skilled workers who could adapt better to future changes in labor market demand, and ensure that job opportunities will continue to exist for low earners who upgrade their skills.

Overall, the chapters in this volume imply that effectively meeting the future demands for a competitive and skilled U.S. workforce will require policy strategies that involve both the demand side of the labor market and the supply side—both are critical in determining the relevant outcomes for American workers and businesses. Policies must focus on raising the skills of workers who are currently underused, while helping businesses and employers in this increasingly competitive world adapt to the changing economic contexts within which they operate. As the current labor force ages, some may be encouraged to remain in the active workforce longer, to capitalize on their skills and experience. Meanwhile, new workers replacing the retirees will need to gain new skills to meet changing demand. Immigrants may fill part of the need for skilled workers, but a critical dimension of national policy should be to improve the skills and productive potential of less-educated native-born workers. Investing in the skills of less-educated workers could enhance the overall aggregate skills of the workforce, particularly if the investments are relevant for sectors and areas expected to grow. At the same time, making these investments will serve the additional, critical goal of improving the earnings and income of the less-educated and equalizing opportunity in society.

NOTES

1. For these projections, see Saunders (2005); Toossi (2005); and the U.S. Census Bureau, "U.S. Interim Projections by Age, Sex, Race and Hispanic Origin," http://www.census.gov/ipc/www/usinterimproj.

2. See Levy and Murnane (2004) and Autor, Katz, and Kearney (2005) for some discussion and evidence on the relatively greater growth of high- and low-wage jobs. On the other hand, employment growth in technical and craft occupations (now called "installation, maintenance and repair" by BLS) and in industries such as construction and health care will no doubt remain robust.

3. Demographic projections of labor force changes (e.g., Toossi 2005) assume little change in retirement behavior over time, or in other market adjustments. The magnitudes of jobs offshored to date have been quite modest, relative to the aggregate creation and destruction in jobs in the United States (e.g., Schultz 2004). Projections of future offshoring vary widely in magnitude, and data on these trends are somewhat conflicting (GAO 2004, 2005).

4. Richard Freeman makes both these arguments in chapter 1.

5. Since payments to health care workers are often affected by Medicare, Medicaid, and other third-party reimbursements that are capped, wage increases might be limited over time in ways that generate shortages when demand growth is strong—as it is expected to be as the boomers age. See, for instance, Stone and Wiener (2001).

6. The most recent evaluation on the Job Corps, based on longer-term follow-up on those who participated in Job Corps versus a control group, shows some fading of its impact over time, though the findings remain largely positive. See Mathematica Policy Research (2006).

7. Osterman acknowledges that some evaluation evidence—such as that on JTPA training and the major welfare-to-work programs—is based on random assignment or more rigorous empirical methods than those used in evaluating the sectoral programs. He also argues that the gains observed in the evaluation of Project QUEST were not likely attributable to the less rigorous evaluation techniques used in that study.

8. This evidence has been disputed by David Card (2001), among others. Card's analysis focuses on differences in earnings and immigrant concentrations across geographic areas, while Borjas has estimated more aggregate

impacts of immigrants over time and across education and work experience groups.

9. In Becker's classic formulation, employers will share the costs of firm-specific training but not general training. But more recent analysis (e.g., Acemoglu and Pischke 1998) that incorporates imperfect and asymmetric information about training between workers and employers suggests these two categories of training are not so easily distinguishable from one another.

10. These supports could take the form of tax credits for training and advancement, technical assistance for firms that attempt to develop new career ladders and credentials, and the kinds of sectoral approaches discussed by Osterman in chapter 5.

REFERENCES

Acemoglu, Daron, and Jorn-Steffen Pischke. 1998. "Beyond Becker: Training in Imperfect Labor Markets." Working Paper 6,740. Cambridge, MA: National Bureau of Economic Research (NBER).

Aspen Institute, The. 2003. *Grow Faster Together or Grow Slowly Apart?* Domestic Strategies Group report. Washington DC: The Aspen Institute.

Autor, David, Lawrence Katz, and Melissa Kearney. 2005. "The Polarization of the U.S. Labor Market." Working Paper 11,986. Cambridge, MA: NBER.

Bardhan, Ashok, and Cynthia Kroll. 2003. "The New Wave of Outsourcing." Working Paper. Berkeley: Fisher Center for Real Estate and Urban Economics, University of California, Berkeley.

Becker, Gary. 1975. *Human Capital: A Theoretical and Empirical Analysis, with Special Reference to Education.* 2nd ed. New York: National Bureau of Economic Research.

Card, David. 2001. "Immigrant Inflows, Native Outflows, and the Local Labor Market Impacts of Higher Immigration." *Journal of Labor Economics* 19(1): 22–64.

GAO. See U.S. Government Accountability Office.

Holzer, Harry J. 2004. "Encouraging Job Advancement among Low-Wage Workers: A New Approach." Welfare Reform and Beyond Brief 30. Washington, DC: The Brookings Institution.

Kletzer, Lori. 1998. "Job Displacement." *Journal of Economic Perspectives* 12(1): 115–36.

Levy, Frank, and Richard Murnane. 2004. *The New Division of Labor.* New York: Russell Sage Foundation.

Mann, Catherine. 2003. "Globalization of IT Services and White-Collar Jobs: The Next Wave of Productivity Growth." Policy brief. Washington, DC: Institute for International Economics.

Mathematica Policy Research. 2006. "Does Job Corps Work? New Mathematica Study Confirms That Job Corps Increases Participants' Earnings, Yet Impacts Decline after Two Years for All but the Oldest Students." Press release. Princeton, NJ: Mathematica Policy Research.

Saunders, Norman C. 2005. "A Summary of BLS Projections to 2014." *Monthly Labor Review* 128(11): 3–9.

Schultz, Charles. 2004. "Offshoring, Import Competition and the Jobless Recovery." Policy Brief 136. Washington DC: The Brookings Institution.

Stone, Robyn, and Joshua Wiener. 2001. *Who Will Care for Us? Addressing the Long-Term Care Workforce Crisis*. Washington DC: The Urban Institute and the American Association of Homes and Services for the Aging.

Toossi, Mitra. 2005. "Labor Force Projections to 2014: Retiring Boomers." *Monthly Labor Review* 128(11): 25–44.

U.S. Government Accountability Office (GAO). 2004. *International Trade: Current Government Data Provide Limited Insight into Offshoring of Services*. GAO 04-932. Washington, DC: United States Government Printing Office.

———. 2005. *International Trade: U.S. and India Data Show Significant Differences*. GAO-06-116. Washington DC: United States Government Printing Office.

PART I

THE LABOR MARKET AND POLICY CONTEXTS

1

IS A GREAT LABOR SHORTAGE COMING? REPLACEMENT DEMAND IN THE GLOBAL ECONOMY

Richard B. Freeman

The sky is falling down, the sky is falling down . . .
I must go and tell the king . . .
A great labor shortage is coming.

In the early 2000s, the business press and media began reporting that the U.S. labor market was on the verge of a major transformation. Retirement of the baby boomers and slow projected growth of the labor force were going to create a great labor shortage. Policymakers should forget about the sluggish real-wage growth of the past three decades, the deterioration in pensions and employer-provided health care, the "jobless" recovery from the 2001 recession, and fears of job loss from offshoring or low-wage imports; they should instead focus on helping business find workers in the coming shortage.

The Hudson Institute's report *Workforce 2020* (Judy and D'Amico 1997) was one of the earliest studies to express concern about the possible future shortage of labor, due to predicted reductions in the growth of labor supply associated with the retirement of the baby boom generation and slackened population growth. Many other groups interpreted government projections of future labor supplies and employment similarly. The National Association of Manufacturers (NAM) warned employers that a gap of 5.3 million skilled workers would develop by 2010 and expand to 21 million by 2020 (NAM 2003). The Chamber of Commerce's 2006 *State of American Business* report declared, "We are staring right in the face of a severe worker shortage as 77 million baby boomers prepare to retire in the next few years— with a fewer number of younger workers available to replace them" (U.S. Chamber of Commerce 2006, 13). According to *Public Power*, the magazine for the electrical utility industry, "The coming labor shortage could become the most significant problem the electrical utility industry will face. . . . The U.S. Bureau of Labor Statistics estimates the United States will face a shortage of 12 million qualified skilled workers by 2010 and 20 million by 2020" (Atkinson 2005). Reporting the consensus from the Aspen Institute's Domestic Strategy Group, David Ellwood wrote, "CEOs, labor leaders, community leaders, all came to the unanimous conclusion that we will have a worker gap that is a very serious one" (cited in Overholt 2004).

Time magazine gave the projected labor shortage a positive spin for workers, calling it the "coming job boom": "The help-wanted ads may look thin—but thanks to aging baby boomers, that's about to change" (Eisenberg 2002). Going further, one pundit dismissed fears that sending good U.S. jobs overseas would harm workers: "The long-term tragedy of offshoring isn't that it's snatching away skilled American jobs but that it isn't snatching enough of them"(Kaihla 2003). The Employment Policy Foundation worried that "if current trends continue, the labor force will only grow to 165 million by 2030, a shortage of 35 million workers . . . (with) serious consequences, slower growth in the standard of living, change in the balance of payments, 'wage-push' inflation, . . . inequality, persistent structural unemployment."[1] Seemingly concerned that readers would find the claimed shortage dubious in light of their job market experiences, *Fortune* headlined its report on the subject, "Believe It or Not, a Labor Shortage Is Coming" (Fisher 2003).

This chapter assesses the shortage claims along with the labor supply and demand projections on which they are based.[2] There is no more reason to believe that the United States faces a great future labor shortage than that Chicken Little got it right about the sky falling down. The retirement of baby boomers and slow growth of the U.S. workforce, on which the shortage claims are based, will most likely have modest and hard-to-detect impacts on the job market. Increased supplies of skilled labor in low-wage countries will affect U.S. workers more than slower increases in domestic labor supply. If there is to be a great labor shortage in the foreseeable future, it will come from something that the shortage soothsayers ignore—a global pandemic that kills millions of people—whose implications would go far beyond assuring that business obtains the labor it may seek 10 or 20 years down the road without incurring higher wages.

This conclusion is based on three findings:

1. The logic of labor shortage analyses is flawed. The most dramatic shortage claims begin with the premise that labor supply should increase to maintain a fixed rate of growth in gross domestic product—a cart-before-the-horse policy from the perspective of standard welfare analysis. In addition, none of the shortage analyses pay adequate attention to the global economy, where the supply of low-wage educated workers in less-developed countries creates a labor surplus worldwide, and where other advanced countries are projected to have greater slowdowns in their labor supplies than the United States.
2. Projections of future demands for skills lack the reliability to guide policies on skill development. Demand for labor in detailed occupations has historically been more greatly affected by changes in technology or unexpected changes in the composition of output among industries than by replacement demand due to retirements. Globalization makes forecasting skill shortages or surpluses in the United States or any specific country more difficult than in the past.
3. Contrary to the assumption implicit in the shortage analyses, demographic changes have not historically been consistently associated with changes in labor market conditions, even for the young workers whose position is most sensitive to changing market realities. The employment and earnings of young workers depends more on macroeconomic conditions, wage-setting institutions, and technological developments than on demography.

DISSECTING SHORTAGE CLAIMS

The most alarmist claims that a great labor shortage is coming assume that the country should increase total gross domestic product (GDP) in the future at a rate comparable to the growth rate in the recent past. From 1980 to 2005, U.S. real GDP grew 3.1 percent annually, with 1.4 percent due to the growth of labor supply and 1.7 percent due to the growth of labor productivity. Given projected declines in labor force growth of 0.7 percent a year, the 3.1 percent growth of GDP will be unsustainable absent increases in labor productivity above historical levels.[3] To maintain past growth of GDP with 1.7 percent growth of labor productivity from 2005 to 2030, the United States would need 200 million workers in 2030. This total is 30 million workers short of the projected labor supply. The shortfall between the projected growth of the labor force and the growth necessary for 3.1 percent growth of GDP defines the coming labor shortage.

The flaw in this mode of thinking is that it treats GDP rather than GDP per capita as the touchstone of economic policy, contrary to virtually all analyses of social welfare. As a wealthy country, the United States can increase the rate of growth of GDP whenever it wants. All the United States has to do is to open its borders to additional immigration. Labor supply would increase as much as desired, raising GDP and returns to capital while reducing wages. Absent an open borders policy, maintaining a desired growth of GDP in the face of slower growth of labor supply requires increased labor productivity, which in turn requires additional investment in physical or human capital or research and development (R&D). Since growth of GDP depends on all factors of production, we could just as well consider the likely slower growth of GDP a coming shortage of capital or R&D and focus policy on ways to create more capital investment and technological advances as well as ways to increase the quality or quantity of labor.

If macrocalculations based on maintaining a given growth rate of GDP were the sole argument for the coming labor shortage, few economists or business leaders would take the claim seriously. What gives credence to the claim are demographic projections that the U.S. workforce will grow more slowly than in the past half-century or so, with the growth concentrated in minority groups that historically have obtained less education and fewer skills than the majority population, and a widespread belief that demographic changes have huge discernible impacts on the economy. Shortage analysts fear that a falling growth rate of skilled labor, in particular, will produce bottlenecks in production that will reduce growth of GDP per capita. Many argue that the country could avoid these problems by preventive investment in education and training directed at likely bottleneck or shortage areas.

Table 1.1 examines the magnitude of the projected reduction in the growth of labor supply. It shows the number of people in the U.S. labor force in each decade from 1950 to 2000, the projected labor force from 2000 to 2050, and the absolute change in labor supply from decade

Table 1.1. Labor Supply, 1950–2000, and Projected Labor Supply, 2000–2050 (millions)

	Labor supply	Change
1950	62.2	
1960	69.6	7.4
1970	82.8	13.2
1980	106.9	24.1
1990	125.8	18.9
2000	140.9	15.1
2010	157.7	16.8
2020	164.7	7.0
2030	170.1	5.4
2040	180.5	10.4
2050	191.8	11.3

Sources: 1950–90, http://www.census.gov/statab/hist/02HS0029.xls; 2000–50, Toossi (2002), table 5.

to decade. From 1950 to 2000 the labor force grew by 78.7 million people, or 127 percent. From 2000 to 2050, the projected growth of the labor force is 50.9 million people, or 36 percent. This deceleration in the rate of growth is expected to be particularly intense from 2010 through 2030, when just 12.4 million additional people are expected to join the labor force. The reason for this timing is the retirement of baby boomers (people born between 1946 and 1964).

The rapid growth of the workforce in the 1950s and 1960s came largely from increased numbers of female workers, primarily white women. In the 1970–90s, growth came from immigration and a continued influx of women into the workforce. In the 2000–50 period, growth of the workforce is expected to come disproportionately from Hispanics and blacks—groups with below-average education levels. The share of the U.S. population from disadvantaged minorities (blacks, Hispanics, American Indians, and Alaska Natives) is projected to rise from 25 percent in 2000 to 37 percent in 2050.[4] Some analysts worry that the U.S. workforce will become less skilled unless the country adopts new policies to help these groups improve their educational skills and attainment. In addition, because the U.S. population will be aging, the number of people in the traditional years of retirement will rise relative to the more slowly growing workforce, burdening the workforce to produce sufficient output to pay the retirement income and health costs of the aging population.

THE GLOBAL CONTEXT

If the United States were the only country in which the growth of the potential workforce was projected to decline rapidly, or if the United

States were a closed economic system with little access to workers in other countries, this focus on domestic labor supply to the exclusion of supply developments elsewhere might be justifiable. But in the global economy, demographic developments and labor conditions in other countries can affect the U.S. labor market. Globalization gives U.S. firms access to labor overseas through foreign direct investment, off-shoring, or subcontracting; globalization also gives access to foreign-born labor that immigrates to the United States. From this perspective, it is incumbent to assess the claims of a coming labor shortage in a global context, rather than to treat the United States as a closed economy, dependent on only domestic labor to produce goods and services.

As a first step in placing the shortage projections into a global context, examine the actual and projected change in the populations of young people (those age 18–23) and of the 15- to 59-year-olds that make up most of the workforce in the United States, Western Europe, Japan, China, and India (table 1.2). The underlying projections are from the United Nations (UN), which forecasts an aging of the world's popula-tion through 2050 (UN 2002) and a slowdown in population growth in much of the world outside of Africa.

The figures in the top half of table 1.2 show a drop in the number of people age 18–23 in the United States from 1980 to 2005 and an expected rise in the numbers to 2030 and 2050. These figures are consis-tent with the slower growth of the workforce over time. But the figures also show that from 1980 to 2005, the number of young people in Western Europe and Japan fell more rapidly than in the United States and will continue to drop thereafter. In 2050, the United States will

Table 1.2. Trends in the Population Age 18–23 and Age 15–59 (millions, except where noted

	U.S.	Western Europe	Japan	China	India	U.S. share of advanced countries' total
Population age 18–23						
1980	26.2	16.3	9.5	109.5	78.1	50%
2005	25.4	13.6	8.7	127.3	125.2	53%
2030	28.3	11.7	6.9	102.6	139.6	60%
2050	28.8	11.9	6.1	88.6	121.3	62%
Population age 15–59						
1975	132	99	71	497	335	44%
2000	176	113	79	829	594	48%
2025	196	100	65	913	869	54%
2050	217	86	49	787	939	62%

Sources: Population age 18–23, National Science Foundation (2006), appendix table 2-36; population age 15–59, UN (2002).

have 13 percent more people in this age group than in 2005, whereas Western Europe will have 13 percent less and Japan 30 percent less. The United States share of 18- to 23-year-olds in advanced countries will continue to trend up.

But the projected reduction in the supply of young people is not limited to the advanced countries. Due to the single-child policy, the projections for China also show a drop in the number of young people, with the result that the ratio of the number of young Americans to the number of young Chinese will increase through 2050. Even India is projected to have decelerated growth in the number of young people from 2005 to 2030 and a decline thereafter. In short, the top half of table 1.2 shows that the projected change in the U.S. youth population does not stand out as creating an extraordinary shortfall compared with the projected changes in the number of young people in the main countries with which the United States is closely tied through the global economy.[5]

The numbers in the bottom half of table 1.2 for the population age 15–59 tell a similar story. The *increase* in the U.S. population in this age bracket drops from 44 million additional people in 1975–2000 to 20 million in 2000–2025 and 21 million in 2025–2050. The projected changes in Western Europe and Japan are much greater, with the population in this age bracket predicted to decline from 2025 to 2050. The U.S. share of the population in advanced countries will thus keep rising. As for the two highly populous developing countries, China's population age 15–59 is projected to rise through 2025 and then to fall through 2050, while India's population is expected to increase throughout the period. The ratio of the Chinese population to the U.S. population will barely change from 2005 to 2050. The UN projects that the proportion of the world's population in India, Africa, and Latin America will rise.

THE DOUBLING OF THE GLOBAL WORKFORCE

In the global economy, where firms "source" labor worldwide, where consumers buy goods and services made in countries that are part of the world trading system, and where immigrants move among countries, labor developments in one country are likely to affect conditions in other countries. In the 1990s, the global labor market changed greatly when China, India, and the ex-Soviet bloc joined the world trading system. Before then, these countries had trade barriers, self-contained capital markets, and only limited immigration to the Western countries, all of which isolated their labor markets from those in the United States and the rest of the capitalist world. The collapse of Soviet communism,

China's decision to "marketize" its economy, and India's rejection of autarky changed all this and brought approximately 1.3 billion new workers into the global capitalist system (figure 1.1). Firms in advanced capitalist countries could suddenly hire low-wage workers in China, India, and the ex-Soviet bloc to perform tasks that might previously have been done in advanced countries or in other developing countries. This roughly doubled the number of workers in the world economy.

Most important, because these countries had relatively little capital, their entry into global capitalism reduced the global capital-labor ratio by about 40 percent, which creates the global opposite of the labor shortage projected for the United States: *an excess of labor at the wages paid in advanced countries.* This excess will affect labor markets in the United States, other advanced economies, and other developing countries. Assuming that globalization continues unabated, United States firms should be able to meet potential shortfalls in domestic labor supplies for tradable goods and services by hiring labor overseas and by seeking immigrant labor to ameliorate potential labor shortages in the production of non-traded goods or services.

Figure 1.1. The Effect of China, India, and the ex-Soviet Bloc on the Global Labor Supply, circa 2000 (millions of workers)

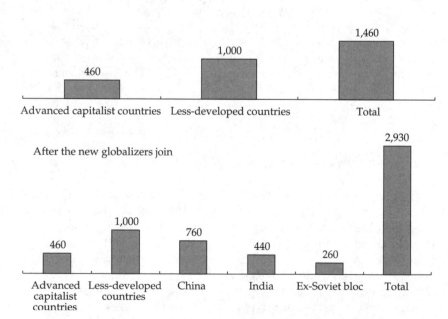

Source: Author's calculations based on International Labour Organisation data, http://www.laborsta.ilo.org.

If workers in China, India, and the ex-Soviet bloc had the same mix of skills as American workers, it would be incontestable that they would compete with American workers and offset, if not overwhelm, any future shortage of U.S. workers. But workers in these countries do not have the same skill set as Americans. A disproportionate number of Chinese and Indians have limited educations; relatively few have the university training of Americans. The ex-Soviet bloc workers are better educated but less numerous, and they have worked under communist conditions. Perhaps the right way to consider these workers is as *complements* rather than *substitutes* for American workers, who will increase U.S. demand for educated labor relative to less-educated labor and thus create a greater potential shortage of skills (rather than workers) in the United States.

This was, after all, the standard assessment of the impact of globalization on the United States when the country was debating the NAFTA treaty with Mexico. Proponents of the treaty argued that the United States would gain high-skilled jobs from increased trade with Mexico while exporting low-wage, less-skilled jobs.[6] The natural policy recommendation from this analysis is that U.S. workers should invest more in human capital. The workers in China, India, and other developing countries would never be able to catch up in skills and adversely affect educated U.S. workers.

This analysis does not seem to characterize the current global labor market. Developing countries, particularly China, are rapidly educating their workforces. The U.S. edge in giving university training to its workforce declined dramatically from the 1970s through the 2000s. In 1970, approximately 29 percent of university enrollments worldwide were in the United States. By 2000, the U.S. proportion of university enrollments worldwide had fallen to 14 percent. Similarly, the U.S. share of doctorates produced around the world has fallen from about 50 percent in the early 1970s to a projected level of 15 percent in 2010. Some of these trends are due to the increased proportion of the world's population in developing countries, but much is due to the spread of mass higher education to most countries.

One consequence of the increase in the supply of highly educated workers around the world is that U.S. multinational firms "globally source for labor" in ways they could not three decades ago. Another consequence is that the United States has been able to meet a large proportion of its rising demands for science and engineering workers through immigration. No readily available dataset measures the increased proportion of foreign-born highly educated workers employed in U.S. multinational companies around the world, but standard government surveys document the importance of immigration of scientists and engineers from overseas.

During the rapid growth of the U.S. economy in the 1990s, the employment of scientists and engineers increased greatly here. It did so despite fairly constant numbers of graduates in these fields among citizens or permanent residents and without markedly raising the salaries of these workers. As table 1.3 shows, the United States was able to meet increased demands for scientists and engineers without huge increases in salaries by "importing" foreign-born specialists in these areas. Some of the foreign-born obtained their education in the United States and later stayed to work here. But most workers with BS degrees and roughly half of those with higher degrees graduated overseas and came to fill jobs. If the U.S. economy demands more highly skilled workers in the period of projected slow labor force growth, it should be able to increase supplies by admitting more immigrants in areas with rising labor demand, as it did in the 1990s.[7]

Finally, while the National Center for Educational Statistics does not provide long-term projections of the number of college graduates, MS degrees, or PhDs, the Center's projections of the supply of highly educated workers show continued growth through 2013 (table 1.4). In the 1970s–2000s, the growth of the supply of college graduates in the United States was spurred by a large increase in the proportion of women obtaining degrees. The proportion of young minority people who obtained bachelor's and higher degrees rose as well. Thus, even though the U.S. edge in higher education will undoubtedly continue to diminish—with Organisation for Economic Co-operation and Development data showing that the United States no longer leads the world in the proportion of young people enrolled in higher education, and

Table 1.3. Foreign-Born Shares of Scientists and Engineers in the United States

	1990	2000
Bachelor's	11%	17%
Master's	19%	29%
PhDs	24%	38%
PhDs younger than 45	27%	52%
Post-docs	51%	60%

Source: Freeman (2005).

Table 1.4. College Graduate Supply, 1988, 2001, and Projected 2014 (thousands)

	Associate's	Bachelor's	Master's	PhD	First professional
1988–89	299	1,019	311	36	71
2002–03	633	1,348	513	46	81
2013–14	735	1,582	693	55	101

Source: Hussar (2005), figure G.

several advanced European Union countries have higher rates of enrollment than we do—the United States will still be producing large and increasing numbers of university graduates (National Science Foundation 2006).

Occupational/Skill Demand Forecasts

Projections of labor shortages require analysts to project labor demands as well as labor supplies. To be useful for education and training decisions, the projections must have some skill or occupation dimension. How does the Bureau of Labor Statistics (BLS) project demand for labor? Are those projections sufficiently precise to guide economic policy?

Every two years, the BLS's Office of Occupational Statistics and Employment Projections publishes the growth of demand in occupations in the *Occupational Outlook Handbook*. At the heart of the BLS occupational projections is an economy-wide "input-output" model, based on fixed coefficients that relate demand for goods and services to employment in various categories. This model begins with projections for the growth of the final demand for various categories of goods and services; it then uses "input-output" tables to translate the projected growth of final demand for goods and services into growth of output in different industries. The BLS then transforms expected industry *outputs* of goods and services into expected levels of industry *employment*, adjusting for projections of employee productivity growth by industry.

Finally, the BLS applies fixed coefficients relating employment in each *occupation* to employment in each *industry* to project the future occupational "needs" associated with the expansion or decline in employment in that industry. The keys to this step are the employment coefficients, which the BLS bases on historical data on the employment of workers in a given occupation within an industry and adjusts with a "change-factor" matrix of likely changes in the use of workers with different skills within industries. The BLS gives the example of systems analysts, which it adjusted upward in its 1990s projections because these workers "would be expected to become a greater proportion of each industry's employment as the number of applications for computer use continues to increase" (BLS 2006, 42). Finally, the BLS sums the estimates of employment in an occupation by industry across all industries to obtain the projected occupational employment.[8]

This technique works reasonably well to forecast the growth of highly aggregated occupations when the economy does not undergo any dramatic changes and when technological change does not greatly alter the demand for skills. It also works well for detailed occupations where most people work in the same industry and where productivity growth and final demands are reasonably stable. In its assessment of the 1984–95 projections, the BLS reports that they "captured the majority of the *general* trends ... [with] the most glaring inaccuracies in the projections of detailed occupations reflect[ing] the conservative nature of projected growth rates" (Veneri 1997, 15); and that the principal source of projection error was unexpected changes in the within-industry usage of different occupations. For instance, the 1984–95 projections were highly accurate for cooks in institutions or cafeterias (18.0 percent projected growth of employment versus 18.1 percent actual growth) but they underpredicted the growth of child care workers; personnel, training, and labor relations specialists; radiological technologists; and various computer specialties; among other occupations. Unfortunately, projections that are reasonably accurate for occupations with relatively stable employment but that fail to foresee big changes in demands for occupations involving new skills are of limited value in assessing future "shortages."

This author's analysis of the accuracy of BLS projections of employment, based on a regression model that links actual changes in occupational employment to the projected changes for 1988 to 2000, tells a similar story. In the author's model, the change in the natural logarithm (or ln) of actual employment is the dependent variable and the ln difference between projected employment and actual employment is the independent variable. Figure 1.2 summarizes the main result. It shows first that the projected growth rates are positively related to ensuing growth of employment, though with a wide band of variation. The estimated constant term is near zero, implying that the projections accurately captured the overall growth of employment.[9] The regression coefficient on the projected ln change term is 0.93, which is only modestly below 1. This implies that, *on average*, an occupation where employment is projected to grow or decline by 10 percent grows or declines at about 9.3 percent.

But the problem is in the fit of the equation. The R^2 is just 0.26, so *three-quarters of the variation in the growth of employment among occupations remains unaccounted for in the analysis*. The figure displays this with a wide range of actual occupational growth rates for any predicted growth rate. Given the variance in the growth of occupations, the standard error for the ln employment growth predicted by the regression is a relatively high 0.30.

The projections have a high standard error for three reasons. First, the industry mix of output or employment can change unexpectedly as a result of changing technology or market conditions. In the global economy, a given demand that domestic producers once met by hiring

Figure 1.2. Predicted and Actual Logarithmic Change in Employment by Occupation, 1988–2000

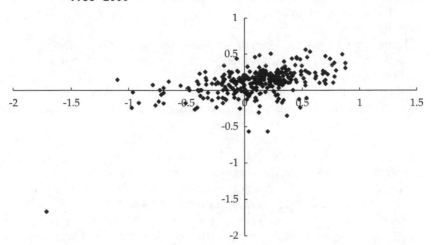

Source: Author's calculations using BLS data on actual and predicted employment, 1988–2000.
Notes: Actual logarithmic change = 0.0 + 0.93 * predicted logarithmic change; R^2 = 0.26. Standard deviation of actual change = 0.34; standard error on the coefficient = 0.09; and the standard error of the regression = 0.30. The sample size is 338.

U.S. workers can be met by foreign competitors, while some other domestic sector may expand to meet foreign demands. Changes like these are not well captured in the input-output model. Second, technical change alters the allegedly fixed coefficients of occupational employment within industries in ways that are difficult to predict. Third, the input-output framework ignores the fact that industry demands for factors of production (like various categories of labor or capital) respond to changes in factor prices. For example, it does not allow employers to substitute against employment in occupations with rapidly rising wages in favor of occupations where wages are falling (Freeman 1980). And by focusing solely on demand adjustments, the projection model ignores possible responses of labor *supply* to market conditions that can greatly affect input coefficients (e.g., through the effect of labor supply on wage rates).

AN EXAMPLE: COMPUTER AND MATHEMATICAL SCIENCES

Because demand for computer specialists has changed greatly (motivating the BLS to adjust the input coefficients for systems analysts mentioned above), it is particularly insightful to examine the projections of employment in this area. The BLS has published projections of future employment in "computer and mathematical sciences" every two years between 1996 and 2002. In each projection, the BLS took as its base actual employment in the year and projected employment 10 years into the future.

Table 1.5 summarizes the projections. In 1996, BLS projected that over the next decade employment would double from 1 million to 2 million jobs—100,000 additional jobs a year. But, at the height of the "dot.com" and high-technology boom of the late 1990s, labor supply increased far more rapidly than the BLS expected. By 1998, just two years after the BLS projected a growth of employment of 100,000 a year, 1.7 million people worked as computer and mathematical scientists—an annual growth of 350,000 employed people in the area. Since universities were not graduating those numbers of specialists, the supply came from people from other disciplines shifting into the computer occupations in response to a booming job market. Starting its 1998 projection at 1.7 million, the BLS projected a 92 percent growth of employment to 2008—1.5 million additional jobs. But in 2000, national statistics showed 3 million computer and mathematical scientists—50 percent more than the BLS had projected for 2006 four years earlier. Given the rapid growth of employment, the BLS raised its projected employment to 5 million by 2010. Then came the dot.com collapse and the offshoring of computer jobs to India and other low-wage countries. The 2002 projection reduced the expected number a decade into the future to 4.1 million—an 18 percent drop in projected employment compared with the 2000 projection for 2010.

The wide variation in the number of workers projected in computer and mathematical sciences reflects the difficulty in foreseeing future demands in an occupation subject to volatile demand from different economic factors. First, computer work in the U.S. market expanded, generating a huge supply response to new job opportunities. But then the availability of qualified labor overseas grew, which allowed firms to offshore work. Over the entire period, employment of computer and mathematical scientists rose sharply, but the market fluctuated so much that new graduates in some cohorts had difficulty finding work, while

Table 1.5. BLS Projections for Computer and Mathematical Sciences, 1996–2002

Year in which BLS made projection	Actual number in projection yr	Year projected	Projected	Number	New jobs
1996	1.0 M	2006	2.0 M	1.0	98%
1998	1.7 M	2008	3.2 M	1.5	92%
2000	3.0 M	2010	5.0 M	2.0	67%
2002	3.0 M	2012	4.1 M	1.1	34%

Sources: Braddock (1999); Hecker (2001, 2004); Silvestri (1997).

experienced programmers and computer specialists could not obtain the type of jobs they expected. In 2000, programmers had an unemployment rate that was among the lowest in the country—1.7 percent, compared with of 3.9 percent for all workers. But by 2001, the unemployment rate of programmers had tripled to 5.1 percent; it now exceeded the national rate, and remained high in succeeding years.[10]

Demography and Replacement Demand

But the projected labor shortage in the United States comes from a presumably well-determined demographic projection based on the retirement of the baby boomers, rather than from detailed projections of demand for specialized workers with wide confidence band. It is natural to think that the coming retirement of the large baby boom generation in the United States will inevitably create job openings and predictable "replacement demand" for new workers. If an occupation has 100 55-year-olds working in 2010, and these workers retire at 65 in 2020, and *nothing else changes*, then employers would seek 100 new workers to replace the retirees. If there is any part of a projection of future labor market balances that would seem likely to prove accurate, projecting replacement demand would be it.

This expectation is wrong. Enough other things change, which labor market models only imperfectly capture, to make projections of replacement demands more complicated and suspect. Changes in retirement behavior—the move to early retirement in the latter part of the 20th century and possible moves to delayed retirement to increase the solvency of Social Security and Medicare—can readily cause divergences between predictions based solely on aging and actual retirements.

In making its projections of replacement demands for labor, the BLS differentiates between *total separations* from an occupation, defined as the flow of individuals leaving an occupation, and *net separations*, defined to include movements of workers into as well as out of an occupation over a specific period. In the retirement age group, the two concepts are similar, since few workers will enter an occupation in that age group from another occupation. But the concepts can differ considerably for younger age groups and across occupations, some of which may traditionally obtain experienced workers from other occupations and others of which traditionally send workers to other occupations. An additional complication occurs between occupations where employment is expected to rise or to fall. For occupations in which employment has been rising, the BLS estimates net separation rates, by age, to estimate replacement needs during the projection period; but it cannot use this procedure for occupations where employment is expected to decline (BLS 2004).

To assess the relation between replacement demand and future job availability for workers of less than retirement age, this author estimated a regression model across occupations in which the dependent variable is the number employed in an occupation in 2000 in some specific age groups: 16–24, 25–34, 35–44, and 45–54. The independent variables are the number of employed people age 55 and older in the occupation in 1990—the likely retirees over the decade—and the number of people in that age group in 1990.

If replacement demands were important in creating jobs for workers below retirement age, the number of people age 55 and older working in 1990 would be positively related to the number of workers in younger age groups in the occupation in 2000. To give equal weight to large and smaller occupations, the variables were scaled by total employment in each occupation in 1990, so each variable is in the form of a rate. The second explanatory variable, the number of people in the specified age group in 1990, again scaled by employment in the occupation in 1990, is designed to deal with the likelihood that some occupations naturally have more or fewer workers in different age groups. With this held fixed, replacement demand should generate positive coefficients on employment for those age 55 and above for employment in that age group.

Table 1.6 gives the regression coefficients, standard errors, and related statistics for this model. The results reject the notion that the rate of likely retirement in an occupation is associated with growth of employment for people in younger age groups. The coefficients on the relative number of people in the retirement-age group are essentially

Table 1.6. Estimated Coefficients and Standard Errors for Relation between Relative Number of People Employed Age 55 and Over in 1990 and Relative Number of People Employed in Younger Age Groups in 2000

	Age Groups in 2000			
	16–24	25–34	35–44	45–54
Relative number of people age 55 and older, 1990	−.01 (.06)	−.27 (.08)	−.25 (.12)	−.07 (.11)
Relative number of people in specified age group in 1990	1.04 (.04)	.26 (.07)	.24 (.12)	.44 (13)
Constant	.00	.21	.28	.21
R^2	.63	.07	.02	.02
Number of observations	473	473	473	473

Source: Bureau of Labor Statistics, Employed persons by detailed occupation, sex, and age, Annual Average 1990 and 2000 (based on CPS).

Note: All variables are scaled relative to total employment in an occupation in 1990.

zero for the 16- to 24-year-olds and for the 45- to 54-year-olds, and are negative and significant for people in the other two age groups. In other words, these results imply that *replacement demand for workers in given occupations is negatively or not at all related to the numbers employed in that occupation for any age group,* rather than positively related.

Why does this occur? The most plausible reason is that older workers tend to be concentrated in older economic sectors, from which demand is shifting toward newer areas. It is this factor that induces the BLS to give different replacement demands for growing and declining occupations. In the 1990s, many workers of retirement age were in the railroad industry and in heavy manufacturing, but few were in the new computer software and "e-economy" sectors where employment was growing. If labor economists had a model that fully accounted for changes in employment due to all factors, replacement demand would inevitably have a positive effect on employment of younger people. Absent such a model, the effects of replacement demand are so dwarfed by changes in market conditions to produce the negative relations in table 1.6. Economic forecasters should not count on replacement demand for retiring baby boomers to create a labor shortage in the occupations with lots of boomers.

DEMOGRAPHY AND LABOR MARKET DEVELOPMENTS

Implicit in the fears that the United States will face a great labor shortage in the next decade or two is a belief that demographic forces have a powerful, predictable effect on economic outcomes. In the past, this has not been the case. Changes in behavior due to changing market incentives often overwhelm demographic factors. In the 1950s and 1960s, analysts projected much smaller growth in labor supply than actually occurred because they failed to foresee the changing labor force behavior of women in response to improved employment opportunities and wages. In the late 1960s and early 1970s, when the "baby boom" generation reached the job market, the earnings and employment of young people worsened relative to the earnings and employment of older workers due to the demographically driven shift in labor supplies. Indeed, this shift was an econometrician's dream exogenous shock for estimating the elasticity of the wages of young people relative to older people to changes in relative supplies (Freeman 1979; Welch 1979).

But when the number of young entrants fell in ensuing years, the earnings and employment of the new smaller cohorts of young workers did not improve. The OECD, among others, expected Western Europe's youth unemployment problems to disappear over time as the supply of young people fell. Instead, other factors—such as national wage policies that affected young workers and the state of the macroeconomy—dominated the youth labor market (Blanchflower and Freeman 2000). In the mid-1970s, this author projected that the rapidly growing supply of graduates would create a long-run relative surplus of college graduates (albeit around "cobweb" fluctuations—see Freeman 1976). Indeed, relative pay of graduates fell in the early and mid-1970s, and then picked up as the growth of supply diminished. But, in the ensuing decade, relative demand for graduates began growing more rapidly than relative supply to produce a rising wage gap between more- and less-educated workers.

As a final point of caution about forecasting economic developments from supply-based projections, consider the slow growth of the labor force in Western Europe and Japan in the 1990s through the mid-2000s. The demography implied that these countries would develop major labor shortages, but they did not. The problem in EU labor markets was quite the opposite: high unemployment and low employment-to-population rates. Perhaps the U.S. economy is so different from those of advanced Europe that the slow projected growth of labor supply in the United States will produce shortages, but perhaps not. The lesson from the historical record is that there is a huge gap between demographic changes and ensuing economic developments.

CONCLUSION

If the analysis of this chapter is correct and the economic sky will not fall down in the face of a slower growth in the U.S. workforce, why do so many people concerned with the well-being of the U.S. economy worry about the great coming labor shortage? Three factors are probably at work.

First, many of those concerned about the possible future shortage do not realize the historically large gap between demographic developments and economic developments. Nor do they recognize that globalization will further widen that gap.

Second, fears of a coming shortage fit with the concerns of various groups. Future shortage or not, business will benefit from policies that increase labor supply to drive down labor costs. Advocates of education and training see the shortage analysis as a way to gain national support for increased spending on training that will benefit workers. Politicians can use the shortage analysis to avoid dealing with policies like minimum wages, mandated health care spending, labor law reform, or enforcement of labor laws, and the like, by endorsing "win-win" education and training policies while sidestepping the fact that someone must pay for these investments.

Third, the shortage analysis offers a more optimistic framework for analyzing the economic future than the view that the biggest problem facing U.S. workers is competition from low-wage labor overseas. If the doubling of the global workforce has weakened the position of workers in the United States, the country has to deal with the rules of the global economy, how to increase savings and the supply of capital, how to retain good jobs and sectors, and how to distribute the gains from globalization to labor as well as capital while deterring protectionism.

That the coming labor shortage is more myth than reality does not invalidate some policies that shortage analysts endorse to help the economy progress. More and better schooling and job training, along with greater provision of occupational information, are potentially critical to preserving the nation's comparative advantage in high-tech sectors under the global competition vision of the future. There is arguably greater need for those policies if global competition places downward pressure on U.S. workers than if a domestic labor shortage puts them in the catbird seat in the economy and places business under pressure to recruit more workers.

If this analysis is wrong and the United States develops a great labor shortage in the future, the government should not intervene to prevent labor costs from rising. If firms demand more labor than workers supply due to a reduced growth of supply, should not a country that relies extensively on unfettered markets allow those markets to raise the price of labor, just as it allowed them to reduce the pay of many in recent decades? Nothing in economics predicts "slower growth in the standard of living, change in the balance of payments, inequality, persistent structural unemployment," or any other economic disasters from the normal functioning of competitive markets in the face of a shift in the supply-demand balance. If there is going to be a great labor shortage that raises wages and benefits for American workers, should we not all cheer the workings of the Invisible Hand, rather than seeing this as a disaster that policy should seek to avoid?

NOTES

The author benefited from the research assistance of Katie Bach.

1. Taken from the Employment Policy Foundation web site, 2001 (web site no longer functional).

2. Economists try to avoid the words "shortage" and "surplus" since, in a well-functioning market, prices or wages adjust so buyers and sellers are in equilibrium, with no one wanting to sell or buy more. One way to interpret the wide use of the terms is that they include changes in prices from long-run

equilibrium values that could have been avoided if market participants had foreseen the shifts in demand or supply better than they did.

3. The data on actual changes in GDP and employment are from the Council of Economic Advisers, *Economic Report of the President 2006* (Washington, DC: U.S. Government Printing Office), tables A-2 and B-36. The projections are from table 1.1 of this chapter.

4. U.S. Census Bureau, "U.S. Interim Projections by Age, Sex, Race, and Hispanic Origin," http://www.census.gov/ipc/www/usinterimproj/natprojtab01a.pdf, table 1a (March 18, 2004). Author estimates the disadvantaged minority group as 1 minus the proportion all white non-Hispanic, all Asian, and all other races.

5. The UN projections on which these data are based show a huge increase in the youth population in Africa, since the UN does not anticipate a fall in birth rate in that continent to the levels elsewhere.

6. This pattern is consistent with the predictions of Heckscher-Ohlin trade theory, in which comparative advantage is exogenous; and with the principal model that economists have used to analyze trade between advanced and developing countries—the "North-South" model in a dynamic context, where the North (i.e., the U.S. and other advanced countries) has a comparative advantage in high-tech sectors.

7. From the mid-1990s through early 2000s, the United States doubled the budget of the National Institutes of Health. This increase had little positive impact on the careers of new U.S. bioscientists, whose pay remained among the lowest among scientists and who had limited career prospects. One reason was the huge supply of "post-docs" and graduate students from foreign countries willing to work at low wages in U.S. labs.

8. See Hecker (2005).

9. The regression model effectively puts errors in projecting the overall growth of employment into the constant term in the regression and thus focuses on the ability of the projections to differentiate employment growth among occupations.

10. See NSF (2006), appendix table 3-8.

REFERENCES

Atkinson, William. 2005. "Confronting the Coming Labor Shortage." *Public Power*, November–December. http://www.appanet.org/newsletters/ppmagazinedetail.cfm?ItemNumber=14824&sn.Item.

Blanchflower, David, and Richard Freeman, eds. 2000. *Youth Employment and Joblessness in Advanced Countries*. Chicago: University of Chicago Press.

BLS. See U.S. Bureau of Labor Statistics.

Braddock, Douglas. 1999. "Occupational Employment Projections to 2008." *Monthly Labor Review* 122(11): 51–77.

Eisenberg, Daniel. 2002. "The Coming Job Boom." *Time*, April 29.

Fisher, Anne. 2003. "Believe It or Not, a Labor Shortage Is Coming." *Fortune*, October 7.

Freeman, Richard B. 1976. *The Overeducated American*. New York: Academic Press.

———. 1979. "The Effect of Demographic Factors on Age-Earnings Profiles." *Journal of Human Resources* 14(3): 289–318.

———. 1980. "An Empirical Analysis of the Fixed Coefficient Manpower Requirements Model, 1960–1970." *Journal of Human Resources* 15(2): 176–99.

———. 2005. "Does Globalization of the Scientific/Engineering Workforce Threaten U.S. Economic Leadership?" Working Paper 11,457. Cambridge, MA: National Bureau of Economic Research.

Hecker, Daniel E. 2001. "Occupational Employment Projections to 2010." *Monthly Labor Review* 124(11): 57–84.

———. 2004. "Occupational Employment Projections to 2012." *Monthly Labor Review* 127(2): 80–104.

———. 2005. "Occupational Employment Projections to 2014." *Monthly Labor Review* 128(11): 70–101.

Hussar, William J. 2005. *Projections of Education Statistics to 2014.* 33rd ed. NCES 2005-074. Washington, DC: U.S. Department of Education, National Center for Education Statistics.

Judy, Richard, and Carol D'Amico. 1997. *Workforce 2020: Work and Workers in the 21st Century.* Washington, DC: Hudson Institute.

Kaihla, Paul. 2003. "The Coming Job Boom." *Business 2.0 Magazine,* September 1. http://money.cnn.com/magazines/business2/business2_archive/2003/09/01/348381/index.htm.

NAM. See National Association of Manufacturers.

National Association of Manufacturers. 2003. *Keeping America Competitive.* Washington, DC: National Association of Manufacturers.

National Science Foundation. Division of Science Resource Statistics. 2006. *Science and Engineering Indicators 2006.* Arlington, VA: National Science Foundation.

NSF. See National Science Foundation.

Overholt, Alison. 2004. "The Labor Shortage Myth." *Fastcompany,* issue 85, August, p. 23. http://www.fastcompany.com/magazine/85/essay.html.

Silvestri, George T. 1997. "Occupational Employment Projections to 2006." *Monthly Labor Review* 120(11): 58–83.

Toossi, Mitra. 2002. "A Century of Change: U.S. Labor Force, 1950–2050." *Monthly Labor Review* 125(5): 15–28.

UN. See United Nations.

United Nations. Department of Economic and Social Affairs, Population Division. 2002. *World Population Ageing 1950–2050.* New York: United Nations.

U.S. Bureau of Labor Statistics. 2004. *Occupational Projections and Training Data 2004–2005 edition.* Bulletin 2572. Washington, DC: U.S. Department of Labor, Bureau of Labor Statistics.

———. 2006. *Occupational Outlook Handbook, 2006–2007 edition.* Washington, DC: U.S. Department of Labor, Bureau of Labor Statistics.

U.S. Chamber of Commerce. 2006. *The State of American Business 2006.* Washington, DC: U.S. Chamber of Commerce.

Veneri, Carolyn. 1997. "Evaluating the 1995 Occupational Employment Projections." *Monthly Labor Review* 120(9): 15–29.

Welch, Finis. 1979. "Effects of Cohort Size on Earnings: The Baby Boom Babies' Financial Bust." *Journal of Political Economy* 87(5): S65–S97.

2

AN OVERVIEW OF U.S. WORKFORCE DEVELOPMENT POLICY IN 2005

Burt S. Barnow and
Demetra Smith Nightingale

Maintaining a skilled workforce involves educating, training, and retraining workers, as well as facilitating job matches between workers and employers and enhancing worker security and safety. Funding for workforce preparation and development come from many sources: the federal government, state and local governments, private employers, and individual workers themselves. This chapter briefly summarizes federal policies related to workforce preparation and development in 2005.

Much of the funding for workforce development comes from the employer or business sector, with some studies estimating that private investment in training may be 10 times higher than public investments (Mikelson and Nightingale 2004). The intent here, though, is to frame considerations for future federal issues and options, which are presented in subsequent chapters. For that reason, this chapter focuses primarily on federal policies and programs, with references as appropriate to state and private policies.

This chapter uses a broad definition of workforce development policy. The typology presented includes policies and programs that provide, fund, or induce increases in employment or skill levels as well as policies that redistribute opportunities for employment and skill increases. This designation also includes workforce preparation that occurs in secondary and postsecondary education institutions. Thus, the broad definition includes, but is not limited to, programs authorized by the Workforce Investment Act (WIA), enacted in 1998 to revamp the nation's employment and training system.

This very broad definition calls attention to the fact that the nation's workforce is affected by an array of policies that may not appear to be directly focused on workforce development. For example, primary and secondary education is often not considered a workforce program, but it is hard to imagine policies more important for shaping the skills of the workforce. Likewise, individual and corporate income tax policies that encourage individuals and firms to invest in education and training are also part of the nation's workforce development portfolio.

TYPOLOGY OF CURRENT POLICIES

One could categorize federal workforce policies in several ways. The general typology presented here categorizes them first by their general purpose or goal and then by the type of policy mechanism used to achieve each purpose. Since the 1960s, Congress has enacted four laws that establish national employment programs and services: the Manpower Development and Training Act (1962), the Comprehensive Employment and Training Act (1973), the Job Training Partnership Act (1982), and the Workforce Investment Act (1998). Each law authorized a number of programs, and each program had various employment-related objectives. Other key employment legislation includes the Wagner-Peyser Act (1933), which authorized the nationwide Employment Service to provide free labor exchange services to workers and employers, and the Social Security Act (1935), which established the framework for unemployment insurance. While the relative priorities and emphasis as well as the specific program objectives have varied somewhat over the years, five broad goals have been central to the development of the nation's workforce development policies:

1. Meet current and future demand for workers by employers
2. Achieve and maintain a highly skilled workforce to increase the nation's productivity

3. Ensure worker security and safety
4. Enhance employment opportunities
5. Reinforce and reward the "work ethic"

Other goals periodically emerge to meet certain special situations. For example, following September 11, 2001 (and, more recently, after the devastating hurricanes in the Gulf states in 2005), special emergency funding was triggered under provisions of WIA's National Emergency grants to address employment and training issues related to economic dislocation or natural disasters. This emergency funding provided resources to states and localities for supplemental unemployment insurance and work programs to clean up and rebuild communities.

The relative priority among the general goals and the mix of programs vary over time, in part reflecting objectives of the executive branch and Congress, the nature of the economic cycle, and social and economic realities. Maintaining the nation's economic competitiveness has been one major goal since World War II. Currently, for example, the context for understanding national workforce policy includes rapid technological changes, globalization factors, and the aging of the population and labor force. While the Bush administration, like all previous administrations since World War II, maintains all five broad goals, the first two are particularly emphasized.

Goals 3 and 4 began with income security programs such as Social Security and unemployment insurance that were enacted in the 1930s as part of President Roosevelt's New Deal policies. Worker security and employment opportunity objectives were addressed through expanded legislation and regulations governing occupational safety and health, equal employment opportunity, and civil rights that emerged decades later. Many programs that fall under the fourth goal emerged out of the Kennedy and Johnson Great Society and War on Poverty policies, including several programs (such as Job Corps, Neighborhood Youth Corps, adult basic education, and Summer Youth Jobs) that specifically targeted economically disadvantaged populations. The final goal—reinforcing and rewarding the work ethic—is somewhat conceptual and overarching, and it can be seen in the work incentives included in welfare reform laws and in the work-test provisions of unemployment insurance, reflecting the historic political culture of a nation that places strong emphasis on individual initiative and responsibility and private entrepreneurship.

As noted in table 2.1, the federal government uses six categories of policy approaches, or mechanisms, to achieve the workforce goals:

1. Insurance and cash payments
2. Regulations and mandates

Table 2.1. Broad National Workforce Policy Purposes, by Policy Mechanisms

	Insurance and cash payments	Regul- ations and mandates	Tax incentives and credits	Human capital investments and services	Labor exchange and information	Social and support services
Meet current and future demand for workers			x	x	x	x
Achieve a highly skilled workforce			x	x	x	x
Ensure worker security and safety	x	x	x			x
Enhance employment opportunity		x	x	x	x	x
Reinforce and reward work ethic	x	x	x	x	x	x

Source: Authors' categorizations.

3. Tax incentives and credits
4. Human capital investments and services
5. Labor exchange and information
6. Social and support services

All five goals employ multiple policy mechanisms, as noted in the table. The first three policy mechanisms involve fiscal, tax, and regulatory strategies, while the last three consist mainly of programs that provide services to individuals directly or through vouchers. An important implication of this distinction is that federal expenditures do not necessarily provide a good measure of the costs or magnitudes of various policies. Regulatory policies, such as minimum wage and occupational safety and health legislation, have virtually no costs as measured by the federal budget, but they may impose substantial costs on employers.

The typology becomes considerably more complex when one also considers the various types of federally funded or sponsored programs or policies, the key ones of which are noted in table 2.2. Each program and policy has specific funding parameters; some are fully federally funded, some use tax-based transfers, and some are federal intergovernmental grants that may or may not require state or local financial

Table 2.2. Categorization of Major U.S. Federal Workforce Development Policies

Policy instrument	Selected key policies and programs
Insurance and cash payments	Unemployment insurance Trade Adjustment Assistance Workers' compensation Social Security Disability Insurance Social Security retirement
Regulations and mandates	Minimum wage (and state/local living wage) Occupational Safety and Health Mine Safety and Health Americans with Disabilities Act Civil rights laws enforced by EEOC Office of Federal Contact Compliance Programs Family leave policies Service priorities for veterans Skills standards, licensing, certification Immigration policies Collective bargaining laws (e.g., National Labor Relations Act) Retirement policies Work tests and work requirements for receipt of some benefits (e.g., welfare, UI)
Tax incentives and credits	Lifelong learning credits Earned income tax credit Work opportunity tax credit Welfare-to-work tax credit Economic development/business creation (Empowerment Zones and Enterprise Zones) Business tax credits for education
Human capital investments and services	Workforce Investment Act adult, dislocated worker, and youth programs K–12 school K–12 vocational education Postsecondary vocational education Postsecondary academics Adult education Vocational rehabilitation Ticket to Work program Veterans benefits Student Postsecondary Education Financial Assistance (grants and loans) Employment programs for specific groups (welfare, ex-offenders, disadvantaged, refugees, tribal members, veterans, older workers, dislocated workers)
Labor exchange and information	Labor exchange services (job matching/Wagner-Peyser) Labor market information
Social and support services	Health coverage Child care Emergency/crisis/disaster assistance Need- and income-based supports (e.g., food stamps, housing assistance)

Source: Authors' compilation.

matching. Many, especially since the mid-1990s, are funded through specially authorized grant programs (usually available for one to three years only) or funds designated by Congress for specific purposes or programs (referred to as "earmarks"). Among the current work-related initiatives funded through federal program grants are the Community-Based Job Training Grants, the Workforce Innovation in Regional Economic Development initiative, the High-Growth Job Training Initiative, the Disability Employment Grants, the Incumbent and Dislocated Worker Skills Shortages Demonstration Grants, the Youth Opportunity Grants (all through the Department of Labor, or DOL); the Jobs for Low Income Individuals grants (through the Department of Health and Human Services), and the reentry grants for programs helping prisoners and ex-offenders return to communities (through the departments of Labor and Justice).

Some permanent and special programs are available to all, while others are targeted. Many programs, such as occupational safety and minimum wage regulations or the public labor exchange and job placement services historically available through local public employment service offices, are universal, meaning that all (or nearly all) persons or businesses are included. A large number of programs and policies, however, are targeted to specific populations, customers, or entities. For example, there are special employment-related programs for refugees, veterans, Native Americans, unemployed workers, welfare recipients, disadvantaged youth and adults, persons with disabilities, workers dislocated from jobs as a result of foreign trade developments, immigrants and the businesses wishing to hire immigrants on special visas, businesses willing to locate in certain neighborhoods, and others.

Most programs commonly referred to as employment and training or workforce development fall within the human capital investment category, including those authorized and funded through the Workforce Investment Act. Bear in mind, however, that human capital investment is only one of several federal policy categories designed to support, enhance, protect, or develop the nation's workforce. Dozens of federal laws, programs, and funding streams are intended to address workforce issues directly or indirectly, including job training, job placement, and other employment services. For example, a recent study identified 69 nonmilitary programs in 2002 that could fund some occupational training for individual workers, including federal student loans and grants for postsecondary education. These programs are administered through seven separate federal departments (Mikelson and Nightingale 2004): Education (13 programs), Health and Human Services (16 programs), Housing and Urban Development (1 program), Interior (3 programs), Justice (1 program), Labor (34 programs), and Veterans Affairs (1 program).

Programs also vary in how they provide services. For example, under WIA, the core labor exchange services (meaning access to job openings and assistance in applying for the jobs) are largely available on a self-service basis, although people who require assistance are helped by staff in local employment offices. Training services under WIA are generally provided through individual training accounts, which are essentially vouchers for programs customers select from an eligible provider list, subject to oversight from the program.

The multiple programs, each with its own definitions, reporting requirements, and fiscal parameters, also make it difficult to estimate precisely how much federal funding is devoted to workforce development. The same study cited earlier determined that federal agencies may spend over $30 billion a year on direct workforce development activities to workers (not counting expenditures for administration or staff development). Of this amount, about $3 to $5 billion is specifically for job training, and the rest is for other employment-related services such as job search assistance, job referral and placement, labor market information, tax credits, and degree or diploma education. This $30 billion in federal spending is, therefore, a lower-bound estimate of the current expenditures on workforce development since it does not include tax-based expenditures (such as the earned income tax credit), regulatory activities, or work supports such as child care or health subsidies for working families.

In addition to the federal investment in workforce development, state governments sponsor employment and training programs. A study for the National Governors Association found that, in 1998, 48 states were using their own funds for workforce development and job training programs. The primary reasons states make such investment, according to the report, are to improve the competitiveness of the state's workforce for economic development and to meet projected labor needs of existing and new businesses and industries in the state (Bosworth et al. 1999).

State investments include direct job training options, such as subsidies and grants for community college occupational certification courses. More typical, though, are strategies where states use state and federal funds to leverage, or partner with, private investment in worker skill development. Although the precise combined total of initial and leveraged funds that result from state investments is not reported, the National Governors Association estimates that states themselves spent about $710 million on job training alone in 1998 (and an unspecified amount on other employment-related activities). Eight states account for about half of all state spending on job training: California, Iowa, Michigan, Missouri, New Jersey, North Carolina, Pennsylvania, and Texas.

While state workforce development spending is important, it represents only a small fraction of federal and private-sector spending, and state spending is highly affected by general economic and fiscal conditions. Expanding upon the NGA estimates, a subsequent analysis found that between 1998 and 2003, states somewhat reduced their spending on job training, to about $500 million (Mikelson and Nightingale 2004). The decrease from 1998 was attributed to less favorable fiscal conditions. As economic conditions worsen, more individuals may be out of work and could benefit from training or retraining, but states' fiscal capacity to invest is diminished, just as private businesses may also reduce their investment in worker training. The federal government can be an important source of stable funding, since it is less susceptible to economic cycles than either private investment or state spending.

CURRENT WORKFORCE INVESTMENT VISION, POLICIES, AND PROGRAMS

Since the term "workforce development" refers to various human capital programs, it is useful to summarize the current scope of those policies. The Employment and Training Administration within the U.S. Department of Labor oversees a large range of training and employment programs. The primary legislation currently governing workforce development programs is the Workforce Investment Act of 1998, which replaced the Job Training Partnership Act and amended laws governing vocational rehabilitation, adult education, and literacy programs. WIA also authorized the formal establishment of a nationwide system of one-stop career centers, intended to improve customer service (to workers and employers), consolidate access to various work-related resources and programs, and make maximum use of information technology resources (box 2.1).

While the legislation provides the framework for the nation's workforce development system, each administration sets priorities and establishes direction. The Bush administration is focusing workforce policy mainly on meeting the labor and skill needs of businesses and industries expected to grow in the future, many of which require new or higher-level skills. The current strategy recognizes two equally important customers—workers and businesses. This broader focus differs somewhat from that of previous administrations, where the basic employment and training system more explicitly emphasized the disadvantaged. The prior system consisted of one part that provided universal labor exchange and job placement services (the Employment Service, authorized by the Wagner-Peyser Act) and one part that focused more on training and employment for disadvantaged or dislocated workers.

**Box 2.1. Workforce Investment Act of 1998
(P.L. 105-220)**

Title I: Workforce Investment System (adults, youth, dislocated workers, One-Stop Career Centers)

Title II: Reauthorization of Adult Education and Family Literacy Programs

Title III: Wagner-Peyser Act Amendments (Employment Service)

Title IV: Rehabilitation Act Amendments

Title V: General Provisions

The current system is more integrated to emphasize the skill needs of both businesses and workers.

The Bush administration's vision for the "workforce investment system" for a new, rapidly changing economy is primarily reflected in the President's High-Growth Job Training Initiative. The initiative was begun in 2002 "to identify high-growth businesses and industries, evaluate their skill needs, and ensure that people are being trained with the skills these rapidly expanding businesses require, . . . [and] . . . to help more Americans gain the skills to find good jobs in our new economy" (DeRocco 2004). The vision includes focusing on high-growth sectors, such as information technology, health care, advanced manufacturing, and biotechnology. It also emphasizes partnerships among government, businesses, and industry, including training providers, community colleges, economic development agencies, and local one-stop career centers.

In DOL's "Workforce Tool Kit," the federal agency further explains to the business community that this vision of the new workforce investment system is a public/private partnership cutting across government agencies and programs:

America's Workforce Network is the name for the newly updated federally sponsored nationwide employment and training system. America's Workforce Network is committed to the nation's workers and their employers: committed to helping workers get the skills they need to succeed in our high-tech world and committed to helping employers find the skilled workers they so desperately need. . . . The new system is called a "network" because it offers a network of services and because it is created and maintained by a network of partners—workers, employers, federal, state and

local governments, educational organizations and community-
and faith-based groups. (DOL 2001, iv)

The tools of the new system, as described by DOL, go beyond funding
job training, providing job placement services, or taking applications
for unemployment insurance (the core services of the "old" system).
They include helping businesses

- "expand your workforce"—by helping businesses find and recruit
  qualified workers through local one-stop career centers and their
  partner providers, including workers from previously "untapped"
  groups such as youth, the elderly, welfare recipients, veterans,
  and persons with disabilities;
- "train your workforce"—especially by upgrading the skills of current workers, through publicly sponsored training programs for
  incumbent workers;
- "restructure your workforce"—including management strategies
  for downsizing, laying off workers, and assisting workers in "transitioning to new jobs";
- "finance your workforce"—by understanding and using various
  tax credits for hiring and training workers; and
- "access workforce resources"—by providing information and
  technical support to use the electronic and technological labor
  market resources available, such as America's Job Bank.

For the worker "customers," the new system also emphasizes partnerships, networks, self-help resources, and technology. Through the
nation's one-stop career centers, over 1,000 local centers provide universal services to any job seeker, worker, or business without regard to
eligibility criteria. Each center has a network of partners that can provide information and resources about training programs and job openings; workshops on career development; job search assistance; and
resource rooms that maintain computers, access online services, and
consult with employment specialists.

Since WIA was enacted in 1998, the primary vehicle through which
individuals receive occupational or vocational training has been individual training accounts (ITAs). Individuals who cannot obtain a job
without additional training can take their ITAs, which are similar to
vouchers, and choose the training they want at certified training providers (usually community colleges, vocational technical schools, or private training institutions). The vision is that through individual choice,
partnerships among providers, and use of the latest and best technological information and resources, the nation's matching of job seekers to

businesses will improve, and individuals will have more control over the direction of their career development choices.

In its budget proposal for fiscal year 2007, the Bush administration has proposed shifting resources away from programs and institutions and more toward individuals. Under this plan, funding for many workforce programs would be combined into a block grant to states, and the states would be required to distribute 75 percent of the funds as career advancement accounts to individuals who would use the funds to purchase training. Most of the remaining funds would be used to fund services through community career centers, which would include one-stop career centers and other community organizations.

Thus, the simple typology presented earlier includes traditional occupational training programs and job placement assistance, as well as loans and grants to individuals and employers for education and worker skills development and tax incentives for individuals and employers to increase employment, education, and training. This policy area is quite broad, encompassing more than just the employment, training, vocational, and adult education programs that fall under WIA and more than just human capital development, which includes education, vocational, and skills training. The different policy mechanisms can work together to achieve certain goals; in some cases, different goals and purposes may appear to counteract each other. Much programmatic restructuring of direct service programs has occurred since enactment of WIA, but, as the typology indicates, the nation's workforce development policy arena encompasses more than just direct programs for workers and businesses.

SUMMARY AND IMPLICATIONS

Workforce development is a broad policy arena encompassing many different notions of what is included in such policy. It includes a range of objectives and missions that sometimes conflict. Although many observers consider WIA the defining policy, it is only one of many federal policies affecting workforce development.

Workforce development requires both public and private responsibilities and resources. While it is impossible to predict with certainty what workforce development policy will look like in the future, one has a good idea about the forces that will be shaping the programs for at least the near term, and more likely for the next decade or more.

The primary factor that will be shaping workforce development policy in the near term is a tight fiscal environment. There will be little if any federal money for program expansions or major new initiatives, and there will be increased pressure to reduce funding. Consequently, it is likely that some programs may be consolidated into fewer funding streams. For example, the current administration has proposed combining Wagner-Peyser and WIA funds. Other consolidation efforts are possible as well, such as combining the Trade Adjustment Assistance program with the WIA dislocated worker program.

States and local governments may also play a larger role in the future, both financially and operationally. Currently, states are under severe fiscal pressure from increasing Medicaid costs, reduced tax revenue during the economic slowdown after 2001, and other factors. States already fund a variety of workforce development programs. They may expand their role, particularly if the federal government decreases its commitment, in large part because states recognize the important role job training plays in their broader economic and business development plans. Local governments have not traditionally been major sponsors of workforce development programs, with the prominent exception of primary and secondary education and vocational education in some states. However, if the federal and state governments decrease their commitments, then local governments may expand their support. For example, Frederick County, Maryland, contributes $900,000 annually to support workforce programs offered by the local workforce agency. This contribution could be indicative of further support by local jurisdictions. Again, the impetus is likely to be a recognition that investments in workforce development contribute to expanded business and economic development.

Another way of coping with shortfalls in federal and state funding is for local governments to undertake fee-for-service activities. Community colleges have long used this strategy to increase their capacity, and a recent evaluation of WIA found some local workforce boards following suit (Barnow and King 2005).

State and local governments are also likely to use strategies to leverage their funding so it stretches farther. Some states and local governments are already combining WIA funds with economic development or workforce funds available from states' Temporary Assistance for Needy Families funds. Such strategies can not only help increase the scale of workforce programs, they can also reduce duplication and fragmentation of programs.

Operationally, the trend over the past three decades has been to devolve authority for program design and service delivery from the federal government to the states or localities. This trend is likely to continue, if for no other reason than that policymakers generally agree that workforce development programs and policies should allow flexibility to respond to local economic needs and business cycles. While some special federal programs and initiatives may continue to be nationally directed (such as Job Corps or services to military veterans), the recent emphasis on state and local discretion will likely expand. Cross-program partnerships between workforce development and other relevant program areas such as economic development, community colleges, and family welfare and self-sufficiency programs have expanded in the past decade and form the basis of many new programs now operating in many communities, both through public agencies and, increasingly, through private institutions and organizations.

As of 2006, one cannot overstate the severity of the fiscal distress facing workforce programs. Since the advent of workforce development programs in the 1960s, however, the nation has been through periods where the federal government was running massive deficits only to be followed by surpluses a few years later. Although workforce development programs are likely to face difficult funding for the next few years, it is unclear what will happen in the longer term. Meanwhile, the range of programs operating at the local level reflect decades of experience as public and private partnering entities and different levels of government attempt to design employment and training programs that meet their immediate and emerging needs.

REFERENCES

Barnow, Burt S., and Christopher T. King. 2005. "The Workforce Investment Act in Eight States: Final Report." Employment and Training Administration Occasional Paper 2005-01. Washington, DC: U.S. Department of Labor, Employment and Training Administration.

Bosworth, Brian, Dan Broun, Eric Foreman, and Cynthia Liston. 1999. *A Comprehensive Look at State-Funded, Employer-Focused Job Training Programs.* Washington, DC: Regional Technology Strategies, Inc., and the National Governors Association Center for Best Practices.

DeRocco, Emily Stover. 2004. Statement of Emily Stover DeRocco, Assistant Secretary of Labor, Employment and Training Administration, before the Committee on Appropriations, Subcommittee on Labor, Health and Human Services, and Education, U.S. House of Representatives, April 1.

DOL. See U.S. Department of Labor.

Mikelson, Kelly S., and Demetra Smith Nightingale. 2004. "Estimating Public and Private Expenditures on Occupational Training in the United States." Report to the U.S. Department of Labor, Employment and Training Administration. Washington, DC: The Urban Institute.

U.S. Department of Labor. 2001. *Workforce Tool Kit: The Resource for Employers.* Washington, DC: U.S. Department of Labor. http://www.doleta.gov/whatsnew/insidebind.pdf.

PART II

SCHOOLING AND TRAINING FOR YOUTH AND YOUNG ADULTS

3

CAREER-FOCUSED EDUCATION AND TRAINING FOR YOUTH

Robert I. Lerman

The idea that American workers are ill-equipped to compete in a world economy has been a longstanding concern of business, political, and academic leaders at least since the beginning of the last century. Since the 1980s, contemporary leaders have worried that the weak educational preparation of American workers will limit the nation's ability to achieve healthy growth in productivity and will prevent the narrowing of large income differences between the highly educated and the less educated (Commission on the Skills of the American Workforce 1990; William T. Grant Foundation 1988). At an October 2005 congressional hearing, future Federal Reserve Chairman Ben S. Bernanke argued for the importance of improving educational attainment and academic achievement as the way to reduce inequality, by lowering the wide earnings differences between college-educated and high school–educated workers.

Of special concern are workers that either do not complete high school or do not learn enough in high school to compete effectively in a modern economy. As Murnane and Levy (1996) succinctly put it, "As a result of the ever-growing mismatch between the skills of most [high school] graduates and the skills required by high-wage employers, a U.S. high school diploma is no longer a ticket to the U.S. middle class." They point to the growing earnings advantage of college-educated workers from the early 1980s to the 1990s. Since 1995, the wage gap between college graduates and both high school graduates and high school dropouts has widened further (Autor, Katz, and Kearney 2005).

Globalization and the changing educational composition of the U.S. workforce only heighten these concerns. Given the increasingly competitive marketplace, an excellent education system is viewed as increasingly critical to a nation's success in the "flat world" described by Thomas Friedman (2005). Based on recent changes in the educational composition of the workforce, U.S. trends look promising. Since 1992, workers with at least some college education have accounted for more than 100 percent of the net growth in the adult (age 25 and over) U.S. labor force.[1] While workers with at least some postsecondary education increased from 1992 to 2004 by 19.6 million, the number of adult workers with no more than a high school degree declined by about 1 million.

This decline took place because the increases in less-educated workers coming from young people entering the job market were more than offset by decreases in the number of older, less-educated workers leaving the job market. The main reason is that cohorts aging out of the workforce had much lower proportions of people attending and completing college than entering cohorts. In the near future, we are not likely to see educational upgrading from this source, because workers reaching 65 over the next decades will have similar levels of education to the young workers replacing them.[2] Thus, the economy of next few decades is likely going to have to absorb a rising number of less-educated workers.

The education and wage patterns add urgency to the question that U.S. policymakers are asking: what are the best ways to educate and train the next generations of workers not likely to obtain BA degrees so they can work in rewarding, good-paying careers? The answer given in the United States in the late 1980s and early 1990s, and still given in other advanced economies, included an important role for career-focused programs. Since the late 1990s, however, U.S. policies have downplayed or ignored these programs, focusing instead on academic standards and on increasing the proportion of workers going to college. In fact, policymakers seem to be pursuing a de facto "college for all" strategy as a goal for the future.[3] They do so without adequately taking into account the current and potential effectiveness of career-based education and training alternatives and despite the reality that many students are and will probably continue to be ill-equipped for college-level courses.

Already, it is clear that the returns to college for the marginal student are far lower than the returns for the average student. Even with a 50 percent increase in the proportions completing a two- or four-year college program, over half of all young people will have no degree beyond high school. Emphasizing a purely academic-oriented definition of skill ignores the critical importance of contextualized knowledge and noncognitive skills that can be developed with work-based learning and career-focused training (Stasz 2001).

This chapter assesses the role career-focused education and training currently plays and should play in the future from theoretical, institutional, and empirical perspectives. Before reviewing the evidence and proposing new policies for career-focused education and training, the chapter discusses the various meanings of career-focused education and the argument that "vocationalism" in education is actually growing (Grubb and Lazerson 2004). Next, the chapter presents the trends in policy and participation in the striking variety of education and training aimed at preparing young people for careers.

The chapter also examines the evidence on the effectiveness of these policies and institutions for various groups of young people. It then draws on this evidence to propose initiatives for helping education and training systems integrate non-BA workers more effectively into rewarding careers. The section suggests promising policies, including some whose effectiveness could and should be tested in demonstration projects. The final section offers some concluding observations.

WHAT ARE THE APPROPRIATE ROLES FOR CAREER-FOCUSED EDUCATION AND TRAINING?

Debates over how best to prepare young people for careers go back centuries and are important in nearly all countries. Even restricting the discussion to recent history and to advanced economies, we find widely varying views on the appropriate roles of high schools, colleges, training institutions, governments, employers, and individuals. Less often discussed but of central importance is how best to define the skills most workers will require for rewarding careers.

At one extreme, schools at all levels should provide a broad range of academic skills and largely ignore any potential connections to the general world of work or to a specific occupation. The education system should limit what Grubb and Lazerson (2004) call "vocationalism," or the use of educational institutions primarily for vocational purposes. Grubb and Lazerson remind us that the debate over how much schools should teach vocational skills goes back at least a century and that national systems vary substantially in this regard.[4] Leading the way toward vocationalizing the school system is an "education gospel" that has vastly exaggerated the role of education in achieving economic growth, reducing economic inequality, and solving an array of the nation's social problems. Grubb and Lazerson worry that educating young people for the job market will end up diverting students from the broader purposes of learning, such as moral and civic education and an appreciation and knowledge of the liberal arts. Schools would become the tools of employers and not primarily concerned with the intellectual development of the individual.

This critique of a vocational orientation comes from the right and left sides of the political spectrum. For example, in critiquing the integrated school and work approach proposed by Marc Tucker, the politically conservative Eagle Forum argues that the plan "would change the mission of the schools *from* teaching children academic basics and knowledge *to* training them to serve the global economy in jobs selected by workforce boards. Nothing in this comprehensive plan has anything to do with teaching schoolchildren how to read, write, or calculate."[5] Others argue that frequent changes in the composition of jobs will make career-focused education and occupational training obsolete and thus less productive than schooling using a purely academic curriculum. Because of this risk and the view that vocational education prepares people for low-status positions, career-focused training will end up trapping many young people in low-wage jobs. Still another critique is that career-focused education in public schools ends up substituting public funding for skills that private employers should be providing and financing.

An alternative view is that schools do and should have a career focus, while at the same time they must better prepare young people with sufficient academic and other skills for the world of work. Few dispute the need to focus on improved academic skills at least through 8th grade. A mix of academic and career-focused approaches, however, might make sense for students in subsequent grades. Schooling should teach academic skills but not become too rigid in making the curriculum entirely academic. Incorporating career-based learning components into the curriculum and extracurricular activities is likely to complement academic courses and to improve the employment opportunities and career-related skills of students when they leave formal schooling. Work-based learning, especially well-structured work experiences, can also play an important role in helping students learn critical workplace competencies, develop confidence, and understand the requirements and operations of specific occupations (Bailey, Hughes, and Moore 2004).

Involving schools in training people for various occupations will make education more relevant for students and thus encourage them to study and learn more (Lerman and Pouncy 1990). Although this strategy cannot solve all social and economic problems, changing the educational system is one of the few public policy instruments that can significantly help people increase their long-term earnings capacities. Advocates of integrated programs have argued that student motivation is central to improving educational outcomes. As Bishop (1990) points out, student effort is a critical, often overlooked input in the educational process. Especially in the high school years, increasing the number and efficiency of student hours on task has more potential than expanding standard school inputs. Requiring students to meet external standards is one way to motivate them. But so is helping students see the relevance of what they learn for their careers and teaching subjects in a real-world context (Hamilton and Hamilton 1997).

Vocationalism embodies two distinct ideas. First, improving career outcomes should be a primary focus of education, especially given the importance of expanding educational attainment for raising the productivity and earnings of the workforce. Second, incorporating career-focused curricula and work-based learning into school programs is an effective strategy for helping students learn relevant skills for the workplace and earn more. Well-structured, career-focused education and training might also serve a useful pedagogical role in improving how well students learn general academic subjects. Making learning relevant to the concerns of students (including what careers they will pursue) can increase their motivation.

Notwithstanding the objections raised by Grubb and Lazerson, policy researchers and the majority of the public support the notion that increasing educational attainment is necessary for career success, high levels of economic growth, and rising productivity.[6] In fact, consensus on this issue has led to the creation of an implicit "college for all" policy that is supported by many political leaders, local school districts, and policy researchers (Rosenbaum 2001). Students and their parents see college as virtually the only route to successful careers. In 2002, about 80 percent of high school sophomores expected to achieve at least a four-year college degree.[7] As James Rosenbaum points out, counselors in U.S. high schools are reluctant to discourage any students from pursuing a college education, no matter how poorly students have performed in high school courses nor how much remedial education they may require before attaining any college credits.

The high and rising wage premium for college graduates over high school graduates provides a straightforward rationale for expanding the college share of the incoming workforce. Although wage differentials favoring college graduates have increased slowly since 1995, the gaps remain high and well above what they were in the 1970s (Autor et al. 2005). By implication, expanding the supply of college graduates should raise the earnings of some workers and lower wage differentials.

One caution is that standard estimates of returns to college may well overstate the contribution of the pure schooling component. Most students work and accumulate substantial amounts of work experience while they are in school, and work experience is known to improve earnings.[8] Two recent studies estimate that a substantial share (25–44 percent) of the estimated returns commonly attributed to two-year and four-year college actually result from the earnings gains caused by the work experience of students (Light 2001; Molitor and Leigh 2005). Other studies find that work during high school and college may have detrimental effects on academic achievement (Stinebrickner and Stinebrickner 2003; Tyler 2003). Another caution is that the added graduates might be poorly matched for formal schooling and for available careers.

A key concern is that the emerging college-for-all policy aims at extending academic learning at the expense of vocational education, training, and work experience. So far, however, the picture concerning shifts from vocational to academic education is mixed. The emphasis on academic standards and academic courses is raising the average number of academic courses taken by high school students and reducing the share of courses with a specific vocational outlet. Yet the absolute number of vocationally related courses has remained constant since 1990 (Silverberg et al. 2004). In addition, the vocational component of postsecondary education clearly remains important. About one-third of all degree-seeking postsecondary students are in sub-baccalaureate vocational degree programs.

Schooling is certainly increasing, but complications arise when we try to examine whether the nation's overall education and training system is tilting away from career-focused skills and toward academic education.[9] The share of 20- to 21-year-olds in formal schooling rose from about 40 percent in 1990 to 48 percent in 2002. Smaller increases took place among 18- to 19- and 22- to 24-year-olds.

Turning to school outcomes, table 3.1 shows the 1992 and 2004 distributions of educational attainment achieved by all noninstitutionalized 25- to 29-year-olds and 30- to 34-year-olds. Increasing percentages of young people have been attending and completing postsecondary programs, most of them academic in orientation. The share of these groups with more than a high school diploma rose from 5 to 12 percentage points. The proportion with an associate's degree in a vocational subject increased by 0.4 to 1.5 percentage points.

Some BA programs are oriented toward specific careers (say, engineering), but they should not necessarily be classified as vocational because many of their courses are clearly academic. The figures in table

Table 3.1. Changes in the Distribution of Educational Attainment by Age and Sex: 1992–2004 (percent)

	Age 25–29		Age 30–34	
	Male	Female	Male	Female
	1992			
Less than high school	13.8	13.5	14.2	12.8
High school only	37.9	36.9	38.8	37.1
Some college	19.3	18.1	17.3	19.7
AA, BA, or post-BA	29.0	31.5	29.6	30.4
Associate's-vocational	3.4	3.9	3.7	4.6
Associate's-academic	2.4	3.6	2.4	3.8
BA	18.4	20.1	16.5	16.6
Post-BA	4.7	3.9	6.9	5.5
	2004			
Less than high school	14.8	12.0	13.8	11.2
High school only	31.8	26.7	29.7	26.6
Some college	20.1	20.8	17.5	19.0
AA, BA, or post-BA	33.3	40.4	39.0	43.2
Associate's-vocational	3.8	4.7	5.2	5.1
Associate's-academic	3.5	4.4	3.9	4.7
BA	21.1	24.8	20.5	23.1
Post-BA	4.9	6.6	9.5	10.2

Source: U.S. Bureau of the Census, http://www.census.gov.

3.1 may well miss graduates of occupational proprietary schools. Even education data sets vastly understate the number of students in these vocational programs (Cellini 2006).[10] These caveats aside, the weight of the evidence indicates that the educational expansion of the 1990s has been largely related to academic subjects.

The drift toward academic education is taking hold in other Organisation for Economic Co-operation and Development (OECD) countries as well. Between 1991 and 2002, the average share of 25- to 34-year-olds in the OECD completing a college education (at the BA level or higher) increased from 20 to 28 percent. The changes differed significantly across countries. Tertiary education completion jumped from 20 to 36 percent in France and from 19 to 31 percent in the United Kingdom, while Germany's rate barely increased from 21 to 22 percent (OECD 2004). Still, even countries with traditions of high-quality vocational education are feeling pressures to expand higher education substantially.

Debates over issues of vocationalism sometimes obscure concrete questions about where and how education and training for careers should take place and about how increases in education and training raise productivity and earnings. In particular, few discussions deal with the likelihood that what works best varies across specific occupations and across individuals. The nature of skills and the relative roles of academic and other skills have little place in current discussions. Almost no attention is paid to the sociocultural approach to examining skills (Stasz 2001), which emphasizes the contextual nature of skills and the importance of non-academic skills often attained in a work environment and through joining experienced workers in a "community of practice."[11] State standards and tests developed to measure student progress at school and to determine eligibility for high school graduation have largely ignored critical non-academic skills required for success at the workplace, as developed and documented by the Secretary's Commission on Achieving Necessary Skills (1992) and others.[12]

Career-focused education, training, and work experience are likely to improve the learning process for many youth and to foster the development of critical Secretary's Commission on Achieving Necessary Skills (SCANS) skills. In any event, it is far from obvious when a course is fundamentally academic or vocational. Even in the largely work-based apprenticeship programs, students take courses that include math, the physics of electricity, and other subject matter that has genuine academic content. Some skills learned at workplaces are applicable beyond the occupation or industry where the training takes place and can apply to aspects of life outside the workplace, such as personal relationships.

In most occupations, work-based learning and career-focused education and training play vital and often distinct roles (Allen and van der Velden 2001). But the timing and framework of this form of learning vary widely among occupational areas at low, medium, and high levels of pay. Attorneys and physicians, two of the highest paid and most prestigious professions, certainly acquire education tailored to their occupations but also rely heavily on internships that combine learning and production at workplaces. In the United States, attorneys' and physicians' work-based learning and practical training take place after at least 16 years of academic schooling and in combination with law and medical schools. Nurses use their combined classroom and work-based learning within a college context or after college.

Other examples of work-based learning occur in formal and informal apprenticeships of varying lengths of time and with varying levels of academic preparation. Formal, registered apprenticeships are most common in the construction and manufacturing industries. Although only a small fraction of the workforce participates or has participated in a formal apprenticeship, the training in such programs is usually intensive in terms of work-based learning and classroom courses.

Governed by State Apprenticeship Councils and the U.S. Office of Apprenticeship Training within the Department of Labor, U.S. apprenticeships are generally undertaken after the high school years, regardless of whether the individual has completed a diploma or GED. Apprenticeships typically require at least 144 hours of classroom training related to the three to four years of work-based training in which workers must gain specified skills at workplaces, mostly as part of the production process. In well-developed apprenticeship programs, even where formal academic entry requirements are minimal, the content of the classroom instruction incorporates applied science and other technical courses, including material that would be taught in a college science class. Indeed, instructors for these programs are often drawn from community colleges. One big advantage is that the apprenticeship trainees receive pay during their work-based learning and as a result bear low costs in terms of forgone earnings. The program imposes a cost in forgone leisure, as apprentices typically take their classroom instruction at night or on weekends.

The dividing line between career-focused and academic approaches to education and training is a thin one, and formal career-focused education and training is included in the trajectories of many types of workers. From this perspective, the key questions become the following:

- What are optimal patterns of purely academic study and of career-focused education and training? Should the interaction between academic courses and career-focused courses and workplace experience begin at varying ages?
- Is a college-for-all policy desirable? If not, what other routes to career success should be emphasized?
- What institutional settings are well-equipped to provide flexibility and heterogeneity that take appropriate account of variations in the interests and capacities of young people and of the complexity of the job market?
- Does having too many options for career preparation hurt the nation's ability to insure all young people meet basic academic standards and other certifications that have credibility with postsecondary education and private firms?

Before turning to these questions, we take a closer look at policies and participation in various types of education and training that youth experience.

POLICY AND PARTICIPATION TRENDS IN CAREER-FOCUSED EDUCATION AND TRAINING

The 10 main institutions preparing youth for careers remain high schools with minimal vocational content, high schools that incorporate career-focused courses and programs, community colleges providing academic and vocational associate's degrees as well as nondegree career-oriented courses, proprietary vocational schools, publicly funded separate training programs (sometimes delivered through community-based organizations), employer-led training, apprenticeships, colleges, universities, and professional schools, usually located within universities. The basic questions about how best to organize these institutions to prepare young people for careers have remained remarkably similar, but the answers have varied over time. Federal, state, and local policymakers have at times placed more or less emphasis on academic-oriented schooling, career-focused education, classroom training, work-based training, work experience, and integrating one or more of these activities. Two key questions are where and when career-focused education should take place. Other concerns have to do with student characteristics (such as academic, racial, ethnic, and disability status) in various institutions and whether to develop tailored, targeted programs or offer a common program for all students.

Evolution of Policies, Programs, and Participation

The policy trends illustrate changing perspectives about national needs. During the 1960s and 1970s, when the critique of mainstream schooling's uneven record in preparing youth for productive careers had not become so strident, the primary concern was the high youth unemployment rates, especially minority teenagers experiencing unemployment rates of over 40 percent (Freeman and Holzer 1986; Freeman and Wise 1982). The national focus was on poor youth, not so much youth in general. The worry was that economically disadvantaged youth lacked the chance to gain valuable work experience and that these early deficits might be a "scarring" experience that could limit their employment and earnings over many years (Ellwood 1982). The Neighborhood Youth Corps, which provided hundreds of thousands of in-school and out-of-school jobs to poor youth, was one response. Ideally, Congress reasoned, the early work experience should reinforce schooling and not substitute for academic learning.

One federal initiative aimed at both reducing youth unemployment and encouraging school completion among low-income youth was the Youth Incentive Entitlement Pilot Project (YIEPP). The purpose of YIEPP was to test the impact of guaranteeing in-school and summer jobs to poor 15- to 19-year-olds as long as they stayed in school (and performed satisfactorily) or returned to school. YIEPP's objective was to increase high school completion and the post-high school employment and earnings of poor youth in selected cities. The YIEPP jobs provided not only work experience and income but also incentives to attain more schooling, culminating with a high school diploma. YIEPP placed little or no emphasis on the content of youth learning in school or at the workplace.

After disappointing findings on the impacts of YIEPP and some youth programs financed by the U.S. Department of Labor, policy interest in and funding for local authorities to finance youth employment and training targeted on economically disadvantaged youth declined. As of 2002, spending on youth employment and training programs through the local workforce investment boards amounted to about $1.2 billion, well below real expenditures in prior years. Only the Job Corps program, an intensive 12-month residential training program for at-risk youth, managed to maintain high levels of funding, at about $1.4 billion. Job Corps financed sufficient training to help participants attain occupational credentials. About 45 percent of Job Corps participants ended up earning a certification in an occupational area.

Still, relative to the size of the youth cohort, or even the disadvantaged youth cohort, these programs are quite small. In 2002, about 53,000 16- to 21-year-olds participated in Job Corps, and about 65,000 took part in other types of training provided under the Workforce Investment Act. By comparison, 4.8 million 16- to 24-year-olds were out of school and out of work in 2000 (Lerman, Moskowitz, and Ratcliffe 2004).

By the 1980s, the policy problem began to shift away from youth unemployment among the disadvantaged toward the low academic achievement of youth in general. A lack of early work experience and the prospects for the disadvantaged no longer were the major concerns. Rather, what was placing the nation at risk was the inability of a large share of students to attain basic skills in reading, math, and writing (National Commission on Excellence in Education 1983). Employers reportedly were dissatisfied with the capacities of the new cohorts entering the workforce, not so much because of a deterioration of basic skills but because of the increasing demand for skills in most jobs. High-paying jobs available to workers with low levels of education were declining in manufacturing and other industries. Policymakers interpreted employers as saying schools should make sure students knew how to read, write, and compute, and were basically work-ready. Employers would take care of the occupation-related and work-related skills. Supporting this view was the expectation that workers were going to undergo frequent changes in occupations and industries, thereby making early career-focused education futile.

This new paradigm contributed to a deemphasis on vocational education in policy circles, as did concerns that vocational education was becoming stigmatized, an outlet for weak students, and ineffective in linking young people to well-paying careers. Instead of abandoning vocational education outright, however, the new goals were to integrate academic and vocational education in various ways. One was to encourage more vocational education students to take higher-level academic classes, including more years of English, math, and science. Influencing this agenda was a proposed "New Basics" curriculum, or the minimum set of courses that all students should take to prepare for a career or postsecondary education (Murnane and Levy 1996). In one elaborate effort to upgrade the academic content of vocational programs, the Southern Regional Education Board developed a vocational education consortium to implement the High Schools That Work (HSTW) project. It began in 1988 as a pilot project with a group of 28 vocational schools across the southeastern United States; by 2000, HSTW had expanded to more than 900 schools.

A second approach to integrate academic and vocational education encouraged close links between career-oriented programs in high schools and related programs in community colleges, especially in technical career fields. Consortia sponsored by the federal government were to develop Tech-Prep programs that built integrated sequential courses of study involving high school and community college programs. Agreements between institutions allowed some courses taken in high schools to count toward a two-year associate's degree. The initial focus of Tech Prep was on increasing education and career opportunities of middle-range students who typically did not complete baccalaureate degrees and often did not graduate from high school with sufficient skills to succeed in the demanding workplace.

Federal grants to implement consortia began soon after Congress passed the Tech-Prep Education Act as part of the Carl D. Perkins Vocational and Applied Technology Education Act of 1990. As of 2003, about 1,000 consortia involving high schools and community colleges were operating, mostly coordinated by community and technical colleges and involving at least articulation agreements allowing the transfer of high school credits. These agreements cover a large share of community colleges and about half the high schools. Over the past decade, Tech-Prep participation has increased substantially, from about 173,000 in 1993 to over 1.2 million in 2001 (Silverberg et al. 2004). The recent figure would suggest that about 10 percent of all high school students are in Tech-Prep. But states vary in how they count participation; often, students reported in Tech-Prep have taken only one vocational course that has transferability.

A separate, but related, effort to integrate academic and career-focused learning was the School-to-Work Opportunities Act (STWOA) of 1994. The stimulus behind STWOA was an emerging consensus among policy researchers and political leaders that the United States lacked an effective system to transition young people from school to work and careers and that the problem was especially serious for the majority of the youth cohort not going on to or expected to complete college (Commission on the Skills 1990; William T. Grant Foundation 1988). Some called for developing intensive youth apprenticeship programs aimed at integrating the last two years of high school with work-based learning, leading to a recognized youth apprenticeship credential (Hamilton 1990; Lerman and Pouncy 1990). Others emphasized less intensive strategies, such as job shadowing, improved career counseling, embedding workplace examples and contextualized learning into academic courses, and short-term internships with employers.

The goals of STWOA were ambitious. STWOA funding was to allow state and local partnerships to bring together education reform, workforce preparation, and economic development. Local plans were to incorporate work-based learning and connecting activities into a well-integrated system for all students. Though STWOA had similar goals to those of HSTW and other efforts to improve the existing system of vocational education (now called career and technical education, or CTE), national officials implementing STWOA generally did not encourage close contact with CTE, partly to avoid potential issues of stigmatization and partly to emphasize career-focused learning in workplaces and not in schools.

Another career-focused education approach is the career academy. While operating within schools and as part of a local school system, career academies are high schools organized around an occupational or industry focus, such as health care, finance, or tourism. They try to weave related occupational or industrial themes into a college preparatory curriculum, enabling students to see relationships between academic subjects and their application to the school's focal area. Data from the Career Academies Support Network document the presence of at least 1,588 academies: 22 percent are in finance, 14 percent in information technology, 12 percent in hospitality and tourism, 8 percent in arts and communication, and 8 percent in health.

Career academies are typically made up of 50–75 students per grade from the 10th through 12th grades within the larger high school. These students take two to four classes a year in the Academy taught by a common team of teachers; at least one course is career- or occupation-focused. Students take other courses in the regular high school. The small learning communities help academies foster a sense of community, personal attention from teachers, and constructive collaboration with peers.

Academies attempt to use applied learning in academic courses as well as career-focused courses. Usually, career academies form partnerships with employers and local colleges, who often contribute money, material resources, speakers, and internships to improve student motivation and achievement. The role of work-based learning varies, however, and long-term internships are often not a part of the student's experience.

Elements of career-focused education and training appear in a range of other high school programs. Wisconsin has established a youth apprenticeship program under which high school juniors in regular high schools enter a combined school-based and work-based course of study leading to an occupational certificate. While undertaking work-based training, students are also paid apprentices taking part in the production process. The Wisconsin Technical College System offers career-focused courses for students while they are apprentices and still in high school. The programs range from automotive technician to finance, from hotel management to architectural drafting, and from travel services to biotechnology. All programs require participating employers to develop a large number of competencies for youth at the workplace. Employers must fill out extensive checklists to document the ability of the apprentice to complete specific tasks and to demonstrate specific skills. Smaller youth apprenticeship programs operate in other states as well.

Other high school systems have offered large-scale internships and other career-focused components. The school system in Philadelphia used school-to-work funds and placed large numbers of students in paid internships. The Boston Private Industry Councils have sponsored large numbers of summer internships and academic coaching at major companies. Other high school programs are linked to the alternative school movement and deal with at-risk youth.

Apprenticeships outside the youth apprenticeship framework remain an important source of intensive, career-focused education and training along with high employer involvement. Gaining registered status for apprenticeship programs requires approval from state or national apprenticeship councils; the programs must meet standards for work-based learning on the job and hours of classroom learning. Although data on apprenticeships are weak, a recent report indicates that apprentices in registered programs have been increasing rapidly, from 346,000 in 1997 to 489,000 in 2003 (Bennici 2004). These numbers are small compared with the size of the student population in vocational education programs at the secondary and postsecondary levels, partly because apprenticeship programs have been concentrated in construction and manufacturing.

An alternative set of figures from household surveys suggests apprenticeship training is much more common than reported on the basis of Labor Department figures. The 2002/2003 National Household Education Surveys (NHES) Program measures involvement in apprenticeships on the basis of respondent reports that they have participated in "a formal program in the 12 months prior to the interview that led to journeyman status in a craft or trade." Using this concept, early data from the NHES indicate that nearly 1.8 million adults (1.5 million of whom were employed) participated in such a formal program, but not necessarily a registered apprenticeship program (O'Donnell 2005).

Recently, the Department of Labor has provided grants to expand the role of apprenticeship to other occupations and industries, including metal-working, nursing, information technology, and geospatial occupations.[13] Many workers enter apprenticeships well after their teenage years. In fact, the median age for U.S. apprenticeship programs is the mid-20s. Thus, certified apprenticeships are not mainly focused on youth.

Apprenticeship programs are closely integrated with individual employers and employer associations but rarely with the educational system. Unlike most other postsecondary programs, even the classroom component of apprenticeships receives little or no government subsidy, even though the courses taught are often comparable in subject matter and at least as high a quality as those taught at community colleges.

Employers often provide other formal and informal career-focused education and training to their workers. Again, data on the details of this phenomenon are limited. Examples of employer-led training include tuition subsidies for classes related to employees' field and specialized courses at the workplace. In 2001, employers apparently provided 30 hours of training for the average worker, mainly in for-credit courses or other courses. Even among young people, employer-provided formal training is common. According to tabulations by Mikelson and Nightingale (2004) based on the NHES, 28 percent of workers age 24 and younger participate in an employer-provided training activity. These forms of training are rarely intensive enough to prepare young people for specific occupational careers, but they do offer a way of upgrading existing workers.

A critical question is the role of conventional high schools in career-focused education and training. About two-thirds of all high schools offer courses and programs designated as vocational education, now called career and technical education. Most students take these courses in one of the 9,500 comprehensive high schools providing CTE courses, including a small number of charter schools, many with an occupational focus. About 1,000 vocational schools emphasize vocational subjects, while also providing a full program of academic courses. In the approximately 800 area vocational schools, students come part-time for vocational courses while continuing to take their academic courses at their home high schools (Silverberg et al. 2004).

Not all CTE courses have an occupational focus. Under the current classifications, CTE courses include family and consumer education, such as home economics or financial literacy, and general workforce preparation skills, such as basic computer skills and learning about the job market (Levesque 2003). The occupational fields vary widely, from business and marketing, to health care and computer occupations, to food service and hospitality, and to construction, printing, and transportation. A renewed emphasis on academic course work for students in vocational tracks is bearing fruit. In 1990, only 19 percent of students with a vocational concentration completed the "New Basics" program of academic courses (four years of English and three years of math, science, and social studies). By 2000, 51 percent of vocational concentrators did so.

The trend of participation in vocational education is mixed. Between 1982 and 2000, public high school seniors reduced the share of their courses in CTE subjects, but mainly because of a rise in the number of academic courses. The average number of academic credits rose from 14.3 to 18.8 over this period, while average vocational credits have remained at about 4.2 since 1990, including a constant 3 credits per student in occupationally focused fields. In addition, the share of students taking any three vocational courses has remained constant, at about 44 percent. Those with at least three courses in one of the broad occupational fields (occupational concentrators), however, dropped from nearly 34 to about 25 percent between 1982 and 1990 and remained at this lower rate through 2000. The proportion of seniors who were occupational concentrators and took at least one advanced course in the occupational field declined from 24 to 14.4 percent from 1982 to 1998.

Some evidence suggests that increasing the number of course credits required for high school graduation played a key role in the declining share of vocational concentrators. Also, schools are perhaps becoming less likely to offer a full range of courses to prepare for an occupation. Still, these figures indicate a large continuing interest and involvement in vocational education. As of 2000, about 750,000 high school seniors were occupational concentrators (Silverberg et al. 2004).

Another way conventional high schools link up with the job market is through work-based learning counted for course credit under general programs or cooperative education. General work experience involves work for course credit that is not connected to a specific occupational program pursued in school. It is often not linked to classroom content. Cooperative education allows students to earn school credit for work related to an occupational program. Schools help place students in jobs that involve supervision by the teacher and employer, with employers evaluating students for their work-based learning and accomplishments. The share of high school graduates experiencing either type of work for class credit has increased over the past two decades, from about 27 percent in 1982 to 32 percent in 1998. Typically, these work experiences provide credit for one course. Still, they account for only a modest share of the total amount of work that high school students experience.

Community colleges, four-year colleges, for-profit vocational schools (generally called proprietary schools), and nonprofit vocational programs all specialize in career-focused education and training, mostly for young people. As of 1999–2000, about 60 percent of degree-seeking undergraduates were enrolled in sub-baccalaureate programs (Silverberg et al. 2004). Of these, about 50 percent had chosen a career major, 25 percent had an academic major, and another 25 percent were undecided. Over half the sub-BA career majors were in technical or paraprofessional fields, but about two-fifths chose majors in occupations that typically require a BA or higher level of education.

In absolute numbers, about 4.9 million undergraduates in 2000 were career majors, or in formal programs offering courses to help students achieve job requirements that are occupationally specific. Not all these sub-baccalaureate vocational students are young. As of 2000, 56 percent were age 24 or older and 34 percent were age 30 or older. Still, younger people recently transitioning from high school made up more than half of those entering associate's degree or certificate programs. Enrollments in vocational associate's degree programs have increased substantially since the 1980s but have leveled off in recent years.

The associate and other sub-baccalaureate vocational programs offer an outlet for students with low academic test scores. As of 1992, two-thirds of students in vocational associate's degree programs had scores in the bottom half of standardized tests of math and reading; the comparable figure for BA students was 22 percent. Still, most sub-baccalaureate vocational students had completed the recommended college preparatory courses in high school, including four years of English and three years of math, science, and social studies. Only 7 percent had high school vocational programs without these academic courses.

Over 80 percent of postsecondary vocational students in 2000 combined schooling with employment. Although 77 percent of BA students also worked, the work commitment by vocational students was substantially higher, as indicated by the fact that 62 percent of BA students, but only 28 percent of postsecondary vocational students, were in full-time, full-year academic programs. It is unclear from the national data what share of working students was in fields related to their school-based programs.

A large number of students use for-profit proprietary vocational schools for their career-focused education and training. Although national data on enrollments and numbers of schools are limited, there is considerable evidence that millions of students enroll in proprietary vocational schools. Even California, a state with perhaps the largest community college system in the country, has more than 3,800 proprietary vocational schools and only 109 community colleges (Cellini 2006). The individual proprietary schools are much smaller; their average enrollment is about 350 students, with 58 percent having 100 or fewer students. In contrast, average enrollment in California's community colleges is over 10,000. Nevertheless, total enrollment in proprietary schools is about 1.3 million in California alone (Cellini 2006), well above the national estimate of 700,000 proprietary school students that was drawn from a U.S. Department of Education data set. Projecting the California estimate to the nation as a whole based on population would imply a national enrollment figure of over 7 million. Even if the presence of proprietary schools was much smaller in other states than in California, U.S. enrollment in proprietary schools could easily number 3–4 million students.

The occupational and industry programs operating in proprietary schools are often similar to programs at community colleges (Cellini 2006). One exception is that the weight placed on computer-related subjects is often higher in proprietary schools than in community colleges. Given the surface similarity between these institutions, it is striking that proprietary schools are able to attract large numbers of students and charge substantially higher tuition than community colleges. One possible explanation is that program flexibility allows proprietary school students to work in their regular jobs and thus reduce the costs in forgone earnings.

Even in four-year BA programs, about 60 percent of students are in programs with a career orientation, such as engineering, accounting, other business fields, teaching, and health care. An examination of the fields in which degrees were awarded in BA and sub-baccalaureate programs in 1984–85 and 2000–01 reveals interesting patterns. For both types of degrees, the share in career majors fell, from 78 to 71 percent among sub-baccalaureate degrees and from 66 to 60 percent in BA degrees. The occupational composition of BA and sub-BA degrees is similar, but with some revealing exceptions. Health care and industry fields are much more common in sub-BA programs, and education degrees are much more common in BA programs.

Worrying Uncertainties about Education and Training Outcomes

Given studies showing the poor job market and social outcomes for dropouts, a major policy goal should be to make sure young people complete high school. Until recently, policymakers could feel encouraged by reports suggesting that only about 13 percent of a young cohort earns neither a standard high school diploma nor a GED. Unfortunately, although National Center for Education Statistics data sets show about 82 percent of individuals earn a high school diploma and about 5 percent earn GED certification by their 20s, evidence from administrative sources suggests the reality is far worse, especially for minorities and for those attaining a high school diploma instead of a GED (Swanson 2004).

Using administrative data, the U.S. Department of Education estimates that the share of youth graduating high school fell from about 77 percent in 1970 to about 68 percent in 1997–98 before rising back to about 75 percent in 2003–04. A study drawing on administrative GED data estimates that nearly 8 percent of 18- to 24-year-olds had obtained GEDs as of 1999 (Chaplin 2002). Without more recent data on GEDs and whether young people are substituting high school diplomas for GEDs, it is unclear how much high school completion rates (including GED attainments) have increased in recent years. In any event, it appears one in four of the nation's young people leaves school without a high school diploma.

High school graduation patterns of black youth are particularly uncertain and potentially of great concern. While reports based on CPS data indicate that 81 percent of black 18- to 29-year-olds earned a high school diploma and another 5 percent earned a GED, analyses using administrative sources project dramatically lower proportions obtaining diplomas. One such study finds that only 50 percent of black students attained a high school diploma in 2001 (Swanson 2004).

Some part of the gap between 81 and 50 percent might be explained by the difference in age categories and the possibility that some people not graduating by age 19 will return to school. But, if this were the main explanation, we would expect large gaps for all groups between the administrative and survey data. In fact, the black-white gap is much larger using administrative data (25 percentage points) than using household data (7 percentage points). Finally, even if the differences narrow with age, it may be quite costly for black students and black workers to attain their high school diplomas past normal graduation dates. Although this chapter deals primarily with career-focused education and training, which set of figures concerning high school graduation is most accurate can color one's analytic and policy perspective.

The Complexity of Career-Focused Education and Training

This review of U.S. institutions providing career-focused education and training yields three interesting outcomes. First, a wide variety of institutions are purportedly training people for work in the same occupations. For example, it is possible to obtain classroom courses and internships dealing with intermediate-level health occupations or hospitality occupations in vocational high schools, community colleges, apprenticeships, proprietary schools, stand-alone training through community-based organizations, and colleges. Second, there are few transparent occupational standards by which to judge the efficacy of training from various institutions. Where the occupational standards are reasonably clear, the variety of institutions can constitute a healthy competition if information about outcomes can be communicated to potential trainees. Still, it is not easy for potential trainees to determine the comparative advantages of one institution or another in obtaining appropriate skills, work experience, and placement in various occupations. Third, though employer involvement could be a very important component of a program, good national information is absent on the nature and intensity of employer participation in the training process through, for example, their willingness to offer workplace learning and to accept accountability for assuring that participants learn from their work-based experiences.

The evaluation record discussed below provides some information on the impacts and outcomes of institutions delivering career-focused education and training, but it does not answer such questions as is a focused high school skill-building program combined with relevant work experience and work-based learning sufficient for a specific occupation, or does it make sense to delay occupation-specific training until students enter a community college or university?

How Effective Are Current Approaches in Improving Careers?

A massive body of literature has studied the effectiveness of a variety of career-focused education and training policies and programs. Conducting such analyses has three intrinsic difficulties. The first, which is inherent and well-recognized in studying youth initiatives, is that understanding long-term consequences requires a long follow-up period. Few evaluations have the resources to conduct studies of 10 to 20 years. In addition, interest in the initial policy may have waned by the end of the follow-up period.

The second issue is how best to define effectiveness and outcomes for a heterogeneous population. Instead of thinking how a policy increases average schooling or average employment levels, it is more appropriate to think of how effectively a set of policies matched young people in varying ways to programs that maximized the productivity and satisfaction of as many young people as possible. Such an analysis is difficult to carry out. It involves viewing youth high school, post–high school, and workplace options as a menu of activities that work together and tailoring participation of each young person to his or her best option. In this respect, the initial assignment to activities may be as important as how well the activities operate.

A third and related issue is how best to group programs that are similar in some respects but differ in others. Vocational education programs vary a great deal, both across schools and within schools. Some have close links with employers and high academic standards, and others do not. Yet it is hard to distinguish among these programs, under the common practice of estimating impacts based on large numbers of students in national data sets. As we review the results of various evaluations and general studies, keep these limitations in mind.

High School Programs

Universal access to schools complicates efforts to stage the random assignment evaluations that can supply convincing evidence on the efficacy of school-based activities. Excluding students from even an optional school program is rarely considered appropriate. A separate issue is the possibility that various forms of contamination, such as peer effects, might not allow experiments to capture the full effects of a program. Nonetheless, this section begins by reviewing the findings from one of the few social experiments of career-focused education and training, the career academies evaluation. It also reviews the Tech-Prep program.

Career Academies

The career academies evaluation began in 1993 and continues to follow experimental and control groups. It has been examining the impact of career academies in eight cities on the labor force outcomes, educational attainment, and social adjustment of students. At the potential entry point of 9th or 10th grade, interested students were subject to a random assignment process that determined whether they could enter the relevant academy. As of 2006, analyses are available based on follow-up information about four years after the student's scheduled high school graduation. Nearly all (85 percent) of the 1,458 students followed in the evaluation are black or Hispanic, reflecting the location of the study sample of schools.

Career academies induced some striking gains (Kemple 2004). Most impressive were the earnings gains experienced by young men in the experimental group. Although career academy participation did not increase the earnings of women, young men assigned to career academies achieved an extraordinary 18 percent average gain in earnings over the four years after scheduled high school graduation. The career academy group earned an average of $1,373 a month, $212 more than the $1,161 a month earned by the control group.

As might be predicted, the earnings gains were concentrated among students with a high or medium risk of dropping out of high school. The earnings effects usually lasted throughout the four years of follow-up. For the high-risk groups, earnings gains actually rose over time and stood at about $240 a month in the last quarter of follow-up. The longevity of the gains is further indicated by the fact that experimentals (in all risk groups) reported a significantly higher likelihood of promotion than controls. The estimates of earnings gains may understate the actual impact of full participation in career academies since nearly 20 percent of the experimental group did not take up the offer of participation and 47 percent were not participating in an academy at the time of graduation.

Both the control and experimental groups completed high school at similar, remarkably high rates (over 90 percent for a minority population in an urban school system). Within the high- and medium-risk groups, controls were somewhat more likely to complete a postsecondary credential, but the differences were small and not statistically significant. Thus, to this point, the earnings gains did not come at the expense of significantly lower amounts of postsecondary credentials.

Overall, the evidence from career academies points to a highly successful intervention for young men and for students at medium or high risk of dropping out of school. Despite not requiring resources for additional schooling, the early percentage returns to career academies for men are as much as two to three added years of education. It is not clear how much of the effect is associated with a small and closely linked learning community or the occupational/industry focus of the programs. Only about 27 percent of experimentals reported their job is or was directly related to their high school program, a rate not particularly high but significantly higher than the 20 percent figure for controls.

Tech-Prep

The Tech-Prep program is another example of high school–based, career-focused education and training. Though the programs vary widely in their occupational focus, structure, and link with existing vocational and technical programs, all use applied learning and career development. After adjusting for selection into Tech-Prep using fixed family effects and other variables, Cellini (2006) finds positive impacts on completing high school and attendance at two-year colleges. But she finds no net gain in college attendance because the negative effects on four-year college participation offset the increases in attendance at two-year colleges.

In a way, this result should not be surprising given Tech-Prep's emphasis on integrating high school and two-year programs through articulation agreements and other relationships. The benefits to high school completion are notable and suggest the value of hands-on learning and applied courses. Because of data limitations, Cellini did not estimate completion at two- and four-year colleges. Shifting some students from four-year to two-year colleges may increase their likelihood of graduating and attaining a relevant credential.

High School Career and Technical Education

Tech-Prep and career academies offer special approaches to combining vocational and academic education. How do other, more common high school–based vocational education programs perform? Before answering this question, it is worth noting that standard high school vocational education in the United States varies widely in intensity, quality, and interaction with employers, including the use of work-based learning. Some high school vocational programs are weak both in academics and in their connections with employers. The impact studies on secondary vocational education come from large, national longitudinal data sets that follow young people through school and into their early careers and do not differentiate students by program quality. Thus, they capture how vocational courses affect the typical young person in such programs.

According to the National Assessment of Vocational Education (NAVE) final report (Silverberg et al. 2004), a higher share of vocational courses added little to academic achievement and did not lower dropout rates or increase postsecondary education. It did, however, raise earnings in the short and medium runs. On a per course basis, the earnings gains averaged 3.2 percent in the short run and 1.9 percent in the medium run (after seven years). By implication, a vocational concentrator with four courses would see 8 to 12 percent increases in annual earnings. The gains were reportedly higher than average for vocational students among at-risk and minority students and in groups taking the New Basics academic curriculum. Work-based learning through cooperative education added to the earnings effects. Although educational gains from vocational education are unproved (and likely small, as in the case of the career academies), the NAVE report documents recent achievement gains in vocational education linked with increases in the number and rigor of related academic courses.

More optimistic results showing higher gains from career and technical education come from another recent study (Bishop and Mane 2004).

The study makes several comparisons among those taking CTE courses, academic courses, and personal interest courses, while controlling for grades, test scores, personal characteristics, family background, school background, 8th grade work experience, 8th grade attitudes and values, region and metropolitan area status, state policies on competency exams, and school completion. Two results are especially notable. First, taking four advanced CTE courses instead of two academic and one personal interest course led to substantial gains in employment and earnings gains about eight years after normal high school graduation. Second, the gains were high for those with no more than a high school diploma but were even higher among college graduates and those achieving an associate's degree or an occupational certificate.

It is important to recognize that these estimates represent the average gains in the existing system of vocational education. Some vocational education settings may have been as well-structured as career academies or Tech-Prep, but many are traditional settings, which may include weak majors. In addition, the observed increases in earnings might (or might not) be much higher for students finding jobs in industries or occupations related to their schooling or for students in schools that have good links with employers.

Although few studies of student impacts distinguish between well-structured and weak CTE programs, Bishop and Mane explore the role of one indicator of program quality—the extent of employer involvement. Using a restricted data set drawn from the National Education Longitudinal Study and information on the degree of employer involvement in individual schools, Bishop and Mane (2003) examine impacts on 1994 labor market outcomes at two years past expected high school graduation. Holding constant various individual, community, and school characteristics, the multivariate analyses yield several positive impacts of employer-school partnerships. The more active the employer-school partnership, the more young people earned, held jobs at higher rates, and avoided unemployment. Even students with low grades did better in the labor market as a result of these partnerships. The job-market gains did not come at the expense of schooling. In fact, employer-school partnerships appeared to raise the share of students graduating on time and with a high school diploma instead of a GED.[14]

Internships, Work-Based Learning, and Other Activities under the School-to-Work Opportunities Act

Another set of heterogeneous career-related interventions in high schools are those encouraged under the 1994 School-to-Work Opportunities Act. Congress had ambitious goals for STWOA, including building well-coordinated state systems that foster effective transitions between school and careers. One goal was to improve the links between work and learning, thereby promoting work-based learning and avoiding the negative effects of work experience on academic performance found in some studies.[15]

While student participation in paid and unpaid school-arranged jobs or internships increased under STWOA, the increases were modest (Haimson and Bellotti 2004). There was only limited involvement in intensive career-focused programs with substantial amounts of work-based learning. By 12th grade, less than 10 percent of students were engaged in intensive, work-based learning activities (Haimson and Bellotti 2001). No more than 3 percent were participating in a school-linked, structured, long-term (one to two years or longer) experience demanding the learning of new skills at the workplace and leading to any type of certification (Hershey et al. 1999).

Most evaluations have focused on specific activities encouraged by STWOA, including job shadowing, mentoring, internships, youth apprenticeships, career majors (coherent sequences of academic and vocational instruction with some work-based learning), and improved links with local employers. Although STWOA did little to stimulate major increases in the more intensive school-to-work (STW) components, it did lead to more career exploration activities, including job shadowing and career counseling through career plans, interest inventories, and scheduled use of career centers (Hershey 2003). In addition, some degree of employer involvement increased in the aftermath of STWOA.

While STWOA did not produce any experimental evaluations, partly because the idea was to alter high school systems as a whole, researchers have attempted to examine the impacts of STW components on the added schooling and earnings of participants. One study of the early experience of minority high school students finds high participation in career majors, with about 30–40 percent of students in or completing 12th grade taking these majors as of 1998 (Rivera-Batiz 2003). The study estimates that participation in a STW activity increased course work in math and science in high schools along with hours worked and reduced the likelihood of dropping out of high school.

A more recent study of how school-to-work activities affect young people a few years after scheduled graduation finds that several components, such job shadowing, mentoring, cooperative education, and internships boost participation in postsecondary education for women and (except for internships) for men (Neumark and Rothstein 2005). The gains in earnings from STW activities are largely limited to men. Especially important are estimates showing STW activities significantly reduce the proportion of young men who are idle (neither working nor in school). The authors provide separate estimates for a group they define as the "forgotten half," the half of the school population less likely to attend college. For this group of men, some STW components (mentoring and cooperative education) increase postsecondary education, while others (cooperative education, school enterprises, and internship or apprenticeship) increase employment and lower the share of youth who are idle after high school. Women in the forgotten half benefit only in terms of earnings and only from the internship or apprenticeship components.

In one large-scale effort to promote internships, Philadelphia used school-to-work funds and demonstrated that even a school system with a largely minority population operating in a city with limited job opportunities could place over 3,000 students in paid internships. Although the initiative was not subjected to a rigorous evaluation, a follow-up survey of the Philadelphia interns and a comparison group yields promising results (Madonna Yost Opinion Research 1999). It finds that interns reported higher satisfaction with their career preparation than the comparison group sample, higher grades, higher attendance, and a higher chance of finding a job with their current employer and in their desired field. In one of the best indicators of a good fit between employers and youth, nearly half the youth interns received a job offer from their employers. Some students worked at internships related to the themes of their small learning communities or career academies.

Internships and other forms of work-based learning were encouraged under STWOA. To see in detail how internships affect the effectiveness of youth in school and careers, Bailey and colleagues (2004) conducted studies involving detailed observations of internships linked to high school and community college programs. They examined the tasks and experiences of 25 interns, focusing on reinforcement of academic skills, work-based skills and career exploration, youth development and engagement, and the stimulus to new modes of thought. Although the internships did not appear to raise academic skills, many helped students learn about potential careers, gain problem-solving and teamwork skills, develop a sense of responsibility and accomplishment, and engage in new modes of thought. These positive outcomes emerged from experiences lasting only about one semester. Long-term, work-based learning could have more constructive impacts, especially since employers would be more likely to reap returns from training and providing responsibility to young workers.

Youth Apprenticeships

Youth apprenticeships go beyond school internships by providing in-depth, work-based learning combined with related course work. Though youth apprenticeships constitute the most intensive form of career-focused education and training, youth apprenticeships and other (including certified) apprenticeships have been the least studied major intervention. Despite the widespread, long-term use of apprenticeships in some countries and their resurgence in others, few rigorous studies have examined how entering and completing apprenticeships in the United States affects the education and job market outcomes of young people. Limited evidence from Wisconsin's youth apprenticeship suggests employers and students believe their involvement is highly beneficial. A follow-up study of high school students who participated in a Wisconsin youth apprenticeship in printing documented participant earnings levels substantially above expected earnings for similar youth (Orr 1995). Other anecdotal evidence suggests that youth apprenticeships motivate participants to do better in school and pursue difficult courses broadly related to their occupational interests (Hamilton and Hamilton 1997).

Postsecondary Career-Focused Education and Training

Community colleges deliver the largest amount of career-focused education. A second major source is occupationally oriented proprietary schools. Second-chance federally sponsored training programs, including Job Corps and programs funded under the WIA, are a third source of postsecondary career-focused education and training, but they cover a small share of young people. Finally, standard apprenticeships provide extensive career-focused education and training after high school. The second-chance programs and apprenticeships are sometimes open to those without a high school diploma or GED. Of these four delivery systems, apprenticeships attract the least in government funding and thus must pass a market test to attract time and money from employers and participants.

Community Colleges and For-Profit Vocational Programs

Many studies have assessed the impacts of community colleges on earnings. The most recent review of evidence (Silverberg et al. 2004) draws primarily from Marcotte and colleagues (2005) and yields separate estimates of the earnings gains of one year of community college and of the receipt of an associate's degree. The distinction is important because less than 30 percent of community college students who expect to obtain an associate's degree actually do so (Bailey, Jenkins, and Leinbach 2005).

Impacts of community college education on earnings vary by gender, by type of degree, by academic disadvantage, and by receipt of a diploma. For men, a year of community college in a vocational program raises earnings by almost 8 percent over men with only a high school diploma. Even young men with the lowest academic test scores gain from a vocationally oriented year of community college. The earnings gain jumps to 30 percent for men with a vocational associate's degree but becomes insignificant for men with a year of academic college work or even an academic associate's degree.

Women do better with academic postsecondary courses when not completing a certificate or degree. A year of community college education raises their earnings by 16 percent (over a high school degree only) when taken in an academic curriculum but has no effect when part of a vocational curriculum. On the other hand, women who complete associate's degrees do better with a vocational concentration (a 47 percent earnings gain versus 40 percent for those earning an academic associate's degree).

Offsetting some of the observed advantages of vocational over academic associate's programs is the finding that community college students are more likely to complete a degree when they choose an academic-oriented major instead of a vocationally oriented major (Silverberg et al. 2004).

When one compares earnings gains among those with a vocational associate's degree to gains among those with a BA, the added benefit for a BA turns out to be remarkably small for men (30 percent for associate's versus 45 percent for BA) but very large among women. Some BA degrees could involve a career concentration as well. As noted above, some of these gains result not from schooling itself but from the work experience that takes place during a two-year or four-year college education.

Estimates of impacts of career-focused, two-year proprietary schools are rare in the literature. One study finds minimal earnings gains associated with these proprietary schools (Grubb 1993), while estimates from another suggest that they induce earnings gains for women but not men (Lyke 1991). In a brief on this subject, Bailey, Badway, and Gumport (2003) argue that earlier studies undertaken in the 1970s and 1980s may not accurately reflect the current groups of for-profit vocationally oriented schools.

According to an evaluation in Washington State, most proprietary school students report that they learned a lot (66 percent), and 96 percent of employers are very or mostly satisfied with the training these students received. On the other hand, only 61 percent report using the skills in their current job during the 2001–02 recession. In addition, attendees of private career schools do not achieve statistically significant gains in earnings over a comparison group with similar characteristics that registered with the state employment service. Completers of career school programs manage to raise their employment by 8 percent and their earnings by $373 a quarter (Washington State Workforce Training and Education Coordinating Board 2004). Still, these gains are much smaller than comparably estimated impacts in Washington for participants in community college programs. Given the study design, it is unclear whether unobserved differences in the student populations accounted for the weak performance of proprietary schools.

This component of career-focused training deserves more study, especially because of extensive government aid for students in these programs. Aid is central for proprietary schools, with nearly 80 percent of their students receiving a federal grant or loan. Among all Pell grant recipients attending programs shorter than four years (mainly community colleges and proprietary schools), about 25 percent are in proprietary schools (Turner 2004). In recent years, state and federal government agencies have strengthened requirements placed on for-profit vocational schools to report on their ability to place their students, and agencies have begun determining whether some schools are fraudulently attracting students helped by financial aid.

Targeted Education and Training for Disadvantaged, Out-of-School Youth

The research on income-targeted programs offering career-focused education and training can help inform policymakers about how to improve career outcomes of youth workers. The two largest evaluations of these programs examined a decentralized, low-intensity program, the Job Training Partnership Act (JTPA) programs; and Job Corps, a nationally operated, intensive, high-cost program.

The youth component of the national JTPA evaluation, which began in the mid-1980s, dealt with programs for out-of-school 16- to 21-year-olds. The first question was, to what extent did the JTPA program cause experimentals eligible for JTPA to obtain more education and training than controls, who could seek education and training outside the program? The results documented that experimental youth spent 180 more hours in training or related activities than did controls. With only about five weeks of additional training, it is perhaps not surprising that JTPA exerted only a modest effect on the attainment of a high school diploma or GED.

The measured effects on earnings were even more disappointing. None of the three youth experimental subgroups saw their earnings rise relative to the earnings of those in the control group. One possibility was that higher earnings in the period after training or employment services offset low earnings during the training period. Unfortunately, no statistically significant positive effects emerged for female or male youth, even five years after signing up for JTPA (U.S. General Accounting Office 1996).

Why did JTPA fail to raise the earnings of out-of-school youth? After all, JTPA increased the amount of education and training, and previous research demonstrated that education and training lead to higher earnings. One important possibility is that greater access to training diverted some JTPA experimentals from taking jobs in the private market. Thus, while experimentals were more likely than controls to accumulate education, training, and other employment services, controls were more likely to gain work experience (Lerman 1996). Another possibility is that the amount of additional education and training was too little to exert a statistically discernible effect.

The national Job Corps evaluation, the largest and most comprehensive recent evaluation, dealt with the oldest and most intensive youth program, one managed directly by the federal government. It used random assignment to designate Job Corps applicants in 1995 as experimentals (and eligible to enter Job Corps—73 percent did enroll) and as controls (ineligible to enter Job Corps). The evaluators from Mathematica Policy Research attempted to determine the impact of Job Corps on employment, earnings, and social outcomes and to calculate whether the benefits generated by Job Corps exceeded the program's relatively high costs.

In 2001, Mathematica released reports of the impacts of Job Corps based on survey data for up to 48 months after application.[16] According to these reports, the opportunity to participate in Job Corps raised youth earnings by an average of $1,258, or 12 percent, during the fourth year after application. With no information on earnings gains beyond four years, the evaluators assumed that the absolute earnings advantage of the Job Corps treatment group would continue for 40 years.[17] This assumption yielded earnings gains that were high enough for the social benefits of Job Corps to exceed its social costs by nearly $17,000. For a net cost to taxpayers of about $3,000, Job Corps participants would obtain a lifetime gain of about $20,000.

Unfortunately, subsequent evidence indicates these evaluations substantially overstated the benefits of Job Corps (Schochet, McConnell, and Burghardt 2003). Administrative data on the earnings of experimental and control group youth through 2001 (almost three years beyond the earlier follow-up) document a rapid erosion of Job Corps earnings gains after the four-year follow-up and a likely overstatement of earlier gains because of differential attrition. For the full sample, earnings gains from Job Corps had eroded completely soon after the 48 month follow-up. The sharp reduction in medium-term and long-term earnings gains meant that projected social benefits per participant were over $10,000 (in 1995 prices) below social costs.

Some subgroups fared better and some worse than the average participant. Those who had entered Job Corps in their early 20s sustained a gain in earnings during the longer-term follow-up. On the other hand, Hispanics and those with serious arrest records before entering Job Corps apparently suffered significant earnings shortfalls by 2000–01 relative to their counterparts in the control group.

Overall, the long-term findings are disturbing but also surprising, given that Job Corps stimulated participants to achieve a GED or a vocational certificate. Among those without a high school degree or equivalent at application, 47 percent of the experimental group attained a diploma or GED, compared with only 34 percent of the control group. The gap in vocational certification was even higher, with 37 percent of the experimental group but only 15 percent of the control group earning a certificate. Additional research is warranted to determine why the initial earnings gains stimulated by Job Corps faded out after a few years.

Job Corps did generate some benefits against crime and welfare dependency but not fertility and nonmarital births. At the four-year follow-up, this highly intensive job training program still left about 40 percent without jobs, modest average earnings, relatively high rates of incarceration, and high rates of nonmarital fertility (40 percent of females).

Positive results from previous Job Corps evaluations led to demonstration projects trying to replicate Job Corps in a nonresidential, less expensive context. These, too, have yielded disappointing results. The major demonstration test of this concept was JOBSTART (Cave and Bos 2003). It integrated instruction in basic skills with self-paced learning; occupational training involving both classroom activity and hands-on experience in high-demand occupations; training-related support services including transportation, child care, and life skills training; and job placement assistance. The model required all sites to offer at least 200 hours of basic education and 500 hours of occupational training and to deal with particularly disadvantaged youth. All participants were high school dropouts. By expanding the amount of education and occupational training received by participants, JOBSTART stimulated an increase in the proportion earning a GED and in the share obtaining a trade certificate. Nevertheless, JOBSTART yielded few or no gains in earnings, employment, reduced childbearing, or criminal activity.

One site within JOBSTART—the Center for Employment Training (CET) in San Jose, California—did manage to generate significantly higher employment and earnings. The CET model emphasized intensive participation in services (having trainees participate full-time), employment and training services that mirror the workplace, skills provision directly relevant to the jobs for which participants are preparing, close involvement of employers to design and deliver training, and operational capacity and stability (Miller and Bos 2003).

The experience of CET and its distinctive model led to a project that replicated and evaluated the CET approach in 12 sites across the country. The results were disappointing. Despite CET's intensive model, being assigned to CET raised participation in education and training activities only modestly. On the positive side, the CET treatment group was much more likely to obtain a training certificate than the control group (39 versus 25 percent). Still, virtually no indicator of employment or earnings showed a statistically significant benefit from CET, as replicated in the 12 demonstration sites. One plausible reason the CET replication sites did not generate earnings gains was the high rate of community college participation by controls. In the sites most effective in replicating CET (the California sites), community colleges are especially strong.

Apprenticeship Training

The review of earnings impacts of standard apprenticeship training in the United States can be brief. Though several studies deal with the effects of apprenticeship training in other countries, few if any have examined how apprenticeship training in general affects employment and earnings. The limited research on apprenticeship represents a major gap in our knowledge of career-focused education and training institutions. One possible reason for the dearth of research on apprenticeships is that such programs receive little government funding.

The evidence that does exist suggests a high degree of effectiveness from apprenticeship training. Using data from the National Longitudinal Survey (Senior) Class of 1972, Cook (1989) compares those taking part in apprenticeships and other work-based learning with those participating in classroom-based postsecondary vocational education. He shows that not only were earnings higher for both apprentices and others taking part in firm-based training than for classroom-based students, but that earnings also rose faster for the two groups receiving mainly work-based learning.

In a more recent study, the Upjohn Institute finds that apprenticeship training generates very substantial gains in earnings, especially for those completing the program (reported in Washington State Workforce Training 2004). Using a matched sample drawn from registrants to the state employment service, the study used administrative data on quarterly earnings and wage rates to follow the earnings pathways of apprenticeship participants, apprenticeship completers, and a matched comparison group of people with similar characteristics who registered with the state's Employment Service.[18] In addition to comparing people in programs to the comparison group, the study compared pre/post gains in earnings for apprentices with pre/post gains for those in other education and training programs.

Under either estimate, the gains associated with apprenticeship training are substantial in the period 8 to 11 quarters after leaving the program. Compared with the main comparison group, all apprentices earn $1,900 more a quarter, and those completing apprenticeships earn nearly $4,300 more a quarter. The earnings gains achieved by apprenticeship completers are nearly three times the comparably estimated gains for those graduating with vocational degrees from community colleges. The Washington State Employment Security Office (1998) touts several other benefits of apprenticeship in addition to these high earnings gains. Apprentice participants have the highest rate of post-program employment, the highest use of training on the job six to nine months after training, and the highest gains in earnings.

Though the evidence on apprenticeship is limited and not experimentally based, the results of the Washington state study and the NLS-Class of 1972 are powerful enough to suggest apprenticeship training is effective and deserves much more detailed study and attention from policymakers.

How Can We Do Better?

The results of this review suggest a mixed picture, with some approaches yielding positive impacts on the job market, others stimulating higher school attainment, and still others doing little to improve labor market or school outcomes. Although career academies provide the most reliable measures of earnings gains, especially for at-risk young men, several other forms of career-focused employment and training are effective as well, including some school-to-work components and, especially, postsecondary vocational education and apprenticeships. Even today's much-maligned vocational education program in high schools shows positive outcomes and considerable improvement in integrating academic instruction and more rigorous course-taking. On the other hand, evaluations show disappointing results for several second-chance programs. What are the implications of these findings for current and future policy initiatives?

Reform High School Curricula

Despite positive indications of the value of work-based learning and career-focused education and training, the emphasis in current policy circles is entirely on academic skills and academic standards in schools. Such an emphasis is understandable and appropriate over the first 8 to 10 years of schooling. But is it appropriate to focus solely on school-based reforms and academic standards?

A recent report published by the National Governors Association (NGA), *An Action Agenda for Improving America's Schools*, indicates the viewpoint of many policymakers (Conklin and Curran 2005). It begins by emphasizing how gaps in learning and inadequate preparation for college or work have "serious implications for our economy and prosperity." According to the report, because future jobs will require more sophisticated skills, all students should have comparable preparation in high school, whether they enter a four-year or two-year college, start postsecondary training, or go directly to work. Yet, although the report focuses on the economic rationale for improving high schools and student preparation for work, the report and many like it pay little attention to the realities of the job market and to sound workforce preparation.

First, the report fails to recognize the heterogeneity of the labor market. Although math skills beyond algebra are useful and intellectually rewarding, large shares of workers will never use such skills on their jobs.[19] The same is no doubt true of advanced classes in other subjects. It is true that upper-level science, math, and social studies are often required by universities; it is far less obvious that such courses are vital to success in the workplace. Further, it is unclear that the high school academic courses offered are the most appropriate for success in the workplace or in other aspects of life. For example, statistics may have broader relevance to jobs than trigonometry, economics more than certain history and civics classes. The potential for misguided state academic standards is real. In recent testimony about the academic standards in Michigan, Timothy Bartik and Kevin Hollenbeck (2006) worry that the proposed curriculum would crowd out high-quality vocational programs and that one approach to education does not fit the needs of all students.

Second, skills that are critical to success in the workplace are largely ignored in recent discussions of high school reforms and appear to have little or no place in the formal curriculum or in formal testing. These skills, drawn from the SCANS, emerged after extensive study about what makes workers successful.[20] In addition to basic academic skills, including reading, writing, and mathematics, the SCANS skills include listening, speaking, decision-making, problem solving, mental visualization, managing time and money, teaching others, negotiating, and many others. Although this formulation of critical skills required at the workplace was published and has been used in workforce circles for well over a decade, few schools and education policymakers have incorporated the findings from the SCANS report into their plans for improving high schools. In order to take seriously high school's role in insuring that students are well prepared for the workplace, school systems must incorporate SCANS or some similar approach into courses and methods of teaching.

Third, while the NGA report and others call on business leaders to advocate for reform, the reports ignore the current and potential future role of businesses in providing work-based learning. It is striking that the NGA report would miss the opportunity to encourage more direct involvement in career-focused approaches, including, but not limited to, work-based learning. Education policymakers often take little account of the large role that work in the job market plays for many students. Even by their sophomore year of high school, 39 percent of students are working and averaging 15 hours a week on the job (Ingels et al. 2005). This is three times the average amount of time all students spend doing homework. The share holding jobs increases as students move to their senior year.

There are several ways to respond to jobholding by students. One common response is to discourage (or ban) market work because it may reduce the ability of many students to perform well in school. Although a recent study finds existing work by 12th graders negatively affects math test scores (Tyler 2003), other studies do not. Further, most researchers find a positive impact of working in high school on subsequent success in the job market (Light 2001; Molitor and Leigh 2005; Ruhm 1997), though some do not (Hotz et al. 2002).

In examining these relationships, it is important to take account of the potential for improving the quality of work experience as well as positive effects of jobholding on other skills, such as SCANS skills, that are significant for career success. Policymakers could respond to student employment by working with employers to make more jobs into constructive learning environments. Transforming more youth jobs into internships and cooperative education positions might allow students to achieve significant improvements in subject matter learning and in the development of SCANS skills. In addition, participating employers might be better able than teachers or even state standards to convince students about the value of meeting standards and of staying in school.

Fourth, many reports on high school reforms are not learning the lessons from the career academies evaluation and from some of the research on vocational education, cooperative education, and youth apprenticeships. At-risk male students find compelling those components with direct links to careers, whether embedded in academic learning, vocational courses, internships, or all three. Although the evidence does not reveal how well each component affects earnings, the activities in career academies certainly proved successful. Encouraging high-risk students to take highly demanding academic courses may work well for some, while providing coherent career majors with work-based learning may be more effective with others.

School systems should encourage the development of more career academies but recognize the importance of up-front investments in planning and engaging employers as well as postsecondary institutions. Ideally, existing and future career academies would include well-structured internships in their programs. Finally, policymakers should pay close attention to initiatives that are improving career and technical education within high schools. Integrating more academic courses is already having some success. Efforts to increase links with employers and postsecondary education and to promote more well-structured work-based learning are ongoing.

One way to reconcile the importance of having all students learn enough to do basic postsecondary work with the diversity of interests and careers might be to adopt a standard that students would be expected to meet by the end of 10th grade or age 16 (Tucker 2003). No one would or should mistake the standard as appropriate for entry into elite colleges and universities. Some students might take the exam later and others earlier. After meeting this standard, however, students could embark on various pathways, some of which would involve education, classroom training, and work-based training focused on careers. Such a strategy might have the best potential to maintain student motivation, a critical ingredient for improving outcomes of the forgotten half of students. At a minimum, state standards should allow for some diversity by having optional standards that incorporate career and technical education, technical English, career-relevant science, and a career major (Bartik and Hollenbeck 2006).

Use the Capabilities of Work-Based Learning

Another approach, one that builds on positive experience of some STW components and apprenticeship, would be to test a high school initiative involving employer-led training in high-wage careers. Even limited, short-term internships are apparently improving workplace skills, enhancing youth development, and widening participants' modes of thought (Bailey et al. 2004). More extensive employer-led training would strengthen these outcomes, by building on components of the time-honored system of apprenticeships and integrating academic skills.

To jump-start this approach, a public-private partnership could sponsor a demonstration with the following components: (1) emphasizing an occupation or industry area that is or is projected to be in high demand, leads to high wages, and does not require a BA degree; (2) insuring industry leadership in program design, in hiring youth for try-out employment, and in long-term work-site training; (3) linking the training to the achievement of a well-recognized credential that has credibility and at least some portability; (4) involving a national or regional industry association and accrediting body; (5) using institutions in selected communities with a good track record in recruitment and teaching work discipline and SCANS skills, and (6) investing significantly in evaluation research, possibly including random assignment.

The departments of Commerce and/or Labor would solicit initiatives from three industries working with national partner organizations or coalitions of local or regional organizations. The project would involve in-depth planning involving each of the three industries and partner groups so the partner organizations recruit appropriate youth, train them in SCANS skills (including the relevant education), and ensure they are properly motivated to work hard enough to achieve success in the relevant career. Industry associations would make sure their member firms know how to deliver work-based learning and to prepare trainees to meet the qualifications required for certification. The project would no doubt require test sites before becoming a national demonstration.

The research on this demonstration would examine impacts not only on the earnings and learning outcomes of youth participants, but also on the hiring patterns and job ladders of employers and the possibility of extending the model nationwide to employers in the same industry. Construction and transportation are two examples of industries that might participate and currently have older work forces, pay good wages, and do not require high levels of educational attainment, though both require sound academic skills.

The demonstration has many potential advantages. Moving youth into these careers could affect their lives significantly, unlike typical programs that offer only a thin set of services to help youth find jobs. Even if only a modest share of young people succeeds in attaining certification and high-wage career jobs, the gains would be substantial. The links with rewarding careers are evident and immediate, improving the incentive for youth to take the program seriously. Much of the learning is learning-by-doing and is accessible to various populations. Although the demonstration could involve implicit targeting by focusing on central cities, the project would avoid concentrating at-risk youth in ways that sometimes lead to deviant peer influences (Dodge, Dishion, and Lansford 2006). Instead, participating young people would be dispersed among employers and would be exposed to an adult and probably a more constructive peer group, at least during their internship. The training would be long-term, but financed largely by firms. Evidence from various studies suggests these investments by firms pay off in terms of higher workforce quality and lower turnover. The serious involvement of employers that hire participants can make the project sustainable and increase the chances for successful replication.

Unlike most demonstrations, this one builds the employer link directly into the model and includes employer groups as key actors and suppliers of services. If the project were successful, other groups could replicate the results at far lower costs. The project includes an important development component beyond the effort to increase the human capital of the participants. It leverages employer training and steers the training toward a useful goal for employers and the youth participants. Finally, the project could achieve high wage levels for many out-of-school youth unlikely to do so through traditional programs, even successful ones.

Expand and Coordinate Postsecondary Apprenticeships

Given evidence indicating high returns to apprenticeship's combination of work-based and school-based learning, the federal government should examine in depth the potential for expanding apprenticeships in several ways. One step is to conduct additional research to verify the high returns found recently in Washington State, to determine the elements that make apprenticeship training valuable,[21] and to analyze concerns about whether the training is unduly narrow, thereby limiting the flexibility of trained apprentices. A second is to continue efforts to expand the scope of apprenticeships to new occupations and industries. As noted earlier, the Department of Labor's Office of Apprenticeship Training is currently sponsoring initiatives to generate apprenticeship programs in four industries. But the modest budget of the national office (about $20 million a year) and state offices limits the ability of apprenticeship professionals to reach enough employers to encourage their adoption of apprenticeships in existing as well as new industries.

A third step would involve consolidating some of existing 858 apprentice occupations into broader categories that allow more worker flexibility over time (Crosby 2002). Even Germany, a country in which 60–70 percent of youth obtain apprenticeships, has only about 300 apprenticeship categories. The U.S. system is especially complex and opaque, since the skills can vary not only between narrowly defined occupations but also among firms within occupations.

Rationalizing the apprenticeship occupations could involve a major effort, especially when such initiatives interact with rationalizing licensures and the variety of state standards for many related occupations. A successful rationalization would make skills more transferable geographically and across fields, would make the skill certification in the job market more transparent, and might encourage more apprenticeship activity. If the experience of the National Skill Standards Board is any indication, however, the development of common skill standards and qualification systems will likely prove difficult. The best strategy might be to sponsor sensible modern occupational qualifications that attract a variety of stakeholders and to allow the old qualification systems to wither away.

Before any of these steps can occur, policymakers and political leaders must begin to look seriously at the possibility of apprenticeship playing a much larger and more constructive role in the U.S. system of career-focused education and training.[22] A common worry is that employers will not find apprenticeships worthwhile because of the threat that trained workers will be attracted to firms not providing training. Although this argument has merit, it ignores the continuing presence of apprenticeship in the United States despite only minimal public support for the system and the resurgence of apprenticeship in the United Kingdom, Australia, and several other advanced countries.

Wagner (1999) points out several benefits for firms that use apprenticeships as a major tool for training and recruitment. Beyond the added output that apprentices produce when working, there is the added flexibility to the production process that apprentices offer by their availability during peak production. Savings in recruitment and initial training are substantial, especially since apprentices newly hired by the firm have a much shorter period of full proficiency than other new hires. Risks that a worker will not fit on the job and will have to be replaced are much lower for apprentices that companies have come to know. Interactions with existing workers provide apprentices with the opportunity for informal learning about occupational skills and company practices that are difficult to codify and teach in a formal setting. Often, existing workers learn from the teaching and mentoring process, as they reflect on what is required to perform tasks at a high level. Finally, companies that poach skilled workers usually must pay a premium.

Incorporate Additional Initiatives for Out-of-School Youth

Expanding apprenticeship options would be especially important for out-of-school youth. As more occupations become apprenticeable, however, sound preapprentice initiatives will become essential to insure access to many out-of-school young people, especially economically disadvantaged youth. One initiative that could be tested with demonstration projects would link employers offering apprenticeships with community organizations with good track records in reaching low-income young people. The community organizations would recruit and teach these young people SCANS-related skills and, where necessary and appropriate, upgrade their basic academic skills. The prospect of entry into an apprenticeship, especially one offering high long-term wages, would serve as a motivating factor for entering and completing the preapprentice program. One component of the preapprenticeship activity would be job shadowing, so participants are fully aware of the occupational areas they will pursue should they enter a full apprenticeship. For programs serving the highest risk youth, the operator of the preapprenticeship program could offer employers a try-out period and offer to serve as the official employer for tax and unemployment insurance purposes.

Other initiatives can extend the basic idea of combining work-based learning, careers, and academic learning. One would involve the armed forces. The military would offer at-risk youth enhanced services, mentoring, education, and counseling that would allow these enrollees to enter the mainstream military training within three to six months if they completed a GED or perhaps other tests indicating high school equivalency. Currently, if at-risk youth are referred or become motivated and try to enlist, the U.S. Army is likely to reject most candidates lacking a high school diploma. Under this initiative, normally unqualified youth could enlist but initially only as participants in the extensive education, training, and behavior skills instruction provided through the special program. Although this initiative may appear risky, the U.S. and other nations' militaries have experience with mainstreaming enlistees initially considered unqualified.

The project has seven potential advantages. First, the program can operate at a large scale with professional management and operations. The program will include case managers and natural mentors. Second, completers of the program end up with reasonably well-paid employment in the military, with attendant educational and other fringe benefits. Third, the chance to succeed in the military and have steady, prestigious employment for at least three years will attract and motivate young people. Many people take pride in serving and in having served in the military. It conveys a sense of prestige in many communities. Fourth, it will ultimately afford at-risk youth training in a range of occupations. Much of the training will be hands-on but other parts will take place in the classroom. Fifth, the army provides a natural place for at-risk youth to learn about discipline and self-discipline. Part of the special program would involve teaching behavioral and other SCANS-type skills, including listening, managing resources, and working well in a team. Sixth, the highly integrated nature of the military will be appealing to minority youth. They will see minorities at the very top of a large organization's hierarchy as well as large numbers of mid-level minority officers. Seventh, upon completing military service, the formerly at-risk youth will have continuing access to various benefits, including education and health benefits.

Like the other demonstration, this project would be led by employers (branches of the military), would leverage funding from a mainstream institution, and would be intensive and long-term. If the program were to succeed, the military would have the capacity to expand the program significantly. The research would learn lessons about training from one of the largest, if not the largest, trainer in the world.

The program could build on the existing National Guard Youth ChalleNGe Academies. In the early 1990s, Congress authorized the National Guard to work with at-risk youth and develop a program to help them learn the values, skills, and self-discipline necessary to succeed as adults. The program focuses on at-risk youth: 16- to 18-year-old high school dropouts who are unemployed but not currently on parole or probation for an adult offense, not convicted of a felony or capital offense, and drug free.[23] The core components of the program are citizenship, academic training toward a GED or high school diploma, life-coping skills, community service, health and hygiene, skills training, leadership, and physical training. The program runs for 17 months, with a five-month residential phase followed by a yearlong mentoring relationship with a specially trained member from each youth's community. Mentorship and follow-up are key elements; participants identify potential mentors in their applications, and mentors are given training.

Extending this approach to the civilian sector, one could provide out-of-school youth with a one- to two-month initial training in SCANS skills and remedial education in preparation for a one- to two-year commitment to AmeriCorps or some alternative community service program. There is already some evidence of the effectiveness of community service programs based on the Youth Conservation Corps demonstration. The program's initial training would deal with relationship skills and job skills as well as problems linked to adolescents in general and disadvantaged youth in particular. The volunteer opportunities would create links to prospective employers and provide work experience (résumé-building). Such social connections offer important help to job-seekers.

CONCLUDING COMMENTS

Efforts to improve the nation's education and training system face many obstacles. Perhaps the biggest are ideological, especially misplaced egalitarianism. Equality of opportunity is too often defined as preserving the chance for all students to attend and graduate from a four-year college, regardless of their performance in academic courses or on external tests. It is certainly desirable to raise the educational competencies of U.S. students to the levels required for college-level work. Some strategies for doing so, however, are crowding out initiatives to improve career-focused education and training and other ways of helping young people prepare for rewarding careers. The likely result is that fewer students will learn important career-oriented skills and earn good salaries. It does no favor to push students to pursue a purely academic-based education when a career-focused, contextualized learning approach would be much more appealing and productive.

Fortunately, the career-focused components of the nation's education and training system are not withering away and indeed have considerable potential for expansion. Even the much-maligned high school vocational system continues to attract students, is strengthening its academic content, and seems to be helping many students do better in the job market without worsening their academic outcomes. According to experimental evidence, career-focused education through career academies can raise the earnings of the most at-risk students without reducing their likelihood of attending college. Students are generally earning good returns on their investment in the vocational features of community colleges as well. Empirical evidence also documents earnings gains accruing to students obtaining other secondary and postsecondary career-focused training, especially apprenticeship programs and components of the school-to-work initiatives. Overall, several existing career-focused approaches are helping young people learn and achieve more in the job market.

At the same time, there is much room for improvement. While over half of all students work for pay during high school and students on average spend as much time working as doing homework, schools are taking little advantage of the opportunity to make existing workplaces into better learning environments. Some programs, such as cooperative education, evaluate work-based learning as courses, but most student work has little or nothing to do with their schooling. Schools rarely instruct students on skills that are critical to success in the workplace, including those recommended by SCANS. There is little interest in developing high school standards that emphasize these and other work-related skills.

The quality of vocational education varies widely, with some programs well-connected with employers and others poorly connected. Evidence suggests that closer employer-school partnerships improve job-market outcomes for students, including students with low grades in school. Over 40 percent of students pursuing vocational degrees in community colleges drop out, but whether they do so after learning as much as they require for their jobs and careers is unclear.

Second-chance employment and training programs are producing uneven results and require serious improvement. Local programs that provide short-term training yield little gain for students. The intensive Job Corps program managed to stimulate short-run earnings gains and an increase in the share with a postsecondary vocational certificate. It is important to learn why the earnings gains eroded and what follow-up efforts might be worthwhile.

A key difficulty with second-chance programs is their limited connection with employers, work-based learning, and programs that emphasize work skills in a disciplined context. Another may be that excessive targeting can concentrate disadvantaged youth and make them subject to deviant peer pressure (Dodge et al. 2006). For this reason, the chapter recommends intensive demonstration projects that integrate at-risk youth into mainstream public and nonprofit employers through Ameri-Corps and the armed forces. Where at-risk youth are necessarily grouped together, it is important to link them around constructive themes and long-term career horizons, as sometimes accomplished with career academies.

Ideally, youth would be dispersed and learn from adult workers. For this reason, the chapter recommend intensive demonstration projects that have close ties with employers, such as preapprentice programs leading to long-term involvement with an employer. Another response is the rigor displayed by the National Guard ChalleNGe Academies. These academies teach at-risk youth the values, skills, and self-discipline necessary to succeed as an adult.

The country is failing to take advantage of opportunities to expand and rationalize the highly successful apprenticeship program. As the Washington State Employment Security Office points out (1998), apprenticeship programs are effective but underused. The programs appear to generate high rates of return, and they already have wide appeal to individuals in their mid-20s and to the many employers that provide and finance work-based and school-based training. Schools should make sure that younger people, including high school students, understand the value of such programs and what students must learn to qualify.

One important next step is to analyze in what ways the high apparent returns to apprenticeship training reflect genuine productivity gains. It is also important to determine the constraints on expansion of apprenticeship and how they might be overcome. In addition, research should be directed toward the relative quality of apprenticeship programs (compared with community colleges and proprietary schools) in teaching not only occupation-specific skills, but also transferable skills. Currently, there is little if any government subsidy for these activities. Were they proved as successful as some data suggest, subsidies to the apprenticeship system would be appropriate, at least in the form of technical assistance and grants for the rationalization and consolidation of occupational definitions.

Overall, career-focused education and training can and should play a significant role in preparing young people for success in the job market. Educational reformers are right to develop policies that lead to proficiency in academic skills. But these policies should complement, not substitute for, career-focused approaches that motivate students, teach academic and occupational skills in context and often outside the classroom, and offer students the chance to learn informal skills and life skills that are often critical to a successful career.

NOTES

The author thanks the Smith Richardson Foundation for helping to support this research and Harry Holzer, Demetra Smith Nightingale, and Betsy Brand for constructive comments.

1. These figures and those in the rest of this paragraph come from http://www.bls.gov, table A-4.

2. Workers now in their 50s have an educational attainment distribution virtually identical to the workers in their 30s and 40s but a much broader distribution than the workers recently reaching their 70s.

3. James Rosenbaum was the first to use this phrase in his book, *Beyond College for All*.

4. See, for example, their discussion of high school reforms initiated in the early part of the 20th century (Grubb and Lazerson 2004, 34–43).

5. See the Eagle Forum web site, http://www.eagleforum.org/educate/marc_tucker/marc_tucker_letter.html.

6. For a recent volume adding to this consensus, see Mayer and Peterson (1999).

7. The 80 percent figure is among the 90 percent of sophomores stating any expectation. See Ingels et al. (2005).

8. The U.S. Bureau of Labor Statistics (2006) recently reported that at least two-thirds of 18-year-olds in high school were working sometime within the prior year. According to calculations by Light (2001), the typical high school graduate accumulates 1,500 hours of work experience between age 16 and graduation, and the typical college student accumulates about 5,000 hours of work experience by graduation.

9. The figures discussed below and in table 3.1 represent the noninstitutional population and thus exclude people in jail or prison. Another problem is the possibility that these data understate the share of young adults who did not complete a high school diploma or GED (Swanson 2004).

10. Using detailed information from California's Bureau of Private Postsecondary and Vocational Education, Cellini estimates that about 1.3 million students enroll in proprietary schools in California, far above a U.S. Department of Education estimate of 700,000 proprietary school students annually in the entire nation.

11. Also see Bailey et al. (2004); Heckman, Stixrud, and Urzoa (2006); and Wenger (1998).

12. In addition to basic skills, the Secretary's Commission on Achieving Necessary Skills stresses thinking skills (problem-solving, creativity, decision-making, learning to learn); personal qualities (responsibility, self-esteem, self-management, and integrity); workplace competencies including resource skills (identifying, organizing, and allocating resources); interpersonal skills (working with and teaching others, teamwork, serving clients, negotiating, and dealing with diversity); information skills (acquiring, using, organizing, interpreting, and communicating information); systems (understanding systems and monitoring and correcting their performance); and technology (working with and selecting technologies and applying them to various tasks). See also the new standards proposed by the National Center for Education and the Economy (1997).

13. See http://www.doleta.gov/atels%5Fbat/cael.cfm, which describes the apprenticeship-related initiative for certified nursing assistants and licensed practical nurses with clinical training linked to an associate's degree in nursing. Geospatial occupations deal with the application of global information and global positioning skills.

14. The Lansing Area Manufacturing Partnership (LAMP) offers a good example of an effective employer-school partnership. Co-sponsored by the United Auto Workers, General Motors, and the local school districts, LAMP exposed students to careers in the auto industry and improved their education and career outcomes (MacAllum et al. 2002).

15. See, for example, Greenberger and Steinberg (1986) and, more recently, Tyler (2003). Most of these studies deal with a broad population of students and do not focus on impacts among low-income and minority students.

16. See Schochet, Burghardt, and Glazerman (2001) for Job Corps impacts on employment and earnings and McConnell and Glazerman (2001) for the benefit and costs of Job Corps.

17. The evaluators argued that this assumption represented a compromise between expecting the percentage gains to last for 40 years and expecting the earnings gains to erode rapidly.

18. The matched characteristics were age, race, sex, disability status, prior education, region of the state, preprogram employment and earnings history, and preprogram receipt of unemployment insurance or public assistance.

19. Murnane and Levy (1996) emphasize the importance of bringing nearly all workers up to 9th grade levels of math and reading, but they point out that many jobs do not require algebra and many require only a rudimentary knowledge of algebra.

20. Also see Murnane and Levy (1996), who focus on the skills required for a middle-class job: "A surprise in the list of New Basic skills is the importance of soft skills. . . . Today, more than ever, good firms expect employees to raise performance continually by learning from each other through written and oral communication and by group problem-solving" (32). These and other skills noted by Levy and Murnane fit well within the SCANS framework.

21. It is possible that some of the returns to apprenticeship reflect the ability of construction and other unions to develop a protected enclave of high-wage jobs that workers can only enter through the apprenticeship program.

22. For an example of renewed interest in apprenticeship training in the United Kingdom, see Apprenticeships Task Force (2005).

23. See http://www.ngycp.org/ for a description of the National Guard Youth ChalleNGe program.

REFERENCES

Allen, Jim, and Rolf van der Velden. 2001. "Education Mismatches vs. Skill Mismatches: Effects on Wages, Job Satisfaction, and On-the-Job Search." *Oxford Economic Papers* 3: 434–54.

Apprenticeships Task Force. 2005. *The Business Case for Apprenticeship*. London: Apprenticeships Task Force.

Autor, David, Lawrence Katz, and Melissa Kearney. 2005. "Rising Wage Inequality: The Role of Composition and Prices." Working Paper 11,628. Cambridge, MA: National Bureau of Economic Research.

Bailey, Thomas, Norena Badway, and Patrick Gumport. 2003. "For-Profit Higher Education and Community Colleges." CCRC Brief 16. New York: Community College Research Center.

Bailey, Thomas, Katherine Hughes, and David Moore. 2004. *Working Knowledge: Work-Based Learning and Education Reform*. New York: RoutledgeFalmer.

Bailey, Thomas, Davis Jenkins, and Timothy Leinbach. 2005. "Graduation Rates, Student Goals, and Measuring Community College Effectiveness." CCRC Brief 28. New York: Community College Research Center.

Bartik, Timothy, and Kevin Hollenbeck. 2006. "Graduation Requirements, Skills, Postsecondary Education and the Michigan Economy." Testimony presented to the Michigan Senate Education Committee, February 20.

Bennici, Frank, with Jeff Strohl and Deborah Posner. 2004. *The Status of Registered Apprenticeship: An Analysis Using Data from the Registered Apprenticeship Information System*. Rockville, MD: Westat.

Bishop, John. 1990. "Incentives for Learning: Why American High School Students Compare So Poorly to Their Counterparts Overseas." In *Research in Labor Economics*, edited by Laurie Bassi and David Crawford (17–52). Greenwich, CT: JAI Press.

Bishop, John, and Ferran Mane. 2003. "The Impacts of School-Business Partnerships on the Early Labor Market Success of Students." In *The School-to-Work Movement: Origins and Destinations*, edited by William Stull and Nicholas Sanders (189–202). Westport, CT: Praeger Press.

———. 2004. "The Impact of Career and Technical Education on High School Labor Market Success." *Economics of Education Review* 23(4): 381–402.

Cave, George, and Hans Bos. 2003. *JOBSTART: Final Report on a Program for School Dropouts*. New York: MDRC.

Cellini, Stephanie Riegg. 2006. "Smoothing the Transition to College? The Effect of Tech-Prep Programs on Educational Attainment." *Economics of Education Review* 25(4): 394–411.

Chaplin, Duncan. 2002. "Tassels on the Cheap." *Education Next* 2002(3): 24–29.

Commission on the Skills of the American Workforce. 1990. *America's Choice: High Skills or Low Wages*. Rochester, NY: National Center on Education and the Economy.

Conklin, Kristin, and Bridget Curran. 2005. *An Action Agenda for Improving America's High Schools*. Washington, DC: National Governors Association and Achieve, Inc.

Cook, Robert. 1989. *Analysis of Apprenticeship Training from the National Longitudinal Study of the Class of 1972*. Rockville, MD: Westat.

Crosby, Olivia. 2002. "Apprenticeships: Career Training, Credentials—and a Paycheck in Your Pocket." *Occupational Outlook Quarterly* (Summer): 2–21.

Dodge, Kenneth, Thomas Dishion, and Jennifer Lansford. 2006. "Deviant Peer Influences in Intervention and Public Policy for Youth." *Social Policy Report* 20(1): 1–20.

Ellwood, David. 1982. "Teenage Unemployment: Permanent Scars or Temporary Blemishes?" In *The Youth Labor Market Problem: Its Nature, Causes, and Consequences*, edited by Richard Freeman and David Wise (349–90). Chicago: University of Chicago Press.

Freeman, Richard, and Harry Holzer, eds. 1986. *The Black Youth Employment Crisis*. Chicago: University of Chicago Press.

Freeman, Richard, and David Wise, eds. 1982. *The Youth Labor Market Problem: Its Nature, Causes, and Consequences*. Chicago: University of Chicago Press.

Friedman, Thomas. 2005. *The World Is Flat: A Brief History of the 21st Century*. New York: Farrar, Straus, and Giroux.

Greenberger, Ellen, and Lawrence Steinberg. 1986. *Why Teenagers Work: The Psychological and Social Costs of Adolescent Employment*. New York: Basic Books.

Grubb, Norton. 1993. "The Varied Economic Returns to Postsecondary Education." *Journal of Human Resources* 28(2): 365–82.

Grubb, Norton, and Marvin Lazerson. 2004. *The Education Gospel: The Economic Power of Schooling*. Cambridge, MA: Harvard University Press.

Haimson, Joshua, and Jeanne Bellotti. 2001. *Schooling in the Workplace: Increasing the Scale and Quality of Work-Based Learning. Final Report*. Princeton, NJ: Mathematica Policy Research, Inc.

———. 2004. "Student Participation in and Use of Work-Based Learning." In *Working Knowledge: Work-Based Learning and Education Reform*, by Thomas Bailey, Katherine Hughes, and David Moore (39–66). New York: RoutledgeFalmer.

Hamilton, Mary A., and Stephen F. Hamilton. 1997. *Learning Well at Work: Choices for Quality*. Washington, DC: U.S. Government Printing Office.

Hamilton, Stephen. 1990. *Apprenticeship for Adulthood: Preparing Youth for the Future*. New York: The Free Press.

Heckman, James, Jora Stixrud, and Sergio Urzoa. 2006. "The Effect of Cognitive and Non-Cognitive Abilities on Labor Market Outcomes and Social Behavior." Working Paper 12,006. Cambridge, MA: National Bureau of Economic Research.

Hershey, Alan. 2003. "Has School-to-Work Worked?" In *The School-to-Work Movement: Origins and Destinations*, edited by William Stull and Nicholas Sanders (79–100). Westport, CT: Praeger Press.

Hershey, Alan, Marsha Silverberg, Joshua Haimson, Paula Hudis, and Russell Jackson. 1999. *Expanding Options for Students: Report to Congress on the National Evaluation of School-to-Work Implementation*. Princeton, NJ: Mathematica Policy Research, Inc.

Hotz, V. Joseph, Lixin Xu, Marta Tienda, and Avner Ahituv. 2002. "Are There Returns to the Wages of Young Men from Working While in School?" *Review of Economics and Statistics* 84(1): 221–36.

Ingels, Steven, Laura Burns, Xianglei Chen, Emily Cataldi, and Stephanie Charleston. 2005. *A Profile of the American High School Sophomore of 2002.* NCES 2005-338. Washington, DC: U.S. Department of Education, National Center for Education Statistics.

Kemple, James, with Judith Scott-Clayton. 2004. *Career Academies: Impacts on Labor Market Outcomes and Educational Attainment.* New York: MDRC.

Lerman, Robert. 1996. "JTPA's Negligible Impacts on the Earnings of Out-of-School Youth." Bethesda, MD: Abt Associates.

Lerman, Robert, and Hillard Pouncy. 1990. "The Compelling Case for Youth Apprenticeship." *The Public Interest* 101: 62–77.

Lerman, Robert, David Moskowitz, and Caroline Ratcliffe. 2004. "A Profile of Out-of-School Youth: Who Are They and How Are They Faring?" Washington, DC: The Urban Institute.

Levesque, Karen. 2003. *Trends in High School Vocational/Technical Coursetaking: 1982–1998.* NCES 2003-025. Washington, DC: US Department of Education, National Center for Education Statistics.

Light, Audrey. 2001. "In-School Work Experience and the Returns to Schooling." *Journal of Labor Economics* 19(1): 65–93.

Lyke, Robert. 1991. *Early Labor Market Experiences of Proprietary School Students.* CRS Report for Congress. Washington, DC: Congressional Research Service.

MacAllum, Keith, Karla Yoder, Scott Kim, and Robert Bozick. 2002. *Moving Forward: College and Career Transitions of LAMP Graduates.* Washington, DC: Academy for Educational Development.

Madonna Yost Opinion Research. 1999. "Work-Based Learning Alumni Survey: Summary of Findings." Unpublished report prepared for the School District of Philadelphia, March.

Marcotte, David, Thomas R. Bailey, Carey Borkoski, and Gregory S. Kienzl. 2005. "The Returns to Education at Community Colleges: Evidence from the National Education Longitudinal Survey." *Educational Evaluation and Policy Analysis* 27(2): 157–75.

Mayer, Susan, and Paul Peterson, eds. 1999. *Earning and Learning: How Schools Matter.* Washington, DC: Brookings Institution Press.

McConnell, Shenna, and Steven Glazerman. 2001. *The National Job Corps Study: The Benefits and Costs of Job Corps.* Princeton, NJ: Mathematica Policy Research, Inc.

Mikelson, Kelly, and Demetra Smith Nightingale. 2004. "Estimating Public and Private Expenditures on Occupational Training in the United States." Washington, DC: The Urban Institute.

Miller, Cynthia, and Johannes Bos. 2003. *Working with Disadvantaged Youth: Thirty-Month Findings from the Evaluation of the Center for Employment Training Replication Sites.* New York: MDRC.

Molitor, Christopher, and Duane Leigh. 2005. "In-School Work Experience and the Returns to Two-Year and Four-Year Colleges." *Economics of Education Review* 24: 459–68.

Murnane, Richard, and Frank Levy. 1996. *Teaching the New Basic Skills.* New York: The Free Press.

National Center for Education and the Economy. 1997. *Performance Standards: Volume 3—High School.* Washington, DC: National Center for Education and the Economy and Learning Research and Development Center.

National Commission on Excellence in Education. 1983. *A Nation at Risk.* Washington, DC: U.S. Department of Education.

Neumark, David, and Donna Rothstein. 2005. "Do School-to-Work Programs Help the 'Forgotten Half?'" Working Paper 11,636. Cambridge, MA: National Bureau of Economic Research.

O'Donnell, Kevin. 2005. *Tabular Summary of Adult Education for Work-Related Reasons: 2002–2003.* NCES 2005-044. Washington, DC: U.S. Department of Education, National Center for Education Statistics.

OECD. See Organisation for Economic Co-operation and Development.

Organisation for Economic Co-operation and Development. 2004. *Education at a Glance: OECD Indicators 2004.* Paris: Organisation for Economic Co-operation and Development.

Orr, Margaret Terry. 1995. *Wisconsin Youth Apprenticeship Program in Printing.* Boston, MA: Jobs for the Future.

Rivera-Batiz, Frances. 2003. "The Impact of School-to-Work Programs on Minority Youth." In *The School-to-Work Movement: Origins and Destinations,* edited by William Stull and Nicholas Sanders (169–88). Westport, CT: Praeger Press.

Rosenbaum, James. 2001. *Beyond College for All: Career Paths for the Forgotten Half.* New York: Russell Sage Foundation.

Ruhm, Christopher. 1997. "Is High School Employment Consumption or Investment?" *Journal of Labor Economics* 12(4): 735–76.

Schochet, Peter, John Burghardt, and Steven Glazerman. 2001. *National Job Corps Study: The Impact of Jobs Corps on Participants' Employment and Related Outcomes.* Princeton, NJ: Mathematica Policy Research, Inc.

Schochet, Peter, Shenna McConnell, and John Burghardt. 2003. *National Job Corps Study: Findings Using Administrative Earnings Data.* Princeton, NJ: Mathematica Policy Research, Inc.

Secretary's Commission on Achieving Necessary Skills. 1992. *Learning a Living: A Blueprint for High Performance. A SCANS Report for America 2000.* Washington, DC: U.S. Department of Labor.

Silverberg, Marcia, Elizabeth Warner, Michael Fong, and David Goodwin. 2004. *National Assessment of Vocational Education: Final Report to Congress.* Jessup, MD: U.S. Department of Education.

Stasz, Catherine. 2001. "Assessing Skills for Work." *Oxford Economic Papers* 3: 385–405.

Stinebrickner, Ralph, and Todd Stinebrickner. 2003. "Working during School and Academic Performance." *Journal of Labor Economics* 21(2): 473–91.

Swanson, Christopher. 2004. *The Real Truth About Graduation Rates.* Washington, DC: The Urban Institute.

Tucker, Marc. 2003. "Discussion of 'Accelerating Advancement in School and Work'," ed. Diane Ravitch. *Brookings Papers on Education Policy:* 367–74.

Turner, Sarah. 2004. "Going to College and Finishing College: Explaining Different Educational Outcomes." In *College Choices: The Economics of Where to Go, When to Go, and How to Pay for It,* edited by Caroline M. Hoxby (13–56). Chicago: University of Chicago Press.

Tyler, John. 2003. "Using State Child Labor Laws to Identify the Effect of School-Year Work on High School Achievement." *Journal of Labor Economics* 21(2): 381–408.

U.S. Bureau of Labor Statistics. 2006. "America's Youth at Age 18: School Enrollment and Employment Transitions between Age 17 and 18." News release USDL 06-320. Washington, DC: U.S. Department of Labor, Bureau of Labor Statistics.

U.S. General Accounting Office. 1996. *Employment Training: Successful Projects Share Common Strategy.* GAO/HHES 96-108. Washington, DC: U.S. General Accounting Office.

Wagner, Karin. 1999. "The German Apprenticeship System under Strain." In *The German Skills Machine: Sustaining Comparative Advantage in a Global Economy,* edited by Pepper Culpepper and David Feingold (37–76). New York: Berghahn Books.

Washington State Employment Security Office. 1998. *Apprenticeship in Washington: Effective, Underutilized.* Olympia: State of Washington.

Washington State Workforce Training and Education Coordinating Board. 2004. *Workforce Training Results: 2004.* Olympia: State of Washington.

Wenger, Etienne. 1998. *Communities of Practice: Learning, Meaning, and Identity.* New York: Cambridge University Press.

William T. Grant Foundation Commission on Work, Family, and Citizenship. 1988. *The Forgotten Half: Pathways to Success for America's Youth and Young Families.* New York: William T. Grant Commission on Work, Family, and Citizenship.

4

HIGHER EDUCATION POLICIES GENERATING THE 21ST CENTURY WORKFORCE

Sarah E. Turner

Whether students from all backgrounds find opportunities for success at colleges and universities is not a challenge new to the 21st century. Yet, the stakes are perhaps greater than ever before as economic rewards to collegiate attainment remain at peak levels. Differences in collegiate attainment by family circumstances limit opportunity and exacerbate inequality across generations. In addition, the collegiate attainment of the coming generation will substantially affect international competitiveness and economic growth.

If we define college participation as enrolling for at least a brief period in a postsecondary institution, more people than ever are participating in higher education. Yet, the rate at which participation has translated into degree attainment has dwindled. What is more, the gap in enrollment by family circumstances is not closing, and differences in completion are even larger than differences in enrollment along this criterion.

Beyond recounting statistics on enrollment rates and college completion rates, this chapter considers how public policies affect the level and distribution of collegiate outcomes. Both state and federal sources face considerable pressure from other budgetary demands such as Medicaid and transportation infrastructure, creating few foreseeable opportunities for dramatic increases in support for higher education policies (Kane and Orszag 2003). The challenge, then, is to consider whether the existing higher education programs use available resources efficiently.

An initial—and nontrivial—task is to outline the public policies that affect higher education. Support for higher education does not come from a single program or piece of legislation but rather a wide range of distinct policies administered by federal and state authorities. At the federal level, public support includes grants, loans, tax credits, and savings incentives. State support includes direct support to public institutions as well as grant aid to students. There is little integration among the various public policies supporting higher education. This may contribute to uncertainty and confusion among potential students about the cost of college.

If there is a general point to make in this chapter, it is that both sides of the market in U.S. higher education—students and colleges—vary considerably. Sweeping "one size fits all" policy proclamations simply fail to fit the data at hand. What is more, the challenges are multifaceted; it is naïve to claim that the demonstrable underrepresentation of low-income students among college graduates is attributable solely to financing, precollegiate achievement, or any other single barrier. It is time to move beyond broad and ill-defined discussions of "access" and "affordability."[1] Instead, the discussion needs to turn to the question of how public resources affect student attainment at the college level. The challenge, then, is to look forward to policies that make the best use of available resources to increase collegiate attainment and provide opportunities for the most economically disadvantaged students.

This chapter focuses on how public policies related to higher education affect the attainment of recent high school graduates—what might be thought of as "traditional" students—at colleges and universities. Necessarily, several types of students are not considered in this analysis. First, graduate study including PhD programs and professional degree attainment are outside the scope of this analysis, though of clear importance for both policy design and workforce issues in the coming years. Second, the question of how higher education policies affect enrollment and attainment of nontraditional students is not answered here.[2] In many regards, the expansion of opportunities in the postsecondary sector for mid-career enrollment and flexibility in opportunities to return to study is one of the great success stories of higher education in the past quarter-century. Significant growth over the past three decades has occurred in the enrollment rates of older and nontraditional students. Yet, of some concern is whether some of the expansion of enrollment at older ages captures barriers to attainment in the original pipeline.

The first section of this chapter reviews the empirical evidence on trends in collegiate attainment and the differential levels of enrollment and attainment by family circumstances. The next section outlines available policies in support of higher education at both the state and federal levels. The final section looks forward to the challenges (and opportunities) ahead for policy design and research.

RECENT TRENDS IN COLLEGIATE ENROLLMENT AND ATTAINMENT

Substantial changes in the structure of earnings and increases in the economic return to a college degree over the past quarter-century motivate much of the discussion about public policies affecting collegiate attainment. To illustrate, the ratio of average hourly wages for college graduates relative to average hourly wages for high school graduates was 1.36 for men and 1.39 for women in 1978. By 2003, these ratios had risen to 1.77 for men and 1.7 for women, an increase of about 30 percent for men and about 22 percent for women.[3] As the returns to education rise, how education opportunities are allocated becomes increasingly important to ensuring intergenerational mobility. In addition, persistently rising returns to education imply that the supply of college-educated workers graduating from U.S. colleges and universities is not keeping pace with the demand. Yet, it is far from clear how public policies can increase collegiate attainment in an economically efficient way.

Overall Trends

While the labor market provides considerable incentives for collegiate attainment in terms of higher wages, the response in collegiate attainment has been anemic. Two empirical points merit note:

- Enrollment rates and participation rates have risen steadily over the course of the past two decades, and now over 65 percent of high school graduates and nearly 60 percent of the total birth cohort record some collegiate participation by their mid-20s (figure 4.1). In addition, while the enrollment rates of black youth still trail behind overall enrollment rates, this group has experienced similar percentage increases in enrollment since the late 1980s.

Figure 4.1. College Enrollment by Year of Birth

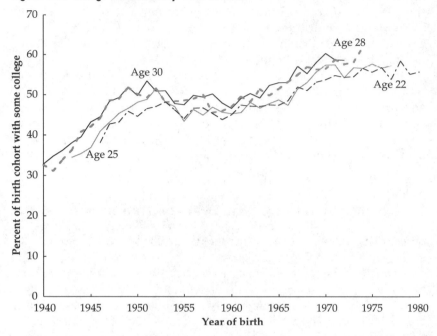

Source: Author's calculations using the October CPS, 1968–2003. See Turner (2004) for details.

- While college enrollment has increased markedly among those born in the late 1960s and 1970s (enrolling in college in the 1980s and 1990s), changes in college completion have lagged. Measured at age 22, the share of college degree recipients among those born in the late 1970s is actually somewhat lower than the share observed for those born in the late 1950s (top chart in figure 4.2). Yet, when we look at attainment as these cohorts age, college completion has increased for recent cohorts. It follows that time to degree completion has increased. Moreover, the share of those starting college who eventually finish has actually declined somewhat if we look at individuals in their early 20s (bottom chart in figure 4.2).

Focusing on the data, figure 4.1 shows college enrollment and figure 4.2 shows completion over time for different age levels. In large part, students who will participate in the collegiate system have had at least some college by their early 20s, as the college participation lines are not appreciably different by age. While many of these students with some participation may return to college (potentially completing

Figure 4.2. College Completion by Year of Birth

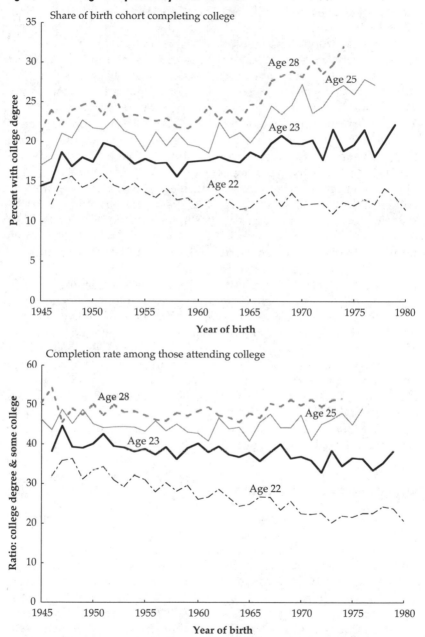

Source: Author's calculations using the October CPS, 1968–2003. See Turner (2004) for details.

Notes: The top figure shows the percent of the total population of a given age who have received a BA or completed 16 years of education. The bottom shows the ratio of college degree recipients to those with at least some college participation at the indicated age.

degrees), few students who have never enrolled by age 22 will do so later in their lives.

Figure 4.2 shows BA degree attainment by year of birth in the top chart and the proportion of those who started college receiving a degree in the bottom chart. With separate lines in the graph indicating age at observation, the figure illustrates substantial divergence by age for recent birth cohorts. For all cohorts, there are gains in BA completion by age, but these differences become particularly pronounced after the 1954 cohort. After this cohort, the share completing a BA by age 22 falls slightly or at least stays steady, while the share completing college by age 25 and older seems to increase slightly. That few of the students beyond age 22 are "new participants" indicates that either the duration of enrollment required to receive a BA has increased or more students complete their degrees after "spells" of discontinuous study. Thus, for students receiving BA degrees at age 28, the total time to degree likely approaches 10 years. Unambiguously, the expected time to BA completion has increased in recent decades, likely resulting in reductions in the supply of college-educated in the labor market.

Taking the last point further, figure 4.3 shows that the share of students finishing undergraduate degrees within four years has fallen over the course of the past two decades. While the full exposition of explanations for increases in time-to-degree must wait for a later analysis (Bound, Lovenheim, and Turner 2006), potential explanations for this observed change include changes in the distribution of student characteristics affecting attainment (e.g., student achievement and finances) and resources at the institutional level that may affect degree completion. While BA degree completion is not the only indicator of collegiate attainment, it is a readily available marker of how collegiate attainment has changed over recent years.

Opportunities by Family Income

Low-income students are underrepresented among students who enroll in college, and differences between low-income students and more affluent students widen as we look at enrollment in four-year institutions or collegiate completion. Figure 4.4 shows the college enrollment rates for students by family income and precollegiate achievement tertile for two different cohorts, students graduating from high school in 1980 and students graduating in 1992. Beyond the overall rise in college enrollments, substantial differences between low-income students and high-income students in the overall likelihood of attending college are apparent. There are differences in college enrollment rates between low-income students and high-income students in all achievement groups. Even among students with high levels of precollegiate

Figure 4.3. Distribution of Time to Degree by Graduation Year

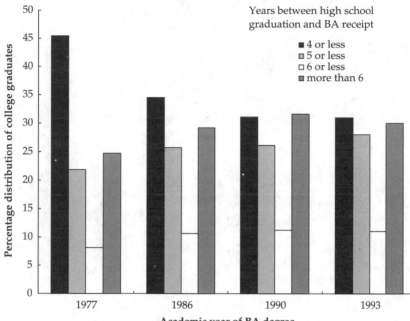

Source: U.S. Department of Education, National Center for Education Statistics, Recent College Graduates Survey for 1977–90 graduates and 1993 Baccalaureate and Beyond Longitudinal Study, First Follow-up (B&B:93/94).

achievement, low-income students are less likely to enroll (82 percent) than students in the top income quartile (96 percent). The differences in enrollment by family income are the widest at the low and moderate levels of achievement, and it is at this margin where enrollment differ ences have *grown* over time.

It is when we go beyond the dichotomous measure of enrollment to consider college choice and collegiate attainment where differences by family circumstances are even larger. Table 4.1 reports enrollment rates by family income and type of enrollment, distinguishing between two-year and four-year institutions and full-time and part-time status. As expected from the earlier indicators, low-income students are appreciably less likely to be enrolled in college; overall enrollment rates for dependent students are 45 percent or less for all income groups below $30,000 in 2003. In contrast, for students from families with incomes over $100,000, college enrollment rates near 70 percent. Another difference—one with substantial implications for degree attainment—is that among high-income students enrolled in college, over 60 percent attend full-time at four-year colleges. Among lower-income students, the share

Figure 4.4. College Enrollment by Family Income

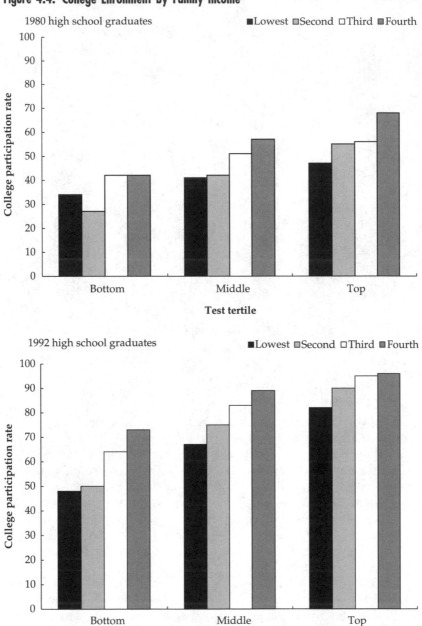

Test tertile

Sources: For 1980, High School and Beyond; for 1992, the NELS-88 survey.
Notes: Data in 1980 chart reflect the high school graduating class of 1980. Data in 1992 chart reflect the high school graduating class of 1992. The data in the figure were computed and reported in Ellwood and Kane (2000).

Table 4.1. College Enrollment Rates for Dependents Age 18–24 by Family Income, 2003

Family income	Two-Year		Four-Year		Total postsecondary
	Full-time	Part-time	Full-time	Part-time	
Less than $10,000	0.04	0.02	0.14	0.01	0.37
$10,000 to $14,999	0.06	0.03	0.20	0.03	0.44
$15,000 to $19,999	0.09	0.05	0.18	0.01	0.44
$20,000 to $29,999	0.09	0.03	0.20	0.02	0.45
$30,000 to $39,999	0.11	0.02	0.24	0.04	0.50
$40,000 to $49,999	0.10	0.07	0.23	0.03	0.50
$50,000 to $74,999	0.11	0.03	0.32	0.03	0.56
$75,000 to $99,999	0.11	0.05	0.38	0.03	0.64
$100,000 to $149,999	0.13	0.03	0.44	0.05	0.71
$150,000 and over	0.10	0.02	0.47	0.03	0.69
Not reported	0.07	0.03	0.31	0.02	0.53
Total	0.10	0.03	0.31	0.03	0.55

Source: U.S. Census Bureau, "Enrollment Status of Dependent Primary Family Members 18 to 24 Years Old, by Family Income, Level of Enrollment, Attendance Status, Type of School, Sex, Race, and Hispanic Origin: October 2003," http://www.census.gov/population/www/socdemo/school/cps2003.html (table 14).

of those enrolled attending full-time at four-year institutions falls appreciably,[4] with these students relatively likely to be attending part-time or at two-year institutions.

These differences also come to light in measures of college completion by family income (a particularly difficult indicator because family income is not observed among college graduates in surveys like the Current Population Survey). Carnevale, Fry, and Turner (2001) use the Panel Study of Income Dynamics and find that the gap between students from the bottom quartile and the top quartile widened appreciably over the past two decades. College completion among those from families in the top income quartile rose from 32 to 47 percent, while it remained stagnant at about 6 percent among those from families in the bottom income quartile, when comparing those age 16 between 1969 and 1973 with those age 16 between 1979 and 1983.[5] These results are consistent with recent calculations by Haveman and Wilson (2005).

Another margin along which differences in collegiate outcomes by family income are apparent is in the representation of students at the most selective colleges and universities. Less than 11 percent of students at some of the most selective institutions come from families in the bottom quartile of the income distribution for families with college-age children (table 4.2). Given the significant underrepresentation of low-income students at these institutions, Bowen, Kurzweil, and Tobin (2005) have asked whether these institutions are "engines of opportunity or bastions of privilege."

Table 4.2. Application, Admission, and Enrollment of Low-Income Students at Private Colleges and Universities, 1995 Entering Cohort (percent)

	Share in Bottom Income Quartile			
	Apply	Admit	Enroll	Graduate
All Expanded College and Beyond	12	9	11	11
Ivy League universities	12	8	9	8
Public universities	12	11	12	11
Liberal arts colleges	11	8	10	10

Sources: Bowen et al. (2005), figure 5.1, and special tabulations from the Andrew W. Mellon Foundation.

Notes: The elite institutions included in the category "All Expanded College and Beyond" are Columbia University, Harvard University, Princeton University, the University of Pennsylvania, Yale University, Barnard College, Bowdoin College, Macalester College, Middlebury College, Oberlin College, Pomona College, Smith College, Swarthmore College, Wellesley College, Williams College, Pennsylvania State University, University of California-Los Angeles, University of Illinois at Urbana/Champaign, and the University of Virginia.

Still, as important as universities like Harvard, Williams, and Amherst may be for providing access to leadership positions, they represent a relatively tiny share of undergraduate enrollment and undergraduate degree attainment among U.S. colleges and universities. To give this point quantitative resonance, the 19 selective institutions represented in data employed by Bowen and colleagues accounted for first-year enrollments of 29,524; first-time undergraduate enrollment in the corresponding year (1995) totaled 2.169 million students (Snyder and Hoffman 2001, table 183), implying that a complete transformation of the enrollment of low-income students at these institutions would hardly make a dent in attainment for low-income students.[6] What is more, the underlying causes of the underrepresentation of low-income students might differ at selective institutions, where students are likely to receive generous grant support, than at other institutions, where credit constraints are likely more significant.[7]

The causal mechanism generating the wide disparities by family circumstances in enrollment and attainment includes the following potential explanations:

- With the widening distribution of family incomes in recent decades, children from the top of the income distribution are likely to be better off in an absolute sense; children from the bottom of the distribution, worse off.
- Persistent difference in precollegiate achievement by family income may lead to differences in college readiness and, in turn, low-income students may be less prepared to attend four-year institutions and relatively selective institutions than their higher-

income peers. To illustrate, about 2.4 percent of students from families with income less than \$24,000 score over 1,300 on their SATs as high school seniors, compared with about 18 percent of students with family incomes above \$92,000 (Hill and Winston 2005).[8]

- Changes in public policy, such as increases in tuition levels or decreases in the real value of student aid, are likely to disproportionately affect low-income students.

While the first two points are of considerable importance, the last one is the focus of the remainder of the analysis. Certainly, other dimensions of public policy should address the causes and consequences of the widening income distribution. Other higher education policies that complement existing student aid, such as outreach initiatives and programs intended to increase students' awareness of collegiate options, should also be weighed against direct aid policies. Further, policies at the elementary and secondary level that increase college preparedness and reduce gaps in achievement by family circumstances are unquestionably important for reducing inequality in collegiate outcomes.

EXISTING HIGHER EDUCATION POLICIES

Public policies in higher education should improve the matching of students with collegiate institutions, specifically resolving the problem of credit constraints caused by the potential inability of individuals to secure loans to finance collegiate investments. Policymakers may also hope to use the financing of higher education to increase the quality and quantity of skilled workers available at the state or national level. The extent to which existing policies accomplish these objectives is a matter of some debate, particularly given the underrepresentation of low-income students in many dimensions of higher education.

There is no single, comprehensive "higher education policy" in the United States. Instead, students (their families) and colleges respond to an array of different policies at the state and federal levels. (The final section of this chapter discusses whether this extraordinary level of decentralization leads to confusion, hampering the capacity of students to make the best investments.) At the federal level, higher education policies include grants, loans, tax credits, and savings incentives. At the state level, students are supported through across-the-board subsidies to colleges and universities (that allow for below-market tuition charges) and direct grants, often conditioned on need or merit.

Noteworthy, then, is how state variation leaves 50 different variants of public policies to higher education.

This section begins with a review of the level and distribution of federal funding for higher education over the course of the past decade. Next, it considers broad variations in the level and distribution of state support. Of final concern is a discussion of the potential inefficiencies in this system of funding higher education.

Federal Policy

The majority of federal funding for undergraduate education comes through three types of aid: Pell grants, student loans, and tax credits. The first two prongs of federal policy—grants and loans—date to the Higher Education Act of 1965, with Pell grants (earlier known as Basic Educational Opportunity Grants) tied to the reauthorization of this legislation in 1972. The primary instruments for federal policy designed to increase collegiate attainment over the past three decades have been the programs under Title IV of the Higher Education Act, notably Pell grants and Stafford student loans. The Tax Reform Act of 1997 added tuition tax credits (under the banner of Hope and Lifetime Learning).[9]

Focusing first on Title IV, the primary student aid programs are the Pell grant program and the Stafford student loan program. Both programs are means-tested and eligibility is determined through the evaluation of a Free Application for Federal Student Aid (FAFSA) form that records student and parental assets and incomes.[10] Applying a nonlinear benefit reduction formula leads to the determination of the expected family contribution, and the difference between allowable college costs and expected family contribution yields aid eligibility.[11] The distribution of aid eligibility under the federal needs analysis formula does not, however, guarantee that a student will have all need met; it is quite possible that the sum of the Pell grant, Stafford loan, and whatever aid is available from the institution may be less than total need in many circumstances.

Title IV financial aid is remarkable in the breadth of the programs covered and the range of potential students eligible to benefit; those who believe that the majority of students receiving aid are recent high school graduates attending full-time residential colleges are simply mistaken. The share of Pell grant recipients who are independent has risen steadily over the past three decades from about 30 percent in 1975 to over 60 percent in the early 1990s, before dipping to about 58 percent in 2003–04. Also in 2003–04, about 46 percent of Pell grant recipients were attending four-year institutions, while 17.1 percent of recipients were attending institutions operating on a for-profit basis.[12] The Title IV financial aid programs are often described as the cornerstone of federal higher education policy; in academic year 2003–04, Pell grant aid totaled $12.6 billion in expenditures, while loan programs provided over $55.4 billion in capital, with about $25 billion of the amount provided through the subsidized Stafford loan program.

Despite the rhetoric surrounding the Title IV programs as the key dimensions of federal policy aimed at eliminating credit constraints, empirical evidence on the behavioral effects of these programs is mixed.[13] Focusing first on the enrollment effects for traditional college-age students (defined as students who are recent high school graduates and still depend on their parents for financial support), evaluations consistently yield no evidence that the program changes enrollment (Hansen 1983; Kane 1994).[14] One explanation for why the Pell grant program has had such modest effects is that the complexity of the program and the difficulty in determining benefit eligibility may impose a high cost, inhibiting many potential students at the margin from applying. According to Dynarski and Scott-Clayton (2006), the federal financial needs analysis mechanism is not only unnecessarily complex, such complexity likely disproportionately burdens those from the lowest income groups, thereby undermining redistributive goals. Beyond financial considerations, another explanation for the underrepresentation of low-income students is that factors beyond financial constraints (including academic achievement) limit college enrollment and college attainment for the low-income student at the margin between attending and not attending college.

While the Pell grant program has not had a discernable effect on the collegiate attainment of traditional students, its effects on college participation for nontraditional students have been marked.[15] The introduction of the Pell program, as well as changes in program eligibility, have significantly affected the college enrollment decisions of older students (Seftor and Turner 2002). Many of the most significant changes in benefit determination associated with the Pell program have affected nontraditional students. As one example, Simmons and Turner (2003) examine the effects of the inclusion of child care expenses under allowable college costs in aid determination and find that the addition of this benefit has affected enrollment for women with children. Expansion of the availability of federal financial aid for undergraduates to older students opens enrollment in higher education to many individuals who would not have been able to enroll in higher education in earlier decades.

It is also worth noting that, today, the maximum Pell grant is $4,050, which is higher in real terms than the award level in the mid-1990s but still well below the constant dollar value of the program award from the mid-1970s (about $4,800). Given that college costs have risen over the past quarter-century, the Pell grant now covers a lower share of the burden of paying for college than it did originally.

Beyond grant funding, low-income students may turn to the federal government for loan assistance in funding college. The mechanics of subsidized student loans are that students can borrow (a limited amount) from the federal government. The government pays interest while the student is enrolled and then offers the student repayment at a subsidized rate when college is completed. Subsidized Stafford loans are awarded based on financial need. The federal government also offers unsubsidized Stafford loans, which are not awarded on the basis of financial need. The interest on these loans is charged to the student as soon as the student receives the money.

Figure 4.5 shows the overall trend in the constant dollar level of federal funding for student loans through the 1990s (see College Board 2004). In reviewing these numbers, note that loans to undergraduate students accounted for only about 70 percent of subsidized loans generated in 2000, down from about 74 percent in 1997 (U.S. Department of Education 2002). While borrowing under the subsidized arm of the program increased (rising about 40 percent in real terms), the most dramatic expansion in credit occurred in the unsubsidized dimensions of the program: unsubsidized Stafford borrowing increased from $2.6 billion in 1993–94 to $23.1 billion in 2003–04, and PLUS (the program allowing parental borrowing) increased from $1.9 billion to about $7 billion.

The overall trends in the availability of loans miss the point that an increasingly smaller share of the available subsidized credit is directed

Figure 4.5. Trends in Federal Student Loans (constant 2003 dollars)

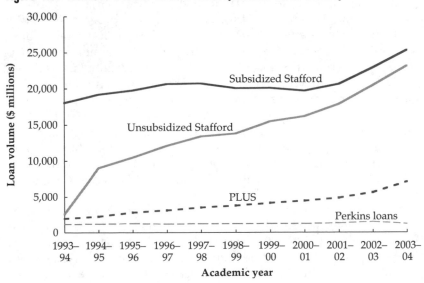

Source: College Board (2004), table 2.

to recent high school graduates attending undergraduate institutions. Loan limits vary by year of study and status as a student (dependent, independent), with dependent undergraduate students limited to borrowing $2,625, while a graduate student may borrow up to $18,500 (with no more than $8,500 in subsidized loans).[16] Table 4.3 shows the applicable loan limits under the federal student loan program.

Examinations of federal loan programs provide strong evidence that students would be better off with more access to credit markets. First, Kane (1999) demonstrates a high degree of stacking in the distribution of student loans, with many students apparently constrained at the lower division limit of $2,625 and the upper division limit of $4,000. In addition, Dynarski (2002) finds significant changes in attendance behavior with the removal of home equity from the needs analysis formula in the early 1990s. When low-income students are limited to federal sources of support to finance college, it is surely possible that they are credit-constrained—perhaps so constrained that they must combine school and work or turn down a residential collegiate program to live at home while attending college.[17]

Table 4.3. Annual Loan Limits for Subsidized and Unsubsidized Stafford Loans

	Dependent undergraduate student	*Independent undergraduate student*	*Graduate/professional student*
First year	$2,625	$6,625–no more than $2,625 may be in subsidized loans.	$18,500–no more than $8,500 may be in subsidized loans.
Second year	$3,500	$7,500–no more than $3,500 may be in subsidized loans.	
Third and fourth years (each)	$5,500	$10,500–no more than $5,500 may be in subsidized loans.	
Maximum total debt from Stafford loans when student graduates	$23,000	$46,000–no more than $23,000 may be in subsidized loans.	$138,500–no more than $65,500 may be in subsidized loans.

Source: "The Student Guide: Types of Federal Student Aid," http://studentaid.ed.gov/students/publications/student_guide/2004_2005/english/types-stafford.htm.

Notes: To qualify for independent status, at least one of the following must be true of a student: born before January 1, 1981; married as of the day of application; is or will be enrolled in a master's or doctorate program (beyond a bachelor's degree) at the beginning of the 2004–05 school year; has children or other dependents who receive half their support from the student; both parents are deceased, or is or was (until age 18) a ward or dependent of the court; is a veteran of the U.S. Armed Forces. For more information, see "The Student Guide: General Information," http://studentaid.ed.gov/students/publications/student_guide/2004_2005/english/general-dependency.htm. The graduate debt limit includes Stafford loans received for undergraduate study.

Tuition tax credits form the final prong of federal aid discussed in this chapter. Most notably, this aid is nonrefundable, implying that eligible students are unlikely to be among the most economically disadvantaged. Long (2004) notes that these credits are aimed at the middle class, with about two-thirds of the population potentially eligible; those with limited tax liability are ineligible, as are those with incomes above a ceiling. The Hope credit, the first arm of the 1997 tax credit program, provides a tax credit equal to 100 percent of the first $1,000 of qualified tuition expenses and 50 percent of the second $1,000 for the first two years of postsecondary education. The Lifetime Learning tax credit, the second arm of the program, covers 20 percent of the first $5,000 in tuition expenditures up to $1,000 and is available for upper-level undergraduates, adults upgrading skills, or graduate and professional students. The College Board (2004) estimates that the implicit tax expenditures through this program have risen from $3.3 billion in 1998–99 to about $6.3 billion in 2003–04. By most accounts, the first-order motivation was the provision of an appealing tax cut to the middle class (not the reform of student aid policy) for political purposes. Many traditional advocates for need-based student aid viewed these tax credit initiatives as crowding out established programs such as the Pell grant and diluting the targeting of need-based aid. This opposition may well have limited the support for the alternative of helping low-income students through a refundable tax credit (Starch 2005).

State Policies

State policies for public higher education have traditionally consisted of substantial direct subsidies to public colleges and universities along with limited portable aid to students.

States have been major direct funders of public colleges and universities throughout the 20th century, with direct funding allowing public colleges to charge relatively low levels of tuition to in-state students. Figure 4.6 illustrates the trend in tuition levels of private colleges and public four-year and two-year institutions. Public institutions continue to post tuition levels well below the level charged by private institutions, with tuition at four-year publics about 25 percent of the private level and tuition at two-year publics about 10.5 percent of the private level. Such steep discounts relative to costs are afforded by large direct appropriations to public institutions from state governments (on average about 45 percent of budgets, down from nearly 60 percent more than a decade ago). In thinking about the distribution of college costs among students, more than 51 percent of students attending four-year institutions full-time faced tuition levels of less than $6,000 (College Board 2005).

Figure 4.6. Average Published Tuition and Fee Charges, 1975–76 to 2005–06 (enrollment-weighted, constant 2005 dollars)

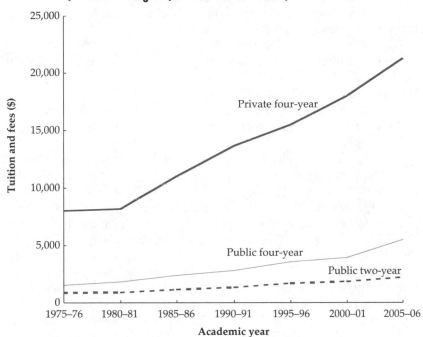

Source: College Board (2005).

Notes: 1997–2005 data weighted by full-time undergraduate enrollment. 1976 to 1987 data weighted by full-time-equivalent enrollment.

That public colleges and universities maintain tuition levels below those charged by private universities reflects the availability of direct subsidies from state governments. The level of per student subsidy varies not only among states but also by type of institution. In general, state flagship universities tend to receive higher per student subsidies than other four-year institutions or community colleges.[18] Yet, state appropriations account for a larger share of per student costs at community colleges than at public research universities, which are likely to draw additional funding from research grants and donative support. State and local appropriations account for nearly 60 percent of revenues at community colleges while making up less than 30 percent of revenues at public flagship universities (Bound and Turner forthcoming). Given this distribution of public subsidies, shocks to public support are likely to have particularly significant effects on community colleges.

Over the past quarter-century, state support as an overall share of public college and university budgets has generally eroded. State appropriations as a share of total educational expenditures at all public colleges and universities fell from 78 percent to 45 percent between 1974 and 2000 (Rizzo 2006). Reductions in state support necessitate either contraction in resources per student or increases in the resources from other sources, including tuition revenues.

The era of very low tuition in all sectors of public higher education is likely coming to an end. In the past two years, public four-year institutions have posted tuition increases of 13 percent and 10 percent (11 percent and 9 percent in constant dollars), above even the rate of increase among private institutions (College Board 2005). Rising costs, including investments in technology and faculty salaries, and substantial fluctuations in state resources over the past two decades create a sharp tension for selective state universities between objectives of excellence and the mission of providing collegiate opportunities for state residents from all backgrounds (Turner 2005).

With increased claims on state coffers from programs like Medicaid and persistent voter pressure for reduced tax burdens, public universities are increasingly hard-hit as higher education is one of the few discretionary items in state budgets (Kane and Orszag 2003). Faced with the realities of limited funding from public sources in the 21st century, public colleges and universities in many states have been forced to reexamine the traditional balance between public subsidy and private tuition payments. In short, state governments can no longer afford to provide across-the-board subsidies to all students.

How well colleges can respond to reduced state support with tuition increases depends largely on their student populations. Flagship state universities with few substitutes are likely to increase prices most dramatically, while open-access four-year institutions may have less latitude in raising tuition if their student populations are more price-sensitive. In addition, the implications of tuition increases for enrollment opportunities of low-income students likely differ appreciably by type of institution, as more resource-intensive institutions may be able to blunt the impact of tuition increases for low-income students with additional financial aid.

Although the capacity—and willingness—of states to provide direct support to public universities over time has dwindled, the role of states in providing grant aid to students has increased markedly over the past decade. Georgia and Arkansas started programs in 1993, with 11 more states adding programs by 2002. The defining characteristic of these programs is that they offer generous aid—often equal to tuition at the public university—for in-state students with academic achievement above a threshold (see Dynarski 2004 for a thorough discussion of these state-level programs). The programs vary in their distributional consequences; some states provide additional aid to the most economically disadvantaged eligible students (Florida and Arkansas), while in other states (Georgia, initially), federal aid led to reductions in state aid for those who were eligible for Pell grants.

What is clear from the available empirical evidence is that these programs have quite sizeable impacts on in-state enrollment decisions. Going somewhat further, Dynarski (2005) finds substantial effects on collegiate attainment, with the introduction of state merit aid programs in Arkansas and Georgia inducing an increase in college completion of about 3 percentage points.

POLICY CHOICES GOING FORWARD

The evidence presented in the first section on the relatively anemic levels of growth in collegiate attainment, which is particularly apparent for low-income students, suggests that current policy tools for financing higher education are not working. To be sure, there are valid concerns about observed levels of precollegiate attainment—particularly for low-income and minority youth—that suggest that even the most generous funding scheme for higher education would not lead to the closure of gaps in attainment (and would likely be an inefficient use of resources). Yet, there is good reason to ask whether the current structure of public policies for higher education is accomplishing the related objectives of increasing the supply of college-educated workers and reducing the inequality of opportunity associated with family circumstances.

Federal Aid

Where federal financial aid programs work least well today is in providing financing to help students enroll full-time in the program that best matches their needs. Because many students—particularly at schools that do not have extensive institutional resources—are left with need not financed by either Pell grants or available student loans, they may be more likely to turn to part-time study, which is not only inefficient but places a further wedge in the opportunities between low-income students and their more affluent peers.[19]

Title IV student financial assistance has contributed to the growth in postsecondary enrollment of older students. Yet, these same federal aid policies do not appear to have affected collegiate attainment for low-income students making initial transitions to college. Reasonable people disagree on the reasons these programs do not appear to change behavior. One argument is that they are simply insufficiently generous to solve the financing problem. A different argument is that the FAFSA form and the associated eligibility rules are not sufficiently transparent to make aid eligibility clear to students early in their college search process. Yet a further explanation is that students (and, perhaps, their parents) are missing more general information about the costs (and benefits) of college attendance.

Perhaps a little humility is in order in thinking through next steps. A first point is that the weaknesses of the existing system of Title IV aid programs are not the exclusive fault of one political party or the other. The basic architecture of the program has been in place for three decades without a substantial reconfiguration from either side of the aisle. Many in the higher education community are reluctant to call for comprehensive—or even partial—restructuring out of concern that any reform might leave students less well off. In addition, stagnant levels of support for policies like the Pell grant make it all too easy to simply blame the lack of progress on a failure of funding. Many economists would concur that there is little empirical evidence supporting a case that the Pell grant program has a substantial effect on college enrollment or attainment of traditional college students.[20]

If the status quo distribution of Title IV aid is ineffective, how should federal student aid policy be restructured? Honesty requires an answer of "uncertain." Yet, we can—and should—use research and policy design to answer this question. Modest experiments (which have been all the rage in the push for scientific-based inquiry at the K–12 level) would help recognize how, for example, a more transparent needs-analysis formula would affect enrollment and college choice. Similarly, experiments offering greater access to subsidized loans will help policymakers understand what student aid tools will yield the largest gains in collegiate attainment at the lowest cost to taxpayers. It is also possible that waivers from the rules of Title IV aid allocation to states or universities might provide opportunities for valuable trials with alternative configurations of the distribution of grants and loans to understand which policy designs have the largest effect on student attainment.

The State–Federal Connection

As federal policymakers think about reforming student aid policy, there is much to be learned—some lessons affirmative, others lessons in what not to do—from the recent innovations at the state level, particularly with the adoption of state merit aid programs. At least two facets of these programs are noteworthy:

- State merit aid programs share many of the same characteristics as the most successful federal initiatives (the G.I. Bill and the Social Security student benefit program). They were very transparent and allowed students to easily determine eligibility, they provided support over a fixed duration encouraging college completion, and they were sufficiently generous to cover a substantial share of college costs.

● State merit aid programs provide the *potential* of benefits to every-one, making these programs enormously popular with voters. Dynarski (2004) argues that the "price of highly progressive spend-ing on need-based aid is that many voters do not see themselves as potential beneficiaries." In turn, "targeting within universality," which can be achieved through merit programs that have a redis-tributive component, may lead to a broader base of support for student aid.[21]

Beyond lessons from merit aid programs, state systems of higher education are increasingly limited in their capacity to maintain low tuitions and the quality of collegiate offerings. Recognizing the fiscal realities and allowing those public institutions serving relatively afflu-ent students to price at market levels (without political retribution) while also making a demonstrated commitment to need-based aid is a first step to greater efficiency and opportunity at the state level. What is more, federal policies that penalize (rather than reward) state spending on higher education while providing matching support for Medicaid expenditures (Kane and Orszag 2003) distort incentives to invest in higher education at the state level.

It is time to celebrate the diversity of opportunities available in U.S. higher education. In doing so, it is time to move beyond models of one-size-fits-all funding for higher education, recognizing that students for whom full-time residential study is the best option benefit from a different type of support for higher education than students attending college at different stages in their lives.

Nevertheless, in thinking about higher education policies, an impor-tant reminder is that colleges and universities stand near the end of a long chain of institutions including families, neighborhoods, and K–12 schools in fostering skill development. Substantial gains in collegiate attainment and reductions in enrollment and college completion associ-ated with family circumstances depend on improvements in precolle-giate achievement. What higher education policies can do is to make clear the opportunities available for collegiate attainment at early ages and to deliver comprehensive policies for students to finance atten-dance at America's colleges and universities.

NOTES

Maria Fitzpatrick provided excellent research assistance with this project. The author thanks Sue Dynarski and Harry Holzer for helpful comments on an early draft of this chapter.

1. Evaluation of public policy in higher education is susceptible to sweeping generalizations about "access" and "affordability," without clear definition of these terms. Reports in the press often focus on questions related to "access," loosely defined as the extent to which individuals from different circumstances enroll in college, to the near-exclusion of questions of attainment. "Affordability" tends to bundle tuition prices and the availability of student aid in aggregate rather than for a specific type of student. Emphasis on "access and affordability" in public discourse has diverted attention from the monitoring of outcomes or "attainment," including courses completed and degrees awarded. For further discussion, see Turner (2004).

2. Fitzpatrick and Turner (forthcoming) discuss the rising collegiate participation and attainment of "nontraditional" students and some potential causes of these changes. They find evidence that enrollment of nontraditional students is not responsive to increases in tuition (within observed ranges) but is responsive to cyclical shocks.

3. See http://www.epinet.org/datazone/05/wagebyed_a.xls, http://www.epinet.org/datazone/05/wagebyed_m.xls, and http://www.epinet.org/datazone/05/wagebyed_w.xls.

4. For example, only 44 percent of those enrolled in college in the $20,000–$29,000 income range were attending four-year institutions (0.2/0.45 in table 4.1).

5. In the Carnevale et al. (2001) analysis, family income quartile is determined on the basis of the person's average family income across ages 15, 16, and 17. Quartiles are computed separately for each cohort, thus the income thresholds for each quartile vary across birth cohorts.

6. One might also consider whether the barriers to enrollment of low-income students at these institutions are somewhat different—less likely to be financial aid resources and more likely to be preparation and recruitment—than in the broader universe of colleges and universities.

7. For clarification, economists typically consider an individual credit constrained if he or she is unable to borrow to finance an investment at the going market rate. Individuals are more likely to face credit constraints in the financing of education than in the financing of property (such as a car or house) because there is no physical property the lender of money used for education can hold as collateral or repossess in the event of a default.

8. Even at more modest levels of achievement, substantial differences by family income persist. Comparing approximately the bottom and top quintiles, Hill and Winston (2005) show that about 22.1 percent of low-income students score above the equivalent of 1,030, while about 67.4 percent of high-income students score above this level.

9. An additional category of aid funded at the federal level is the specially directed aid aimed at specific populations to achieve objectives other than meeting financial need; these programs include G.I. benefits and the Social Security student benefit program. Notably, both the G.I. Bill and the Social Security student benefit program had generally significant effects on collegiate enrollment and completion (Bound and Turner 2002; Dynarski 2003). The G.I. Bill and the Social Security student benefit program share several design features including the transparency of eligibility determination, meaning that potential beneficiaries knew their eligibility and the level and duration of benefits without additional calculations or waiting for the results of a bureau-

cratic process, and the substantial size of the benefits, often covering the majority of college costs.

10. This section follows the exposition in Turner (2004).

11. In essence, a tax rate is applied to a measure of available resources, both income and assets, with fixed adjustments for family size and number of members of the family in college to determine the student's "ability to pay." If this amount is less than allowable college costs, the student is aid-eligible.

12. The inaugural Higher Education Act (passed in 1965) separated academic and vocational training in determining program eligibility. Most programs funded under the 1965 Higher Education Act were campus-based (providing resources to institutions rather than portable aid to students). According to Gladieux (1995), Title IV was the first explicit federal commitment to equalizing college opportunities for needy students, to be achieved through means-tested grant aid and student support programs (Upward Bound, Talent Search, and the programs now known as TRIO). The primary means-tested aid vehicle was the Student Educational Opportunity Grants; award of aid under this program was administered by colleges and universities, which were required to "make 'vigorous' efforts to identify and recruit students with 'exceptional financial need.'" (See Gladieux 1995 for additional history.) Under the 1972 reauthorization of the Higher Education Act, Congress substituted the word "postsecondary education" for "higher education," intending to broaden the range of options beyond traditional baccalaureate programs. In this regard, the Basic Educational Opportunity Grants (known now as the Pell grants) included two- and four-year colleges and proprietary schools from the inception. Thus, the 1972 changes widened students choice sets to include more short-term, non-baccalaureate degree and vocational programs under Title IV.

13. To illustrate the symbolic attachment to these programs, both candidates in the 2004 presidential debate on domestic policy invoked the Pell grant as a policy tool; Kerry mentioned the program twice and Bush mentioned it six times (http://www.cnn.com/2004/ALLPOLITICS/10/13/debate.transcript/).

14. In one initial assessment of the program using time series data, Hansen examined the relative enrollment rates of more and less affluent students before and after the introduction of the Pell program. Hansen writes: "These data force one to conclude that the greater availability of student financial aid, targeted largely toward students from below-median-income families, did little, if anything, to increase access. The results certainly do not accord with expectations that access would increase for lower-income dependents relative to higher income dependents" (Hansen 1983, 93).

15. Under Title IV of the Higher Education Act, federal financial aid policy makes a statutory distinction between "dependent" and "independent" students in the determination of program eligibility. Eligibility for independent students rests only on the financial position of the applicant and his or her spouse, relative to direct college costs and other demands on resources including the number of children in the family. To be eligible for aid as an independent student, an individual must not be claimed as a dependent in the prior or current year for tax purposes and may only receive limited cash and in-kind contributions from parents. Eligibility for students claiming independent status has become more restrictive since the inception of the program. The 1986 amendments to the Higher Education Act required students to be at least 24 years old, married, or with children to qualify for aid as independent students.

16. These loan limits are set in statute at nominal levels and have not been adjusted since the 1980s. In discussing this point, one policy expert noted that adjusting loan limits for first- and second-year students would likely entail huge costs because there would also be pressure to up the loan limits for first- and second-year independent students (which are already at $6,625).

17. Researchers disagree about the magnitude of credit constraints, but most analysts agree that credit constraints limit enrollment and choice for some students. Even those skeptical of the argument that limited access to financial aid is the major barrier to collegiate attainment for low-income students acknowledge that financing may limit opportunities for some students. For example, Carneiro and Heckman state, "We present evidence that a small group of people is credit-constrained in this short-run sense, and that policies that relieve the constraints this group faces may be cost effective" (2004, 81).

18. The discussion of the trade-offs between a "high tuition, high aid" strategy and across-the-board low tuition has surfaced in research and policy discussion for more than three decades. Late in the 1960s, Hansen and Weisbrod (1969) made the case that large state subsidies to support low tuition were both inequitable and inefficient and, instead, that tuition should more accurately reflect cost of instruction, with public subsidies targeted to low-income students in the form of higher financial aid. The crux of the Hansen and Weisbrod argument, which derived largely from a case study of California, is that students from relatively affluent families are represented disproportionately in flagship universities that receive the largest per student appropriations from the state.

19. The suggestion of credit constraints in this case does not rely on strict causal evidence, but is instead based on the plausibility that a student limited to $2,625 in loans and $4,050 in Pell grants will have difficulty financing a full-time residential course of study at a four-year institution without institutional support.

20. The counterfactual of what enrollment would look like today, in an era in which real tuition levels are much higher than when the Pell program was introduced in the 1970s, is not observed. A related concern is that the elimination of the program would lead to a dramatic reduction in enrollment, with the effects most severe for low-income students. In thinking about alternatives for policy, most critique focuses on the return to additional spending on the existing student aid programs; for example Carneiro and Heckman write, "The limited role short-run credit-constraints play in explaining contemporary American educational gaps is, no doubt, in part due to the successful operation of policies that were designed to eliminate such constraints. Substantial reductions in the generosity of educational benefits would undoubtedly affect participation in college" (2004, 127).

21. This argument follows Dynarski (2004) and draws on points made in the context of explaining the popularity of Social Security relative to other means-tested transfer programs by Skocpol (1991) and Wilson (1987).

REFERENCES

Bound, John, and Sarah Turner. 2002. "Going to War and Going to College: Did the G.I. Bill Increase Educational Attainment?" *Journal of Labor Economics* 20(4): 784–815.

————. Forthcoming. "Cohort Crowding: How Resources Affect Collegiate Attainment." *Journal of Public Economics.* Corrected proof at http://www.sciencedirect.com/science/article/B6V76-4M33VVH-1/2/c3824aa84b4ae19b95650f72090d11ff.

Bound, John, Michael Lovenheim, and Sarah Turner. 2006. "Understanding the Increased Time to the Baccalaureate Degree." Mimeo, University of Virginia.

Bowen, William G., Martin Kurzweil, and Eugene Tobin. 2005. *Equity and Excellence in American Higher Education.* Charlottesville: University of Virginia Press.

Carneiro, Pedro, and James Heckman. 2004. "Human Capital Policy." In *Inequality in America,* by James J. Heckman and Alan B. Krueger (77–240). Cambridge, MA: MIT Press.

Carnevale, Anthony, Richard Fry, and Sarah Turner. 2001. "Growing Inequality in Collegiate Attainment: Evidence on the Role of Family Income." Unpublished manuscript.

College Board. 2004. *Trends in Student Aid.* Washington, DC: College Board.

————. 2005. *Trends in College Pricing.* Washington, DC: College Board.

Dynarski, Susan. 2002. "Loans, Liquidity, and Schooling Decisions." Working paper, Kennedy School of Government, Harvard University.

————. 2003. "Does Aid Matter? Measuring the Effect of Student Aid on College Attendance and Completion." *American Economic Review* 93(1): 279–88.

————. 2004. "The New Merit Aid." In *College Choices: The Economics of Which College, When College, and How to Pay for It,* edited by Caroline M. Hoxby (63–100). Chicago: University of Chicago Press.

————. 2005. "Building the Stock of College-Educated Labor." Working Paper 11,604. Cambridge, MA: National Bureau of Economic Research.

Dynarski, Susan, and Judith Scott-Clayton. 2006. "The Cost of Complexity in Federal Student Aid: Lessons from Optimal Tax Theory and Behavioral Economics." *National Tax Journal* 59(2): 319–56.

Ellwood, David T., and Thomas J. Kane. 2000. "Who Is Getting a College Education? Family Background and the Growing Gaps in Enrollment." In *Securing the Future: Investing in Children from Birth to College,* edited by Sheldon Danziger and Jane Waldfogel (283–324). New York: Russell Sage Foundation.

Fitzpatrick, Maria, and Sarah Turner. Forthcoming. "Blurring the Boundary: Changes in the Transition from College Participation to Adulthood." In *The Price of Independence: Economics of the Transition to Adulthood,* edited by Sheldon Danziger and Cecilia Rouse. New York: Russell Sage Foundation.

Gladieux, Lawrence E. 1995. "Federal Student Aid Policy: A History and an Assessment." Paper presented at National Conference on the Best Ways for the Federal Government to Help Students and Families Finance Higher Education, Washington, D.C., October.

Hansen, W. Lee. 1983. "The Impact of Student Financial Aid on Access." In *Crisis in Higher Education,* edited by Joseph Froomkin (84–96). New York: Academy of Political Science.

Hansen, W. Lee, and Burton A. Weisbrod. 1969. "The Distribution of Costs and Direct Benefits of Public Higher Education: The Case of California." *Journal of Human Resources* 4(2): 176–91.

Haveman, Robert, and Kathryn Wilson. 2005. "Economic Inequality in College Access, Matriculation, and Graduation." Mimeo.

Hill, Catharine B., and Gordon C. Winston. 2005. "Access to the Most Selective Private Colleges by High Ability, Low-Income Students: Are They Out

There?" Discussion Paper 69. Williamstown, MA: Williams Project on the Economics of Higher Education, Williams College.

Kane, Thomas J. 1994. "College Entry by Blacks since 1970: The Role of College Costs, Family Background, and the Returns to Education." *Journal of Political Economy* 102(5): 878–911.

———. 1999. *The Price of Admission: Rethinking How Americans Pay for College.* Washington, DC: Brookings Institution Press.

Kane, Thomas J., and Peter Orszag. 2003. "Higher Education Spending: The Role of Medicaid and the Business Cycle." Policy Brief 124. Washington, DC: The Brookings Institution.

Long, Bridget. 2004. "The Impact of Federal Tax Credits on Higher Education Expenses." In *College Choices: The Economics of Which College, When College, and How to Pay for It*, edited by Caroline M. Hoxby (101–65). Chicago: University of Chicago Press.

Rizzo, Michael. 2006. "State Preferences for Higher Education Spending." In *What's Happening to Public Higher Education*, edited by Ronald G. Ehrenberg (3–35). Westport, CT: Praeger.

Seftor, Neil, and Sarah Turner. 2002. "Federal Student Aid and Adult College Enrollment." *Journal of Human Resources* 37(2): 336–52.

Simmons, Sarah, and Sarah Turner. 2003. "Taking Classes and Taking Care of the Kids: Do Childcare Benefits Increase College Attainment?" Mimeo, University of Virginia.

Skocpol, Theda. 1991. "Targeting within Universalism: Politically Viable Policies to Combat Poverty in the United States." In *The Urban Underclass*, edited by Christopher Jencks and Paul Peterson (411–36). Washington, DC: Brookings Institution Press.

Snyder, Thomas D., and Charlene M. Hoffman. 2001. *Digest of Education Statistics, 2000.* Washington, DC: National Center for Education Statistics, U.S. Department of Education.

Starch, Patricia. 2005. "The Politics of Policy Design: Federal Funding for Higher Education." Mimeo, State University of New York.

Turner, Sarah. 2004. "Going to College and Finishing College: Explaining Different Educational Outcomes." In *College Choices: The Economics of Which College, When College, and How to Pay for It*, edited by Caroline M. Hoxby (13–56). Chicago: University of Chicago Press.

———. 2005. "Higher Tuition, Higher Aid, and the Quest to Improve Opportunities for Low-Income Students in Selective, Public Higher Education." Mimeo, University of Virginia.

U.S. Department of Education. Office of Postsecondary Education, Office of Policy, Planning, and Innovation. 2002. "Federal Student Loan Programs Data Book: Fiscal Years 1997–2000." Washington, DC: U.S. Department of Education.

Wilson, William Julius. 1987. *The Truly Disadvantaged.* Chicago: University of Chicago Press.

PART III

TRAINING FOR ADULTS

5

EMPLOYMENT AND TRAINING POLICIES: NEW DIRECTIONS FOR LESS-SKILLED ADULTS

Paul Osterman

A mericans of virtually all economic circumstances confront a more complicated and challenging job market now than at any time in the postwar period. Frontline workers face job insecurity from outsourcing and reengineering, and large numbers of working poor have not shared in America's prosperity. Even CEOs must cope with a world in which their job security is suddenly at risk. While the problems of CEOs may not be an appropriate topic for public policy, the more widespread challenges certainly are. This chapter thinks through what role the public employment and training (E&T) system can play in helping people succeed in today's job market.

More than a decade after President Clinton campaigned on the theme of "making work pay," a remarkably large number of adult Americans work yet are poor or near-poor. In 2004 the poverty rate among people who work was 6.1 percent, an increase from 5.8 percent in 2003. In fact, 2,896,000 adults worked full-time year-round in 2004 yet lived in poverty. More strikingly, 5,062,000 families had a member who worked full-time year-round yet had household incomes below 150 percent of the federal poverty level, and 9,230,000 families with full-time, full-year workers had incomes below 200 percent of the poverty level.[1]

The characteristics of jobs confirm this picture. In 2001, 21.6 percent of all hours worked in the economy were in jobs that paid less than two-thirds of the median wage (i.e., less than $8.67 an hour). If the cut-off is set at less than $8 an hour, then 16.3 percent of all hours were in these jobs (Bernstein and Gittleman 2003).[2]

The economic straits of the working poor might seem more tolerable if today's difficulties were simply a prelude to tomorrow's upward mobility. That, however, seems untrue. Harry Holzer followed the economic mobility of low earners for six years beginning in 1993–95. During this period of remarkable economic strength, only 27 percent of his sample consistently raised their incomes enough to rise above the poverty level for a family of four (Holzer 2004).

Additional confirmation that economic mobility is difficult comes from comparing young men that entered the job market between 1980 and 1991 with men that entered between 1970 and 1979. Among the earlier entrants, 60 percent of all men and 71 percent of college-educated men attained earnings of at least twice the poverty level by the time they turned 30. Among the later entrants, the rates were 42 percent and 56 percent (Duncan, Boisjoly, and Smeeding 1996).

Studies of family income mobility show a similar pattern. Bradbury and Katz (2002) find that among families that started in the bottom quintile of income in 1969, 49 percent remained in that quintile 10 years later. When the starting point was 1988, however, the proportion stuck in the bottom quintile in 1998 increased to 53 percent.

In short, the numbers of working poor are high and their prospects for upward mobility are low and falling. But what is striking about the current period is not just low-wage workers find themselves in difficulty. The increased volatility of the job market has taken its toll on more experienced and skilled employees as restructuring has increased the rate of layoffs. For two decades, the Current Population Survey has tracked the experience of these dislocated workers. According to Henry Farber (2005), while the business cycle is the dominant driver of dislocation nonetheless, after taking the cycle into account, the rate is trending upward; this trend is affecting the better-educated as well as those at the bottom of the skills distribution. In the most recent Current Population Survey, covering 2001–03, the dislocation rate was 12 percent for workers with a high school education and 9 percent for college-educated workers. In addition, the fraction of the unemployed who were long-term jobless—that is, unemployed for six months or longer—had risen to roughly 20 percent and held at this level for an unprecedented period (Allegretto, Bernstein, and Shapiro 2005).

The consequences of this dislocation are severe. Among high-school-educated workers, only 54 percent reported themselves reemployed; for college-educated workers, the rate was only 71 percent. Reemployment itself does not make employees whole. Thirteen percent of those losing full-time jobs were reemployed in part-time work, and among those who did manage to find new full-time work, the average wage loss was 11 percent for high-school-educated workers and 13 percent for those with college educations (Farber 2005). According to the evidence, these earning losses persist (Kletzer 1998).

With these significant employment patterns, the case for a more effective E&T and job-matching system has now gone beyond the traditional concerns with poverty and welfare. The labor market is increasingly difficult to navigate for people higher up in the job queue; hence, it is reasonable to believe that the substantive and political case for effective policy is becoming more compelling.

THE ROLE OF THE EMPLOYMENT AND TRAINING SYSTEM

The classic function of the E&T system is to improve the skill levels of people in difficulty, and there is good evidence that this function is important. A significant segment of the American labor force lacks the skills necessary to compete successfully for good jobs. This statement is about the nature of both labor supply and demand. Turning first to the workforce, 42 percent of the total labor force age 25 and older has only a high school degree or less education (Aspen Institute 2003). In fact, the problem may be getting worse: the rate of high school completion fell throughout the 1990s (Barton 2005).

More direct measurement of skill points in the same direction. A 2003 survey of adults in several OECD nations directly measured literacy skills. The survey in the United States was a random representative sample of 3,400 adults and directly tested respondents on three types of literacy: prose skills, document interpretation skills, and numeracy. Five levels were identified, with level one signifying very low level skills.[3] In the United States, 20 percent of adults scored at level one in prose and document interpretation skills, and 26 percent scored at level one in numeracy skills. By comparison, the shares at these levels in Canada were 14 percent, 15 percent, and 19 percent; in Norway, the shares were 7 percent, 8 percent, and 10 percent (OECD and Minister of Industry Canada 2005).

When these results are combined with the high school dropout data, it seems apparent that a substantial segment of the workforce has a significant skill problem. At the same time, the economy is demanding more, not less, skill in order to do well. Many commentators have pointed to new skill and technological demands of jobs, and workers in many settings face new requirements. The spread of new work systems involving teams, job rotation, and quality programs have contributed to this trend (Osterman 1994, 1995, 2000). In industries as disparate as telecommunications, banking, and auto parts manufacturing, technology is making it harder for the less skilled to get by (Appelbaum, Bernhardt, and Murnane 2003). Overall, occupational projections suggest that the skill requirements of jobs are trending up.

The Employment Exchange

If improving skills is a core function of the E&T system, then a second standard objective is job matching. In a volatile job market, the role of intermediaries in helping match employees and employers becomes more important. Indeed, the increased volatility in the labor market had been met by a rise in private-sector intermediaries. This rise is partly the result of technology, such as the rise of Internet-based job searching, but also partly the result of new institutions. Notable among these are temporary help firms, which have grown explosively (although they still account to a relatively small fraction of total employment).

These firms have a clientele disproportionately weighted to the working poor. For example, 15 percent of those employed by temporary help firms in 1999 were high school dropouts, and 21 percent were college graduates. The comparable figures for people in traditional employment arrangements were 11 percent and 31 percent. Blacks and Hispanics accounted for 34 percent of temporary workers, compared with 21 percent of people in traditional occupations (DiNatale 2001).

Although for-profit intermediaries, such as temporary help agencies, can improve labor market efficiency, it is not their responsibility to be concerned with distributional issues or improving the economic circumstances of the working poor. The evidence on their impact along these dimensions is mixed. Andersson, Holzer, and Lane (2005) use longitudinal data to track employment outcomes for people who began the 1990s with very low wages. The researchers find that among people who changed jobs during this period, initial experience in a temporary help agency was correlated with 6 to 10 percent higher subsequent earnings.[4] But another recent examination of the role of temporary agencies in welfare-to-work job placement finds that people randomly assigned to temporary help agencies for placement do no better, and in some cases worse, in the long run than others who navigate the labor market on their own (Autor and Houseman 2005).

Additional evidence on this point comes from a study of intermediaries in the Silicon Valley and Milwaukee. In a random sample of interviews with employees in the two regions, workers reported that, beyond placements, they received relatively little assistance from for-profit temporary help firms compared with nonprofit intermediaries. For example, 60 percent of people who worked with nonprofit agencies received assistance in job-hunting skills, compared with 30 percent who worked with temporary help firms. Less than 7 percent of those who worked with for-profit agencies received training in computer skills, compared with 33 percent who worked with nonprofit placement agencies. Finally, less than 3 percent received mentoring from for-profit temporary agencies, compared with 18–34 percent receiving mentoring from nonprofits (Pastor, Leete, and Dresser 2003).

It seems fair to conclude that comprehensive, well-designed E&T system entails an important role for a public labor market intermediary. While private intermediaries have grown rapidly in a more volatile job market, they either do not help people at the bottom of the labor market or they play a positive role but the gains are relatively modest. Therefore, the public sector has a crucial gap to fill.

Beyond a Pure Training Strategy

Not surprisingly, the E&T system has traditionally focused on improving the circumstances of people in difficulty by augmenting their skill levels and helping them find jobs. But it has other potential roles. Most important, the E&T system might move beyond a pure training strategy by working with firms to modify their human resource (HR) policies to redound to the benefit of low-wage employees. An additional objective might be to help firms become more competitive in order to lessen the problems of dislocation. Working on the demand side is important because if all the E&T system does is enable some people to move into better jobs, then what will ensue is a game of musical chairs in which others move into the bad jobs left vacant. The quantity of substandard employment will remain unchanged.

The case for improving the human resource practices of low-wage firms is strengthened by the fact that in many industries employing low-wage adults—sectors such as hotels, restaurants, and nursing homes—conditions have stagnated or deteriorated. But technology and skill are not the culprit (Appelbaum et al. 2003). This condition implies a negative feedback loop in which the human resource practices of firms reinforce the difficulties of low-wage workers.

One element of this negative feedback loop is the low level of training to the least-skilled employees. It is true that American firms devote considerable resources to training their workforce. The American

Society for Training and Development (2005) estimates that firms spent 2.5 percent of their payroll on "learning expenditures" in 2004, an increase from 1.9 percent in 1999. In addition, private-sector training leads to economic gains for employees who receive it (Lynch 1992). The problem, however, is that training in private firms is biased away from low-skilled frontline workers. People with higher levels of education receive disproportionately more training.[5] According to the National Household Education Survey of 1995, 22 percent of workers in the bottom quintile of earnings reported receiving employer-supported education, compared with 40 percent in the top quintile (Ahlstrand et al. 2001). International comparisons make the same point. The International Adult Literacy Survey compared the relative participation in occupational training of those with less than a high school degree with those with a university degree and found the ratio lower in the United States than in Canada, Germany, Sweden, and the United Kingdom (Kletzer and Koch 2004).

The failure to train lower-wage workers makes it harder for them to advance in the firm. Other HR practices contribute to these difficulties. These include the growing tendency to outsource lower-skilled work and hence to remove the jobs from the firms' internal labor market or job ladders as well as a more general deterioration of internal mobility paths.

The more innovative E&T programs work with firms to make their HR practices more favorable to low-wage workers. By operating on the demand and the supply sides, these efforts could widen, not simply redistribute, opportunities. Put differently, the E&T system can make bad jobs good and improve access to jobs.

What the Employment and Training System Cannot Do

While the E&T system has an important role to play in addressing the challenges set forth above, the system can only address a portion of the underlying causes.

One clear contributor to the challenges facing low-wage adults is the long-term decline in the real value of the minimum wage. The real value of the minimum wage in 2004 was 26 percent lower than it was in 1979, and all the gains from the 1996 increase have been erased by inflation. In fact, as a fraction of the average wage for private nonsupervisory workers, the minimum wage today is at its lowest level (32 percent) since 1949. If the minimum wage were increased to $7.25, 72 percent of the beneficiaries would be adults.[6] More formal economic analysis also suggests that the falling value of the minimum wage has been an important contributor to growing wage inequality (Card and DiNardo 2002).

A second force driving the low-wage labor market is the recent surge in immigration. The basic facts are well-known: whereas in 1970 just under 5 percent of the U.S. population was foreign-born, by 2000 the figure stood at 11.1 percent. Immigration will account for 32 percent of the projected growth of the U.S. adult labor force by 2020 (Aspen Institute 2003). This demographic development has had a substantial impact on the bottom of the labor market. The wage disadvantage of immigrants relative to natives increased for men by a factor of four between 1960 and 2000, and while immigrants (men and women) accounted for about 10 percent of the workforce, they accounted for about 25 percent of workers in the bottom 20 percent of the wage distribution (Borjas 2003). At least some of this disparity is due to a skills gap: 32 percent of the immigrant population in 2000 were high school dropouts, compared with 11 percent of natives (Borjas 2003). While immigration trends are determined by policy considerations outside the purview of E&T policy, to the extent that skill gaps lead to immigrants facing labor market difficulties, E&T policy is an important part of the solution.

A third factor outside the purview of E&T policy that has altered the low-wage labor market is the decline of unions. Substantial research shows that unions equalize the wage distribution and, in particular, push up wages at the bottom of the distribution. Yet only 8.6 percent of the private-sector workforce was represented by unions in 2004; in two industry sectors that employ large numbers of low-wage workers (leisure/hospitality and wholesale/retail trade), the figures were 3.6 percent and 5.9 percent, respectively (U.S. Bureau of Labor Statistics 2006).

In short, the minimum wage, immigration policy, and unionization rates are all important determinants of economic outcomes in the low-wage labor market. Nonetheless, the E&T system's array of tools—training, intermediary services, and working with firms—have a significant role to play.

THE CONTOURS OF THE SYSTEM

A useful first step is to ask about the E&T resources currently devoted to problems facing relatively unskilled or dislocated adults. There are six main buckets of programs. The first are those funded by the Workforce Investment Act (WIA) and aimed at poor adults. The second are programs funded by WIA and the Trade Adjustment Assistance (TAA) Act aimed at dislocated workers. Third are programs funded by the Department of Education (and states) that fall under the broad rubric of adult basic education (ABE). Forth, community colleges are a major source of occupational training for adults. Fifth, some states have funded training programs aimed at incumbent workers. Finally, the Employment Service or one-stop system serves as a labor market intermediary for people in difficulty.

Turning first to WIA, the Government Accountability Office (GAO) estimates that local workforce investment boards (WIBs) trained 416,000 adults in program year 2003 (GAO 2005b). Of these, about 235,000 were poor adults and the remainder were dislocated workers. Clearly these numbers are far below any estimate of the universe of need. A crude estimate of the expenditures per trainee (arrived at by summing the GAO estimate of $929,000 as the funds expended on training and dividing by the number of trainees) is $2,233. This sum cannot buy extended or intensive training, although the resources are modestly increased when TAA training is added in.[7]

WIA appropriations are larger than the figure cited above for training; according to the GAO, WIBs spent only 40 percent of their available funds on training (GAO 2005b). In fact, the shift from the Job Training Partnership Act (JTPA) to the Workforce Investment Act reduced the relative proportion of resources spent on training. Under WIA, 32.3 percent of adults and 39.6 percent of dislocated workers exiting in program year 2000 received training, while the comparable figures for JTPA carry-over participants were 73.6 and 65.8 percent (King 2004). Between the end of JTPA and the 2002 WIA program year, the number of adults who received training fell by 17 percent (Frank and Minoff 2005). More striking, among adults who received training, the share who were low-income fell from 96 percent under JTPA to 82.4 percent in 2000 and 68.4 percent in 2003. As might be expected, the average length of time adults spend in WIA has fallen relative to JTPA, a fact that also implies less intensive services (D'Amico and Salzman 2004).

These data make it clear that the federal commitment to training the working poor and dislocated via programs delivered through the Department of Labor is limited and shrinking. By any reasonable measure, these efforts fall far short of the universe of need. But to stop here would miss a crucial point: a large number of the working poor and dislocated adults receive public training via other channels.

One source of skills building for adults is the adult basic education system, now funded at the federal level by the Adult Education and Family Literacy Act and by the states through their own appropriations. In 2000, the federal appropriation of $442 million accounted for about a quarter of total spending (U.S. Department of Education 2004). The system provides English for Speakers of Other Languages (ESOL) training, pre-general-equivalency-diploma (GED) (or ABE) training, and preparation for the GED. In 2000, about 2.6 million adults received some services, of which about half were in ESOL programs (U.S. Department of Education 2004).

The services provided by the ABE system vary widely and are delivered in an array of settings: churches, community colleges, libraries, prisons, schools, and social service agencies. The intensity of service is very low: only 21 percent of participants receive more than 150 hours of instruction (Comings, Sum, and Uvin 2000). Indeed, 50 percent of those in adult education classes drop out before completing 35 hours or 10 weeks (Jobs for the Future 2004).

The real center of gravity for the adult training system is America's roughly 1,200 community colleges. The numbers are quite striking: among all college students in 2000, 29.6 percent were in community college occupational training programs, and another 28.7 percent were in other community college tracks. Of the students enrolled in occupational training, 64 percent were in associate's degree programs and the remainder were in certificate programs (Bailey et al. 2004).

The profile of the students suggests that community colleges touch the working poor to a nontrivial extent. Fifty-five percent of students in occupational programs are age 24 or older, 39 percent are minority, and 66 percent attend part-time (Bailey et al. 2004). Eighty percent of community college students work full- or part-time while in school (Brock and LeBlanc 2005). Among first-time community college students between the ages of 25 and 64 in 1995–96, 71 percent were in the lower two income quintiles, compared with 50 percent of younger students (Prince and Jenkins 2005).

The final significant source of support for training adults comes from a disparate set of state programs. These programs are typically aimed at helping firms compete more effectively, and as such are driven by job retention or attraction. Although not directed at dislocated workers per se, these programs are in an important sense an "antidislocation" set of programs, and they can be construed as improving the skills of employees so they can fare better when dislocation occurs. Most of these programs are run through companies, sometimes with the assistance of an intermediary organization or a labor union. The programs typically are aimed at improving the skills of incumbent workers, although some also assist in training new hires. Some programs are funded with general state tax revenue but the most common source of funds is employer taxes, often a small fraction of the unemployment insurance tax and sometimes another revenue stream. In 2002, 23 states used employer taxes to fund training programs and total expenditures were $278 million (GAO 2004b). In some states, including California, the programs were quite large, while in others they were small and mainly symbolic.

In summary, setting community colleges aside, the total training resources devoted to adults in difficulty due to low skills or to dislocation are small relative to the universe of need and have been shrinking.

Adding community colleges to the mix leads to a somewhat more optimistic view. As we will see, however, community colleges have multiple missions that limit their effectiveness in this particular arena.

The Employment Exchange

The Employment Service (ES) is a federal–state program funded at the federal level by Wagner-Peyser monies. These funds have declined sharply; between 1984 and 2003, they fell in real terms by 40 percent (Smole 2004). With the advent of WIA, however, labor exchange services are now provided in one-stops; WIA funds may underwrite these services, and WIA staff may join with ES staff to provide the services. A nontrivial fraction of WIA funding is directed to the one-stops (of which there are about 3,400), a fact rationalized by many states' "jobs-first" philosophy (i.e., an emphasis on placement and not on training). In fact, less than half of WIA funding goes for training. In addition, a few states have used their own funds to partially compensate for the decline in Wagner-Peyser funding (Ridley and Tracy 2004). The bulk of recipients of labor exchange services receive only a job referral and many of the rest get simple job search assistance. Hence the cost per recipient is very low.

In 1999–2000, about 17 million people came to ES offices for service. Of these, a bit over a third were unemployment insurance recipients who were required to register at ES offices. This still leaves a substantial number of job seekers who turn to the ES for help (O'Leary 2004).

EFFECTIVENESS OF THE SYSTEM

As is apparent, there are multiple elements of the broadly construed E&T system. Our knowledge about their effectiveness is uneven; some components have been extensively evaluated while others have little information available. This section begins by reviewing what we know about the effectiveness of training programs and next turns to the employment exchange and to community colleges. The section concludes with an assessment of the system as a whole based on the evaluation evidence. Subsequent sections of the chapter ask some broader questions about the effectiveness of the E&T system.

The Effectiveness of Training

A challenge faced by the E&T system is that it is widely perceived as ineffective. Some observers believe that it is not possible to improve the economic situation of working adults through job training programs. This perspective, however, is incorrect. Careful evaluations have demonstrated that E&T programs can pay off for adults.

One important study, the national JTPA evaluation, showed a statistically significant gain for adult women and men enrolled in JTPA (Bloom et al. 1997).[8] Men earned about $1,400 more over their two post-program years than did the control group, and females earned about $1,700 more. These results were statistically significant and the gains showed no evidence of decay. Nonetheless, the gains are small. Two facts are important in assessing these magnitudes. First, these gains were relative to the control group; a large fraction of the controls received training services from other sources. Second, the JTPA intervention itself was fairly small, with an incremental investment over the control group of just over $1,000 per man and $1,300 per woman. Given this modest investment, a modest return is not surprising.

A sense of the potential gains from a longer-term investment in people can be gained from an evaluation of Project QUEST in San Antonio, Texas. This program, which has won national awards, trains working adults for 18 months and cooperates closely with employers to identify job needs and design the training curriculum. Although QUEST has not been evaluated using random assignment, two independent pre/post evaluations found very substantial wage gains. One study reported an income increase of between $5,000 and $7,500 a year for QUEST participants (Osterman and Lautsch 1996); this increase was confirmed by another independent evaluation (Grote and Roder 2005).

Another example is a Portland, Oregon, program aimed at low-wage adults and evaluated as part of the National Evaluation of Welfare to Work Strategies. The program randomly assigned over 5,000 people into treatment and control groups. The program placed relatively more emphasis on training and education services than the typical welfare-to-work intervention, and it involved a high level of cooperation between the welfare, JTPA, and community college systems. Based on a two-year follow-up evaluation, the program raised employment rates by 11 percentage points versus the control group and increased earnings by 35 percent (Scrivener et al. 1998).[9]

The foregoing discussion of impact described what we know about programs typically aimed at the poor or working poor. Our knowledge of the effectiveness of training for dislocated workers is thinner. What data we do have, however, suggest that short-term training leads to small or nonexistent gains. On the other hand, more substantial long-term training seems to improve the earnings of dislocated workers to an important degree. In this sense, the story is optimistic.

The weak results regarding short-term training come from evaluations conducted in the 1980s in diverse locations (Texas, Michigan,

New York, and New Jersey). The benefits of short-term classroom training were very modest (Leigh 2000). By contrast, a TAA evaluation in the late 1980s that studied long-term training found gains of between $1,400 and $3,100 a year, while an early 1990s study of vouchers (valued at $4,000) found training gains in the $2,000–$3,600 range. One reviewer of this evidence concludes that "there is room for cautious optimism" about training (Leigh 2000, 254).

Support for this optimism is found in a study using Washington State data to track outcomes for dislocated workers who enrolled in community college training programs (Jacobson, LaLonde, and Sullivan 2005). About 11 percent of dislocated workers over age 35 enrolled, and they were compared (after statistical controls) with dislocated workers of the same age who did not take these courses. The earnings gains for dislocated workers over age 35 was between 8 and 10 percent for a full year of coursework (women were at the higher end). In fact, the typical dislocated worker attended about eight months of school. Further, if people enrolled in more technical occupational courses, then the gain was a third higher for men and double for women. The authors control for selection issues via both the standard statistical controls and fixed effect models, but they remain concerned that the people who enrolled in community colleges differ in some ways from those who did not. Nonetheless, the authors also believe that these results point to real gains for dislocated workers from community college training.

Effectiveness of the Employment Exchange

The demand for employment exchange services is substantial, but the response of the system is very uneven. About 19 percent of the unemployed turn to the ES today, compared with about 30 percent three decades ago (Eberts and Holzer 2004). Part of this decline is no doubt due to the emergence of alternative intermediaries. But the performance of the ES itself is an issue. Only about 10 percent of people who seek jobs through the ES are placed into jobs via an ES referral (O'Leary 2004). More to the point, very few employers use the ES to fill openings. In one study, only 2.6 percent of employers reported that they had used the ES to fill their last job opening (Eberts and Holzer 2004). A similar pattern emerged from a survey tracking the use of labor market intermediaries in the Silicon Valley and Milwaukee. Among all jobs obtained in the three years before the survey (conducted in 2001 and 2002), only 2.7 to 4.4 percent were obtained via a nonprofit or government agency. Since this category is broader than just the ES/one-stop system, its share is even smaller than the figures indicate (Pastor et al. 2003).

Those jobs that do get filled by the ES tend to be low-level. Fully one-third of these jobs are temporary, lasting less than 150 days (Jacobson 1995). What success the ES has is in a very limited range of the labor market. In one dataset from the mid-1980s, the average male job placement was in a job paying $10,700 a year, and the average female job placement was in a job paying $8,700. As one researcher notes, "What is clear is that certain types of employers rely heavily on the ES. Those firms generally employ workers of few specialized skills, are willing to accept high turnover, and therefore pay low wages" (Jacobson 1995, 6).

Because of the low cost per client, the ES passes a cost-benefit test. As it stands now, however, the ES (and by extension the one-stop system) is very far from being an effective labor exchange capable of helping people surmount the challenges of today's job market.

Effectiveness of Community Colleges

Community colleges are a key source of training for working adults. The policy community is interested in making these institutions even more central to a national training effort than they are now. This is apparent both in the efforts of several national foundations and in the fact that the Bush administration has worked to transfer training resources to the community college system.

Given this considerable interest, what do we know about the returns to a community college education? The patterns are surprisingly mixed. For students who enroll for a substantial amount of credits (e.g., a full year's worth) or who receive an associate's degree, the payoff is clear. Research for both the 1980s and the late 1990s find (after controls for test scores, family background, and a range of demographic characteristics) that a full-time-equivalent (FTE) year of study returns about a 6 percent annual income gain and that an associate's degree (AA) returns about a 14 percent gain—that is, what one would expect from two years of study (Kane and Rouse 1999; Marcotte et al. 2005).

There are, however, nontrivial flies in this ointment. A strikingly low fraction of students who enter community colleges attain even an FTE year of credits, much less an associate's degree. Despite the fact that a majority of 1992 high school graduates who entered postsecondary education went to community colleges, 28 percent had earned a bachelor's degree by 2000, only 5 percent had an AA degree, and only 6 percent had a community college certificate (Marcotte et al. 2005). Among students who entered community colleges and who did not receive an associate's degree, the average amount of schooling received was 0.16 FTE year. Completing only a semester of community college courses produces no economic benefit for men but some gain for women; thus, it is reasonable to believe that the 0.16 FTE year leads to no gain for anyone.

The bottom line on community colleges is that students benefit substantially when they attend for a year or longer, regardless of whether they receive a degree. This is as true, and perhaps more so, for occupational programs as for academic ones. But most people who attend community colleges do not manage to stay in long enough to reap these benefits; for these people the rate of return appears close to zero.

Effectiveness of the System as a Whole

Examples have demonstrated that effective programs can be designed for working adults. The purely pessimistic view of the possibilities of training efforts seems misguided. But it is one thing to argue that effective programs can be designed and delivered; it is quite another to claim that these models can be successfully implemented nationwide with consistent quality. This claim produces more reason to worry. Consider, for example, that replications of Centers for Employment Training, another effective program that did very well in a random assignment evaluation at its original site, have not gone smoothly. The Portland program is the most successful of those that were part of the national evaluation; other efforts have not gone as well. This result suggests that scale is difficult, even with designs that work well.

With this in mind, it is not surprising that if we ask what we know about the effectiveness of the E&T system as a whole, the picture becomes much murkier. Consider the following comments drawn from several GAO reports on the E&T system:

On state programs: "None have used sufficiently rigorous research designs to allow them to make conclusive statements about the impact of their programs" (GAO 2004b, 4).

On one-stops: "While [The Department of] Labor currently tracks outcome data—such as job placement, job seeker satisfaction, and employer satisfaction . . . little is known about the impact of various one-stop delivery approaches on these and other outcomes" (GAO 2003b, 28).

On TAA: "No information is currently available to accurately measure program effectiveness" (GAO 2004a, 45).

On WIA adult training: "Substantial Funds Are Used for Training, but Little Is Known Nationally about Training Outcomes" (title, GAO 2005b); and "Labor's Office of the Inspector General has said that there little assurance that the states' performance data for WIA programs are either accurate or complete" (GAO 2005b, 4).

STRUCTURAL CHALLENGES FACING THE E&T SYSTEM

The foregoing discussion assesses the E&T system using fairly traditional criteria: the impact upon individuals. It is, however, also worthwhile to step back and ask about the overall structure of the system. By and large, the system is not well connected to the core concerns of the economy, nor are its many parts well articulated.

Connection to the Economy

The federally funded components of the E&T system do not effectively connect to firms. Most employers view the system as an extension of the welfare system and do not turn to it for assistance with their human resource needs.

The disconnect between the E&T system and the private economy is longstanding. A study in the 1980s found that people who applied for jobs and had subsidies from federal programs did worse than comparable people without the subsidies because employers did not wish to work with the programs (Burtless 1985). This pattern does not seem to have changed. A recent survey of manufactures found that only 4.6 percent of responding firms reported using WIB or one-stops to meet their human resource needs, whereas 30.8 percent used community colleges, 46 percent used industry associations, and 40 percent used temp firms (Partnership for Employer-Employee Responsive Systems 2003). In a survey of intermediary use in Silicon Valley and Milwaukee, among people who found jobs via intermediaries, the use of nonprofits and government agencies was a distant third behind temporary help firms and community colleges (Leete et al. 2004). Finally, in a recent series of focus groups of employers in three industry clusters (fabricated metals and industrial machinery, transportation/distribution/logistics, and health care), the participants were generally positive about the role of community colleges in meeting their workforce needs but perceived community-based E&T organizations as unstable, slow, and lacking professionalism. Participants also characterized state and federal programs as non-service organizations with little screening or training capacity. The researchers summarized their findings as a "complete disconnect between employer perceptions of preferences for workforce programs and the programs themselves" (Laufer and Winship 2004, 216).

This disconnect between the E&T system and firms is not only substantive but also seems to occur at the level of governance. Although the Workforce Boards are intended to provide a key role for firms (as were the Private Industry Councils that preceded them), this has not generally happened. A recent assessment of implementation of WIA found that "business role was strong in only a few of the sample states" (Barnow and King 2003, 11); at the local level, "employer involvement in the governance of WIA and related workforce programs was generally limited to moderate" (14).

On the more positive side, a recent survey of firms conducted by the GAO found widespread employer awareness of one-stops; among firms aware of one-stops, three-quarters expressed satisfaction with their services (GAO 2005a). But neither this survey nor Department of Labor data provide information on the extent of actual use (for example, the number and quality of jobs that are filled via the one-stops).

Absence of Effective Ladders

A standard charge against the E&T system is that it consists of many programs that do not work well together. For example, the GAO identified 44 programs that provided some training in 2001 (GAO 2003a). This complaint, however, is unfair. Although there are a large number of individual programs, 73 percent of total federal spending on employment and training is accounted for by four programs: vocational rehabilitation, TANF, Job Corps, and WIA (GAO 2003a). For purposes of this chapter, only WIA is relevant, hence the system does not appear scattershot in terms of funding streams.

Where the system does fail, however, is that the main building blocks are not well articulated on the ground, in states and in communities. If the system worked well, it would function as a ladder that adults could use to move from basic education to credentialed education or job training and then into good jobs. The rungs of the ladder—the ABE system, the community college system, and the job training system—would work together to support people and smooth hand-offs. But this ladder does not typically exist.

Starting at the bottom of the ladder, the ABE system has historically been distinct from the employment and training system. At the federal level, a major effort at integration was the incorporation of the Adult Education and Family Literacy Act as Title II of WIA. This led to improvements in the performance standards of the ABE system and in the overall quality of data collection. But there is still considerable national variation in the links between the systems; in many states, the ABE system is managed by the state Department of Education and not by the agency that manages the E&T system. The Workforce Alliance, an organization representing community-based organizations that engage in training, recently observed that "many . . . community-based organizations cite concerns about local workforce development systems in which basic education and occupational skills training services operate independently of each other" (2003, 40).

The evidence suggests this finding is true. A sense of the disconnect between the systems, and the failure to build effective ladders, can be gained from careful study of the Massachusetts system. In 1999, the one-stop system made only 314 referrals to the ABE system statewide, and only 557 ABE participants reported that after completing their program, they were referred to the E&T system (Comings et al. 2000).

Related to this problem, community colleges typically do a poor job of linking remedial classes (such as English as a second language or adult basic education) to for-credit academic subjects. In the words of one recent assessment, "while many community colleges possess extensive basic education and ESOL programs, these are often disconnected from the rest of the institution and staffed by people who are uninvolved in the colleges' central activities" (Jobs for the Future 2004, 4). Because of this difficulty, the institutions do not reach their potential as sources of assistance for the working poor. The same report goes on to note that for low-skilled adults, community colleges "do not connect educational milestones to meaningful credentials, articulated career ladders, and economic payoffs" (Jobs for the Future 2004, 9).

These national patterns were replicated in a recent study using Washington State administrative data combined with unemployment insurance earnings records. There was a return (using pre/post methodology) to the completion of an AA degree. But among students who entered community colleges by taking ESOL courses, only 13 percent received any college credits after five years. Of those who entered taking ABE or GED courses, only 30 percent received any college credits after five years (Prince and Jenkins 2005).

In addition, many observers believe that community colleges often are reluctant to work with the WIA system either because they feel that they do not need the funds or because they are reluctant to comply with WIA data requirements. This impression is supported by a GAO survey of workforce boards (GAO 2005b).

The pieces of the WIA system itself also frequently do not work well together. One reason that the coordination function of the local boards has not performed as hoped is that many workforce boards see themselves essentially as extensions of the Department of Labor and as such have not been imaginative or inclusive. A recent study of eight states and 16 local areas representative of the nation found that "most states have kept the major workforce development programs relatively separate, with traditional structures that mirror federal funding 'silos'"

(Barnow and King 2003, 13). The same study went on to find that, at the local level, only half the boards studied had achieved any degree of meaningful integration. In short, the federal divisions become templates for comparable divisions at the state and local levels.

INNOVATION

The foregoing discussion leads to a relatively pessimistic view of the E&T system. The worst rap on the system, that effective programs cannot be designed and delivered, is wrong. It is true, however, that we do not have the basis to be confident about the overall performance of the system as a whole. In addition, the system is isolated from firms, and its pieces do not fit well together. When these worries are added to modest and declining resources, then there is a lot about which to be concerned.

There is, however, good news. While in recent years the employment and training system has been starved for resources at the federal level, there has been substantial innovation in the field. Supported by state governments, foundations, and (to a lesser extent) firms and unions, a range of new models have been implemented. Many models are intended to directly address the weaknesses of the broader system. Given the range of innovation in the field, it would be fair to say that in the past decade there has been more programmatic creativity than at any time since the War on Poverty.

This burst of local creativity is very consistent with the history of innovation in labor policy in America. Many institutions that now are thought of as national and federal were invented locally. This is true of unemployment insurance and the Employment Service as well as much of the core regulatory structure such as the Fair Labor Standards Act.

To pin down the nature of this innovation more concretely, the next few pages describe seven prototypical program models and show what they have in common and how they vary along several dimensions.

Project QUEST

QUEST is a training program in San Antonio, Texas, aimed at working poor adults with high school degrees. The program works with firms in San Antonio to identify job openings and the skills required. The firms then make a good-faith pledge to hire program graduates. The jobs must meet living wage standards. The training is provided by local community colleges and typically lasts one and a half years. The program provides modest financial support and extensive counseling to clients. QUEST is organized and managed by a nonprofit organization that is closely linked to a community-based organization. Over 2,000 people have gone through the program. An evaluation in the mid-1990s found that annual earnings increased for participants by between $4,923 and $7,457 a year. The model has been replicated in Austin, McAllen/Brownsville, Tucson, and El Paso (Osterman and Lautsch 1996).

Wisconsin Regional Training Partnership

The Wisconsin Regional Training Partnership (WRTP) is a union–employer partnership that includes 125 firms in Wisconsin. The sectors include manufacturing, finance, construction, and hospitality. The partnership, managed by a nonprofit organization, works with firms to help them improve their production processes and organizes training programs for upgrading incumbent workers. The training takes place both in the firm and in community colleges. To date, 6,000 employees have been trained. WRTP also manages a training program for entry-level employees from inner-city areas in Milwaukee and has trained 1,500 through this program (Giloth 2004).

WIRE-net

Affiliated with the Cleveland Chamber of Commerce, via the Chamber's Jobs and Work Force Initiative, WIRE-net aims to increase the labor supply of entry-level machinists for small Cleveland firms while at the same time providing training opportunities for Cleveland's working poor. The program provides orientation, job readiness workshops, and intensive skill training. In addition, WIRE-net works with firms and assists them in assessing the skill levels of their workforce and in developing training plans. Since the program's inception, 213 trainees have entered the program and 140 have graduated; of these graduates, 115 have been placed in 80 firms (Berry 2004).

Cooperative Home Care Associates

Cooperative Home Care Associates works with low-paid home health care aides and has sought to transform the nature of their work by creating a workers' cooperative, providing more training and skill than is typical, and leveraging this to charge a higher-than-average wage/benefit package and a larger proportion of full-time work than is the norm. The model has been successful in New York City and is replicated in other locations by the Paraprofessional Health Care Institute.

AFSCME 1199c Training and Upgrading Fund

This is a joint training and career ladder fund in Philadelphia operated by the local union and funded by a 1.5 percent of gross payroll paid by hospitals, nursing homes, and other health care providers. In addition to a wide range of courses, the program works to create career ladders from certified nursing assistants (CNAs) to licensed practical nurses (LPNs). With an overall budget is over $4 million, the career ladder program has helped 103 CNAs advance to LPN positions (Fitzgerald 2006).

Massachusetts Workforce Training Fund

Funded by the State of Massachusetts using a small portion of the employer unemployment insurance tax, the Workforce Training Fund provides grants to firms for training incumbent workers. The grants can range from less than $50,000 to $1 million. Special programs include incentives to train employees in adult basic education and English as a second language.

Portland Community College

Working with Mt. Hood Community College, Portland Community College (PCC) has integrated funding streams to create modular career pathways that move from adult basic education and E&T programs to college certificates and degree programs. These pathways, which have been structured in cooperation with local employers, are multiple entry/exit to accommodate working adults. In addition to the education and training, PCC provides support services and job search assistance. The modules are linked to employer needs so students—who are recruited from one-stops, ESOL programs, TANF, and GED programs—can get immediate payoffs as they work toward a degree or certificate. In addition, the college has integrated credit faculty with the teaching of ESOL and ABE courses. The integration of programs and funding streams is facilitated by the governance structure in Oregon in which the community colleges, E&T programs, and ABE programs are all in the same agency. The 13 pathways accommodate about 250 students a year (Jobs for the Future 2004).

Hosiery Technology Center

Located at North Carolina's Catawba Community College, this center is a cooperative venture of the community college, a business association (Carolina Hosiery Association), the U.S. Manufacturing Extension Partnership, and the U.S. Department of Labor. It provides firms in the area with technical assistance on new technology, helps with marketing and development of new markets, runs seminars for firms on business practices, and is an industry testing center that certifies that producers meet quality standards. It also trains a range of workers, virtually all of whom are in jobs that do not require more than a high school education. The training content ranges from the highly skilled (e.g., machine repair) to machine operation and ESOL. Observers, as well as the firms, believe that the center can claim credit for helping the industry maintain local employment in the face of potential overseas competition (Willis, Connelly, and DeGraff 2003).

The eight new program models vary along a number of dimensions: target groups, the auspices under which the programs are managed, and the nature of the services provided. What is striking, however, is that they have also coalesced around a common set of what might be termed "best practices" elements. These elements move these innovations beyond the traditional approach of E&T programs and make these new programs distinctive and important.

The most important of these best practice elements is an understanding that employment and training efforts work best if they connect effectively to both sides of the labor market—employers and employees. In order to accomplish this, the programs work hard to become knowledgeable about the human resource needs of their target group of firms; in some cases, they also seek to understand how they can contribute to the competitive success of the firms. In short, they appeal to firms as a business proposition, not as a charity, public relations, or welfare effort.

The second feature that the new programs share is that they invest substantially in their clients. The new programs reject the quick and dirty training, short-term investments, and simple job search assistance models that characterize much of the traditional E&T system. The investments that the new programs make take a variety of forms: long training periods, more sustained involvement with firms, and higher levels of support to clients in terms of financial assistance and counseling.

There are, however, important differences across the programs. Their auspices vary and include community groups, unions, community colleges, employer organizations, and state governments. The programs also vary in how much they work with incumbent workers versus job seekers. In addition, the programs differ in whether they take the existing nature of jobs for granted or seek to transform the nature of work by creating job ladders or in other ways improving wages and other conditions of employment.

Much, but not all, of the discussion around these new models tends to focus on two broad program categories: labor market intermediaries and sectoral programs. Labor market intermediaries are organizations that consciously look both ways in the job market, attempting to work with both employers and individuals. For firms, intermediaries provide a range of services, including assistance in recruiting labor and, on occasion, assistance in designing career ladders. For individuals, the intermediaries are a source of both job training and placement. Sectoral programs perform the same functions as intermediaries, but they have the added characteristic of specializing in a particular industry. They seek to develop deep knowledge of the markets, technology, and labor market circumstances of the industry and, through this knowledge, to contribute to both the human resource and also the economic growth and development needs of the industry. Both sets of organizations seek to not only to improve access to jobs but also to help make bad jobs better and to create more good jobs. The relative weight placed on these goals varies across different programs.

While the intermediary and sectoral models have gained substantial attention, they are not the only approaches worth considering. More traditional occupational training, of the sort embodied in the community college or 1199 union models, are alternatives. Unlike older occupational training, the newer incarnations take care to work closely with employers in order to link training to real needs and to improve the prospects of clients.

Although these new models have gained substantial attention in policy circles, there are limited data on either their diffusion or effectiveness. A 2002 survey by the National Network of Sector Partners identified 243 organizations that met four criteria: they worked with both employees and employers, they targeted low-wage workers, they provided a mix of services and not simply job placement, and they invested in longer-term career advancement past the placement stage. More than half these programs were less than 10 years old, and two-thirds of them served 500 or more people a year. They were housed in a wide range of different organizations (Marino and Tarr 2004).

The evaluation evidence on these initiatives is promising but incomplete and thin. As already noted, a pre/post evaluation of Project QUEST found very large gains for participants, and a study of participant files suggested that creaming and self-selection effects could not explain away the gains (Osterman and Lautsch 1996). A qualitative evaluation reached positive conclusions about the ability of sectoral programs to achieve their goals (Pindus et al. 2004) and a pre/post evaluation of six intermediary and sectoral programs by Public/Private Ventures found gains in hourly wages for five organizations 24 months after program completion; these gains ranged from $1 to $5 an hour (Grote and Roder 2005).

MOVING AHEAD

The foregoing is a good news, bad news story. The bad news is that if one were to step back and assess the employment and training system from a distance, one would conclude that it is scattered, poorly articulated, underfunded, and of uncertain overall impact. The good news is that we have solid evidence that well-designed programs can make a difference in people's lives, that many building blocks of an effective system are in place, and that there is considerable local creativity, energy, and innovation. The question, then, is how to move ahead.

What seems most helpful is not to endorse particular program design or detailed policy proposals. Rather, this discussion will proceed in three stages. First, it will describe the most important long-run goals of the system. Second, it will lay out a strategy for accomplishing these goals. Finally, it will outline some tactical innovations that will help make this strategy more attainable.

Long-Run Goals

The most fundamental goal should be to build a ladder for the working poor and dislocated that enables them to move, as needed, from adult basic education to a higher education degree and skills training. People would enter this ladder at the appropriate point and then move up. For this vision to be a reality, each stage or rung must be effective on its own terms, and the different rungs must be well-linked or articulated. It also requires that people be given the appropriate supports—financial and otherwise—that enable them to succeed.

A second key strategic objective is attaining scale or impact. Many of the innovative programs described above are impressive but work with only small numbers of people. For example, one of the largest, long-standing, and effective efforts—Project QUEST—has served roughly 2,000 people in San Antonio over a decade. While commendable, this total is a drop in the bucket of the San Antonio labor market. The scale problem is made even more difficult because the better programs work closely with multiple constituencies, particularly employers, and this is time-consuming and very hard work.

One solution to the scale concern is replication. For example, Project QUEST has been replicated in half a dozen cities in the Southwest. A second solution is to take seriously the notion of institutional change. An effective program does not simply affect its immediate clients but also seeks to change the behavior and outcomes of other actors in the labor market. Project QUEST, for example, encouraged the San Antonio community college system to make itself more accessible to large numbers of working people. Cooperative Home Care Associates has influenced public policy in a variety of ways to improve the conditions of home health care workers who are not members of the cooperative.

A third strategic objective is that the E&T system should work on the demand and supply sides of the labor market. This involves two distinct issues. First, in contrast to the system's history of training people and then throwing them over the wall in the hopes that they will land a job, programs need to work better with firms to identify openings and the skills required. But working with employers is more than this simple prescription. It also means seeking to improve the nature of jobs and the career opportunities that people confront. It is unrealistic to believe that a pure training strategy is adequate. Without adequate numbers of good jobs, the trainees who benefit will to some extent simply displace other people who would have obtained the jobs. This displacement effect is typically ignored in the evaluation literature, but it has to be taken seriously. The implication is that efforts to help firms improve their human resource practices, augment the amount of training they provide, and build career paths are all important components of successful program design.

A Strategy for the System

The system's goals should be ladders, scale, and impact on the demand side. In thinking about how to achieve these goals, one question that immediately comes to mind is whether it makes sense to move in these directions through WIA or other equivalent programs or instead to fold everything into the much larger and more institutionalized community college system. That path has been advocated by some proponents of community colleges (Grubb 2001). The case for this approach points to the greater funding and reach of community colleges, their more professionalized staffing, and their more regularized curriculum.

These arguments are all persuasive. Set against them, however, is the fact that community colleges have multiple missions and multiple constituencies, and building ladders for the working poor and dislocated workers would not rank at the top of the list. The danger is that this objective would be compromised and sacrificed to other priorities. A focus on the working poor and the dislocated and a constituency for them needs to come from an E&T system that is their advocate and has a clear mission. The E&T system should be the driver of this agenda. In this context, the community colleges are key players, perhaps central ones when it comes to delivering training, but they cannot be expected to drive the system.

Having said this, WIA and the traditional E&T system should rethink their mission and operational strategy. In the past, WIA and its predecessors were basically sources of funding for program operators. This

led to some good programs and some bad programs, but, more fundamentally, it did not significantly change the opportunities available to
the large numbers of people the system was trying to serve. To make
a real difference, WIA needs to recognize that while it is small relative
to the universe of need, the network of community colleges is much
larger and the investment that employers devote to their human
resources is larger yet. This implies that the best way to think about
WIA is as a source of leverage for these larger systems and a catalyst
for systems change.

In this view, WIA is less about delivering services than it is about
using its scarce resources to shape what other, larger systems deliver.
This is not to say that WIA does not fund service provision, but rather
that it thinks about its funding very strategically. The best analogy is
that WIA should think of its strategy in the same way as do foundations.
Foundations fund services but they do so to leverage larger systems and
encourage innovation. In short, WIA needs to fundamentally rethink its
role and its strategy.

It is important to understand that the present proposal is not a call
for more of the coordination and planning efforts that have periodically
swept through the E&T system and that are at the heart of much of
what propelled WIA in the first place. Too often these efforts are simply
process-oriented rote exercises. By contrast, the proposal here is to use
WIA resources to encourage the other actors in the system to improve
their practices and to fill gaps in the system, in the ladder, that currently
impede progress. To make this happen, the managers of the WIA
system and federal actors would have a strategic view of what they
want to accomplish, and they would use their resources to leverage
additional resources from larger actors and to propel other players and
the system forward. WIA in this view is not a forum for planning or
coordination. It is a resource for experimentation, for systems change,
and for filling programmatic gaps.

How can the WIA system play these roles? One tactic is to systemati-
cally fund policy entrepreneurship. As already noted, the past decade
has seen an impressive flowering of new program designs. These have
been implemented by a wide range of actors—community groups,
business associations, unions, and other nonprofits—and they have
been supported by foundations, by state training funds, and by demonstration grants from the Department of Labor. What is particularly
attractive about these innovations is that they seek to address many
of the historical limitations of the E&T system. The innovations work
closely with employers to understand their labor force needs as well
as their competitive positions. The programs also attempt to improve
the quality of jobs rather than focus entirely on the supply side of the
labor market. They also are open to providing longer-term training

rather than the quick-and-dirty interventions that typified many previous efforts.

At the same time, unanswered questions about these efforts need to be studied and evaluated, not the least of which is the standard question about impact. In addition, these programs vary considerably in their auspices (who sponsors and runs them), in the role played by support services, and in whether they aim at particular industries or sectors or whether they provide broad occupational training.

Given the promise of these efforts and given the long American history of innovation in labor policy springing from local efforts, it seems important to encourage, support, and fund policy entrepreneurship, particularly when that entrepreneurship is combined with careful assessment. Local WIBs should support these innovations; in addition, there is a strong case for a federal fund for supporting innovation and evaluation for new models of intermediary, sectoral, and occupational training programs.

Using WIA to match and stimulate state training funds is worthwhile because it levers additional resources. This is particularly true because these efforts are typically aimed at incumbent workers at risk of dislocation. In return for federal matching, the state training funds should establish procedures to ensure that any support provided to firms represents a net addition to the firms' training efforts (and does not simply substitute for what the firm would otherwise have done) and that the programs are subject to credible evaluation. All these efforts could be funded either through general revenue or, perhaps more appropriately, by more creative federal use of unemployment insurance funds.

Third, the WIA system needs to find ways to work more effectively with the community college system. Community colleges are the nation's largest source of occupational training and, while the system has significant blemishes, it nonetheless must be a centerpiece of any effort to create a real ladder of opportunity for the working poor and dislocated workers. Within community colleges, there is often a disconnect between the nondegree remedial programs and the degree or occupational training programs. This disconnect is a major problem for people attempting to move up and should be remedied through the kinds of innovations described earlier at Portland Community College.

In addition, the completion rates for low-income people, and in particular part-time students, in community colleges are very low. Several national demonstrations are under way that address some of these issues, but improved supportive services is one key. National data show that the ratio of students to counselors in community colleges is 1,000 to 1 (Grubb 2001). By contrast, Project QUEST trains its clients in community colleges and has very high retention rates because it provides well-staffed, intensive supportive services.

The nature of community college cooperation with WIA is also very uneven. The use of local WIA funds as matching and challenge grants to community colleges to address the limitations described above, combined with more flexibility on data and reporting requirements, could go a long way toward focusing community colleges more effectively on a mission of improving the prospects of low-earning adults and dislocated workers.

The other major source of training resources lies, of course, with firms themselves. As we have seen, firms spend a great deal on training and on career systems, albeit with their spending biased away from employees at the bottom of their job ladders. Many firms in a wide range of industries have found that investing in their human resources leads to significant gains in productivity and profits (Jobs for the Future 2003; Osterman et al. 2001). The challenge lies in diffusing these examples and in overcoming the obstacles—lack of knowledge, scarce managerial time, short time horizons—that limit the adoption of these best practices. Making progress in the face of these market failures is a very legitimate policy goal of the system.

WIA resources can be used to encourage new HR practices in firms, but the federal system has a very spotty history of working effectively with employers. Intermediary organizations—business associations such as the Chamber of Commerce, the National Association of Manufacturers, and industry-specific organizations as well as nonprofits such as the Council for Adult and Experiential Learning—have much better track records. The federal system needs to work effectively with these intermediaries in order to leverage the training resources of firms and to encourage more progressive human resource practices.

Redesigning WIA

All the strategies described above are very much in line with the present tactics of the national foundations active in this arena. But potential federal resources are much more substantial and long-lasting than those of foundations, and the federal government has other tools, such as tax incentives, at its disposal that the foundations lack. But for the WIA system to rethink itself as a instigator of innovation and systems change, it must become much more flexible and much less rule-bound than it currently is.

As the system stands now, federal regulations can lead to risk-averse and overly cautious behavior. In part, this is because many preexisting JTPA regulations were simply transferred into the new WIA system. In addition, the fear of an audit or a disallowed cost pushes WIBs into unimaginative actions. Too often these workforce boards come to think of themselves as extensions of the federal Department of Labor.

The WIA system also has built-in programmatic requirements that are, simply put, untested. These requirements include the idea of one-stops, individual training accounts, the sequence of services, and the specific composition of WIB boards. Some of these ideas have a commonsensical quality and are attractive in many ways, but it is easy to think of offsetting arguments regarding each. Yet the point is not whether the ideas are good and are worth trying out—in most cases, they are. The point is they are untested hypotheses that are nevertheless mandated in the system. These mandates are costly and soak up resources that could be devoted to system-leveraging activities like those described earlier. Moving away from directives of this kind seems an important component for providing more state and local initiative and creativity.

If the new role of WIA is to stimulate innovation and to instigate broader institutional change in the broadly conceived E&T system, then performance standards also need to be reconsidered. A simple model in which funds that would otherwise go to WIA or its equivalent are distributed to the states with no strings attached is undesirable. Rather, the appropriate federal role can be derived from how effective corporate headquarters operate and from lessons drawn from the quality movement that has transformed firms in the past two decades. Firms have learned that if they set goals and objectives while providing more opportunity and authority to employees and operating units, the result is greater commitment, increased productivity, and higher quality. By the same token, the federal government should establish broad objectives for the use of its funds and then use performance standards to determine whether these goals are achieved.

In effect, the federal government would start a conversation with each state to reach a mutual agreement regarding the broad goals and strategies of the programs, the purposes to which funds will be put, and targets for the amount of services rendered to specific groups. These objectives, which are important but which should also be less constraining than the present system, can be combined with a new set of performance standards. The federal government would use the standards to measure a state's progress toward a broadly defined outcome. Under this arrangement, detailed program management, of the sort embodied in current performance standards, would be left to the states.

Finally, it is important to understand that there remains an important role for federal creativity at the national level. Demonstration funding remains central to efforts to design and test new program models. An excellent example, particularly for dislocated workers, is experiments with lifetime learning accounts, which enable people to accumulate funds for retaining in the event of job loss or other forms of dislocation.

Funding

The goals of E&T policy should be to build ladders of opportunity on a scale large enough to affect and improve firms' HR practices concerning frontline employees. The strategy should reconceive the federal system as a source of leverage and systems change for the larger labor market institutions—firms and community colleges—that can substantially affect the lives of low-wage workers. This reconception implies a new model for WIA and federal programs. To move in this direction, the federal government needs to take several important tactical steps.

First, it is important to address funding. The scale of WIA funding falls far short of the universe of need, with numerous negative consequences. One obvious effect is that training for less-skilled adults is not effectively addressed. An additional underappreciated, but important, point is that an effective employment and training system needs a modern administrative structure and a professional, well-trained staff. Skilled professionals need to be confident that they can build careers in the system. It is difficult to build such an infrastructure in an unstable and declining funding environment.

A second funding issue lies in the financial aid system for higher education. One central element in building ladders is improving the ability of low-wage and dislocated adults to attend higher education, particularly community colleges. Financial aid is a central determinant of whether people can follow this path. The most important federal financial aid program, Pell grants, is targeted to low-income families. According to estimates, about 33 percent of Pell funding supports occupational training (Spence and Kiel 2003), and 90 percent goes to families with annual incomes below $30,000 (Choitz, Dowd, and Long 2004). The problem, however, is that few working adults are able to use this program. In 2000, only 1 percent of Pell recipients were enrolled less than half-time, and only 3.5 percent of working parents who took classes less than half-time received Pell grants (Choitz and Widom 2003). Other federal financial support, notably the Hope and Lifetime Learning tax credits, do not reach the working poor. There are various ideas for making these programs more accessible to people who have to work full-time (see, for example, Choitz et al. 2004 and Bosworth and Choitz 2004). These ideas should be explored in more detail and taken seriously.

CONCLUSION

There are many ideas—good ideas—available for improving America's employment and training system. But what is missing in the discussion is a broader vision and a compelling mission for the system. For all its weaknesses, in the past, the employment and training system was connected in the public mind to important national concerns. That is not true today.

The modern E&T system took shape in the late 1950s and early 1960s with the passage of the Manpower Development and Training Act. This legislation, and the interest in improving the nation's training infrastructure, was driven by worries about the impact of automation on the employment of skilled (typically male) workers. There was a serious national discussion of this concern, and the E&T system was seen as central to any solution.

Beginning in the mid-1960s, the War on Poverty was a central theme in domestic national political discourse; again, the E&T system was center stage. A wide range of new program models emerged, and the federal government, states and localities, and the private foundation world were all active players. Late in this period, as the consequences of the oil shocks played out, the E&T system took on the additional burden of providing public service jobs to ease the consequences of job loss by experienced workers.

In the late 1980s and early 1990s, widespread concern about America's competitive position in the world economy led policymakers to focus on the skill level of the U.S. workforce. Along with school reform, job training was seen as important, and several initiatives emerged: the attempt to implement a system of skills standards, programs encouraging a version of the German apprenticeship model, and enhanced training of incumbent workers. All this activity added up to a central role for the E&T system.

From the impact of automation to poverty to national competitiveness, the E&T system has been seen as an important player in addressing national domestic policy concerns. Today the system is floundering, in part because it does not connect to a driving narrative that justifies a strong system and makes it central to contemporary concerns. But the elements of that narrative seem fairly clear. Today's labor market is volatile, and there is widespread understanding that up and down the income scale, people need skills to do well. Experts broadly understand the importance of labor market institutions that enable people to make successful transitions. Firms also face a newly competitive environment, and many recognize that a key to their success is the quality of their human resources. In short, success in a volatile world points to the case for a strong E&T system, a system in which the federal role is to stimulate innovation and to leverage other labor market actors to build ladders that lead to success.

NOTES

1. Taken from the U.S. Bureau of the Census web site, http://www.census.gov/hhes/www/poverty/poverty.html.

2. These data are from the National Compensation Survey of Occupational Wages, which represents all private-sector jobs regardless of establishment size and all state and local government employment in establishments with 50 or more employees.

3. The figures in the text refer to skills below level 2. Level 2 prose skills refer to the ability to locate a single item of information in a text with several distractors or plausible but incorrect pieces of information present. Level 2 document interpretation skills require the respondent to match a single piece of information with distractors present. Level 2 numeracy skills require one- or two-step processes involving whole numbers and percents and interpreting simple graphs.

4. Andersson and colleagues also find that the temporary work itself pays low wages. The implication, then, is that something about the experience of temporary work leads to good outcomes via subsequent mobility.

5. Lerman, McKernan, and Riegg (2004) review the literature on this topic.

6. See the Economic Policy Institute web site, http://www.epinet.org/content.cfm/issueguides_minwage_minwagefacts.

7. Funds made available under the TAA Act for retraining in 2004 totaled $269 million, which supported the training of about 45,000 workers (GAO 2004a).

8. The national JTPA evaluation was a random assignment study of 15,981 people. They were tracked for 30 months after leaving the program by 1989. The sample was drawn from 16 service delivery areas (SDAs) around the country and, while the SDAs were not chosen randomly, they were representative of the nation. Within the relevant SDAs, random assignment was used to assign clients to the program or to a control group. People in the control group could not receive JTPA training, but they could obtain training and services from other sources (Bloom et al. 1997).

9. See also Greenberg et al. (2005). They attempt to understand these results in the context of other welfare-to-work programs and conclude that location-specific effects played a role in the program's success but that design features (i.e., training) were also important.

REFERENCES

Ahlstrand, Amanda, Max Armbruster, Laurie Bassi, Dan McMurrer, and Mark Van Buren. 2001. "Workplace Education Investments and Strategies for Lower-Wage Workers." In *Low-Wage Workers in the New Economy*, edited by Richard Kazis and Marc S. Miller (327–46). Washington, DC: Urban Institute Press.

Allegretto, Sylvia, Jared Bernstein, and Isaac Shapiro. 2005. "The Lukewarm 2004 Labor Market: Despite Some Signs of Improvement, Wages Fell, Job Growth Lagged, and Unemployment Spells Remained Long." Issue brief. Washington, DC: Economic Policy Institute.

American Society for Training and Development. 2005. *2005 State of the Industry Report*. Alexandria, VA: American Society for Training and Development.

Andersson, Fredrik, Harry Holzer, and Julia Lane. 2005. *Moving Up or Moving On: Who Advances in the Low Wage Labor Market?* New York: Russell Sage Foundation.

Appelbaum, Eileen, Annette Bernhardt, and Richard Murnane, eds. 2003. *Low-Wage America: How Employers Are Reshaping Opportunity in the Workplace*. New York: Russell Sage Foundation.

Aspen Institute, The. 2003. *Grow Faster Together or Grow Slowly Apart: How Will America Work in the 21st Century?* Washington DC: The Aspen Institute.

Autor, David, and Susan Houseman. 2005. "Do Temporary Jobs Improve the Labor Outcomes for Low-Skilled Workers? Evidence from Random Assignments." Working paper. Cambridge, MA: Massachusetts Institute of Technology.

Bailey, Thomas, Timothy Leinbach, Marc Scott, Mariana Alfonso, Gregory Kienzl, and Benjamin Kennedy. 2004. "The Characteristics of Occupational Students in Postsecondary Education." CCRC brief 21. New York: Community College Research Center, Institute on Education and the Economy, Teachers College, Columbia University.

Barnow, Burt, and Christopher King. 2003. "The Workforce Investment Act in Eight States: Overview of Findings from a Field Network Study." Albany, NY: Nelson A. Rockefeller Institute of Government.

Barton, Paul. 2005. *One-Third of a Nation: Rising Dropout Rates and Declining Opportunities*. Policy Information report. Princeton, NJ: Educational Testing Service.

Bernstein, Jared, and Maury Gittleman. 2003. "Exploring Low-Wage Labor with the National Compensation Survey." *Monthly Labor Review* 126(11/12): 3–12.

Berry, Daniel. 2004. "Creating and Sustaining a Coherent Voice for Employers in Workforce Development: The Cleveland Experience." In *Workforce Intermediaries for the Twenty-First Century*, edited by Robert Giloth (193–215). Philadelphia, PA: Temple University Press.

Bloom, Howard, Larry Orr, Stephen Bell, George Cave, Fred Doolittle, Winston Lin, and Johannes Bos. 1997. "The Benefits and Costs of JTPA Title II-A Programs: Key Findings from the National Job Training Partnership Act Study." *Journal of Human Resources* 32(3): 549–76.

Borjas, George. 2003. "Comment." In *Inequality in America: What Role for Human Capital?* by James Heckman and Alan Krueger (241–52). Cambridge, MA: MIT Press.

Bradbury, Katharine, and Jane Katz. 2002. "Are Lifetime Incomes Growing More Unequal? Looking at New Evidence on Family Income Mobility." *Regional Review (The Federal Reserve Bank of Boston)* 12(4): 3–5.

Bosworth, Brian, and Victoria Choitz. 2004. "Title X: A New Federal-State Partnership in Higher Education for Working Adults in the 21st Century." Arlington, MA: FutureWorks.

Brock, Thomas, and Allen LeBlanc, with Casey McGregor. 2005. "Promoting Student Success in Community College and Beyond: The Opening Doors Demonstration." New York: MDRC.

Burtless, Gary. 1985. "Are Targeted Wage Subsidies Harmful? Lessons from a Voucher Experiment." *Industrial and Labor Relations Review* 39(1): 105–14.

Card, David, and John DiNardo. 2002. "Skill-Biased Technological Change and Rising Wage Inequality: Some Problems and Puzzles." Working Paper 8,769. Cambridge, MA: National Bureau of Economic Research (NBER).

Choitz, Victoria, Laura Dowd, and Bridget Terry Long. 2004. "Getting Serious about Lifelong Learning: Improving the Use and Value of the Hope and Lifetime Learning Tax Credits for Working Adult Students." Full report. Arlington, MA: FutureWorks.

Choitz, Victoria, and Rebecca Widom. 2003. "Money Matters: How Financial Aid Affects Nontraditional Students in Community Colleges." New York: MDRC.

Comings, John, Andrew Sum, and Johan Uvin. 2000. "New Skills for a New Economy: Adult Education's Role in Sustaining Economic Growth and Expanding Opportunity." Boston: MassINC.

D'Amico, Ronald, and Jeffrey Salzman. 2004. "Implementation Issues in Delivering Training Services to Adults under WIA." In *Job Training Policy in the United States*, edited by Christopher O'Leary, Robert Straits, and Stephen Wander (101–34). Kalamazoo, MI: W.E. Upjohn Institute for Employment Research.

DiNatale, Marisa. 2001. "Characteristics of and Preferences for Alternative Work Arrangements, 1999." *Monthly Labor Review* 124(3): 28–49.

Duncan, Greg, Johanne Boisjoly, and Timothy Smeeding. 1996. "The Economic Mobility of Young Workers in the 1970s and the 1980s." *Demography* 33(4): 497–509.

Eberts, Randall, and Harry Holzer. 2004. "Overview of Labor Exchange Policies and Services." In *Labor Exchange Policy in the United States*, edited by David Balducchi, Randall Eberts, and Christopher O'Leary (1–33). Kalamazoo, MI: W.E. Upjohn Institute for Employment Research.

Farber, Henry. 2005. "What Do We Know about Job Loss in the United States? Evidence from the Displaced Workers Survey, 1984–2004." Working Paper 498, Industrial Relations Section. Princeton, NJ: Princeton University.

Fitzgerald, Joan. 2006. *Moving Up in the New Economy: Career Ladders for U.S. Workers*. Ithaca, NY: Cornell University Press and the Century Foundation.

Frank, Abby, and Elisa Minoff. 2005. "Declining Share of Adults Receiving Training under WIA Are Low-Income or Disadvantaged." Washington, DC: Center for Law and Social Policy.

Giloth, Robert. 2004. "Introduction." In *Workforce Intermediaries for the Twenty-First Century*, edited by Robert Giloth (193–215). Philadelphia, PA: Temple University Press.

GAO. See U.S. General Accounting Office, U.S. Government Accountability Office.

Greenberg, David, Karl Ashworth, Andreas Cebulla, and Robert Walker. 2005. "When Welfare-to-Work Programs Seem to Work Well: Explaining Why Riverside and Portland Shine So Brightly." *Industrial and Labor Relations Review* 59(1): 34–50.

Grote, Mae Watson, and Anne Roder. 2005. "Setting the Bar High: Findings from the National Sectoral Employment Initiative." New York: Public/Private Ventures.

Grubb, Norton. 2001. "Second Chances in Changing Times: The Role of Community Colleges in Advancing Low-Skilled Workers." In *Low Wage Workers in the New Economy*, edited by Richard Kazis and Marc Miller (283–306). Washington, DC: Urban Institute Press.

Holzer, Harry. 2004. "Encouraging Job Advancement among Low-Wage Workers: A New Approach." Policy Brief #30. Washington, DC: The Brookings Institution.

Jacobson, Louis. 1995. "The Effectiveness of the Employment Service." Advisory Commission on Unemployment Compensation. Washington, DC: U.S. Government Printing Office.

Jacobson, Louis, Robert LaLonde, and Daniel Sullivan. 2005. "The Impact of Community College Training on Older Displaced Workers: Should We Teach Old Dogs New Tricks?" *Industrial and Labor Relations Review* 58(3): 398–415.

Jobs for the Future. 2003. *Hiring, Retaining, and Advancing Front-Line Workers: A Guide to Successful Human Resource Practices.* Boston, MA: Jobs for the Future.

———. 2004. *Breaking Through: Helping Low-Skilled Adults Enter and Succeed in College and Careers.* Boston, MA: Jobs for the Future.

Kane, Thomas, and Cecilia Rouse. 1999. "The Community College: Educating Students at the Margin between Education and Work." *Journal of Economic Perspectives* 13(1): 63–84.

King, Christopher. 2004. "The Effectiveness of Publicly Financed Training in the United States: Implications for WIA and Related Programs." In *Job Training Policy in the United States*, edited by Christopher O'Leary, Robert Straits, and Stephen Wander (57–100). Kalamazoo, MI: W.E. Upjohn Institute for Employment Research.

Kletzer, Lori. 1998. "Job Displacement." *Journal of Economic Perspectives* 12(1): 115–36.

Kletzer, Lori, and William Koch. 2004. "International Experience with Job Training: Lessons for the United States." In *Job Training Policy in the United States*, edited by Christopher O'Leary, Robert Straits, and Stephen Wander (245–88). Kalamazoo, MI: W.E. Upjohn Institute for Employment Research.

Laufer, Jessica, and Sian Winship. 2004. "Perception vs. Reality: Employer Attitudes and the Rebranding of Workforce Intermediaries." In *Workforce Intermediaries for the Twenty-First Century*, edited by Robert Giloth (216–40). Philadelphia, PA: Temple University Press.

Leete, Laura, Chris Benner, Manuel Pastor Jr., and Sarah Zimmerman, 2004. "Labor Market Intermediaries in the Old and New Economies: A Survey of Worker Experiences in Milwaukee and the Silicon Valley." In *Workforce Intermediaries for the Twenty-First Century*, edited by Robert Giloth (263–92). Philadelphia, PA: Temple University Press.

Leigh, Duane. 2000. "Training Programs for Dislocated Workers." In *Improving the Odds: Increasing the Effectiveness of Publicly Funded Training*, edited by Burt Barnow and Christopher King (227–60). Washington, DC: Urban Institute Press.

Lerman, Robert, Signe-Mary McKernan, and Stephanie Riegg. 2004. "The Scope of Employer-Provided Training in the United States: Who, What, Where, and How Much." In *Job Training Policy in the United States*, edited by Christopher O'Leary, Robert Straits, and Stephen Wander (211–43). Kalamazoo, MI: W.E. Upjohn Institute for Employment Research.

Lynch, Lisa. 1992. "Private-Sector Training and Its Impact on the Earnings of Young Workers." *American Economic Review* 82(1): 299–312.

Marcotte, David, Thomas Bailey, Carey Borkoski, and Greg Kienzl. 2005. "The Returns of a Community College Education: Evidence from the National

Education Longitudinal Survey." *Educational Evaluation and Policy Analysis* 27(2): 157–75.

Marino, Cindy, and Kim Tarr. 2004. "The Workforce Intermediary: Profiling the Field of Practice and Its Challenges." In *Workforce Intermediaries for the Twenty-First Century*, edited by Robert Giloth (93–123). Philadelphia, PA: Temple University Press.

OECD. See Organisation for Economic Co-operation and Development.

O'Leary, Christopher. 2004. "Evaluating the Effectiveness of Labor Exchange Services." In *Labor Exchange Policy in the United States*, edited by David Balducchi, Randall Eberts, and Christopher O'Leary (135–77). Kalamazoo, MI: W.E. Upjohn Institute for Employment Research.

Organisation for Economic Co-operation and Development (OECD) and Minister of Industry Canada. 2005. *Learning a Living, First Results of the Adult Literacy and Life Skills Survey.* Paris: OECD.

Osterman, Paul. 1994. "How Common Is Workplace Transformation and Who Adopts It?" *Industrial and Labor Relations Review* 47(2): 173–88.

———. 1995. "Skill, Training, and Work Organization in American Establishments." *Industrial Relations* 34(2): 125–46.

———. 2000. "Work Organization in an Era of Restructuring: Trends in Diffusion and Impacts on Employee Welfare." *Industrial and Labor Relations Review* 53(2): 179–96.

Osterman, Paul, and Brenda Lautsch. 1996. "Project QUEST: A Report to the Ford Foundation." Cambridge, MA: Massachusetts Institute of Technology.

Osterman, Paul, Thomas Kochan, Richard Locke, and Michael Piore. 2001. *Working in America: A Blueprint for a New Labor Market.* Cambridge, MA: MIT Press.

Pastor, Manuel, Laura Leete, and Laura Dresser. 2003. "Economic Opportunity in a Volatile Economy: Understanding the Role of Labor Market Intermediaries in Two Regions." Santa Cruz, CA, and Madison, WI: Working Partnerships USA and the Center on Wisconsin Strategy.

Partnership for Employer-Employee Responsive Systems. 2003. *Workforce Intermediaries: Generating Benefits for Employers and Workers.* Boston, MA: Jobs for the Future.

Pindus, Nancy, Carolyn O'Brien, Maureen Conway, Conaway Haskins, and Ida Rademacher. 2004. "Evaluation of the Sectoral Employment Demonstration Program." Washington, DC: The Urban Institute.

Prince, David, and David Jenkins. 2005. "Building Pathways to Success for Low-Income Adults Students: Lessons for Community College Policy and Practice from a Statewide Longitudinal Tracking Study." New York: Community College Research Center, Institute on Education and the Economy, Teachers College, Columbia University.

Ridley, Neil, and William Tracy. 2004. "State and Local Labor Exchange Services." In *Labor Exchange Policy in the United States*, edited by David Balducchi, Randall Eberts, and Christopher O'Leary (73–100). Kalamazoo, MI: W.E. Upjohn Institute for Employment Research.

Scrivener, Susan, Gayle Hamilton, Mary Farrell, Stephen Freedman, Daniel Friedlander, Marisa Mitchell, Jodi Nudelman, and Christine Schwartz. 1998. "Implementation, Participation Patterns, Costs, and Two-Year Impacts of the Portland (Oregon) Welfare-to-Work Program." New York: Manpower Development Research Corporation.

Smole, David. 2004. "Labor Exchange Performance Measurement." In *Labor Exchange Policy in the United States*, edited by David Balducchi, Randall Eberts, and Christopher O'Leary (101–34). Kalamazoo, MI: W.E. Upjohn Institute for Employment Research.

Spence, Robin, and Brendan Kiel. 2003. "Skilling the American Workforce 'On the Cheap': Ongoing Shortfalls in Federal Funding for Workforce Development." Washington, DC: The Workforce Alliance.

U.S. Bureau of Labor Statistics. 2006. "Union Members in 2005." News release USDL 06-99. Washington, DC: U.S. Department of Labor, Bureau of Labor Statistics.

U.S. Department of Education. 2004. *Adult Education and Family Literacy Act Program Year 2002–2003: Report to Congress on State Performance.* Washington, DC: U.S. Department of Education.

U.S. General Accounting Office. 2003a. "Multiple Employment and Training Programs: Funding and Performance Measures for Major Programs." GAO-03-589. Washington, DC: U.S. General Accounting Office.

———. 2003b. "Workforce Investment Act: One-Stop Centers Implemented Strategies to Strengthen Services and Partnerships, but More Research and Information Sharing Is Needed." GAO-03-725. Washington, DC: U.S. General Accounting Office.

———. 2004a. "Trade Adjustment Assistance: Reforms Have Accelerated Training Enrollment, but Implementation Challenges Remain." GAO-04-1012. Washington, DC: U.S. General Accounting Office.

———2004b. "Workforce Training: Almost Half of States Fund Employment Placement and Training through Employer Taxes and Most Coordinate with Federally Funded Programs." GAO-04-282. Washington, DC: U.S. General Accounting Office.

U.S. Government Accountability Office. 2005a. "Employers Are Aware of, Using, and Satisfied with One-Stop Services, but More Data Could Help Labor Better Address Employers' Needs." GAO-05-259. Washington, DC: U.S. Government Accountability Office.

———. 2005b. "Workforce Investment Act: Substantial Funds Are Used for Training, but Little Is Known Nationally about Training Outcomes." GAO-05-650. Washington, DC: U.S. Government Accountability Office.

Willis, Rachel, Rachel Connelly, and Deborah DeGraff. 2003. "The Future of Jobs in the Hosiery Industry." In *Low-Wage America: How Employers Are Reshaping Opportunity in the Workplace,* edited by Eileen Appelbaum, Annette Bernhardt, and Richard Murnane (407–45). New York: Russell Sage Foundation.

Workforce Alliance, The. 2003.*Workforce Development Policies: Background and Current Issues.* Washington, DC: The Workforce Alliance.

6

OVERCOMING EMPLOYMENT BARRIERS: STRATEGIES TO HELP THE "HARD TO EMPLOY"

Dan Bloom and David Butler

Millions of Americans face serious obstacles to steady work. These individuals often become enmeshed in costly public assistance and enforcement systems; just as important, many find themselves living in poverty, outside the mainstream in a society that prizes work and self-sufficiency.

Interest in the "hard to employ" surged in the 1990s, when the strong economy, rising employment-to-population ratios, and dramatic declines in the welfare caseload all combined to focus a spotlight on groups that had been "left behind." For the first time on a large scale, welfare agencies began developing or brokering services for recipients with mental health conditions, substance abuse problems, disabilities, and other serious barriers to work. Parallel changes were occurring in other systems: criminal justice officials began to focus on the daunting problems facing prisoners returning to their communities, and the rapid growth of disability programs led policymakers to look for ways to encourage work among beneficiaries. These discussions are ongoing today.

As discussed elsewhere in this volume, with the baby boom generation approaching retirement age, labor markets may tighten in the not-too-distant future. If the 1990s are an accurate guide, if the unemployment rate stays low for an extended period, part of the hard-to-employ population will be swept into the labor force: employers will be willing to take a second look at groups that would otherwise be ignored.

But while tight labor markets may provide a rare opportunity to engage the persistently unemployed, this problem is not likely to solve itself. If those farther back in the queue are not ready and able to work, policymakers and employers will adjust to tight labor markets in other ways—for example, by easing restrictions on immigration or shipping more jobs overseas. Given this reality, there are several compelling reasons to spend more time, energy, and money improving the employment prospects of those facing serious barriers to steady work.

First, it is costly for taxpayers to support individuals who, with appropriate help, could work. Spending money on effective services for the hard-to-employ may generate offsetting savings in public assistance, incarceration, or other public costs. Even when income support programs are cheaper than services, Americans are typically willing to spend more if the money is used to increase self-sufficiency.

Second, although many of these connections are not proven, there may be broader consequences for society when people do not work steadily—for example, deleterious effects on public safety, family structure, child well-being, and the health of particular communities. Bringing more of the hard-to-employ into the economic mainstream may help to address some of these persistent social problems.

Third, many of the hard-to-employ very much want to work. While our society has been unwilling to guarantee a job to everyone, there is a strongly held conviction that everyone deserves a chance.

Fourth, helping the hard-to-employ find and keep jobs is critical to improving their economic well-being—a more realistic goal now that expanded work supports are in place to supplement low-wage jobs. This may be particularly beneficial for children: The best evidence we have suggests that simultaneously raising parents' employment and income can generate significant improvements in their children's school performance and other outcomes (Morris, Gennetian, and Knox 2002).

Finally, at least some employers will prefer a solution that maximizes use of our own human resources. Many corporations are concerned about the health of the communities in which they operate—and about their public image. And it is clear that some people considered hard-to-employ actually make highly reliable employees under the right conditions.

These arguments are persuasive, but they do not address the crucial question of what exactly should be done. Public dollars will be scarce for some time to come so major increases in government spending seem unlikely. Even if funding were more readily available, it is unclear that throwing money at this problem would solve it. For one thing, we simply do not know enough about what works. More broadly, many policies, systems, and programs that interact with the hard-to-employ are designed in ways that actually make employment less likely. Thus, while additional funding is certainly needed in some areas, we also have to do much better with what we already have, while simultaneously building our knowledge about which programmatic strategies are most cost-effective.

After a general description of the problem, this chapter explains why public systems are critical to any serious effort to help the hard-to-employ. It focuses in detail on three such systems: welfare, disability assistance, and criminal justice. These systems are not the only relevant ones, but they are critical to any large-scale effort to assist the hard-to-employ. Because the specific problems and opportunities differ by system, the systems are discussed separately. The final section draws cross-cutting lessons and offers some recommendations for policy and practice.

WHO ARE THE HARD-TO-EMPLOY?

There is no universally accepted definition of the term "hard to employ." In fact, the definition can fluctuate over time with shifting political or ideological currents. Groups for whom employment was once considered inappropriate—for example, single mothers with pre-school-age children—are now widely expected to work. Others that were thought of as unemployable not so long ago, such as the disabled, are now seen as employable but in need of special supports. As noted earlier, labor market conditions also play a role: when the labor market is tight, employers are willing to hire individuals whose personal characteristics would otherwise eliminate them from consideration.

The definition is also fuzzy at the individual level. Some people are able to work but only part-time or only under special conditions. Others have chronic health conditions that wax and wane: they are able to work sometimes but not others. Still others are able to find jobs but seem unable to hold them.

With no clear definition, it is difficult to count the hard-to-employ. The Annie E. Casey Foundation's Kids Count project estimates that more than 2 million custodial parents are persistently unemployed. A broader definition of the hard-to-employ—including adults who are not living with children, and individuals who are able to work but cannot maintain steady employment—would yield a much larger estimate. Even after dramatic declines in the welfare caseload, there are still about 1 million adults receiving Temporary Assistance for Needy Families (TANF). Another 4 million working-age adults receive Supplemental Security Income (SSI), and 6 million receive Social Security Disability Insurance (SSDI) benefits. Of course, many of those receiving disability benefits are unable to work at all, and some receiving TANF benefits are not truly hard-to-employ. On the other hand, these figures do not include the large numbers of hard-to-employ adults who are incarcerated, or those who are supported by family members and do not receive public assistance.

ASSISTING THE HARD-TO-EMPLOY

To devise effective services, it is first necessary to understand the personal characteristics that make people hard to employ. These barriers might be grouped into three broad categories:

- **Human capital deficits**, including very low basic skills, limited English proficiency, and lack of work experience.
- **Health problems**, including disabilities, behavioral health conditions (depression, substance abuse), and chronic physical health problems (hypertension, obesity) that can affect employability.
- A diverse **"other"** category that includes situational barriers (e.g., lack of transportation, the need to care for a disabled dependent, and so on) and having a **criminal record**, a factor that deserves special emphasis. While individuals may wind up in the criminal justice system in part because they face the barriers described above, involvement in the system creates its own distinctive employment barriers, since convicted felons are legally barred from many occupations and are considered highly undesirable by employers.

This categorization is obviously oversimplified. In reality, many people face more than one barrier, and many people who face the barriers described above are able to work. According to research conducted on the welfare system, the accumulation of many barriers, rather than the presence or absence of any single barrier, makes people hard to employ (University of Michigan 2004).

In addition, this scheme does not address the behavior of employers who, for both legitimate business reasons and because of discrimination and fear, are reluctant to hire many people who face the barriers described above. Employer policies related to health insurance and sick leave, and the behavior of supervisors, may also affect employment retention for these groups.

Nonetheless, a categorization of this type is useful because different barriers require different services or supports. Services might also be grouped into a few broad categories:

- **Treatment services.** There are efficacious treatments for many of the health conditions listed earlier, but the hard-to-employ often need help accessing high-quality medical care and remaining in treatment over time.
- **Employment and training services.** This category runs the gamut from traditional classroom-based education and vocational training to work-based approaches including transitional and supported employment. It also includes labor exchange services designed to connect the hard-to-employ with employers who are willing to hire them and follow-up services designed to promote job retention.
- **Incentives.** While we assume that the hard-to-employ require services to address their barriers, financial incentives targeted both to the hard-to-employ and to employers may also play a role.
- **Workplace accommodations.** This category includes assistive technologies, measures to make workplaces more accessible, and other strategies to improve the functional capacity of individuals with disabilities.

There are many important questions about which services are most effective for individuals facing specific barriers. For example, there are long-running debates about the role of education and training versus work-based approaches, the most appropriate ways to combine treatment and employment services, and whether incentives can change employers' hiring decisions. Many of these issues are discussed below.

But barriers and services are only part of the puzzle. As noted earlier, many of the hard-to-employ become enmeshed in public systems or programs: both *assistance programs,* such as welfare, food stamps, SSI/SSDI, and Medicaid; and *enforcement systems,* such as criminal justice, child support enforcement, and child welfare. It is almost impossible to discuss the effectiveness of a particular service strategy without considering the system context in which it is delivered. In some instances, characteristics of the systems can actually make success more difficult.

For example, interventions in the disability system must address the serious financial disincentives to work and the conflicting messages of a system that makes permanent disability an eligibility requirement but also is trying to encourage more employment. Reentry programs for ex-prisoners must operate within the constraints of systems like parole that have deemphasized rehabilitation and may impose rules and requirements that make employment more difficult.

Finally, in order to deliver services, it is often necessary to forge links between the assistance and enforcement systems mentioned above and service delivery systems, such as mental health and substance abuse treatment, employment and training, and vocational rehabilitation. In addition to the usual challenges to developing such links, the service systems have their own special characteristics that may help or hinder effective programming. For example, many substance abuse treatment providers believe that work is not appropriate, at least in the early stages of treatment. The employment and training system, driven by performance standards, is sometimes reluctant to serve groups that tend to have relatively poor outcomes.

Because the issues differ in each system—and because funding for both services and research tends to flow through the systems—much of what we know about services for the hard-to-employ comes from system-specific studies. Thus, the following sections focus on three key systems—welfare, disability assistance, and criminal justice—that serve substantial numbers of the hard-to-employ. Although the timing and the specific issues differ, each system has struggled to balance a focus on employment for its "clients" with other, potentially competing elements of its mission.

Interestingly, one could argue that the importance of these three systems to the overall hard-to-employ issue is inversely related to the amount of attention the systems have received from policymakers and the media in recent years. The welfare system received extensive coverage for many years (though somewhat less so lately) but directly affects the fewest people. The criminal justice system affects a larger number of people and receives a great deal of general attention, but the subjects of rehabilitation and prisoner reentry have only recently reemerged in public debates after a long period of neglect. Finally, disability assistance programs may serve more people than the other two systems combined—and have grown very rapidly in recent years—but have received comparatively little attention of any kind.

THE WELFARE SYSTEM

The main cash assistance program for nondisabled adults, Temporary Assistance for Needy Families, mostly serves families headed by single mothers.[1] After a dramatic decline in the caseload during the second half of the 1990s, fewer than 2 million families remain on assistance today. Of these, nearly half are "child only" cases in which no adult is counted in the grant. Moreover, the TANF caseload is highly concentrated in a few states—about 45 percent of the national caseload is in California, New York, Texas, Ohio, and Pennsylvania. Combined federal and state spending on TANF is around $25 billion a year.

Many, perhaps most, people who ever receive TANF cash assistance might not be classified as hard to employ—they receive benefits for short periods after a personal or family crisis or because they lose a job and do not qualify for unemployment compensation. But a substantial share of the caseload at any time is made up of long-term recipients, many of whom face significant barriers to employment.

The Policy Context

Of the three systems discussed in this chapter, the welfare system has gone furthest in promoting work and self-sufficiency for its recipients. The first federal rules explicitly designed to promote work among welfare recipients emerged in the 1960s, though most states did not start to enforce work-related mandates for recipients until the 1980s. Although the welfare caseload has always included people with physical and mental health problems, educational deficits, and other employment barriers, recipients facing the most serious barriers were often exempted or deferred from mandatory participation in the early welfare-to-work programs.

In the 1990s, states, initially operating under waivers of federal rules, began to impose work requirements more broadly and to strengthen the penalties for noncompliance with those requirements. The federal Personal Responsibility and Work Opportunity Reconciliation Act of 1996, which further shaped state policies, limited exemptions from federal work requirements, imposed time limits on the receipt of federally funded assistance, and pushed states to emphasize quick employment. Narrower exemptions have pushed states and localities to work with more hard-to-employ recipients that were previously exempted or deferred, while the potential impact of time limits and stricter penalties for noncompliance (i.e., sanctions) on this more vulnerable population have raised the stakes for states to help these recipients become self-sufficient. TANF was reauthorized in early 2006, with new rules that could force states to engage an even greater share of their caseloads in work activities.

The unprecedented caseload declines in the 1990s led to a focus on two issues: the status of families that had left the rolls and the characteristics of those still receiving benefits. A number of states conducted "leavers studies," finding that a high percentage of leavers were employed, although many had difficulty sustaining employment and a minority were neither employed nor living with employed household members (Acs and Loprest 2001). Families that left assistance because of sanctions appear to have particularly low rates of employment, and several studies find that sanctioned recipients are much more likely than other leavers or current recipients to face various barriers to employment (Bloom and Winstead 2002).

Although program operators frequently report that individuals facing serious barriers to employment increasingly dominate the shrunken welfare caseload, some empirical studies have questioned this assumption (Moffitt and Stevens 2001). Nevertheless, it is undoubtedly true that because more hard-to-employ recipients are expected to work, line staff are more likely than in the past to be actively working with this group, and the barriers faced by hard-to-employ welfare recipients can be daunting. One study synthesized results from a common survey that was administered to welfare recipients in six states in 2002. It found that 40 percent of recipients across the six states lacked a high school diploma or GED, 21 percent had a physical health limitation, 30 percent met the diagnostic criteria for major depression or were experiencing severe psychological stress, and 29 percent had a child with health problems (Hauan and Douglas 2004).

Early welfare-to-work programs were designed as joint initiatives between the welfare system and the broader workforce development system. Over time, many state welfare agencies assumed control over employment programming for their caseloads (often through contracts with nonprofit organizations, community colleges, or other entities). During the past few years, as states have increasingly begun to work with recipients facing more severe barriers, welfare agencies have again begun to look outward, to agencies and systems with more specialized expertise—notably vocational rehabilitation, mental health and substance abuse treatment, and domestic violence agencies.

What We Know

Over the past 30 years, a series of random assignment studies has provided a rich body of evidence about the effectiveness of different kinds of employment interventions for welfare recipients, including those who face severe obstacles to finding and sustaining employment.

Most of the rigorous studies looked at broad-coverage welfare-to-work programs that served a wide array of recipients and mandated participation in job search activities, vocational training, adult basic education, or, in a few cases, unpaid work experience (i.e., workfare). Some programs used a fixed sequence of activities for all or most recipients while others used various assessments to sort recipients into different service tracks. An analysis of the results of 20 broad coverage programs for various subgroups concluded that the programs increased earnings about as much for the most disadvantaged recipients (defined as long-term welfare recipients with no high school degree and no recent work history) as for less disadvantaged groups. Individuals in the most disadvantaged subgroup, however, earned only about one-sixth as much as those in the least disadvantaged group, indicating that the programs left many in the most disadvantaged group far from self-sufficiency—and these programs, mostly operating in the late 1980s and early 1990s, typically did not serve people with serious physical or mental health problems. The most effective programs used a mix of job search activities and short-term education and training, while maintaining a strong emphasis on employment (Michalopoulos and Schwartz 2000).

Other studies examined programs that supplemented the earnings of welfare recipients to encourage work and increase income. These programs also raised employment levels and earnings, and the effects for the most disadvantaged recipients—those least likely to work in the absence of the programs—were, if anything, larger than for other subgroups. Again, however, the outcome levels for the most disadvantaged were quite low (Michalopoulos 2005).

There have been far fewer studies of welfare-to-work initiatives targeted to specific hard-to-employ subgroups within the welfare population. The National Supported Work Demonstration, implemented in the 1970s, still provides the most comprehensive evidence about the effects of an employment program specifically targeted to long-term welfare recipients (as well as three other hard-to-employ groups). In the supported work model, participants were typically assigned to work crews, and workplace demands were gradually increased over time. Revenues from the goods and services produced by participants helped finance the programs, as did welfare grant diversion. The supported work model had its largest impacts on post-program employment and earnings for the long-term welfare recipient target group. Impacts appeared particularly large for the most disadvantaged recipients within the group (e.g., very long term recipients and those with no high school diploma). Supported work was expensive—more than $20,000 per person in today's dollars—but the value of the output produced by participants was also substantial (Manpower Demonstration Research Corporation Board of Directors 1980).

A more recent study, the Substance Abuse Research Demonstration, evaluated a case management intervention for female substance abusers on TANF in New Jersey. The intervention used a combination of services and sanctions or incentives to get these women to first participate in treatment and then transition to employment and leave welfare. The program increased participation in treatment and led to some reductions in substance use, but these gains did not translate into positive impacts on work and training participation (Morgenstern et al. 2002).

The knowledge base about programs for specialized populations will likely grow substantially in the near future. As part of two multisite research projects, the U.S. Department of Health and Human Services (HHS) is sponsoring several random assignment evaluations that will yield results in the coming years. These include studies of a large-scale employment program for welfare recipients with work-limiting medical conditions, a case management program for welfare recipients with substance abuse problems (similar to the New Jersey project described above), a telephonic care management program for Medicaid recipients with depression, and a test of alternative employment strategies for long-term TANF recipients. One strategy being tested in the latter study is a large-scale transitional employment program in which participants are placed in temporary, wage-paying jobs in nonprofit or public agencies and receive a range of supports. Some experts see transitional employment as a particularly promising employment strategy for hard-to-employ groups (Kirby et al. 2002; Waller 2002).

In addition to providing new evidence on the effectiveness of various approaches for "special populations," these studies will say a great deal about the challenges involved in creating and managing interagency links. For example, some of the HHS-sponsored studies mentioned earlier will examine the differences in philosophy and practice among the welfare, vocational rehabilitation, and substance abuse treatment systems.

THE DISABILITY ASSISTANCE SYSTEM

Two major federal programs provide cash assistance for people with disabilities.[2] The Supplemental Security Income program is the means-tested income assistance program that provides cash assistance to people over the age of 65 or people under 65 who are blind or disabled. The Social Security Disability Insurance program is the disability insurance program for working-age adults and their dependents. SSDI has no means test, but benefits are only paid if an individual has worked long enough in covered employment to be insured. These two programs dwarf TANF, with a combined 10 million working-age recipients and benefit expenditures exceeding $100 billion a year.

The disability eligibility criteria are the same in both programs. To qualify for benefits, a disability must be *permanent and severe* enough to prevent someone from engaging in "substantial gainful activity." But the populations in the two programs differ somewhat. By virtue of the eligibility criteria, most SSDI recipients have substantial work histories. In contrast, SSI recipients are likely to have lower skills and less work experience in addition to their health problems.

In either case, it is difficult to know what proportion of disability recipients can in fact work—and how much work can reasonably be expected of this group. We know, however, that disability is not a static condition: many disorders abate, recur, and newly emerge. In addition, some percentage of the DI caseload—estimates are as high as 75 percent—will experience some type of full or partial recovery during their spell (Benitez-Silva, Buchinsky, and Rust 2003).

Policy Trends

Despite 20 years of advocacy and legislation designed to expand employment opportunities for the disabled (e.g., the Americans with Disabilities Act, New Freedom Initiative, Ticket to Work), the number of people with disabilities who work has remained persistently low, and the disabled have become increasingly dependent on SSI and SSDI for income support. During the economic boom of the 1990s, when employment increased for almost all groups, it declined among people with disabilities, and their poverty rates went up. During the decade when welfare caseloads declined by half, the numbers of SSDI and SSI beneficiaries almost doubled (Stapleton and Burkhauser 2003).

There are competing theories about why the caseloads have been increasing, as well as why employment rates among adults with disabilities have declined.[3] Whatever the explanation, it is unlikely the trend will reverse in the near future since very few beneficiaries of disability benefits work. Only about 7 percent of SSI beneficiaries work part-time while receiving benefits, and less than 1 percent ever leave the rolls because of excessive income. Employment rates among SSDI beneficiaries are even lower.

Surprisingly, the recent growth in the disability programs has managed for the most part to avoid serious budgetary and political scrutiny. It is hard to imagine that it will continue to do so for much longer in this environment of expanding deficits, calls for reforms in Social Security retirement programs, and enormous new budget pressures from national security and disaster relief. Thus, there is a compelling need to learn if more disability beneficiaries can work and reduce their dependence on cash assistance without increasing poverty and to learn which policy options are likely to be most effective.

The Social Security Administration (SSA) has focused on three basic approaches to try to increase employment:

- **Incentives.** In recent years, SSA has implemented policy changes to decrease work disincentives by allowing beneficiaries to keep more benefits when they work, expanding the availability of health coverage and other supports for beneficiaries who leave the rolls, and making it easier for people who lose their jobs to quickly get back on benefits. Some of these policy changes are generous (for example, eight years of continued Medicare eligibility for employed SSDI beneficiaries who leave the rolls) and provide potentially strong work incentives.
- **Increasing participation in employment supports.** The Ticket to Work program has been the primary SSA initiative intended to expand program options and choice, but program implementation has turned out to be a massive and difficult undertaking. In theory, all SSI and SSDI beneficiaries are eligible for vocational rehabilitation (VR) services, but state VR agencies typically have long waiting lists. Also, applications can be denied if the VR agency can show that the applicant is unlikely to benefit from services. VR agencies have an incentive to be selective since, under Ticket to Work rules, they are only paid for getting jobs for beneficiaries who earn enough to lose cash benefits. Initiatives designed to better coordinate existing services have been more promising and have led to some increased participation, especially when benefit counseling about SSA rules and incentives was combined with services planning and case management.
- **Targeting specific groups for early intervention.** One ambitious new initiative is the Youth Transition Demonstration (YTD), which targets youth age 14–25 who are on SSI or at risk of entering the system. YTD is intended to improve outcomes by removing barriers to accessing existing education and employment services, adding services to fill unmet needs, changing SSI rules that discourage work and education, and counseling families about the economic and other implications of transition. YTD will be tested in a random assignment evaluation. SSA is testing a different strategy in the SSDI program with the Accelerated Benefits Demonstration. This project will use a random assignment design to assess the impact on employment, health, and benefit receipt of allowing new beneficiaries with certain health conditions to receive immediate health coverage (rather than waiting 29 months as under current rules).

All these strategies hold promise, though it is unclear whether these incremental approaches can significantly increase employment or service participation in a voluntary system, given the contradictory messages about work and disability. As long as being permanently disabled and unable to work are the defining conditions of eligibility for benefits, it will be difficult to persuade beneficiaries to increase their work effort.

What We Know

The limited evidence from evaluations of programs for people with disabilities suggests that employment rates can be increased in this population, more so perhaps through interventions that operate outside the benefit system. However, the employment gains generated by all these programs were mostly through part-time work with low hours.

Structured Training and Employment Services (STETS), a supported work program for mentally retarded youth tested in the early 1980s, had impressive impacts on employment and earnings and was a major influence on policy and practice in the disability field for years (Kerachsky et al. 1985). Another very successful program that has been rigorously evaluated is the Individual Placement and Support (IPS) model of supported employment. Designed for adults with severe mental illness, IPS is a work-first approach that relies on rapid placement in unsubsidized jobs coupled with postemployment supports and accommodations. This model had large effects on earnings and employment compared with other program models, including preemployment training and transitional work (Bond et al. 1999).

Both IPS and STETS were "stand-alone" programs that recruited and selected volunteers from the community. They did not operate inside the SSI system or attempt to reach a broader group of beneficiaries. Since many of the rules and operations of the benefit system are themselves significant employment barriers, it is important to also look at programs that have operated in the system. Only a handful of these studies have been done, but the story has been largely one of low participation rates, small impacts on earnings and employment, and no reductions in disability benefits. Even the more substantial earnings and employment gains experienced by a few subgroups in these studies translated into negligible reductions in benefit payments. This was because most working participants had earnings below the threshold that would result in losing benefits (Decker and Thornton 1995).

Fortunately, more data about the effectiveness of employment-oriented strategies operating within the disability system will be forthcoming in the next few years. SSA has initiated an ambitious set of demonstration projects with rigorous evaluations, some of which were mentioned earlier.

THE CRIMINAL JUSTICE SYSTEM

For better or worse, the criminal justice system is one of the only public systems that has extensive interaction with hard-to-employ men who are not disabled and do not live with their children (the child support enforcement system is another). After a 25-year incarceration binge, more than 2 million people—1 out of every 140 U.S. residents—are currently incarcerated in state and federal prisons and local jails, and more than 5 million adults have previously been incarcerated. The growth in incarceration has disproportionately affected African American men. One recent study found that 20 percent of black men born between 1965 and 1969 had served time in prison by their early 30s; among black men born during that period who were high school dropouts, a staggering 60 percent had been incarcerated by 1999 (Pettit and Western 2004).

Since almost all prisoners are eventually released, an incarceration boom necessarily translates into a reentry boom. In fact, some 630,000 people are released from prison or jail each year. Unfortunately, most end up back in the criminal justice system before long: two-thirds of released prisoners are rearrested within three years, and half return to prison (Langan and Levin 2002).

States and localities bear most of the budgetary costs of incarceration: in 2004, states spent about $41 billion on corrections, a total that does not include the cost of arresting and trying the people who are eventually incarcerated (National Association of State Budget Officers 2005).

Policy Trends

For most of the 20th century, rehabilitation and reintegration were central to the mission of the criminal justice system. This began to change in the 1970s, when "other concepts—just desserts, retribution, and incapacitation for crime control purposes" began to dominate public discussions and state laws (Travis 2005, xix). States and the federal government began to institute mandatory minimum sentences, eliminate or restrict discretionary parole, and create a new set of "collateral sanctions"—for example, by making convicted felons ineligible for certain public assistance and student loan programs, denying them the right to vote, and restricting them from holding many kinds of jobs.

During a period when the prison population grew dramatically, employment and other services for prisoners were scaled back, and parole agencies began to focus more on monitoring and surveillance and less on providing services to aid the reentry process. Parole officers' caseloads are typically quite large, and the rules they must enforce—for example, curfews and reporting requirements—can, in some instances, restrict employment opportunities. Today, about one-third of prison admissions are for technical violations of parole conditions, rather than convictions for new crimes (Petersilia 2003).

The pendulum has begun to swing back in the past few years, thanks in part to the work of Jeremy Travis and others who have focused public attention on the issue of prisoner reentry (see, for example, Travis 2005 and Petersilia 2003). State budget problems have helped create an eager audience for this message since breaking the cycle of recidivism is one clear way to shrink the prison population and reduce corrections costs.

But the high budgetary cost of incarceration is only one reason it makes sense to try to improve reentry outcomes. Obviously, public safety will be improved if released prisoners commit fewer crimes. And it is becoming increasingly clear that mass incarceration can have devastating effects on families and communities. At least half of state prisoners are parents and, while research on this topic is still limited, some studies suggest that parental incarceration may be associated with negative outcomes for children (Parke and Clarke-Stewart 2003). It is also clear that prisoners disproportionately come from—and return to—particular inner-city neighborhoods that also experience high rates of public assistance receipt, single parenthood, and other social problems (Cadora 2003; Clear, Rose, and Ryder 2001). Very high levels of incarceration may further erode the fabric of these communities, exacerbating these problems.

Ex-prisoners face daunting obstacles to successful reentry, but employment may be the biggest challenge of all. Most released prisoners have characteristics that limit their employability—low levels of education and work experience, health problems, substance abuse, or mental illness—and a large proportion are members of racial and ethnic groups that experience employment discrimination. Unfortunately, the blue-collar jobs that might best suit released prisoners are increasingly scarce, while the sectors least likely to hire this population are growing fastest.

And then there are the direct effects of incarceration. As noted earlier, many states have enacted laws that prohibit people with prior convictions from working in certain jobs. More broadly, studies have shown that employers consider individuals with criminal records among the least desirable job applicants, with black ex-prisoners experiencing a double dose of employment discrimination (Holzer, Raphael, and Stoll 2003; Pager 2003). In other words, individuals often enter the criminal justice system hard to employ and emerge even harder to employ.

What We Know

Evidence indicating that people with criminal records have a difficult time in the labor market does not necessarily mean that improving the employment rates and earnings of ex-prisoners will reduce recidivism.

Nevertheless, there is a strong theoretical link between employment and crime, and many reentry programs focus on employment as a key strategy for improving reentry outcomes.

Unfortunately there is very little hard evidence about effective employment-oriented reentry strategies. In the 1970s, a controversial research review helped buttress the retreat from rehabilitation by concluding that prison-based education and training did little to reduce recidivism (Martinson 1974).

There have been many studies since that time, but the evidence base remains very thin. Several recent reviews and meta-analyses have examined the results of dozens of evaluations of work-focused reentry programs. For example, Wilson, Gallagher, and MacKenzie (2000) analyze the results of 33 evaluations of corrections-based education, training, and work programs. The authors conclude that, overall, the programs reduced recidivism. But Wilson and colleagues also note that almost all the evaluation designs were weak, limiting the authors' ability to draw firm conclusions about program effectiveness.

Similarly, Visher, Winterfield, and Coggeshall (2005) examine the impact of community-based employment programs that served people with a criminal record and were evaluated using random assignment designs. They find only eight relevant studies and conclude that, overall, these programs did not reduce recidivism. However, they also note that the research evidence is limited and that many promising new programs have not been evaluated.

Reflecting on many of these results, Bushway (2003) speculates that employment-oriented programs may "only help offenders who have taken the first step and are motivated to stop offending" (8). He notes that a reanalysis of results from the National Supported Work Demonstration by Uggen (2000) concluded that this program, which had no impact on recidivism for the ex-offender target group, had positive results for individuals over 26 years old, a group more likely to have matured enough to have decided to "go straight." Bushway concludes that reentry programs may need to focus on "motivating individuals to change rather than simply providing skills or a job" (9).

As in the welfare and disability systems, the recent surge of interest in prisoner reentry has triggered a new round of rigorous research. For example, the U.S. Department of Health and Human Services is sponsoring a random assignment study of the Center for Employment Opportunities, a large-scale transitional employment program for ex-prisoners, the U.S. Department of Justice is leading a multiagency test of reentry programs for violent offenders, and the Joyce Foundation is sponsoring a random assignment study of reentry programs using a transitional employment model. These studies should begin to yield results in the coming years.

WHAT NEXT?

Demographic trends could soon create a rare opportunity to bring traditionally excluded groups into the economic mainstream. Policymakers and administrators will need to take affirmative steps to make this outcome more likely, and the welfare, disability, and criminal justice systems will need to play key roles in this process.

The rest of the chapter suggests three parallel tracks for action, based on the framework described earlier. First, some key systems that serve the hard-to-employ will need to change in order to promote the goal of employment for their "clients." Second, policymakers will need to continue building supports for low-wage workers that both improve the incentives to work and allow individuals to survive with low earnings. Third, researchers should continue to build knowledge about the most effective service strategies for addressing the employment barriers laid out at the beginning of the chapter.

Systems Change

This chapter has emphasized the importance of seeing employment initiatives for the hard-to-employ in the context of the public benefit and enforcement systems in which they operate. These systems, for better or worse, will help determine the success of efforts to increase employment, and the chapter has discussed various ways in which the rules and operations of the disability assistance and criminal justice systems can create additional employment barriers for their "clients."

The most difficult barriers emerge when efforts to encourage and support employment interfere with the ability of these systems to fulfill their core missions, either in practical ways—for example, by increasing the workload of an overburdened parole system—or by creating a systems version of cognitive dissonance, for example by expecting the disability system to encourage employment when eligibility for benefits is based on permanent disability. Overcoming these mission-driven barriers may ultimately be impossible unless the criminal justice and disability assistance systems are prepared for fundamental changes that make employment and self-sufficiency part of their core missions.

But are these systems changes realistic? Are they affordable, and will the public support them? Can they be implemented without undermining the ability of programs for people with disabilities to provide financial support or the ability of the criminal justice system to protect public safety? And is it more than a blind leap of faith to think that these kinds of changes will make a significant difference in employment outcomes? These complex questions can only be answered if we are prepared to test alternative approaches. But the experience of the welfare system is instructive since it shows that it is possible to change systems and make employment a central mission-driven goal while continuing to address the core responsibilities of an income assistance program.

There is an anecdote from the early 1980s about a deputy welfare commissioner with an artistic flair who would display a large drawing he made to demonstrate his agency's success in managing what was then termed the "recipient employability pool." The elaborate illustration of an actual swimming pool with swimmers in different parts of the pool was designed to show that he could account in detail for all the employability statuses of his large caseload. As the story goes, he once proudly showed his drawing to a senior government official, who responded with some surprise, "That's very impressive but what about employment: how many people did you help finds jobs?" The deputy commissioner replied, "I don't know, we don't track that, employment isn't our responsibility." Certainly today, or probably at any time over the past 15 years, such a response might have cost the deputy commissioner his job.

This may not seem very remarkable now, 10 years after the passage of national welfare reform, but one should recall that during the 1970s and '80s, considerable doubts were expressed about whether such a change was possible or even desirable. The same questions posed above about the feasibility of mission change in the disability and criminal justice systems were raised then about welfare. If the system reduced its focus on controlling error rates and fraud and abuse, some argued, this would further undermine public confidence and support for an already beleaguered benefit program. Others were skeptical that the system could be changed given an entrenched culture of practices, rules, and attitudes that discouraged employment.

History has proven these skeptics wrong, and the welfare system has been able to make employment an integral part of its core mission. And while we cannot know to what extent the increases in employment and reductions in caseloads in the 1990s are the result of changes in the welfare system versus the strong economy or other factors, most researchers agree that the impact of systems change was considerable.

It would be a mistake to push the welfare analogy too far. Many would argue, with fairly convincing evidence, that the welfare system has tipped the balance too far, in some cases neglecting its original mission of providing income assistance. Moreover, unlike ex-prisoners and people with disabilities, welfare recipients had considerable work experience and capacity to build on. In other words, the leap of faith was a smaller one, as were the risks of failure. Nevertheless, it would be useful to examine whether lessons from the welfare system are directly applicable to the disability and criminal justice systems.

The first step may be to alter each system's understanding of its responsibilities. Once this occurs, and is broadly accepted by the key stakeholders in the system, administrators will begin to respond with operational changes that will ripple throughout the systems. Not so long ago, as the earlier anecdote illustrated, most welfare administrators believed they had no control over how many of their clients found jobs—just as police departments may have believed they could not prevent crimes from being committed. In both instances, once it was accepted that these outcomes could and should be achieved, the systems had the impetus to align policies, operating practices, accountability systems, and staff incentives to promote these outcomes.

If the parole system's effectiveness were measured by the number of people who successfully completed parole, or the disability system was evaluated based on the number of recipients who worked at least part-time, administrators might begin to make operational changes to promote those goals. Parole officers might develop better links with local workforce development and mental health treatment agencies, and disability program staff might find better ways to explain and market the work incentives that have recently been built into their programs. Pressure from criminal justice agencies and disability programs might, in turn, force service systems like vocational rehabilitation, workforce development, and substance abuse treatment to focus more on achieving employment outcomes for hard-to-employ groups.

Ultimately, a change in mission might even trigger bigger changes— or at least experimentation. For example, disability programs could introduce participation requirements modeled on the welfare system. Though likely to be controversial, this approach may be worth testing.

Another even more ambitious approach would be to test a two-tiered disability system that would start everyone in a temporary, time-limited program requiring beneficiaries to participate in rehabilitation, receive regular assessments, and prepare for reemployment. Those who demonstrate that they cannot work would become eligible for permanent disability benefits. Others would return to full employment and benefits would end. This alternative model would resolve the contradiction in the current system of expecting people to work who have proven they are permanently unable to work. Proponents of a two-tiered approach point to examples from several European countries (e.g., Germany, Sweden, and the Netherlands) that successfully return many people with disabilities to work from the temporary program.

Similarly, in the criminal justice system, redefinition of the mission might eventually lead to larger changes in state policy (these changes are already beginning in some places). For example, a system with the goal of successful reintegration might reconsider "collateral sanctions" such as restrictions on employment, voting, and housing assistance that have no obvious public safety benefit and that may well make successful transitions more difficult.

Work Supports

In a labor market increasingly bifurcated along skill lines, many of the hard-to-employ will only be able to obtain low-paying jobs. Thus, work supports are particularly critical for this population.

Most analysts agree that financial incentives played a key role in driving the increases in labor force participation among single mothers and the corresponding welfare caseload declines in the 1990s (Hotz and Scholz 2003). The welfare system included both financial sticks and carrots—harsher penalties for noncompliance with work-related requirements and new rules allowing recipients to keep more of their benefits when they go to work (i.e., earnings disregards). Perhaps even more important were changes outside the welfare system that built new work supports for recipients who left the rolls for low-wage jobs. The 1993 expansion of the earned income tax credit, broader eligibility for publicly funded health insurance (particularly for children), and increased state and federal spending on child care assistance altered the benefit-cost calculation for recipients considering work. There are still important gaps in this package of supports, but the incentives are certainly much better aligned than they were 20 years ago.

As discussed earlier, the disability system is now experimenting with some of the same changes instituted in the welfare system: allowing beneficiaries to keep more benefits when they work, expanding the availability of health coverage and other supports for beneficiaries who leave the rolls, and making it easier for people who lose their jobs to quickly get back on benefits. The challenge is certainly greater in the disability system, but these steps are nonetheless important.

Work incentives are much less favorable for returning prisoners. The extensive set of work supports described earlier is targeted mostly to custodial parents. The earned income tax credit for childless workers is quite small, and eligibility for Medicaid coverage for adults working in low-wage jobs is still limited. Moreover, many ex-prisoners have substantial child support obligations, including current support orders and huge arrearages that may have accumulated while they were incarcerated. Some believe that recent improvements in the child support enforcement system's ability to locate noncustodial parents and garnish their wages drive low-income absent fathers out of the formal labor market (Holzer, Offner, and Sorensen 2005). This tendency, in turn, may reduce the likelihood that these men will stay out of the criminal justice system.

There have been several proposals for changes in tax policies that would improve the work incentives facing ex-prisoners, particularly those with child support obligations. Most recently, New York Governor George Pataki proposed a state tax credit for noncustodial parents who meet their child support obligations. It might also be worth considering a transitional earnings supplement for recently released prisoners working in low-wage jobs. There are valid arguments against such policies, and they could produce unintended side effects and would certainly cost a substantial amount. Nevertheless, at a minimum, a rigorous experiment seems worthwhile.

In addition to the nature of the work supports themselves, it is critical to consider how they are administered. Currently, no single agency sees supporting the working poor as its primary mission. Some supports are delivered through the welfare system, but many working poor are reluctant to become involved with that system. Some have argued that it makes more sense to build a focus on work supports into the operation of the workforce development system, which can also deliver services designed to promote employment retention and career advancement.

Finally, it is important to consider the other side of coin—incentives, usually in the form of targeted tax credits, designed to persuade employers to hire members of disadvantaged groups. These chapter authors view those approaches with some skepticism. A recent report reviewed the research on the targeted jobs tax credit, which existed from 1978 to 1994, and conducted new analysis on the current work opportunity and welfare-to-work tax credits. In short, there is very little evidence that these credits appreciably change employer hiring practices (Hamersma 2005). This view is supported by anecdotal evidence from many discussions with job developers in employment programs, who typically say that tax credits can be useful "perks" but rarely persuade an employer to make a hire. At least one study suggests that these tax credits can make disadvantaged job seekers less employable by labeling them as potentially problematic employees.[4]

On the other hand, more research is needed on one particular employer-targeted policy—the federal bonding program, which offers fidelity bonds to anyone ineligible for commercial bonding. In theory, this program should make ex-prisoners less undesirable to employers. Research is needed to better understand how extensively the program is used, whether its administration could be improved, and whether it affects hiring decisions (if employers are reluctant to hire ex-prisoners because they think they will be unreliable employees, the bond will not make much difference).

Building Knowledge

The brief review of research evidence embedded in the earlier sections of this chapter suggests that we know a fair amount about how to address some key barriers facing the hard-to-employ. For example, a great deal is known about the most effective treatments for health, mental health, and substance abuse problems. We also know a lot about how to run effective labor exchange programs and strong supported and transitional employment programs (although we need to learn more about which groups benefit most from these models). Similarly, the disability field has made significant strides in developing technologies for assisted employment and workplace accommodations. In short, we know a lot about how to treat health problems and how to connect people with jobs.

In other key areas, however, the knowledge base is much thinner. Thus, along with efforts to reform systems and improve incentives, it will be critical to continue building evidence about the most effective service strategies for the hard-to-employ. Three examples follow.

First, we know considerably less about how to build skills than about how to connect people with jobs. Evaluation evidence from the welfare system has largely discouraged the use of mainstream adult basic education programs for recipients with very low reading and math skills. Recipients who were required to participate in such programs usually left them quickly without building their skills much. Similarly, there are few examples of successful vocational training models for high school dropouts. The good news is that many of the hard-to-employ may be able to find jobs even without building their skills—and the emerging system of work supports will supplement their earnings. But it will be very hard for these individuals to move up to middle-class wages without further education or training. Many individual programs and experts claim to know a great deal about how to successfully teach low-skilled adults, but there is little hard evidence to validate these approaches.

Second, we need to learn more about how to connect people with the efficacious medical treatments mentioned earlier. The health and behavioral health fields have been grappling for years with the challenge of how to increase engagement and ongoing participation in treatment and get patients to adhere to appropriate treatment guidelines. The criminal justice, disability, and welfare systems now face the challenge as well for their hard-to-employ populations, as health, mental health, and substance abuse treatment have increasingly become an important part of their efforts to increase employment.

The obstacles to participation are many and varied, depending upon the nature of the health problem itself, the availability and accessibility of services, and the attitudes and motivations of individuals with the condition. Whatever the particulars, it appears that without considerable support, guidance, and encouragement many people are not able to stay engaged in treatment. One promising strategy that has emerged to address this problem is the use of care managers to encourage people to accept the need for treatment, help them access care, monitor their progress, and keep them engaged. More research is needed to understand which specific strategies are most effective.

Finally, we need to learn more about how to assess employment barriers. One common strategy is to place people in structured work activities for limited periods, generally without prior screening and assessment, and evaluate their job performance to assess employment skills, productivity, and level of work readiness. This approach provides practical information about work capacity and limitations but is less useful as tool for understanding *why* someone is unable to work.

The other common approach relies on various screening and clinical or vocational assessments to identify employment barriers and determine employability. Such assessments are clearly necessary to determine who may need treatment services, but they are not especially useful in sorting out who can work. Extensive screening for barriers can also shift the focus of staff and participants away from employment. Further evidence is needed on the most effective ways to combine these two approaches.

Fortunately, as noted in earlier sections, the surge of interest in the hard-to-employ has triggered a new round of rigorous research, much of it federally funded, that will address these and other key issues. It will be critical to translate what is learned into concrete lessons for policy and practice, and to continue building knowledge as we move forward. A growing base of knowledge about what works, along with the systems changes and expanded work supports discussed earlier, could make a real difference in improving the employment and life prospects of the hard-to-employ.

NOTES

1. Some states still have General Assistance programs that provide cash assistance to nondisabled adults ineligible for TANF, but these programs have been drastically scaled back in the past two decades. (See, for example, Zimmermann and Tumlin 1999).

2. In fact, more than 200 federal programs provide assistance to people with disabilities; these two programs are the largest.

3. For example, Autor and Duggan (2002) argue that caseload increases are explained by more liberal disability program rules combined with declining employment opportunities for the low-skilled unemployed.

4. Similarly, some believe that regulations stemming from the Americans with Disabilities Act, designed to promote employment among people with disabilities, have actually made employers less likely to hire the disabled because of concerns about the costs of required workplace accommodations (DeLeire 2003).

REFERENCES

Acs, Gregory, and Pamela Loprest. 2001. "Initial Synthesis Report of the Findings from ASPE's 'Leavers' Grants." Washington, DC: The Urban Institute.

Autor, David H., and Mark G. Duggan. 2003. "The Rise in the Disability Rolls and the Decline in Unemployment." *Quarterly Journal of Economics* 118(1): 157–205.

Benitez-Silva, Hugo, Moshe Buchinsky, and John Rust. 2003. "Using a Life-Cycle Model to Predict Induced Entry Effects into the SSDI Program." Manuscript, Department of Economics, Stony Brook University.

Bloom, Dan, and Don Winstead. 2002. "Sanctions and Welfare Reform." In *Welfare Reform and Beyond: The Future of the Safety Net*, edited by Ron Haskins, Andrea Kane, Isabel V. Sawhill, and R. Kent Weaver (49–58). Washington, DC: Brookings Institution Press.

Bond, Gary R., Robert E. Drake, Deborah R. Becker, and Kim T. Mueser. 1999. "Effectiveness of Psychiatric Rehabilitation Approaches for Employment of People with Severe Mental Illness." *Journal of Disability Policy Studies* 10(1): 18–52.

Bushway, Shawn. 2003. "Reentry and Prison Work Programs." Paper presented at the Urban Institute Reentry Roundtable "Employment Dimensions of Reentry: Understanding the Nexus between Prisoner Reentry and Work," New York, May 19–20.

Cadora, Eric, with Charles Swartz and Mannix Gordon. 2003. "Criminal Justice and Health and Human Services: An Exploration of Overlapping Needs, Resources, and Interests in Brooklyn Neighborhoods." In *Prisoners Once Removed*, edited by Jeremy Travis and Michelle Waul (285–311). Washington, DC: Urban Institute Press.

Clear, Todd R., Dina Rose, and J. Ryder. 2001. "Incarceration and Community: The Problem of Removing and Returning Offenders." *Crime and Delinquency* 47(3): 335–51.

Decker, Paul, and Craig Thornton. 1995. "The Long-Term Effects of Transitional Employment Service." *Social Security Bulletin* 58(3): 71–81.

DeLeire, Thomas. 2003. "The Americans with Disabilities Act and the Employment of People with Disabilities." In *The Decline in Employment of People with Disabilities: A Policy Puzzle*, edited by David C. Stapleton and Richard V. Burkhauser. Kalamazoo, MI: W.E. Upjohn Institute for Employment Research.

Hamersma, Sarah. 2005. "The Work Opportunity and Welfare-to-Work Tax Credits." Tax Policy Issues and Options Brief 15. Washington, DC: The Urban Institute.

Hauan, Susan, and Sarah Douglas. 2004. "Potential Employment Liabilities among TANF Recipients: A Synthesis of Data from Six State TANF

Caseload Studies." Washington, DC: U.S. Department of Health and Human Services, Office of the Assistant Secretary for Planning and Evaluation.

Holzer, Harry J., Paul Offner, and Elaine Sorensen. 2005. "Declining Employment among Young Black Less-Educated Men: The Role of Incarceration and Child Support." *Journal of Policy Analysis and Management* 24(2): 329–50.

Holzer, Harry J., Steven Raphael, and Michael A. Stoll. 2003. "Employment Barriers Facing Ex-Offenders." Paper presented at the Urban Institute Reentry Roundtable "Employment Dimensions of Reentry: Understanding the Nexus between Prisoner Reentry and Work," New York, May 19–20.

Hotz, V. Joseph, and John Karl Scholz. 2003. "The Earned Income Tax Credit." In *Means-Tested Transfer Programs in the United States*, edited by Robert A. Moffitt (141–97). Chicago: University of Chicago Press.

Kerachsky, Stuart, Craig Thorntorn, Anne Bloomenthal, Rebecca Maynard, and Susan Stephens. 1985. "The Impacts of Transitional Employment for Mentally Retarded Young Adults: Results from the STETS Demonstration." New York: Manpower Demonstration Research Corporation.

Kirby, Gretchen, Heather Hill, LaDonna Pavetti, Jon Jacobson, Michelle Derr, and Pamela Winston. 2002. *Transitional Jobs: Stepping Stones to Unsubsidized Employment*. Princeton, NJ: Mathematica Policy Research, Inc.

Langan, Patrick A., and David J. Levin. 2002. "Recidivism of Prisoners Released in 1994." Bureau of Justice Statistics Special Report. NCJ 193427. Washington, DC: U.S. Department of Justice, Bureau of Justice Statistics.

Manpower Demonstration Research Corporation Board of Directors. 1980. *Summary and Findings of the National Supported Work Demonstration*. Cambridge, MA: Ballinger Publishing Company.

Martinson, Robert. 1974. "What Works? Questions and Answers about Prison Reform." *The Public Interest* 35: 22–54.

Michalopoulos, Charles. 2005. *Does Making Work Still Pay?* New York: MDRC.

Michalopoulos, Charles, and Christine Schwartz. 2000. "What Works Best for Whom: Impacts of 20 Welfare-to-Work Programs by Subgroup." Washington, DC: U.S. Department of Health and Human Services and U.S. Department of Education.

Moffitt, Robert, and David Stevens. 2001. "Changing Caseloads: Macro Influences and Micro Composition." Chicago: Joint Center for Poverty Research.

Morgenstern, Jon, Kimberly Blanchard, Katharine McVeigh, Annette Riordan, and Barbara McCrady. 2002. "Intensive Case Management Improves Substance Abuse and Employment Outcomes of Female Welfare Recipients." Washington, DC: Office of Planning, Research, and Evaluation, Administration for Children and Families, U.S. Department of Health and Human Services.

Morris, Pamela A., Lisa Gennetian, and Virginia Knox. 2002. "Welfare Policies Matter for Children and Youth." New York: Manpower Demonstration Research Corporation.

National Association of State Budget Officers. 2005. *2004 State Expenditure Report*. Washington, DC: National Association of State Budget Officers.

Pager, Devah. 2003. "The Mark of a Criminal Record." *American Journal of Sociology* 108(5): 937–75.

Parke, Ross D., and K. Alison Clarke-Stewart. 2003. "The Effects of Parental Incarceration on Children: Perspectives, Promises, and Policies." In *Prisoners Once Removed*, edited by Jeremy Travis and Michelle Waul (189–232). Washington, DC: Urban Institute Press.

Petersilia, Joan. 2003. *When Prisoners Come Home: Parole and Prisoner Reentry.* New York: Oxford University Press.

Pettit, Becky, and Bruce Western. 2004. "Mass Imprisonment and the Life Course: Race and Class Inequality in U.S. Incarceration." *American Sociological Review* 69(2): 151–69.

Stapleton, David, and Richard V. Burkhauser. 2003. *The Decline in the Employment of People with Disabilities: A Policy Puzzle.* Kalamazoo, MI: W.E. Upjohn Institute for Employment Research.

Travis, Jeremy. 2005. *But They All Come Back: Facing the Challenges of Prisoner Reentry.* Washington, DC: Urban Institute Press.

Uggen, Christopher. 2000. "Work as a Turning Point in the Life Course of Criminals: A Duration Model of Age, Employment, and Recidivism." *American Sociological Review* 65(4): 529–46.

University of Michigan. 2004. "Women's Employment Study: Summary of Findings, 5 Survey Waves." Ann Arbor: Michigan Program on Poverty and Social Welfare Policy, Gerald R. Ford School of Public Policy, University of Michigan.

Visher, Christy, Laura Winterfield, and Mark Coggeshall. 2005. "Ex-Offender Employment Programs and Recidivism: A Meta-Analysis." *Journal of Experimental Criminology* 1(3): 295–315.

Waller, Margy. 2002. "Transitional Jobs: A Next Step in Welfare-to-Work Policy." Washington, DC: The Brookings Institution.

Wilson, David B., Catherine A. Gallagher, and Doris L. MacKenzie. 2000. "A Meta-Analysis of Corrections-Based Education, Vocation, and Work Programs for Adult Offenders." *Journal of Research in Crime and Delinquency* 37(4): 347–68.

Zimmermann, Wendy, and Karen Tumlin. 1999. *Patchwork Policies: State Assistance for Immigrants under Welfare Reform.* Washington, DC: The Urban Institute. *Assessing the New Federalism* Occasional Paper 24.

PART IV

OTHER POLICIES TO INCREASE THE SUPPLY OF SKILLS

7

IMMIGRATION POLICY AND HUMAN CAPITAL

George J. Borjas

The United States offers unequaled social, political, and economic opportunities to anyone lucky enough to enter its borders. Because of these opportunities, many more people want to come to the United States than the country is willing to admit. As an example of the excess demand for entry, consider the "diversity lottery" that the United States has held annually since 1995. Each year, some visas are made available to persons originating in "countries with low rates of immigration to the United States." Persons living in the eligible countries can apply for a random chance at winning one of the coveted entry visas. Potential migrants applied for the 2006 drawing by submitting an application between November 5, 2004, and January 7, 2005. This lottery drew 6.3 million qualified applications for the 50,000 available visas.

Because of the excess demand for entry visas, immigration policy has to specify rules to pick and choose from the many applicants. These rules may stress family ties (as is currently done for the bulk of legal immigrants), or national origin (as used to be done), or skills (as is done in other countries).

Before 1965, immigration to the United States was regulated by the "national origins quota system." In that system, the fixed number of entry visas was allocated on the basis of national origin, with each country's share depending on the representation of that ethnic group in the U.S. population as of 1920. As a result, Germany and the United Kingdom received almost two-thirds of the available visas. Immigration from Asia was effectively banned. Until the early 1960s, for instance, India and the Philippines were each allotted 100 visas annually. Finally, few persons migrated from Latin America. Although the national-origins quota system did not set a numerical limit on migration from countries in North and South America, the migration of Latin Americans may have been discouraged through unofficial means, such as consular officials simply refusing to grant entry visas to the applicants.

The resurgence of large-scale immigration has its roots in the 1965 amendments to the Immigration and Nationality Act. The 1965 amendments (and subsequent minor legislation) repealed the national origins quota system, set a worldwide numerical limit, and enshrined a new objective for awarding entry visas among the many applicants: the reunification of families. Congress passed the 1965 amendments when the civil rights movement was at its peak, and the legislation can be interpreted as one in the series of civil rights statutes enacted during that period.

As a result of the 1965 amendments, the United States sets aside the bulk of the visas (54 percent) to people who have relatives already residing in the country, including the adult children and siblings of U.S. citizens as well as the spouses and minor children of permanent resident aliens. "Immediate" relatives of U.S. citizens—such as spouses, parents, and minor children—are exempt from the numerical limits and are entitled to immediate entry. In the mid-1990s, 32 percent of the immigrants entered with an "immediate relative" visa that did not count against the limit, and over 70 percent entered through one of the family reunification provisions of the law.

The 1965 amendments also changed the national origin mix of the immigrant population. Over two-thirds of the legal immigrants admitted during the 1950s originated in Europe or Canada, 25 percent in Latin America, and 6 percent in Asia. By the 1990s, only 16 percent originated in Europe or Canada, 49 percent in Latin America, and 32 percent in Asia.

There has also been a substantial increase in illegal immigration. The latest wave of illegal immigration began in the late 1960s after the end of the bracero program, an agricultural guest worker program for Mexicans that was discontinued because of its perceived harm on the economic opportunities of competing native workers. To address the problems created by illegal immigration, Congress enacted the 1986 Immigration Reform and Control Act (IRCA). This legislation gave amnesty to 3 million illegal aliens and introduced a system of employer sanctions designed to stem the flow of additional illegal workers. This legislation obviously did not solve the illegal immigration problem. The most recent estimates indicate that over 10 million illegal immigrants resided in the United States as of 2003 (Passel 2005), with almost 60 percent originating in Mexico.

The 1965 policy shift had a historic impact on the number of immigrants living in the United States. Even though only 250,000 legal immigrants entered the country annually during the 1950s, almost 1 million were entering by the 1990s. Figure 7.1 illustrates the impact of this resurgence of legal immigration (combined with the remarkable increase in illegal immigration) on the immigrant presence in the labor market. In 1970, there were 3.2 million foreign-born workers in the labor market, accounting for 4.9 percent of the workforce. By 2000, there were 15.4 million foreign-born workers, accounting for 13.4 percent of the workforce.

This chapter summarizes how the large-scale resurgence of immigration to the United States altered the skill endowment of the U.S. workforce in the past three decades. As a result of this shift, the immigration policy pursued by the United States has dramatically increased the number of workers with very low levels of skills, defined here as educational attainment and years of work experience. This increase in

Figure 7.1. Immigration and the Workforce, 1960–2000

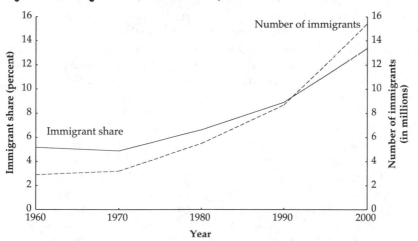

Source: Author's calculations from U.S. censuses.
Note: The workforce is all adults age 18 to 64 who are not enrolled in school and who worked in the civilian sector at least one week in the year before each decennial census.

less-skilled immigrants makes it increasingly more difficult and more expensive to pursue the kinds of equalizing human capital investment policies typically proposed in policy debates.

THE SKILLS OF IMMIGRANTS

The skill composition of the immigrant population—and, particularly, how the skills of immigrant workers compare with those of native workers—is the key determinant of the economic impact of immigration on the United States. The point that the *relative* skills of immigrants matter can be easily grasped through an example. Suppose that all the immigrants who entered the United States between 1940 and 2000 had 12 years of schooling. The labor market impact of immigration would differ greatly over time because most natives in 1940 were high school dropouts while most natives in 2000 had some college education. In 1940, immigration would increase the supply of relatively high-skilled workers; in 2000, immigration would increase the supply of relatively low-skilled workers.

The skill distribution of immigrants has consequences on the U.S. labor market. The relative skill mix of immigrants clearly determines which native workers are most affected by immigration. Low-skilled immigrants will typically harm low-skilled natives, while high-skilled immigrants will harm high-skilled natives. Skilled immigrants might also assimilate more quickly. They might be more adept at learning the tools and "tricks of the trade" that can increase the chances of economic success. In addition, the relative skills of immigrants determine the economic benefits from immigration. The United States may benefit from immigration because it can import workers with scarce qualifications and abilities. Because of the crucial role the relative skills of immigrants play in any analysis of the economic consequences of immigration, a great deal of research attempts to measure the level and trend in the relative skills of foreign-born workers in the United States.

The evidence in this chapter is based on data drawn from the 1960–2000 Integrated Public Use Microdata Series (IPUMS) of the U.S. Census.[1] Table 7.1 documents the trend in the distributions of educational attainment for native and immigrant workers. The table shows a significant decline in the *relative* education of the foreign-born workforce between 1960 and 2000. In 1960, for instance, 59.4 percent of immigrant workers were high school dropouts and 9.7 percent were college graduates. This educational mix was only slightly worse than that of native men, where 49.3 percent were high school dropouts and 9.7 percent were college graduates. By 2000, however, natives were more likely to have a college degree (28.2 percent versus 25.9 percent

Table 7.1. Educational Distribution of Native and Immigrant Workers, 1960–2000 (percent)

	1960	1970	1980	1990	2000
Natives					
High school dropouts	49.3	35.3	20.6	10.5	7.2
High school graduates	31.2	39.9	42.7	36.8	32.9
Some college	9.7	11.9	17.6	28.7	31.7
College graduates	9.7	12.9	19.1	24.0	28.2
Immigrants					
High school dropouts	59.4	44.6	37.0	30.6	29.4
High school graduates	21.2	28.1	27.9	26.1	25.9
Some college	9.7	12.1	14.5	19.7	18.7
College graduates	9.7	15.2	20.6	23.6	25.9

Source: Author's calculations from U.S. censuses.

Note: The statistics are calculated in the sample of persons age 18–64 who are not enrolled in school and worked at least one week in the year before the census.

of immigrants) and were far less likely to be high school dropouts (7.2 percent versus 29.4 percent). As a result of the relative increase in the number of immigrants who lacked high school diplomas, the immigrant share in the population of working high school dropouts rose from 6.1 percent in 1970 to 38.7 percent in 2000 (figure 7.2). Among

Figure 7.2. The Immigrant Share of the Workforce, by Educational Attainment, 1960–2000

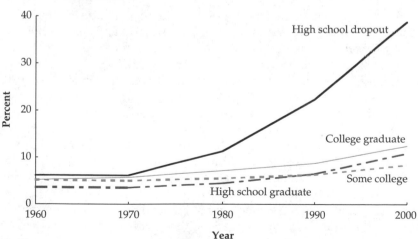

Source: Author's calculations from U.S. censuses.

Note: The workforce is all adults age 18 to 64 who are not enrolled in school and who worked in the civilian sector at least one week in the year before each decennial census.

college graduates, the increase was much more modest, from 5.7 percent to 12.4 percent.

This relative decline in the human capital of the foreign-born population underlies many trends in labor market characteristics at the core of today's immigration debate. Table 7.2 summarizes the trends in key labor market characteristics for immigrants and natives over the past 40 years, reported separately for men and women. The top half of the table shows that immigrant men have only slightly lower employment rates than native men, and that the employment rate of both groups declined at roughly the same rate over the past few decades. By 2000, 88.7 percent of native and 87.9 percent of immigrant men worked at some point during the year. Immigrant men also tend to work slightly fewer hours per year than native men.

The large differences between immigrant and native men tend to show up not in terms of employment but in terms of wages. Table 7.2 also reports summary statistics on income earned in the calendar year before the census, as well as the log wage differential, which approximately measures the percent wage differential between immigrant and native men.[2] In 1960, immigrants had slightly higher annual earnings: about $25,300, compared with $25,000 for natives. By 2000, however, immigrants had substantially lower annual earnings: natives earned $36,000 annually compared with $29,300 for immigrants. In terms of hourly wage rates, the percent wage differential between immigrant and natives stood at +6.5 percent in 1960, declined to −7.3 percent in 1980, and declined further to −19.1 percent by 2000. This decline in relative wages can be partly attributed to the decline in relative educational attainment documented earlier.

The bottom half of the table reports the respective statistics for immigrant and native women. Immigrant women tend to have much lower employment rates than native women. In 2000, for example, 77.2 percent of native women worked, compared with only 64.2 percent of immigrant women. These large differences in employment rates imply that the wage trends for immigrant and native women are likely to be contaminated by selection biases arising from differences in the work decision. In fact, the trend in the log wage differential between immigrant and native women resembles that found among men, but the decline is not as steep. In 1960, immigrant women earned 2.8 percent more than native women; by 2000, immigrant women earned 9.8 percent less. Because of the likely importance of the selection that generates the sample of working women, most of the evidence reported below focuses on describing and explaining the trends for working men.

It is important to analyze how the earnings potential of immigrant workers adapts to the host country's labor market.[3] By tracing the evolution of earnings over time (as natives accumulate more labor

Table 7.2. Labor Market Characteristics of Natives and Immigrants

	Natives					Immigrants				
	1960	1970	1980	1990	2000	1960	1970	1980	1990	2000
Men										
Employment rate (%)	95.3	94.1	90.8	90.2	88.7	93.9	93.8	89.8	89.1	87.9
Annual hours worked (1,000s)	2.17	2.19	2.10	2.12	2.18	2.09	2.11	2.02	2.03	2.05
Unemployment rate (%)	4.7	3.5	6.2	5.8	4.6	4.6	3.2	5.8	6.7	5.4
Annual earnings ($1,000)	25.0	33.3	33.1	32.9	36.0	25.3	33.2	30.9	29.1	29.3
Hourly wage rate	12.5	16.4	16.7	16.0	16.9	13.2	17.0	16.2	14.7	15.0
Log wage differential	—	—	—	—	—	.065	.016	−.073	−.138	−.191
Women										
Employment rate (%)	48.4	57.3	65.0	74.5	77.2	44.0	54.2	59.5	64.5	64.2
Annual hours worked (1,000s)	1.60	1.61	1.55	1.68	1.77	1.61	1.60	1.56	1.68	1.72
Unemployment rate (%)	5.3	5.0	6.2	5.5	4.5	6.2	5.5	7.4	8.2	7.7
Annual earnings ($1,000)	11.7	15.1	14.7	17.4	20.8	11.7	15.1	14.6	16.9	19.1
Hourly wage rate	8.6	10.7	10.4	10.7	12.2	8.7	10.9	10.4	10.6	11.9
Log wage differential	—	—	—	—	—	.028	.030	−.015	−.038	−.098

Source: Author's calculations from U.S. censuses.

— not applicable

Notes: The statistics are calculated in the sample of persons not enrolled in school age 18–64 as of the census year. The employment rate gives the percent of persons who worked at least one week in the year before the census; annual hours worked and the self-employment rate are calculated in the sample of workers; the unemployment rate is calculated in terms of the labor force participant's status in the survey week. The means of the earnings variables are calculated in the sample of workers age 25–64 who are not enrolled in school and are employed in the civilian sector.

market experience and immigrants accumulate both more labor market experience and more time in the United States), it is possible to determine if the earnings of immigrant and native workers converge over time. It is typically found—in cross-section data—that recently arrived immigrants earn less than native workers, while immigrants who have been in the United States a relatively long time earn more than native workers.

Two distinct arguments have been used to explain these results. At the time of arrival, immigrants earn less than natives because they lack the U.S.-specific skills rewarded in the American labor market (such as English proficiency). As these skills are acquired, the human capital stock of immigrants grows relative to that of natives, and immigrants experience faster wage growth. The human capital investment hypothesis, however, does not *by itself* generate an overtaking point. After all, why would immigrants accumulate more human capital than natives? The overtaking point was instead interpreted in terms of a selection argument: immigrants are more able than native workers. This assumption was typically justified by arguing that only the most driven and most able persons have the ambition and wherewithal to pack up, move, and start life anew in a foreign country.

This optimistic appraisal of immigrant adjustment was initially challenged by Borjas (1985), who argued that the positive *cross-section* correlation between the relative wage of immigrants and years-since-migration need not indicate that the wage of immigrants converges with that of natives. The basic problem with this interpretation of the data is that it infers how the earnings of immigrant workers evolve over time from a single snapshot of the immigrant population. But newly arrived immigrants might differ inherently from those who migrated 20 years ago. Hence, the current labor market experiences of those who arrived 20 years ago cannot forecast the future earnings of newly arrived immigrants.

In the past two decades, the literature has concentrated on measuring both the "assimilation" and "cohort" effects that lie at the core of these varying interpretations of the cross-section data. To identify these effects separately, researchers need to track specific immigrant and native workers over time, or use a series of repeated cross-sections (such as the various censuses) to track specific groups of immigrant and native workers. Because large longitudinal samples of foreign-born workers are relatively rare, the literature has focused instead on measuring the two effects using the repeated cross-section method.

To illustrate the nature of the evidence, figure 7.3 begins by describing the trend in cohort effects over the past 40 years. The line labeled "1–5 years in U.S." describes the trend in the *relative* wage of immigrants who—as of the time of each census—have been in the United States

Figure 7.3. Trends in the Relative Wage of Immigrant Men, 1960–2000

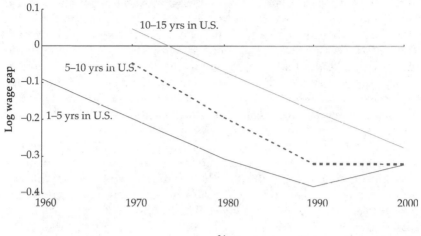

Year

Source: Author's calculations from U.S. censuses.

Note: The relative wage is calculated in the sample of working men age 25–64 who are not enrolled in school and who worked in the civilian sector. The hourly wage rate is defined as the ratio of total income earned annually to annual hours worked in the calendar year before the census.

one to five years. More precisely, this line illustrates the trend in the unadjusted log wage differential between the immigrants who arrived in the five-year period before the census and native workers in each census since 1960.

The figure clearly shows that the relative wage of newly arrived immigrants declined precipitously between 1960 and 1990.[4] In 1960, the typical male immigrant who had just arrived in the United States earned 9.1 percent less than his male native counterpart. By 1990, a new arrival was earning 38.0 percent less than his male native counterpart.

The figure indicates, however, that this trend was reversed in the late 1990s. By 2000, the newly arrived immigrant still had a sizeable wage disadvantage, but substantially less than the disadvantage observed for the respective cohort 10 years earlier. In particular, the newly arrived immigrant in 2000 had a 32.2 percent wage disadvantage. Figure 7.3, therefore, summarizes an important trend in the relative skills of successive cohorts of immigrant men: a steep decline through 1990 and a reversal of this trend in the 1990s.

Recent research by Borjas and Friedberg (2004) has documented that the uptick in cohort quality for immigrants who arrived in the late 1990s can be explained by a simple story that has significant policy relevance. In particular, the entire uptick disappears when the relatively small number of immigrants who are employed as computer scientists and engineers is excluded from the analysis (figure 7.4). The figure illustrates two basic trends. The first is simply the replication of the trend line first reported in figure 7.3 showing the steep decline and then the increase in the relative skills of newly arrived immigrant men. The second is the trend line obtained when the immigrant sample omits all workers classified as computer scientists or engineers in any given census year. Before 1990, the two trend lines correspond with each other very closely (with the sample excluding high-tech workers, of course, having lower relative earnings). Between 1990 and 2000, however, the trend lines diverge.

In particular, the comparison of the actual cohort effects to the counterfactual (i.e., a labor market where no foreign-born computer scientists or engineers had been admitted) indicates that the uptick is completely driven by the admission of a large number of foreign-born computer scientists and engineers in the late 1990s. In both 1980 and 1990, fewer than 5 percent of newly arrived immigrants worked in these high-tech occupations. By 2000, however, 11.1 percent of newly arrived immigrants worked in these occupations.

Although the census data do not provide information on the type of visa immigrants use to enter the country, it is probably not a coincidence that this increase in the relative number of high-tech immigrants occurred at the same time that the size of the H-1B visa program grew

Figure 7.4. The Effect of High-Tech Immigration on the Relative Wage of Newly Arrived Immigrant Men, 1960–2000

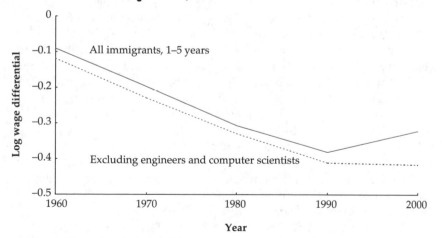

Source: Author's calculations from U.S. censuses.
Note: The relative wage is calculated in the sample of working men age 25–64 who are not enrolled in school and who worked in the civilian sector. The hourly wage rate is defined as the ratio of total income earned annually to annual hours worked in the calendar year before the census.

substantially. This program allows employers to sponsor the entry of temporary workers in "specialty occupations." In fact, most workers entering the country with an H-1B visa (70 percent in 2000) are employed either in computer-related occupations or in engineering (U.S. Immigration and Naturalization Service 2002). Between 1990 and 1994, the number of H-1B visas hovered around 100,000 annually. This number increased to 144,548 in 1996, to 240,947 in 1998, and to 302,326 in 1999 (U.S. Immigration and Naturalization Service various years). It seems, therefore, that this "importation" of high-tech workers through the H-1B program reversed the long-standing trend of declining relative skills in successive cohorts of new immigrants.

The 1960–2000 census data can also be used to measure the extent of "economic assimilation," the improvement in the relative wage of a specific immigrant cohort over time. In particular, one can use the decennial censuses to calculate the wage differential between newly arrived immigrants and natives as of 1970, to recalculate the wage gap between these same two groups in 1980, and to recalculate it again later in 1990 and 2000. Figure 7.5 summarizes the economic assimilation trends experienced by men who arrived in the United States when they were 25 to 34 years old.

Consider first the immigrant men who arrived in the late 1960s when they were 25 to 34 years old. These immigrants earned 13 percent

Figure 7.5. Economic Assimilation of Immigrant Men, 1960–2000

Relative wage of immigrants who arrived when they were 25–34 years old

Source: Author's calculations from U.S. censuses.

Note: The relative wage is calculated in the sample of working men age 25–64 who are not enrolled in school and who worked in the civilian sector. The hourly wage rate is defined as the ratio of total income earned annually to annual hours worked in the calendar year before the census.

less than comparably aged native workers at the time of entry. Move forward in time to 1980, when both the immigrants and the natives are 35 to 44 years old. The wage gap between the two groups has narrowed to 3 percent. Move forward in time again to 1990, when both immigrants and natives are 45 to 54 years old. The wage gap between the same immigrants and natives has disappeared, and immigrants now have a slight wage advantage of +1 percent. Finally, move forward in time to 2000, when the two groups are 54 to 65 years old. This immigrant cohort does not achieve any additional wage improvement and is at parity with native workers.

Overall, the process of economic assimilation exhibited by this cohort reduced the initial wage disadvantage of these immigrants by about 13 percentage points over 30 years, with most of the growth occurring in the first 10 years after immigration. Because this immigrant cohort had a relatively high entry wage, the process of economic assimilation allowed the immigrants to narrow the wage disadvantage and "catch up" with natives.

With the exception of the immigrant cohort that entered in the late 1990s, the young immigrants who arrived after 1970, however, faced a much bleaker future—simply because they started out with a much greater disadvantage. Consider those who arrived in the late 1970s. They entered the country with a 24 percent wage disadvantage. As with the earlier cohort, they too were able to narrow the gap by 10 percentage points in the first decade, to 14 percent. But the 2000 Census does not reveal any further narrowing. Even after 20 years in the United States, these immigrants still earn 14 percent less than comparably aged natives. The evidence, therefore, suggests that most immigrants who arrived in the 1970s and 1980s will not accumulate sufficient human capital to close the wage gap.

Up to this point, this chapter has simply documented how the immigrant supply shock has altered the skill distribution of the U.S. workforce. It is likely that the entry of large numbers of low-skilled immigrants will itself alter the wage of low-skilled workers already residing in the United States (and of high-skilled workers as well). After all, the textbook model of a competitive labor market has clear and unambiguous implications for how wages and employment opportunities in a particular country should adjust to these labor supply shocks, at least in the short run. In particular, immigration should lower the wage of competing workers and increase the wage of complementary workers, whose skills become more valuable because of immigration.

Despite the commonsense intuition behind these theoretical predictions, the economics literature has—at least until recently—found it very difficult to document the inverse relation between immigrant-induced supply shocks and wages. Much of the literature attempts to estimate the labor market impact of immigration in a receiving country by comparing economic conditions across local labor markets in that country. Although there is a great deal of dispersion in the measured impact across studies, there is a consensus that the estimates cluster around zero. This finding has been interpreted as indicating that immigration has little impact on the receiving country's wage structure (Card 1990, 2001; Friedberg and Hunt 1995).

Borjas, Freeman, and Katz (1997) challenge this conventional wisdom by arguing that the spatial correlation—the cross-city correlation between labor market outcomes and immigration—may not truly capture the economic impact of immigration if native workers respond by moving their labor or capital to localities seemingly less affected by the immigrant supply shock. Borjas (2003) uses the insight that the labor market impact of immigration may be measurable only at the national level to examine how the wages of U.S. workers in particular skill groups—defined by both educational attainment and years of work experience—relate to the immigrant supply shocks affecting those groups. The national-level labor market evidence is striking, showing robust evidence of an inverse relation between supply increases and wages in the short run. In rough terms, a 10 percent immigrant-induced increase in the labor supply of a particular skill group lowers the relative wage of that group by 3 to 4 percent. The magnitude of the wage response suggests that as much as half the decline in the relative wage of high school dropouts in recent decades can be directly linked to the entry of sizeable numbers of low-skilled immigrants.

Over the long run, as the capital stock adjusts to the immigrant influx, the adverse wage effect on the typical worker is muted. It is important to note, however, that *relative* wage effects will remain even in the long run, simply because immigration has changed the relative supply of the various skill groups. As a result, immigration has likely reduced the relative wage of low-skilled workers even in the context of a long-run equilibrium that allows for full adjustments in the economy's capital stock.

THE ECONOMIC CASE FOR SKILLED IMMIGRATION

The deteriorating economic status of the immigrant population has sparked a heated debate over whether the goal of immigration policy should shift away from family reunification and focus instead on the potential economic impact of immigrants. The case that can be made for preferring one type of immigrant to another will ultimately depend on what one *assumes* about the host country's policy objectives. More specifically, what should the United States seek to accomplish from immigration?

Different policy goals will inevitably lead to different decisions about the composition of the immigrant population. For example, if immigration policy should strive to relieve the tax burden on native-born taxpayers, it would be fiscally irresponsible to admit millions of less-skilled immigrants who have a high propensity for participating in public assistance programs. In contrast, if the goal were to help the poor of the world by giving many of them an opportunity to live and work in the United States, the increased cost of maintaining the welfare state is the price that Americans are willing to pay for their generosity.

The case for skilled immigration is based on *one* particular assumption about the policy goal. In particular, suppose that immigration policy should seek to improve the economic well-being of the population currently residing in the United States (that, for simplicity, is referred to as "natives").

One could obviously argue over whether this policy goal accurately represents what Americans *should* want to accomplish from immigration. Nevertheless, the economic well-being of the native-born population has always played a very influential role in determining the shape and direction of immigration policy. In the early 1960s, the bracero program was halted because of its perceived harmful impact on the job opportunities of American workers. In the late 1990s, the H-1B visa program was expanded because of its perceived beneficial impact on the job opportunities of American workers.

Suppose then that the goal of immigration policy were to maximize the economic well-being of the native population. And suppose that native economic well-being depends on both per capita income and the distribution of income in the native population. In particular, the country wants to pursue an immigration policy that makes natives wealthier but does not increase the income disparity among workers already in the country. What type of immigration policy should the United States then pursue? More specifically, which types of immigrants should the country admit, skilled or unskilled workers?

A strong case can be made that the economic well-being of natives would increase most if the country adopted an immigration policy that favored the entry of skilled workers. The argument in favor of this policy contains three distinct parts. Consider first how the fiscal impact of immigration affects the native population. Skilled immigrants earn more, pay higher taxes, and require fewer social services than less-skilled immigrants. Put simply, skilled immigration increases the after-tax income of natives, while the tax burden imposed by the immigration of less-skilled workers probably reduces the net wealth of native tax-payers. From a fiscal perspective, therefore, there is little doubt that skilled immigration is a good investment, particularly compared with the immigration of less-skilled workers.

The second part of the case for skilled immigration relies on how immigrants alter the productivity of the native workforce and of native-owned firms. These productivity effects depend entirely on how the skills of immigrants compare with those of natives. Skilled native workers, for example, have much to gain when less-skilled immigrants enter the United States. Skilled natives can specialize in their professions, while the immigrant workforce complements the native workforce by taking on various service jobs. It does not seem far-fetched to assume that the American workforce, particularly compared with the workforce of many source countries, is composed primarily of "skilled" workers. On aggregate, therefore, it would seem as if the typical American worker would gain from and would prefer to have *less-skilled* immigration.

But there is a third part of the story. Immigration also affects the profits of native-owned firms. Firms that use low-skilled workers in the production line, such as sweatshops, gain from the immigration of the less skilled. Other firms, however, might be better off with skilled immigrants. In fact, many studies of the American economy suggest there is more complementarity between skilled labor and capital than between unskilled labor and capital. In other words, the machines and capital that are now used in the production process become more productive when combined with a skilled worker than with an unskilled worker. Most firms, therefore, would gain more if the immigrant flow were composed of skilled workers.

In short, there is a conflict between the type of immigrant that the "typical" native worker favors and the type of immigrant that the "typical" firm favors. The typical native worker would be better off with unskilled immigrants, while the typical native-owned firm would be better off with skilled immigrants. Because the productivity of capital is very sensitive to the presence of skilled workers, the available evidence suggests that per capita income in the United States would rise most if immigration policy favored skilled persons (Borjas 1995b).

The gains from skilled immigration would be even larger if immigrants had "external effects" on native productivity. One could argue, for example, that immigrants bring in knowledge, skills, and abilities that natives lack, and natives can somehow pick up this know-how by interacting with immigrants. In fact, many arguments that stress the beneficial impact of immigrants on particular industries—such as the role played by immigrants in the creation and growth of Silicon Valley—stress these externalities. Although there is no hard evidence that such externalities exist, these gains would probably be larger if natives were to interact with highly skilled immigrants.

Finally, skilled immigration has favorable distributional effects. The skilled workers who already reside in the United States will face more job competition and lower wages. As a result, there will be less, rather than more, income inequality. On both efficiency and distributional grounds, therefore, it would seem that the United States would be better off if the immigrant flow were skilled.

How can the United States select skilled workers from the pool of visa applicants? In the past few decades, Australia, Canada, and New Zealand have all instituted point systems that reward certain socioeconomic traits in the admissions formula. In Canada, for example, visa applicants are graded in terms of their age, educational attainment, work experience, English or French language proficiency, and occupation. Those applicants who score enough points qualify for entry into Canada, while those who fail the test are denied entry.

Needless to say, any point system is inherently arbitrary. It is unclear, however, that the Canadian point system—with its detailed gradations for different types of jobs and different types of workers—is any more arbitrary than the one currently used by the United States, where entry, for the most part, is determined by the answer to a single question: does the applicant have relatives already residing in the United States? Those who have relatives in the United States are granted an entry visa; those who do not are denied entry.

Finally, it is worth stressing that adopting a skills-based point system addresses only the "demand side" of the immigration market. In the end, the United States can attract only those immigrants who wish to enter the country—*regardless* of what the admissions formula says. The United States seems to attract many low-skilled workers originating in less-developed countries. If a skills-based point system were adopted, the United States would wish to grant most visas to skilled workers, but it might find relatively few skilled workers taking up the offer. The possibility that the market may not clear should not be ignored. The United States currently permits the "sale" of roughly 10,000 visas annually to entrepreneurs who are willing to invest $1 million (and create some jobs in the process). In 2004, however, only 129 such visas were sold.

There is a possibility, therefore, that adopting a skills-based point system might greatly reduce the number of immigrants admitted, simply because many people who might meet the requirements would not bother to apply for entry. One should not view this potential outcome as a flaw of the point system. It simply means that the types of workers the United States wants to buy are not available at the price the country is willing to offer. When such things happen in other markets, consumers typically do one of two things. First, they raise the price they are willing to pay. The United States could offer financial incentives to the immigrants it truly wants—as Australia did for many years when it chose to pay some immigrants for the expense of getting there. Second, consumers withdraw from the market. The United States could simply wait for economic conditions to change until it can again recruit the types of workers most beneficial for the country.

It is also important to note that a curtailing of legal immigration along the lines discussed above would obviously increase the incentives for many workers to instead migrate illegally to the United States. It seems, therefore, that the effectiveness of any sensible proposal to reform legal immigration would require a concurrent reappraisal of our "policy" regarding illegal immigration, a policy that has permitted the entry of millions of undocumented workers into the country.

The economic case for skilled immigration hinges entirely on an *assumption* about the country's policy objectives. Skilled immigration is the best policy if the United States wishes to pursue an immigration policy that maximizes the economic well-being of the native population. This assumption obviously ignores the impact of immigration on many other constituencies, such as on the immigrants themselves (who would clearly prefer to be reunited with their families) and on the vast population that remains in the source countries. The United States, for instance, might choose to drain the labor markets of many source countries from particular types of skills and abilities (such as high-tech workers). Such a brain drain would probably have a detrimental effect on economic growth in those countries.

In short, there are difficult trade-offs. Pursuing a particular immigration policy might help some groups, such as native workers, but may hurt others. As a result, the adoption and implementation of any specific immigration policy will leave winners and losers in its wake. In the end, the goals of immigration policy must inevitably reflect a political consensus that inevitably incorporates the conflicting social and economic interests of various demographic, socioeconomic, and ethnic groups, as well as political and humanitarian concerns.

NOTES

1. In 1960 and 1970, the data provide a 1 percent random sample of the population. In 1980, 1990, and 2000, the data provide a 5 percent sample. Throughout the study, noncitizens and naturalized citizens are classified as immigrants; all other people are classified as natives. The samples are restricted to adults age 18 to 64 who are not in the military and are not enrolled in school.

2. Income earned in the past year includes both earnings from salaried jobs and income from self-employment.

3. Representative studies on this topic include Chiswick (1978) and LaLonde and Topel (1992).

4. To interpret the trend in the relative wage of immigrants (both within and across cohorts) as a measure of relative changes in skills, one must assume that period effects influence the wages of immigrants and natives by the same relative amount. It is well known that there were historic changes in the U.S. wage structure during the 1980s and that these changes did not affect all skill groups equally (Katz and Murphy 1992). Borjas (1995a) shows that detailed controls for period effects do not explain the downward trend in the relative wage of successive immigrant cohorts.

REFERENCES

Borjas, George J. 1985. "Assimilation, Changes in Cohort Quality, and the Earnings of Immigrants." *Journal of Labor Economics* 3(4): 463–89.

———. 1995a. "Assimilation and Changes in Cohort Quality Revisited: What Happened to Immigrant Earnings in the 1980s?" *Journal of Labor Economics* 13(2): 201–45.

———. 1995b. "The Economic Benefits from Immigration." *Journal of Economic Perspectives* 9(2): 3–22.

———. 2003. "The Labor Demand Curve *Is* Downward Sloping: Reexamining the Impact of Immigration on the Labor Market." *Quarterly Journal of Economics* 118(4): 1335–74.

Borjas, George J., and Rachel M. Friedberg. 2004. "What Happened to Immigrant Earnings in the 1990s?" Working paper, Harvard University.

Borjas, George J., Richard B. Freeman, and Lawrence F. Katz. 1997. "How Much Do Immigration and Trade Affect Labor Market Outcomes?" *Brookings Papers on Economic Activity* (1): 1–67.

Card, David. 1990. "The Impact of the Mariel Boatlift on the Miami Labor Market." *Industrial and Labor Relations Review* 43(2): 245–57.

———. 2001. "Immigrant Inflows, Native Outflows, and the Local Labor Market Impacts of Higher Immigration." *Journal of Labor Economics* 19(1): 22–64.

Chiswick, Barry R. 1978. "The Effect of Americanization on the Earnings of Foreign-Born Men." *Journal of Political Economy* 86(5): 897–921.

Friedberg, Rachel M., and Jennifer Hunt. 1995. "The Impact of Immigration on Host Country Wages, Employment, and Growth." *Journal of Economic Perspectives* 9(2): 23–44.

Katz, Lawrence F., and Kevin M. Murphy. 1992. "Changes in the Wage Structure, 1963–87: Supply and Demand Factors." *Quarterly Journal of Economics* 107(1): 35–78.

LaLonde, Robert J., and Robert H. Topel. 1992. "The Assimilation of Immigrants in the U.S. Labor Market." In *Immigration and the Work Force: Economic Consequences for the United States and Source Areas*, edited by George J. Borjas and Richard B. Freeman (67–92). Chicago: University of Chicago Press.

Passel, Jeffrey. 2005. "Unauthorized Migrants: Numbers and Characteristics." Washington, DC: Pew Hispanic Center.

U.S. Immigration and Naturalization Service. 2002. *Report on Characteristics of Specialty Occupation Workers (H-1B): Fiscal Year 2000.* Washington, DC: U.S. Immigration and Naturalization Service.

———. Various years. *Statistical Yearbook of the Immigration and Naturalization Service.* Washington, DC: U.S. Immigration and Naturalization Service.

8

POLICIES TO PROMOTE LABOR FORCE PARTICIPATION OF OLDER PEOPLE

Alicia H. Munnell

That older people will need to work longer in order to ensure a secure retirement is undeniable. Social Security, the backbone of the retirement system, will not replace as much preretirement income in the future as it does today. Employer-sponsored pensions also involve considerably more uncertainty given the shift from defined benefit to 401(k) plans. With institutional saving arrangements on the decline, one might have thought that people would be saving more on their own. But personal saving outside of pension plans is virtually nonexistent. Combine the retirement income crunch with the dramatic increase in life expectancy, and continued employment in later life appears a promising option for ensuring the financial security of older Americans. The hard questions are whether older people will offer their services and whether employers will retain or hire them.

On the supply side, despite the need to build up their stock of "retirement wealth," older people may find the availability of Social

Security benefits at age 62 too tempting and continue to retire early. And not all older people can work. Some have health problems or have been laid off and cannot find another job, and others see continued employment as simply too onerous. For those who want to work, meaningful jobs may continue to require full-time employment, an arrangement inconsistent with the desires of many older people.

On the demand side, the decline in fertility rates that followed the boom will cause labor supply to grow more slowly than in the past. Slow labor force growth may create a tight labor market overall or in certain locations and sectors, thereby improving the employment prospects of older workers. Offsetting potentially tight labor markets, however, are three factors. First, older workers are expensive. They are paid more, sometimes in excess of their productivity. They involve expensive health care costs and rapidly rising pension costs under traditional defined benefit pension plans. Second, employers generally resist part-time employment, which is the preferred mode for many older workers. Third, age discrimination, while technically illegal, probably exists. Thus, it is not clear that the demand for older workers will materialize.

This chapter explores the potential supply of and demand for older workers and looks at proposals to help increase the labor force participation of this group. With today's retirement patterns, pressure on the nation's retirement programs will require older people to work longer. But several impediments keep older people out of the labor force— namely, the availability of Social Security benefits at 62, the health and employment limitations of some workers, and the potential lack of jobs with enough flexibility.

Shifting to the employers' side, the potential increase in the demand for labor can be looked at as the ratio of older people to those of working age increases. Employers can respond by adding more capital, tapping immigrants and women, or outsourcing, but it is unclear that these responses will alleviate the pressure on wages. Another option is to employ more older workers, given they will be healthier and better educated than in the past and that jobs will be less physically demanding. But older workers also have some disadvantages. The most important is that they tend to be expensive.

Some policy proposals could improve both the supply of and demand for older workers. Unfortunately, other than increasing Social Security's earliest eligibility age from 62 to, say, 64, the realistic options are few. Keeping older workers in the labor force may be good for both workers and employers, but it is not obvious that it will happen.

WORKERS: THE NEED FOR CONTINUED EMPLOYMENT

The first decision when discussing older workers is to identify the group under consideration. The Age Discrimination in Employment

Act protects workers age 40 or older. People can withdraw money without penalty from their 401(k) plans at 59½. And people are eligible for unreduced Social Security benefits at age 66. This analysis focuses on adults age 55 to 70, because at age 55 the labor force activity of both men and women starts to decline markedly and by age 70 most people should have accumulated enough resources to be able to support themselves comfortably in retirement.

Today, both men and women continue to retire early. As shown in figure 8.1, labor force participation drops about 15 percentage points between age 50 and 60. By age 60, only 72 percent of men and 56 percent of women are in the labor force.

This decline in labor force participation shows up in a reduction in earnings as a percentage of income as the age of the household increases. For those in the middle quintile of the income distribution, earnings account for 80 percent of income for households age 55 to 61, but decline to 57 percent for those 62 to 64, 24 percent for those 65 to 69, and become trivial for those over 69. The typical household over age 69 gets the bulk of its income from Social Security and employer-sponsored pensions. Both these sources will provide less in the future than they do today.

Figure 8.1. Labor Force Participation by Age and Gender, 2004

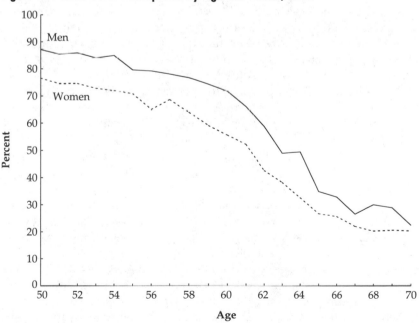

Source: U.S. Bureau of Labor Statistics and U.S. Census Bureau (2005).

204 ■ Other Policies to Increase Supply of Skills

The Outlook for Social Security

Today, the hypothetical "average earner" retiring at 65 currently receives benefits of $1,180 a month, or about 42 percent of previous earnings. After paying the Medicare Part B premium, which is automatically deducted from Social Security benefits before the check goes in the mail, the replacement rate is 38.7 percent, or $1,090. Under *current law*, Social Security replacement rates—benefits as a percent of preretirement earnings—are scheduled to decline at any given retirement age for three reasons. First, the current increase in the normal retirement age, from 65 to 67, is equivalent to an across-the-board cut. Second, Medicare Part B premiums are slated to increase sharply owing to rising health care costs. (Premiums for the new Part D drug benefit will also claim an increasing share of the Social Security check.) Finally, Social Security benefits will be taxed more under the personal income tax, as the exemption amounts are not indexed to inflation. These three factors will reduce the net replacement rate from 38.5 percent today to 29.4 percent in 2030, or $830 in today's terms (Munnell 2003). Restoring solvency through cuts in benefits would reduce this level of support still further.

The Outlook for Private-Sector Employer-Sponsored Pensions

With a diminished role for Social Security, retirees will be increasingly dependent on employer-sponsored pensions. One problem is that at any moment in time, only about half the private-sector workforce age 25 to 64 participates in an employer-sponsored plan of any type, and this fraction, which has remained virtually unchanged since the late 1970s, is unlikely to improve.[1] Since pension participation tends to increase with earnings, only middle- and upper-income individuals can count on receiving meaningful benefits from employer-sponsored pension plans.

The other issue is that the nature of pension coverage has changed dramatically. Twenty years ago, most people with pension coverage had a traditional defined benefit plan that paid a lifetime annuity at retirement.[2] Today the world looks very different. Most people with a pension have a defined contribution plan—typically a 401(k). In contrast to defined benefit plans, 401(k) plans are like savings accounts. Generally the employee, and often the employer, contributes a specified percentage of earnings into the account. These contributions are invested, usually at the direction of the employee, mostly in mutual funds consisting of stocks and bonds. Upon retirement, the worker generally receives the balance as a lump sum, albeit with the option to roll it over to an individual retirement account (IRA).

In theory, workers could accumulate substantial pension wealth under 401(k) plans. But *in practice*, they do not. For example, simulations suggest that the worker in the middle of the earnings distribution, who contributes regularly throughout his worklife, should end up at retirement with about $300,000 in his 401(k) account or IRA. (Most IRA assets are rolled-over balances from 401(k) plans.) This amount, when combined with Social Security, would provide an adequate retirement income. But reality looks quite different. The Federal Reserve's 2001 Survey of Consumer Finances reports that the typical individual approaching retirement had 401(k)/IRA balances of only $42,000 (figure 8.2). Younger cohorts also do not seem to be on track for an adequate retirement income. The average 401(k)/IRA holdings for those age 45 to 54 are only $37,000, compared with a predicted $155,000.

A critical factor explaining these low balances is that the entire burden has shifted from the employer to the employee. In these plans, workers must decide whether to join, how much to contribute, how to invest the assets, when to rebalance, what to do about company stock, whether to roll over accumulations when changing jobs, and how to withdraw the money at retirement. A significant fraction of participants make serious mistakes at every step along the way. A quarter of those eligible to participate choose not to do so. Over half

Figure 8.2. 401(k)/IRA Actual and Simulated Accumulations, by Age Group, 2001

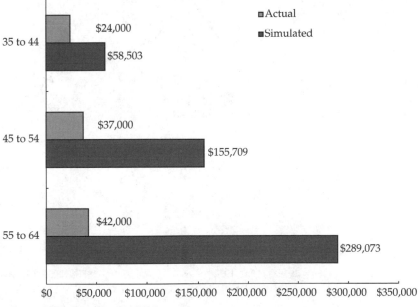

Source: Munnell and Sundén (2004).

fail to diversify their investments. Many overinvest in company stock. Almost no participants rebalance their portfolios as they age or in response to market returns. Most important, many cash out when they change jobs and very few annuitize at retirement. The basic problem is that financial decisions are difficult. Most participants lack sufficient financial experience, training, or time to figure out what to do.

Personal Saving

Given the projected decline in Social Security and increased uncertainty surrounding employer-sponsored pensions, one might have expected to see people of working age increase their personal saving. But a recent study of the U.S. National Income and Product Accounts personal saving rate revealed that virtually all the saving undertaken by the working-age population occurred in pension plans, as shown in figure 8.3 (Munnell, Golub-Sass, and Varani 2005). In recent years, saving outside of pensions has actually been negative.

Figure 8.3. NIPA Personal Saving Rate: Working-Age Population with and without Pensions, 1980–2003

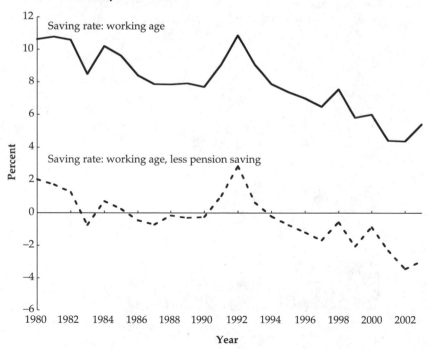

Source: Munnell, Golub-Sass, and Varani (2005).

Thus, the outlook for retirement income for future cohorts of retirees is dismal. People are not going to be able to continue to retiree at 62 and 63 and maintain their preretirement living standards over an increasingly long period of retirement. Working longer is an obvious solution.

The Impact of Working Longer on Retirement Income

Each additional year in the workforce increases income directly through earnings from work and investments. It also actuarially increases Social Security benefits by 5 to 8 percent and reduces the number of years over which retirement savings need to be spread. The financial implications are striking. A couple in the middle of the income distribution could reduce the assets required to replace 80 percent of its after-tax preretirement income from $511,000 to $118,000 by delaying retirement from 62 to 70 (table 8.1).

In summary, Social Security replacement rates are scheduled to decline even under current law, 401(k) plans have made income from employer-sponsored pensions more uncertain, and the working-age population saves virtually nothing on its own. People will not be able to maintain their preretirement standards of living if they continue to retire in their early 60s. Delaying retirement is clearly a desirable goal. But is it realistic?

WORKERS: IMPEDIMENTS TO CONTINUED EMPLOYMENT

Recent trends in retirement and various survey results provide some encouraging evidence that older workers will stay in the labor force

Table 8.1. How Retirement Age Affects Assets Needed in Retirement, Married Couple Earning $58,560 after Taxes (2004 dollars)

Retirement age	Annual Social Security payments[a]	Additional retirement income needed to achieve 80 percent of after-tax preretirement income ($46,848)	Assets needed at retirement to produce that additional income[b]
62	20,888	26,270	510,757
66	27,648	19,200	298,380
70	38,136	8,712	117,651

Source: Congressional Budget Office (2004).
[a] Taken from the Social Security Administration's "Social Security Quick Calculator," http://www.ssa.gov/OACT/quickcalc/calculator.html.
[b] The figures are based on the cost of an annuity through the Federal Thrift Savings Plan.

longer. Other pieces of information, however, suggest that people often do not follow through on their good intentions. After reviewing the labor force trends, this section discusses some possible reasons people continue to withdraw early from the labor force.

Current and Projected Labor Force Trends

The most important development on the retirement front is an apparent pause, if not end, to the pattern of earlier and earlier retirement. The average retirement age can be defined in several ways. But for this discussion it is the age at which 50 percent of the age cohort is out of the labor force (Burtless and Quinn 2002). For men, the retirement age dropped from 66 in 1965 to 63 in the early 1980s, where it has remained (figure 8.4). For women, the pattern differs slightly because of a cohort effect: as the increase in participation rates at younger ages feeds

Figure 8.4. Average Retirement Agea, by Age and Gender, 1961–2003

Sources: U.S. Bureau of Labor Statistics and U.S. Census Bureau (1962–2005) and author's calculations.

Note: Retirement is defined as the age at which more than 50 percent of the cohort is out of the labor force, as in Burtless and Quinn (2002).

through, the average retirement age of older women has increased. By 2003, the average retirement age for women was 62.

With regard to the future, people say that they plan to work longer. For example, the 2004 EBRI Retirement Confidence survey shows that almost half of today's workers plan to retire at age 65 and older, implying that the average retirement age in the future will rise to 65 from its current level of 63 (Employee Benefit Research Institute 2004). Similarly, surveys sponsored by AARP in 1998 and 2004 report that 80 percent of baby boomers expect to work in retirement (AARP 1998, 2004).

It is unclear, however, whether these expectations will be realized. Since 1994 the Retirement Confidence Survey has asked individuals when they plan to retire and has asked retirees when they actually retired. An average of the results over the full period shows that the typical worker has expected to work until age 65, and the typical retiree has left the workforce at about age 62 (Employee Benefit Research Institute 1994–2004). This finding suggests that individuals often end up retiring earlier than they had initially planned.

Current data also show some discouraging trends, particularly for men in their 50s. Figure 8.5 depicts the labor force participation rates

Figure 8.5. Labor Force Participation by Age and Gender, 1984 and 2004

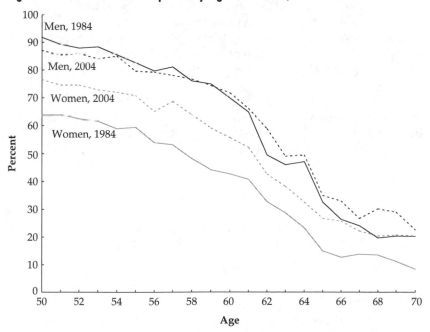

Source: U.S. Bureau of Labor Statistics and U.S. Census Bureau (1985, 2005).

by age from 1984 through 2004. At older ages, a greater proportion of men is in the labor force in 2004 than in 1984. But at younger ages— that is, between 50 and 58—the labor force participation rate for men is below that of 20 years ago.

One final piece of evidence is the reaction of voters to the proposal to help close the Social Security financing shortfall by raising the age at which one can receive benefits. Regardless of party affiliation, survey respondents overwhelmingly reject the notion of raising the Social Security retirement age.[3] Perhaps voters recognize this proposal as a benefit cut and simply oppose all benefit cuts. More likely, however, people resist legislation that sounds like it will keep them in the labor force longer.

Thus, it may be a mistake to take today's workers at their word that they plan to work longer than their predecessors. That is unfortunate, since, as discussed above, people will need to stay in the labor force at older ages to secure an adequate retirement income. A lot of survey respondents talk about work later in life, but many do not follow through. The question is why.

The Availability of Social Security Benefits

Much has been made of the extension of the normal retirement age under Social Security from 65 to 67. Some commentators imply that this change is an important incentive to remain in the labor force (OECD 2005). To the extent that an incentive to remain in the labor force exists, it takes the form of a cut in benefits at age 62 from 80 percent of full benefits with a normal retirement age of 65 to 70 percent with a normal retirement age of 67. That is, people retiring at 62 would take a bigger hit for claiming early.

The problem is that most researchers have found people very sensitive to the availability of benefits and much less sensitive to changes in benefit levels (Gruber and Coile 2000). Despite the reduction in the monthly benefit amount, most people claim benefits at age 62 (U.S. Social Security Administration 2005a). The impression one gets is that a large number of people are tolerating their jobs just long enough to acquire sufficient income to stop working, and as soon as that income becomes available, they grab it. The implication is that as long as the early eligibility age remains at 62, a large percentage of people are likely to claim earlier than they would otherwise and withdraw from the labor force.

Work Limitations

The discussion so far has proceeded as if all workers have the capacity and opportunity to work as long as they want. This is clearly untrue.

Three pieces of information suggest that between 30 and 40 percent of workers leave involuntarily. First, the Health and Retirement Study (HRS) asks why people retired. Of those who had retired by age 65, 65 percent said they retired voluntarily, 18 percent for health reasons, 6 percent because their business closed, 7 percent because they were laid off, and 4 percent for family reasons (University of Michigan 1992–2002). Similarly, a recent survey by Prudential Financial of a nationally representative sample found that 38 percent of retirees claimed they had retired involuntarily. Finally, a recent study, which used the HRS to explore the impact of work on physical and mental health, found that about one-third of older workers were employed in positions where the demands of the job were judged excessive or job satisfaction was very low (Calvo 2006). Many in this group will not view their ultimate retirement as voluntary.

The Lack of Flexible Jobs

Another hurdle to continued employment is that older people consistently report that they want to work part-time. For example, a study based on the Health and Retirement Study reports that 56 percent of respondents age 55 to 65 in 1996 said they would prefer to gradually reduce their hours as they age (U.S. General Accounting Office 2001). And older self-employed people tend to reduce hours worked as they approach retirement. But few older workers have part-time positions, and part-time employment does not appear to be increasing (figure 8.6).

Currently, part-time employment is concentrated in small establishments and in establishments in the service sector (Montgomery 1988). This is true even after controlling for other factors that would affect demand, such as wages, fringe benefits, seasonal fluctuations in demand, and hiring costs. It is not exactly clear why this is the case. Large firms might avoid part-time workers because they tend to have higher turnover rates than full-time employees (Tilly 1991). Part-time work might be more common in the service sector because it is labor-intensive and faces fluctuations in demand, and because employers find it is easier to meet these fluctuations with part-time workers. While all these theories are plausible, they have not been supported by rigorous empirical studies (Hutchens 2001). Without an increase in the availability of part-time employment, however, many older people may be unwilling to keep working.

EMPLOYERS: POTENTIAL DEMAND FOR OLDER WORKERS

The United States, like virtually every other developed country, is about to experience a radical transformation of its labor markets. The

Figure 8.6. Percent of Workers Age 55 to 70 Employed Part-Time, 1980–2004

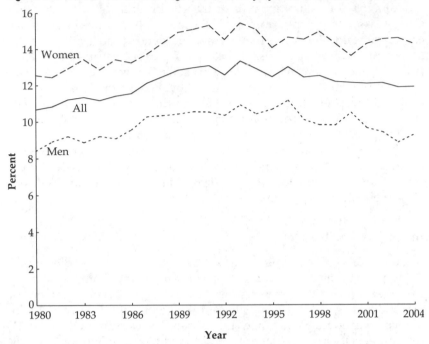

Sources: U.S. Bureau of Labor Statistics and U.S. Census Bureau (1981–2005).

ratio of those age 65 and older to the working-age population will increase significantly. The ratio increases very rapidly as the baby boomers retire between 2010 and 2030 and then rises slowly thereafter, reflecting continuing increases in longevity (figure 8.7). With a rising ratio of consumers to workers, labor demand is likely to rise relative to labor supply, putting upward pressure on wages.

At the same time, the composition of the labor force will change. As the baby boomers age, those 55 and older will compose a larger share of workers, rising from 13 percent in 2000 to about 19 percent by 2030 (figure 8.8). Thus, the relative glut of older workers may put downward pressure on their wages relative to their younger counterparts. That is, the same crowding effect that placed downward pressure on the wages of the baby boomers when they were young may follow them into their late 50s and 60s (Triest, Sapozhnikov, and Sass 2005; Welch 1979). And the downward pressure may persist as older workers continue to constitute a large share of the workforce. Thus, boomers may face two types of wage pressures—downward due to their large cohort and upward due to the slow growth in the labor force.

Figure 8.7. Population of the United States 65 and above as a Percent of Population Age 20 to 64, 1950–2050

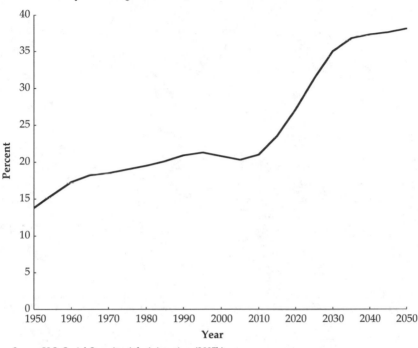

Source: U.S. Social Security Administration (2005b).
Note: Numbers after 2005 are projections.

Possible Employer Responses to the Coming Wage Pressure

In theory, employers could respond to the upward pressure on overall wages by using more capital, by tapping immigrants and women, or by relocating jobs. Each of these options is likely to provide only limited relief, however, suggesting that employers may become more receptive to the continued employment of older workers.

Use More Capital

Employers have an incentive to respond to higher wages by using more equipment and advanced technology to automate their production processes. The problem is that the purchase of capital needs to be financed.[4] And the same demographic trends that lead to the aging of the population are likely to reduce both personal and government saving, leading to an increase in the cost of financing new capital investment. On the personal side, the dissaving by large numbers of retirees as they leave the labor force is likely to swamp the saving

Figure 8.8. Percent of the Labor Force Age 55 and Older, 1980–2050

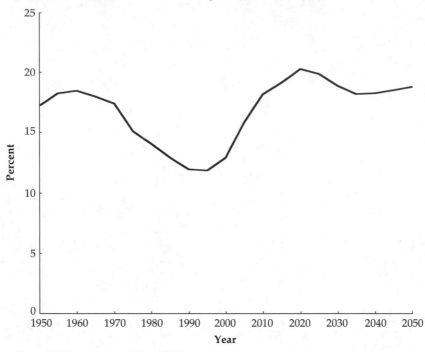

Source: U.S. Department of Labor (2005).
Note: Numbers after 2005 are projections.

undertaken by smaller incoming cohorts. On the government side, the claims of retiring workers on Social Security and Medicare are likely to reduce government saving. With lower levels of personal and government saving, the only way to finance investment is to borrow from abroad. That approach worked in the 1980s. But the U.S. current account deficit is now so large relative to GDP that further borrowing to offset the projected decline in national saving seems unlikely. As a result, lower national saving is likely to limit how much capital employers can use to alleviate wage pressure.

Tap Immigrants and Women

An alternative to adding more capital is to increase the labor force by turning to untapped sources, such as immigrants and women. The problem is that immigration is relatively high by historical standards. The United States went from very high immigration rates in the early part of the century to extremely low rates during the Depression and World War II. After the war, immigration rates increased steadily to a post-war high in 2000. The Census Bureau's middle assumption for net immigration, which underlies its labor force projections, is about 900,000 a year including both legal and those classified as "other-than-legal." This level would be in keeping with the pattern of the 1990s. Higher levels of immigration seem unlikely for the foreseeable future in the wake of September 11, 2001.

Women have contributed enormously to the growth in the labor force over the past 40 years (figure 8.9), but a significant increase in their labor force participation seems unlikely. Women born in 1940 and thereafter came into the labor force at ever increasing rates, and they stayed in the labor force at higher levels than those born before them. This pattern came to a halt, however, with those born around 1965, when labor force participation reached a plateau (Nyce and Schieber 2002). By the 1990s, the continued increase in female labor force participation reflected the retirement of older women, who had relatively low lifetime participation, and their replacement by younger women with higher labor force activity. The current gap in participation between men and women age 35 to 44 has narrowed to 15 percentage points (90.1 percent versus 75.4 percent in 2004), and this discrepancy

Figure 8.9. Labor Force Participation Rates for Men and Women, 1960–2004

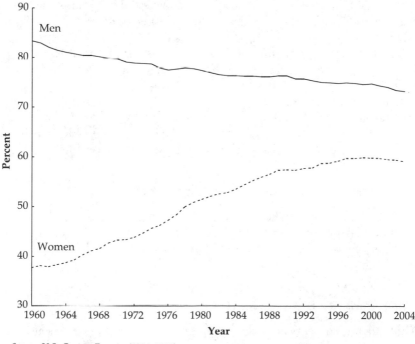

Source: U.S. Census Bureau (1996, 2002).

comes from the significant difference in participation between married men and married women. Given that women remain primarily responsible for the care of the home and children, they are likely to need higher pay or substantial improvement in child care facilities to enter the labor force in greater numbers.

Relocate or Outsource Overseas

Firms might respond to the pressure on wages by relocating overseas or "outsourcing."[5] The growth and advance of the global communications infrastructure and the rise of English as the global language has allowed American companies to look abroad in order to cut costs. Here too, however, the potential may be limited. Most manufacturing now occurs offshore, so further movement must come primarily from the service sector. While the phenomenon has received a lot of attention, the numbers involved are sketchy and tend to suggest that no more than 100,000 jobs a year are outsourced. According to the Bureau of Labor Statistics, only 4 percent of the roughly 900,000 layoffs a year (2002–03) are from overseas relocation (U.S. Bureau of Labor Statistics 2004). A survey of call-center and software operators in India shows that around 350,000 jobs have been created in India from March 2000 to March 2004. Goldman Sachs estimates about 500,000 jobs were outsourced jobs from 2000 till 2004. Other surveys show more substantial numbers. The most cited report by Forrester Research Inc. claims that over 3.3 million white-collar jobs will be shipped overseas by 2015 (McCarthy et al. 2004). The future of outsourcing is clearly uncertain, but if it remains modest, it will not alleviate the wage pressure created by an increasing ratio of consumers to workers.

If increased capital, a surge of immigrants, more female workers, and relocation do not relieve the pressure on wages, will employers turn to older workers? In many ways, relying more on older workers seems the logical response to the coming labor force pressure.

Why Employers Should Rely More on Older Workers

Tomorrow's older workers will be well-educated, they will have a lifetime of experience, they will be healthier than workers in the past, and the jobs employers need filled have become much less physically demanding.

Older Workers Are Well Educated

The educational gap between older and younger workers is now a thing of the past. Individuals 65 and over have substantially less education than their younger counterparts (table 8.2). But educational levels for men age 55 to 64, which includes the bulk of the baby boomers, are better than levels for younger men. The picture for women is more complicated, given that the educational attainment of each succeeding cohort surpasses that of earlier cohorts. But even here, the gap between women age 55 to 64 and younger groups is much less than with women 65 and over. In short, older workers will look much like younger workers in terms of their educational attainment.[6]

Older Workers Have a Lifetime of Experience

Older workers have logged many years in the labor force and have generally acquired valuable skills in the process. These skills are not just useful to their current employer. Most older workers have a diverse work history and experience with many different employers, as the U.S. workforce is extremely mobile.[7] The median job tenure is about 10 years for workers age 55 to 64; fewer than one in five wage and salary workers age 60 to 64 has more than 25 years of tenure (Copeland 2003). Today's older workers are generally efficient, versatile, able to display good judgment, and capable of adjusting to workplace changes.

Older People Are Healthier Now than in the Past

Between 1982 and 1999, the share of those 65 and older with severe disabilities, measured roughly in terms of lack of ability to function independently with ease, declined from 26.2 to 19.7 percent (Manton and Gu 2001).[8] This is a 25 percent cumulative reduction in the disability rate, or 1.7 percent a year. What is more, the rate of reduction is increasing over time.[9] The dramatic improvement in the health status of those age 65 and older suggests that those in their late 50s and early 60s must also be healthier.

The outlook for the future depends on the cause of these health improvements (Cutler 2001). If they are largely due to public health changes at the beginning of the 20th century, they will fade over time

Table 8.2. Percent of U.S. Population with a Bachelor's Degree or More, 2004

Age	Men	Women
25 to 34	27.43	33.13
35 to 44	28.99	30.80
45 to 54	30.59	28.58
55 to 64	32.48	24.83
65 and over	24.81	14.30

Sources: U.S. Bureau of Labor Statistics and U.S. Census Bureau (2005) and author's calculations.

as people born well after these improvements were instituted enter old age. If the improvements are primarily due to new medical treatments, such as drugs for arthritis or cataract surgery for eye problems, they are likely to persist over time. Similarly, if people are healthier mainly because of behavioral changes, such as a reduction in smoking or fat consumption, or improved education and thus better access to medical care and greater understanding of appropriate behavior, the trend toward continued improvement is likely to persist.

Jobs Are Less Physically Demanding

The nature of employment has changed dramatically in the past 20 years. As manufacturing declined, the service sector exploded. This expansion reflects the job growth in places such as universities, hospitals, software developers, and management consulting firms. Even within manufacturing, the nature of jobs has changed, as firms have automated or outsourced production and now employ more managers, engineers, and technicians (Massachusetts Office of the Governor 2001). Generally, jobs now involve more knowledge-based activities. Employers looking to fill less physically demanding knowledge-based jobs should be more willing to hire older workers who offer a wealth of skills and experience.

In summary, employers are likely to face wage pressures as the population ages. Using more capital, tapping women and immigrants, and outsourcing may help, but such measures may not restrain labor costs significantly. Increased employment of older workers seems a natural solution.

EMPLOYERS: IMPEDIMENTS TO HIRING OLDER WORKERS

Although increased employment of older workers seems like it would alleviate the problems of workers and employers alike, four impediments stand in the way. First, older workers are expensive. Second, employers resist part-time employment, which older workers disproportionately favor. Third, personnel considerations make phased retirement difficult. Finally, age discrimination, while illegal, probably continues to exist at least to some extent.

Older Workers Are Expensive

Older workers are expensive for several reasons. First, earnings rise with age, often more than can be justified by productivity.[10] Economists explain this phenomenon in terms of implicit contracts between employers and workers whereby younger workers are underpaid and older workers are overpaid to encourage workers with firm-specific skills to remain with the company (Lazear 1979). This pattern may be less prevalent than in the past with the onset of tight labor markets and the pressure of global competition. Nevertheless, older workers tend to be paid somewhat more than younger workers on a quality-adjusted basis (Altonji and Williams 1998).

In addition to cash earnings, the cost of fringe benefits—health insurance and pensions—are high for older workers. Health insurance costs increase for two reasons. First, the percentage of workers covered rises with age. In 2003, 82 percent of full-time workers age 55 to 64 had employer-provided health insurance, compared with 74 percent of 25- to 44-year-olds and 52 percent of 16- to 24-year-olds (Employee Benefit Research Institute 2005). Second, the cost of health insurance increases with age. Private health insurance costs for full-time year-round workers are between $1,000 and $1,500 for those age 20 to 44, compared with almost $2,000 for workers 45 to 54 and almost $3,000 for workers 55 to 64 (figure 8.10). If the employer self-insures, hiring an older

Figure 8.10. Per Worker Health Care Expenditures Paid by Private Insurance, 1998–2000 (2002 dollars)

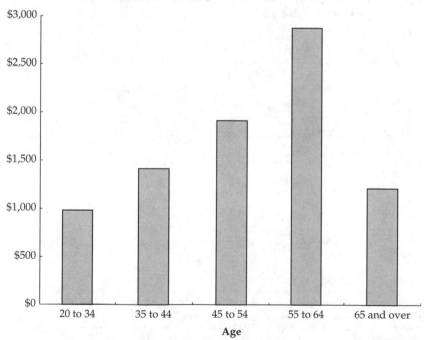

Source: Holahan (2004).

220 ■ Other Policies to Increase Supply of Skills

worker—all else equal—will drive up health care costs. If the employer purchases insurance from a carrier, hiring older workers will raise the cost of the policy.

In the case of pension costs, the impact of hiring older workers depends on the type of plan provided. With 401(k)s, the employer's contribution is generally a fixed percentage of salary and therefore rises in line with pay increases. If the older worker's salary simply reflects greater productivity, then 401(k) contributions raise no cost issue. To the extent that older workers' salaries are higher because of implicit contracts, the 401(k) contribution adds to the extra expense. On the whole, however, 401(k) plans are not a major factor in the hiring of older workers. Neither are the cash balance plans that some employers have adopted to replace their traditional defined benefit plans.

The real pension issue with older workers arises in traditional defined benefit plans. Figure 8.11 shows the average accrual rate in a sample of traditional private-sector defined benefit plans by age—that is, the increase in the present discounted value of pension benefits as a percent of earnings for each age group. The accrual rate rises sharply from 2.1 percent for those age 26 to 30 to 12.0 percent for those age 51 to 55.[11] Defined benefit plans also make *hiring* older workers costly.[12]

Figure 8.11. Average Accruals in Private Defined Benefit Plans, for Workers Starting at Age 25

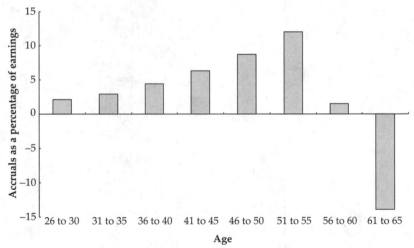

Source: Penner, Perun, and Steuerle (2002).

Notes: The analysis is based on a sample of 340 salary-based defined benefit plans in the private sector. Accrual estimates assume that workers join the firm at age 25 and leave at the age that maximizes the present discounted value of pension benefits (or age 70). The analysis assumes that wages grow at the average age-specific rate for college-educated male workers with defined benefit plans. The real interest rate is set at 3 percent and the inflation rate at 3.3 percent. Estimates are weighted by firm size.

Several other items make older workers more expensive to retain or hire (Committee for Economic Development 1999). One is paid leave. Both vacation days and sick leave tend to increase with tenure, so older workers are generally entitled to more days off than younger ones. Another is life insurance costs. Many employers provide term life insurance for their employees, and the cost of these policies is directly related to the age of the workforce. Finally, the cost associated with work injury and disability tends to be higher for older workers.

In short, the current compensation structure tends to make older workers expensive. If they are more productive because they have spent years on the job, some of the disadvantage to retaining older workers disappears. But for workers in jobs that require little training, the cost disadvantage of older workers is a serious problem.

Employers Resist Part-Time Employment

Today, two part-time people are more expensive than one full-timer because a number of costs, such as supervising and record keeping, hiring and training new workers, and fringe benefits like health insurance, are unrelated to hours worked. In the future, the price of part-time workers could decline if large numbers of older workers were willing to accept lower wages in order to attain a part-time slot. Economists do not have a good idea, however, how much compensation would have to decrease relative to full-time workers to spur demand. That is, it is unclear whether part-time compensation would have to fall by 5 percent or even 20 percent relative to full-time to persuade employers to hire more part-time workers (Hutchens 2001).

Personnel considerations also may help explain why employers resist having workers move from full-time to part-time work. For instance, it is difficult to think how a manager could function effectively coming in three days a week. Similarly, activities requiring teamwork would not lend themselves to one person working part-time. Yet, in some cases, employers clearly find a continuing part-time relationship advantageous. When they do, they generally rehire retired employees on a part-time or temporary basis or hire retirees as contractors (Brown and Schieber 2003). The rehiring approach allows employers to pick and choose those older workers with whom they would like a continuing relationship. (In the past, having employees separate from the firm was the only way employees could both continue working and claim defined benefit pension benefits before the normal retirement age. New Treasury proposals will make separation unnecessary in the future, so it will become clearer whether the pattern is driven by personnel considerations or pension rules.)

In short, older workers consistently report that they would like to reduce their hours as they age, and this preference is clearly evident in the behavior of the self-employed, who cut back gradually as they approach retirement. But employers outside the service sector and small firms appear reluctant to hire part-time workers.

Age Discrimination

Age discrimination is one barrier that should have been removed with the passage of the Age Discrimination in Employment Act (ADEA). But evidence suggests that age discrimination still exists, at least to some extent, and it may shape workplace culture affecting retention and hiring decisions. Secondary effects are also likely, since workers' perceptions of employers' practices are likely to influence their workforce decisions.

One problem in gauging the importance of age discrimination is the lack of definitive measures. Unlike other types of discrimination, age discrimination is very difficult to detect. Studies on race and gender discrimination proceed on the assumption that, all else equal, minorities and women are as productive as white and male workers, respectively. Any remaining differences in earnings can therefore be attributed to discrimination. This approach is not suitable to age discrimination since the very process of aging affects productivity, both positively and negatively. Further, as noted earlier, firms may have legitimate concerns about the cost of employing older workers.

Because of the difficulty of testing for discrimination with conventional techniques, researchers rely primarily on self-reported information. The findings suggest that managers value older workers. Managers indicate that older workers often work harder and are more reliable and motivated than their younger counterparts. They also state that older workers display good judgment, quality control, and attendance, and have lower turnover (Sterns and McDaniel 1994). On the other hand, employers express concern that older workers are less willing to adapt to changing technologies or workplace practices and are more likely to have difficulty learning new skills.

These negative perceptions of older workers appear to be reflected in hiring and training decisions. In one study, résumés for an older and younger worker with equal qualifications were mailed to nearly 800 firms in the United States. When a position appeared vacant, the older worker received a less favorable response about 25 percent of the time (Bendick, Jackson, and Romero 1996). Another study looked at employers' reactions in Massachusetts and Florida to résumés submitted in response to help wanted ads and found younger workers were 40 percent more likely to be called for an interview than older workers (Lahey 2005). Other studies explored the likelihood of older workers receiving training. One based on a nationally representative sample of nearly 1,500 employers with 50 or more employees found that about 70 percent of employees in general received formal training in the previous year, compared with only about 50 percent of employees age 55 years and older. Of those who were trained, older employees also had far fewer hours of training than employees age 25 to 54 (Frazis et al. 1998).

Beyond the direct effects of age discrimination by employers on recruitment and training, age discrimination creates an additional, more subtle, barrier to work through the perceptions of older workers. According to data from the HRS, between 10 and 20 percent of older workers indicate that younger workers are given preference over older workers and that their employers exert pressure on them to retire. This perception of discrimination on the part of workers significantly increases the likelihood that older workers will leave their jobs and the workforce.

POLICIES TO PROMOTE GREATER LABOR FORCE PARTICIPATION AMONG THE ELDERLY

In order for greater numbers of older people to remain in the workforce, they must be willing to participate—that is, they must be willing to *supply* their labor—and employers must be willing to hire them—that is, employers must *demand* their labor.

Changes to Date

Several important changes have occurred in the past 20 years that changed employer attitudes toward older workers or alleviated older workers' disincentives to work: the elimination of mandatory retirement, the shift from defined benefit to defined contribution plans, and changes in Social Security.

On the employers' side, a major intervention to affect employer behavior has been amendments to the ADEA that outlawed mandatory retirement before age 70 in 1978 and effectively abolished it altogether in 1986. A study of the retirement patterns in educational institutions in the wake of the elimination of mandatory retirement found that retirement rates fell by two-thirds for faculty who had reached the former mandatory retirement age (Ashenfelter and Card 2002). With regard to the *hiring* of older workers, the evidence about the antidiscrimination thrust of the legislation is somewhat murkier. Some critics charge that the legislation may have made employers less willing to hire older workers for fear of being sued (Posner 1995). Nevertheless, on balance, the legislation has probably eliminated an obstacle to continued employment.

Changes incurred in the structure of employer-sponsored plans have also reduced incentives to retire early. Provisions in many traditional defined benefit plans offer a significant subsidy for early retirement, while 401(k) plans are neutral with respect to retirement age. The subsidy arises because companies offer benefits at an early retirement age, such as 55, that are not adjusted sufficiently to reflect the fact that retirees will receive benefits for 10 years longer than if they retired at age 65.[13] The subsidy implicit in the less-than-actuarially-fair reduction then gradually declines and disappears entirely at the normal retirement age.[14] This pattern produces a strong incentive to retire early. In contrast, 401(k) plans work like savings accounts and contain no incentives to retire at any particular age. A series of studies has documented that workers covered by 401(k) plans retire a year or two later on average than similarly situated workers covered by a defined benefit plan (Friedberg and Webb 2000; Munnell, Cahill, and Jivan 2003).

On the defined benefit side, the Internal Revenue Service has issued proposals to improve the possibility of phased retirement. Formerly, employees covered by a defined benefit plan could not receive any pension benefits as they moved to part-time employment until they had reached the plan's normal retirement age.[15] A plan that paid such benefits could lose its tax-qualified status, since it was permitted to pay benefits only in the event of death, disability, termination of employment, or at the normal retirement age. To the extent that workers who reduce their hours need to supplement their earnings with pension benefits, the previous regulations made continued employment with the same firm difficult. In November 2004, the Internal Revenue Service issued a proposal that would allow employers to pay a pro rata share of the employee's benefits before the normal retirement age, assuming the employee cut his or her hours by 20 percent or more. The proposal was generally well received, and final regulations are expected shortly.

Finally, several changes to the Social Security program have made it more age-neutral with respect to retirement. The first change pertains to the earnings test. Since Social Security was insurance against loss of income due to retirement, the government imposed an earnings test. But the earnings test encouraged people to retire early because it seemed like a tax. Most beneficiaries were unaware that the reduction in benefits while working triggered an increase in benefits later. In recent years, Congress increased the exempt amount for all beneficiaries subject to the earnings test. And, for pensioners between the normal retirement age and 69, it first reduced the benefit loss for each dollar earned over that exempt amount (from 50 to 33 cents) and then eliminated the test altogether beginning in 2000.

Congress also increased the reward that workers receive for delaying initial benefit receipt past the normal retirement age. When this formula change is fully implemented, for workers attaining age 62 after 2004, the adjustment for delayed benefit receipt will be much closer to actuarially fair, or age-neutral. This means that, for a worker with average life expectancy, lifetime Social Security benefits will be about the same regardless of whether the pension begins at age 62, age 65, or age 70. Thus, the incentives to retire early have been substantially reduced.

Proposals to Increase the Supply of Older Workers

One powerful way to encourage later withdrawal from the labor force is to change the age at which people first qualify for Social Security benefits. As discussed earlier, Social Security's earliest eligibility age (EEA) allows workers to claim reduced benefits as early as age 62. And the vast majority of both men and women jump at this option. Many people find work onerous and seize retirement benefits as soon as they become available.

The problem with claiming early is that the monthly benefit is actuarially reduced.[16] And the reduction is scheduled to increase from 20 to 30 percent as the normal retirement age moves from 65 to 67 (table 8.3).[17] The reduction in monthly benefits can have a profound impact as retirees age, since the elderly tend to spend down their other retirement assets and rely increasingly on Social Security. In essence, as life expectancies lengthen, keeping the EEA at 62 shifts more Social Security benefits toward "middle age" (Steuerle and Spiro 1999). Raising the EEA to, say, 64—in step with the two-year increase in the normal retirement age—would counteract this shortsightedness and prevent incomes from falling to inadequately low levels.

More important for the purpose of this analysis, raising the EEA is likely to encourage people to work longer. Currently, retirement rates, as measured by the percent decrease in participation rates, spike sharply at age 62 for both men and women (figure 8.12). Increasing labor force participation among those in their early 60s is possibly the best solution to keeping people in the labor force longer.

Table 8.3. Benefits as a Percent of the Worker's PIA

Full retirement age	Workers Retiring at			
	62	65	67	70
65 in 2002	80.0	100.0	113.0	125.0
66 in 2009–2020	75.0	93.8	108.0	132.0
67 in 2027	70.0	88.0	100.0	124.0

Sources: U.S. Social Security Administration (2005b) and author's calculations.

Figure 8.12. The Percent of Working People Who Retire at a Given Age (Hazard Rate), 1992–2002

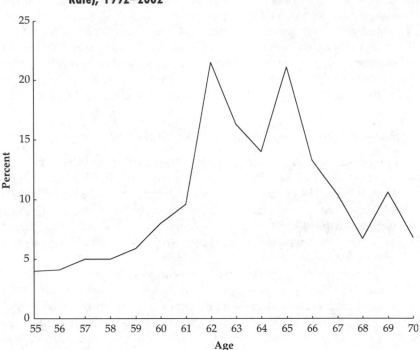

Sources: University of Michigan (1992–2002) and author's calculations.

Not everyone is convinced, however, that raising the EEA is a good idea. Opponents claim that many individuals can neither work longer nor save more for retirement. Raising the EEA could impoverish these groups as well as strain social programs like Disability Income and Supplemental Security Income that would likely end up serving more people. Finally, critics contend that withholding benefits until a later age hurts those with shorter life expectancies and shifts more retirement wealth to those with longer lives.

Both criticisms have some merit, but they need to be put in perspective. First, four studies have found the majority of workers who claim benefits early have significant non–Social Security income (Burkhauser, Couch, and Phillips 1996; CBO 1999; Munnell and Sundén 2004; Panis et al. 2002). This suggests that, if the EEA were raised, retirees could use their own assets during ages 62 and 63. Among those without alternative income sources, many could remain at work beyond age 62. Nevertheless, a sizeable minority—about 10 percent of early claimers, or 4 percent of all those age 62—are in poor health and do not have a source of income other than Social Security. This group would need assistance between age 62 and 64 through either the Disability Insurance or the Supplemental Security Income program. Even these individuals, however, would be better off in the long run because they would receive higher monthly Social Security benefits. On the other hand, it may be too cavalier to say that anyone capable of work can work, since recent studies suggest that continued work might be a real hardship for some individuals.

Withholding Social Security benefits until age 64 would hurt those with shorter life expectancies, and these people tend to be African Americans—particularly men. Such knowledge of an inequitable outcome across different groups makes it difficult to enact legislation to increase the EEA. However, the impact is relatively small—2 to 3 percent of lifetime Social Security benefits—and should be considered in the context of the entire Social Security program. Many of those who would be hurt by a higher EEA tend to have lower earnings. As such, they gain from the progressivity of the Social Security benefit formula, which awards proportionately greater benefits to low earners.

Thus, despite the obvious negatives, raising the EEA may be a desirable policy. But it is a hard sell politically. It does nothing to eliminate Social Security's long-term financing gap and would probably require greater current outlays by other programs. The best that could be said on the financing side is that it may pave the way for future increases in the normal retirement age, which does improve solvency. Raising the EEA thus is probably a realistic option only as part of a package of other changes that restore financial balance and maintain equity in the Social Security program.

Proposals to Increase the Demand for Older Workers

The only real way to increase employer demand for older workers is to reduce their cost. The most common proposal is to eliminate the requirement for those age 65 and older that Medicare serve as the secondary payer. That is, workers would be covered by Medicare rather than their employer's plan, relieving companies of a substantial expense. In the short run, this change would only cost 1.5 percent of Medicare spending since so few people work past 65, but, if the change were successful, costs would rise and further burden a program already facing enormous long-term deficits (U.S. House Committee 2000). At this time, unfortunately, such a proposal is fanciful given that the program already faces enormous long-term deficits and medical costs are growing at unprecedented rates (Penner, Perun, and Steuerle 2002; U.S. House Committee 2000).

A more modest, yet slightly more realistic, proposal is to exempt older workers from the Social Security payroll tax once they reach the earliest eligibility age. This change would cost money at a time that Social Security also faces a long-term deficit. But the amounts are probably relatively small.

The other way to make older workers attractive is to improve their skills so employers get better value for the wage. Most studies looking at the prospects for older workers conclude with extensive recommendations about expanding training programs.[18] As desirable as training might be, it seems unlikely to be the answer in the United States. A recent study by the United Nations of 20 European and North American countries revealed that the United States spent less (as a percent of GDP) than any other country on these programs (United Nations Economic Commission for Europe 2003). A major initiative in this area seems unlikely.

CONCLUSION

Current sources of retirement income will likely be inadequate for low- and middle-income individuals. The Social Security program will be significantly less generous in the future than it is today, and employer-sponsored pensions, where coverage has moved from traditional plans to 401(k)s, will provide less reliable retirement income. Because of these impending shortcomings in traditional sources of retirement income, people will need employment later in life to ensure adequate retirement income.

The same demographic shifts that will cause Social Security to be less generous may put employers in a tight situation as well. They will no longer be able to rely on a rapidly growing group of younger workers in the future. So how will employers respond to a stagnating supply of labor in the face of a major increase in those age 65 and older? They will expand their use of women, immigrants, and capital, and some firms may relocate. But these responses may not be enough to make up for the slow growth in the labor force. Older workers are well educated and healthier than in the past and have a lifetime of experience.

Although the stage appears set for hiring older workers, impediments exist. First, older workers are expensive. They are paid more, sometimes in excess of their greater productivity. They involve expensive health care costs and rapidly rising pension costs under traditional defined benefit plans. Second, most existing employment policies have been geared to encouraging early retirement. Incentives to retire early rather than late are the hallmark of traditional defined benefit plans. Although these plans are significantly less important in the private sector than they were 20 years ago, they are still the dominant plan for states and localities. Third, employers resist part-time employment, which is the preferred mode for older workers, and it is unclear that employer preferences will change in the future. Finally, age discrimination, while technically illegal, probably exists.

Increased employment of older workers may well be in the interest of both workers and employers. But mutual interest is not enough. And no silver bullets exist to solve the problem. The United States has already eliminated mandatory retirement and most of the incentives to retire early in its private and public pension programs. The only remaining option to increase the supply of older workers is to deny them Social Security benefits until, say, age 64. In terms of making older workers more attractive, exempting them from payroll taxes would help somewhat. But the usual proposals to make Medicare the primary health insurance payer and increase training are simply unrealistic at this point. Progress in terms of continued employment of older workers, to the extent that it occurs, will result from a myriad of small efforts on the part of both employees and employers to be more flexible in their requirements.

NOTES

The author thanks Francesca Golub-Sass and Marric Buessing for valuable research assistance.

1. The pension coverage data discussed above apply only to individual workers at any given point in time. Over a lifetime and on a household— rather than an individual—basis, coverage rates are somewhat higher. For households age 55 to 64, the 2001 Survey of Consumer Finances shows that approximately 65 percent of households had some sort of pension coverage in 2001. Pension coverage is much more extensive for high-income households.

2. The annuity might be a dollar amount per month for each year of service, say $50; so workers with 20 years of service would receive $1,000 per month at age 65. The benefit could also be a percentage of final salary for each year of service, say 1.5 percent; so workers with 20 years would receive 30 percent (20 years at 1.5 percent) of final salary for as long as they live. The employer finances these benefits by making pretax contributions into a pension fund, holds the assets in trust, directs the investments, and bears the risk. The Pension Benefit Guaranty Corporation (PBGC) insures benefits up to specified limits. The PBGC monthly guarantee limit in 2003 is $3,665 at age 65 and declines to $1,649 at age 55. Employers pay for this insurance with premiums largely determined by the plan's funding status.

3. See CBS News and *New York Times*, "Poll: The Social Security Debate Continues," 2005.

4. On the other hand, a lower rate of investment will be needed in the future to increase the amount of capital per worker than was true in the past when the labor force was growing more quickly.

5. This discussion is based on Bardhan and Kroll (2003), Brainard and Litan (2004), Mann (2003), McKinsey and Company (2003), and Schultze (2004). See also Jon Hilsenrath, "Behind Outsourcing Debate: Surprisingly Few Hard Numbers," *The Wall Street Journal*, 12 April 2004, A1.

6. Recent studies show that the use of computers among workers age 50 and older has doubled since the mid-1980s, and the entire population, including older workers, has now become familiar with computers, the hallmark of the "new economy" (Friedberg 2001).

7. While the workforce in the United States is and has been highly mobile, there is some dispute over whether the mobility of the U.S. workforce has increased in recent decades. See Munnell and Sundén (2004).

8. The conclusion that the health of older workers is improving is a relatively new finding. Demographers who examined the issue in the 1970s concluded that the elderly were increasingly less healthy. But these early conclusions may have been based on less than ideal data that allowed multiple interpretations. A new survey of those 65 and older designed in part to solve these data problems—the National Long-Term Care Survey—was first conducted in 1982 and now challenges this view. It asks detailed questions about disability in a consistent manner over time and now provides almost 20 years of information (Cutler 2001).

9. Between 1982 and 1989, disability rates fell by 1.0 percent a year; between 1989 and 1994, by 1.6 percent a year; and between 1994 and 1999, by 2.6 percent a year.

10. Cross-section data on earnings by age typically show a hump-shaped pattern, but longitudinal data sets generally show real wages rising at least for men into their 60s (Hurd 1996; Johnson and Neumark 1996).

11. The reason for this increase is the multiplier effect inherent in the traditional defined benefit formula. Assume that the formula provides 1.5 percent of final salary for each year of service and a 54-year-old with 20 years of service works for another year. That worker's replacement rate will increase from 30 to 31.5 percent. In addition, the entire 31.5 percent will apply to salary earned in that 21st year of service, increasing the value of all the previously earned pension credits. For this reason, defined benefit pension accruals rise much faster than salary, making the retention of older workers very expensive.

12. Suppose the plan provides 1.5 percent of final salary and that the employee earns $35,000 during the first year of employment. Both the older and younger worker will be entitled to benefits of $525 a year (1.5 percent of $35,000) when they retire. The older worker, however, can retire in five years at age 60, while the younger worker has to wait 35 years. That means in terms of calculating the present value of the accrued pension benefit at age 60, the $525 for the older worker is discounted by five years while the $525 for the younger worker is discounted by 35 years. The fewer years of discounting means a much larger required contribution to the pension plan for the older worker, making the hiring of older workers in firms with traditional defined benefit plans very expensive.

13. For example, suppose a person will live for 20 years and is entitled to a pension of $15,000 at age 65; lifetime benefits will equal $300,000 (20 × $15,000). To keep lifetime benefits constant, if that employee retired at 55, his annual benefit should be only $10,000 a year (30 × $10,000 = $300,000). But traditional defined benefit plans typically provide far more because they use

an actuarial reduction that is smaller than the full reduction. That is, they pay, say, $12,000 at age 55, which means that the worker in this example who retires at 55 would receive substantially more in lifetime pension benefits than if he or she were to retire at 65. The exercise is actually somewhat more complicated because the employee adds to his pension if he continues to work.

14. Often working beyond the normal retirement age results in negative pension accruals. The law requires that the wage increases of those who work beyond the normal retirement age be reflected in higher retirement benefits. But it does not prevent firms from capping the years of service used to calculate benefits; nor does it require firms to provide actuarial adjustments for the fact that participants will receive benefits for fewer years (McGill et al. 1996).

15. Participants in 401(k) plans who reach age 59½ can continue to work for their employer and receive distributions from their account. Before age 59½, any distribution—in service or not—is subject to a 10-percent excise tax in addition to ordinary income taxes. The law provides two exceptions. First, distributions may begin as early as 55 if the employee separates from his employer under an early retirement plan. Second, if benefits are paid as a lifelong annuity, they can begin at any age. Thus, these plans do not preclude part-time work and pension receipt.

16. Benefits are reduced by $\frac{5}{9}$ of 1 percent for each month they are received prior to the normal retirement age up to 36 months and by $\frac{5}{12}$ of 1 percent for each month thereafter. This is equivalent to a 6.67 percent reduction for the first three years prior to the normal retirement age and 5 percent thereafter.

17. The increase began with individuals born in 1938, for whom the normal retirement age (NRA) is 65 plus two months, and increases two months a year until it reaches age 66. Then, after a 12-year hiatus, the NRA again increases by two months a year until it reaches age 67 for individuals born in 1960 or later.

18. For example, see OECD (2005).

REFERENCES

AARP. 1998. "Baby Boomers Envision Retirement." Washington, DC: American Association of Retired Persons.

————. 2004. "Baby Boomers Envision Retirement II." Washington, DC: American Association of Retired Persons.

Altonji, Joseph G., and Nicolas Williams. 1998. "The Effects of Labor Market Experience, Job Seniority, and Mobility on Wage Growth." In *Research in Labor Economics*, edited by Solomon W. Polachek (233–76). Stamford and London: JAI Press.

Ashenfelter, Orley, and David Card. 2002. "Did the Elimination of Mandatory Retirement Affect Faculty Retirement?" *The American Economic Review* 92(4): 957–80.

Bardhan, Ashok Deo, and Cynthia A. Kroll. 2003. "The New Wave of Outsourcing." Research report. Berkeley: Fisher Center for Real Estate and Urban Economics, University of California, Berkeley.

Bendick, Marc, Jr., Charles W. Jackson, and J. Horacio Romero. 1996. "Employment Discrimination Against Older Workers: An Experimental Study of Hiring Practices." *Journal of Aging and Social Policy* 8(4): 25–46.

Brainard, Lael, and Robert E. Litan. 2004. " 'Offshoring' Service Jobs: Bane or Boon and What to Do?" Policy Brief 132. Washington, DC: The Brookings Institution.

Brown, Kyle N., and Sylvester Schieber. 2003. "Structural Impediments to Phased Retirement." Mimeo, Watson Wyatt Worldwide.

Burkhauser, Richard V., Kenneth A. Couch, and John W. Phillips. 1996. "Who Takes Early Social Security Benefits? The Economic and Health Characteristics of Early Beneficiaries." *Gerontologist* 36(6): 789–99.

Burtless, Gary, and Joseph F. Quinn. 2002. "Is Working Longer the Answer for an Aging Workforce?" Issue in Brief 11. Chestnut Hill, MA: Center for Retirement Research at Boston College.

Calvo, Esteban. 2006. "Does Working Longer Make People Healthier and Happier?" Work Opportunities Brief 2. Chestnut Hill, MA: Center for Retirement Research at Boston College.

CBO. See Congressional Budget Office.

Committee for Economic Development. 1999. *New Opportunities for Older Workers*. New York: Research and Policy Committee of the Committee for Economic Development.

Congressional Budget Office. 1999. *Raising the Earliest Eligibility Age for Social Security Benefits.* Washington, DC: U.S. Government Printing Office.

———. 2004. "Retirement Age and the Need for Saving." Economic and Budget Issue brief. Washington, DC: Congressional Budget Office.

Copeland, Craig. 2003. "Employee Tenure." *Employee Benefit Research Institute Notes* 24(3): 1–10.

Cutler, David M. 2001. "The Reduction in Disability among the Elderly." *Proceedings of the National Academy of Sciences of the United States of America* 98(12): 6546–47.

Employee Benefit Research Institute. 1994–2004. *Retirement Confidence Survey: Summary of Findings.* Washington, DC: Employee Benefit Research Institute.

———. 2005. *Databook on Employee Benefits.* Washington, DC: Employee Benefit Research Institute.

Frazis, Harley, Maury Gittleman, Michael Horrigan, and Mary Joyce. 1998. "Results from the 1995 Survey of Employer-Provided Training." *Monthly Labor Review* 121(6): 3–13.

Friedberg, Leora. 2001. "The Impact of Technological Change on Older Workers: Evidence from Data on Computer Use." Working Paper 8,297. Cambridge, MA: National Bureau of Economic Research.

Friedberg, Leora, and Anthony Webb. 2000. "The Impact of 401(k) Plans on Retirement." Discussion Paper 2000-30. San Diego: Department of Economics, University of California, San Diego.

Gruber, Jonathan, and Courtney Coile. 2000. "Social Security Incentives for Retirement." Working Paper 7,651. Cambridge, MA: National Bureau of Economic Research.

Holahan, John. 2004. "Health Insurance Coverage of the Near Elderly." Washington, DC: Kaiser Commission on Medicaid and the Uninsured.

Hurd, Michael D. 1996. "The Effect of Labor Market Rigidities on the Labor Force Behavior of Older Workers." In *Advances in the Economics of Aging*, edited by David A. Wise (11–58). Chicago and London: The University of Chicago Press.

Hutchens, Robert. 2001. "Employer Surveys, Employer Policies, and Future Demand for Older Workers." Paper prepared for a Roundtable on the Demand for Older Workers, sponsored by the Retirement Research Consortium, Washington, D.C., March 23.

Johnson, Richard W., and David Neumark. 1996. "Wage Declines among Older Men." *Review of Economics and Statistics* 78(4): 740–47.

Lahey, Joanna N. 2005. "Do Older Workers Face Discrimination?" Issue in Brief 33. Chestnut Hill, MA: Center for Retirement Research at Boston College.

Lazear, Edward P. 1979. "Why Is There Mandatory Retirement?" *Journal of Political Economy* 87(6): 1261–84.

Mann, Catherine L. 2003. "Globalization of IT Services and White Collar Jobs: The Next Wave of Productivity Growth." International Economics Policy Briefs PB03-11. Washington, DC: Institute for International Economics.

Manton, Kenneth G., and XiLiang Gu. 2001. "Changes in the Prevalence of Chronic Disability in the United States Black and Nonblack Population above Age 65 from 1982 to 1999." *Proceedings of the National Academy of Sciences of the United States of America* 98(11): 6354–59.

Massachusetts Office of the Governor. 2001. *Massachusetts toward a New Prosperity: Building Regional Competitiveness.* Boston: Massachusetts Office of the Governor.

McCarthy, John C., Christine Ferrusi Ross, William Martorelli, Christopher Mines, and Adam Brown. 2004. "Near-Term Growth of Offshoring Accelerating: Resizing U.S. Services Jobs Going Offshore." Forrester Research *Trends.* Cambridge, MA: Forrester Research.

McGill, Dan M., Kyle N. Brown, John J. Haley, and Sylvester J. Schieber. 1996. *Fundamentals of Private Pensions.* 7th ed. Philadelphia: University of Pennsylvania Press.

McKinsey and Company. 2003. *Offshoring: Is It a Win-Win Game?* Perspective. New York: McKinsey and Company.

Montgomery, Mark. 1988. "On the Determinants of Employer Demand for Part-Time Workers." *Review of Economics and Statistics* 70(1): 112–17.

Munnell, Alicia H. 2003. "The Declining Role of Social Security." *Just the Facts on Retirement Issues.* Chestnut Hill, MA: Center for Retirement Research at Boston College.

Munnell, Alicia, and Annika Sundén. 2004. *Coming Up Short: The Challenge of 401(k) Plans.* Washington, DC: Brookings Institution Press.

Munnell, Alicia H., Kevin E. Cahill, and Natalia A. Jivan. 2003. "How Has the Shift to 401(k)s Affected the Retirement Age?" Issue in Brief 13. Chestnut Hill, MA: Center for Retirement Research at Boston College.

Munnell, Alicia H., Francesca Golub-Sass, and Andrew Varani. 2005. "How Much Are Workers Saving?" Issue in Brief 34. Chestnut Hill, MA: Center for Retirement Research at Boston College.

Nyce, Steven A., and Sylvester J. Schieber. 2002. "The Decade of the Employee: The Workforce Environment in the Coming Decade." *Benefits Quarterly* 1: 60–79.

OECD. See Organisation for Economic Co-operation and Development.

Organisation for Economic Co-operation and Development. 2005. *Ageing and Employment Policies: United States.* Paris: Organisation for Economic Co-operation and Development.

Panis, Constantijn, Michael Hurd, David Loughran, Julie Zissimopoulos, Steven Haider, Patricia St. Clair, Delia Bugliari, Serhii Ilchuk, Gabriela Lopez, Philip Pantoja, and Monika Reti. 2002. "The Effects of Changing Social Security Administration's Early Entitlement Age and the Normal Retirement Age." Santa Monica, CA: RAND Corporation.

Penner, Rudolph G., Pamela Perun, and Eugene Steuerle. 2002. "Legal and Institutional Impediments to Partial Retirement and Part-Time Work by Older Workers." Washington, DC: The Urban Institute.

Posner, Richard A. 1995. *Aging and Old Age*. Chicago: University of Chicago Press.

Schultze, Charles. 2004. "Offshoring, Import Competition, and the Jobless Recovery." Policy Brief 136. Washington, DC: The Brookings Institution.

Sterns, H.L., and M.A. McDaniel. 1994. "Job Performance and Older Workers." In *Older Workers: How Do They Measure Up?* edited by Sara E. Rix (27–51). Washington, DC: American Association of Retired Persons.

Steuerle, C. Eugene, and Christopher Spiro. 1999. "Adjusting for Life Expectancy in Measures of Labor Force Participation." Straight Talk on Social Security and Retirement Policy 10. Washington, DC: The Urban Institute.

Tilly, Chris. 1991. "Reasons for the Continuing Growth of Part-Time Employment." *Monthly Labor Review* 114(3): 10–18.

Triest, Robert K., Margarita Sapozhnikov, and Steven A. Sass. 2005. "Population Aging and the Structure of Wages." Paper prepared for the 7th Annual Conference of the Retirement Research Consortium: "Towards a Secure Retirement System," Washington, D.C., August 11–12.

United Nations Economic Commission for Europe. 2003. *Trends in Europe and North America: The Statistical Yearbook of the Economic Commission for Europe, 2003*. Geneva: United Nations Economic Commission for Europe.

University of Michigan. 1992–2002. *Health and Retirement Study*. Ann Arbor: University of Michigan.

U.S. Bureau of Labor Statistics. 2004. "Extended Mass Layoffs Associated With Domestic and Overseas Relocations, First Quarter 2004." Washington, DC: U.S. Department of Labor, Bureau of Labor Statistics.

U.S. Bureau of Labor Statistics and U.S. Census Bureau. 1962–2005. *Current Population Survey*. Washington, DC: U.S. Bureau of Labor Statistics and U.S. Census Bureau.

U.S. Census Bureau. 1996. *Statistical Abstract of the United States: 1995*. Washington, DC: U.S. Census Bureau.

———. 2001. *Statistical Abstract of the United States 2001*. Washington, DC: U.S. Census Bureau.

———. 2002. *Statistical Abstract of the United States 2002*. Washington, DC: U.S. Census Bureau.

———. 2005. *Statistical Abstract of the United States 2004–2005*. Washington, DC: U.S. Census Bureau.

U.S. Congress. House. Committee on Ways and Means. 2000. *The 2000 Green Book Background Material and Data on Programs within the Jurisdiction of the Committee on Ways and Means*. Washington, DC: U.S. Government Printing Office.

U.S. Department of Labor. 2005. *Labor Force Data Files*. Washington, DC: U.S. Department of Labor.

U.S. General Accounting Office. 2001. *Older Workers: Demographic Trends Pose Challenges for Employers and Workers*. GAO-02-85. Washington, DC: U.S. General Accounting Office.

U.S. Social Security Administration. 2005a. *Annual Statistical Supplement, 2004*. Washington, DC: U.S. Social Security Administration.

———. 2005b. *The 2005 Annual Report of the Board of Trustees of the Federal Old-Age and Survivors Insurance and Disability Insurance Trust Funds*. Washington, DC: U.S. Government Printing Office.

Welch, Finis. 1979. "Effects of Cohort Size on Earnings: The Baby Boom Babies' Financial Bust." *Journal of Political Economy* 87(5): S65–S97.

PART V

OTHER PROBLEMS: INSURING AGAINST RISK, BALANCING WORK AND FAMILY

9

INCOME SUPPORTS FOR WORKERS AND THEIR FAMILIES: EARNINGS SUPPLEMENTS AND HEALTH INSURANCE

Gary Burtless

Advances in technology, changes in consumer tastes, and shifts in world trade inevitably lead to labor market disruption. By definition, improvements in productivity mean that fewer workers are needed to produce the same amount of goods and services. When productivity in an industry climbs fast enough, the need for employees in the industry will decline, forcing many long-service workers to find jobs in another industry or occupation. Shifting consumer tastes and swings in global trade also lead to substantial worker displacement. On humanitarian, social, and political grounds, it is essential to lessen the economic injury that job loss entails.

Some of the financial hardship that follows job loss is offset by unemployment insurance. Experienced U.S. workers who are laid off from their jobs can claim unemployment benefits that replace about half their lost earnings, at least up to a maximum weekly benefit amount. Since this maximum payment represents roughly half the wages earned by an average worker covered by the unemployment insurance system, laid-off workers who earn above-average wages collect benefits that replace a smaller percentage of their lost earnings. Unemployment insurance benefits are time-limited as well. Under ordinary circumstances, benefits are restricted to just 26 weeks. Laid-off workers who fail to find work within six months of losing a job will run out of unemployment benefits before they start earning another paycheck.

Further, the unemployment insurance system only replaces the money wages that workers lose when they are laid off. It does not insure workers against the loss of health insurance or other fringe benefits that are tied to the lost job. For a private-sector employee, the employer's contribution for health, retirement, and insurance benefits, excluding mandatory social insurance, averages about 16 percent of the worker's money wage (BLS 2005). The loss of fringe benefits is particularly important for workers who depend on their employers for health insurance. Insurance purchased outside an employer's health plan is so costly that few unemployed workers can afford it.

Laid-off U.S. workers face considerable income and health insurance risks in the 21st century labor market. In particular, the income replacement provided under the unemployment insurance system is decreasing, and the significance of lost health insurance when workers are laid off from their jobs is increasing. The design and reach of the unemployment insurance system might account for the declining effectiveness of the program in protecting the incomes of the nation's unemployed.

Long-tenure workers sustain economic losses when they are permanently dismissed from their jobs. Displacement and the welfare losses caused by displacement could represent more serious problems today than they did in the earlier post-war period. One of the most important differences between today's job market and that of the early post-war era is that health insurance has become a major component of worker compensation. Thus, displacement poses serious risks, both for workers who lose their jobs and for active workers and their families.

Possible solutions include severing the tie between employment and health insurance, subsidizing health insurance for unemployed workers, lengthening or broadening the reach of unemployment compensation, or supplementing traditional unemployment benefits with earnings insurance. Implementing any of these changes, however, requires a major shift in America's perspective on unemployment and health insurance.

UNEMPLOYMENT COMPENSATION

The United States offers one principal form of insurance to workers who lose their jobs as a result of a temporary or permanent layoff—unemployment compensation. The U.S. system was established in the Great Depression as part of the Social Security Act. It assumed its present-day form and scale shortly after World War II. The system serves two critical functions. It provides workers with essential income protection when they are temporarily unemployed as a result of a layoff. And by helping unemployed workers maintain their consumption in bad times, it gives the nation valuable macroeconomic stimulus in periods when overall unemployment is high or rising.

Administration and Financing

Unemployment insurance is provided under a complicated federal–state administrative arrangement. The federal government collects unemployment insurance payroll taxes from employers in all the states and gives partial rebates of those taxes to states maintaining unemployment insurance programs that conform to broad federal requirements. Not surprisingly, all states have set up qualifying programs. If a state failed to do so, the federal government would collect the full federal unemployment tax, but none of the collected funds would be used in the state to pay for program administration or insurance benefits.

State employment security agencies are responsible for determining eligibility, calculating and paying weekly benefits, providing employment services to the unemployed, and ensuring that unemployed workers who file claims continue to make good-faith efforts to find a job. Under broad federal guidelines, state legislatures make laws setting state payroll tax schedules as well as payment levels and eligibility standards for benefits. State payroll tax revenues are deposited in separate trust fund accounts for each state, and the federal payroll tax is deposited in a small number of federal unemployment trust funds. Most benefit payments are paid out of the separate state trust funds.

The federal government pays for nearly all the administrative cost of state programs. A federal unemployment insurance trust fund also pays for half the cost of extended benefits, a special compensation program that provides three extra months of compensation to unemployed workers in states with exceptionally high unemployment rates. All regular benefits—that is, all benefits paid during the first six months of unemployment—and half the cost of extended benefits are financed out of state unemployment insurance payroll taxes. If a state's unemployment trust fund contains too little money to pay for current benefits, the federal government lends the state program money from a federal trust fund. States are obliged to repay these loans (with interest). The federal government imposes penalty unemployment payroll taxes on employers in states that fail to repay loans in a timely manner.

The tax used to pay for unemployment benefits has two unusual features. First, it is a payroll tax imposed mainly on employers, but the annual wages subject to tax are low in relation to average wage levels.[1] The federal portion of the unemployment tax is only imposed on the first $7,000 of a worker's annual earnings, and this taxable wage limit has remained unchanged since 1983. In contrast, the taxable wage base for the Social Security Old-Age, Survivors, and Disability Insurance program was $90,000 in 2005, and this base is adjusted every year in line with the growth in wages. More than half the states have an unemployment tax wage base higher than $7,000, but only a few have a wage base above $20,000, and only one state had a wage base over $30,000 in 2005. A full-time worker who earns the U.S. minimum wage and is employed 52 weeks a year earns about $10,700. The federal unemployment insurance wage base is less than two-thirds of this earnings amount. Only 20 of the 50 states have a taxable wage base that is higher than $10,700. In effect, the unemployment insurance tax represents a head tax on company employment rather than an ordinary payroll tax on company wage payments.

A second unusual feature of the U.S. unemployment tax is experience rating. Each company's payroll tax rate is based on the employer's unemployment insurance claims experience. In other words, each company faces a tax rate determined by the cost of insurance claims filed by its laid-off workers. Firms with poor lay-off experiences and a high rate of claims for unemployment benefits pay a higher payroll tax rate than employers with good lay-off experiences. In nearly every other country with an unemployment insurance payroll tax, all employers or employees face an identical unemployment payroll tax rate.

Benefits

U.S. unemployment benefits are notably less generous than the norm in other rich industrialized countries. Analysts usually assess the generosity of an unemployment system by calculating the benefit replacement rate, which is the percentage of net earnings lost as a result of a layoff that is replaced by the after-tax value of the unemployment benefit. Among 20 rich countries around the world, the United States ranks 16th in the unemployment insurance replacement rate it provides to unemployed workers in the first few months after a layoff.[2]

Jobless workers' precise benefits depend on the state where a claim is filed, the level and pattern of earnings over the last 15 months on a job, and, in many states, on the number of a worker's dependents. The

Organisation for Economic Co-operation and Development (OECD) calculates that U.S. workers earning two-thirds of the average wage who live in single-earner households obtain a net replacement rate of 52–62 percent. Workers who steadily earn the average wage typically receive net unemployment benefits that replace 53–57 percent of their net wages, and workers earning one and one-half times the average wage obtain a replacement rate of 38–40 percent of their net wages. These replacement rates are lower than rates available in most other rich countries, and the gap is particularly large in the case of unemployed workers with dependents or above-average earnings.

Figure 9.1 shows the net replacement rate for a laid-off married worker who has a nonworking spouse and two dependent children and who earned the average production worker's wage before losing his or her job. OECD estimates are displayed for 20 rich countries ranked according to the replacement rate that unemployed workers receive in the first six months after losing a job. For this type of unemployed worker, the United States ranks 19th out of 20 countries, though its rank varies depending on the exact wage and family circumstances of the laid-off worker. For workers at other wage levels and in other family circumstances, the replacement rate in the United States may be 4 to 26 percentage points (or 6 percent to 36 percent) below the average replacement rate available to similar workers in the other 19 countries.

Figure 9.1. Percent of Net Earnings Initially Replaced by After-Tax Value of Unemployment Benefits in 20 OECD Countries, 2004

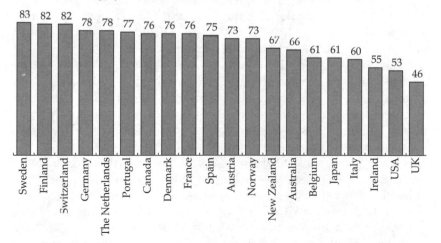

Source: OECD (2004).

Note: Rate shown is for married single earner with two children who is paid the average wage.

The overall replacement rate in the United States reflects an average of replacement rates that diverge widely across states and among workers within the same state. State governments determine exact benefit levels, but all states follow similar general principles in establishing their payment formulas. Weekly benefit amounts typically replace between 50 and 60 percent of a worker's average gross earnings, but the exact percentage can vary depending on the pattern of earnings over the worker's base period and on the number and ages of the worker's dependents. Benefit payments are treated as ordinary taxable income in the U.S. income tax and most state income tax systems. States' payment formulas differ in how they treat earnings fluctuations during the base period and how they adjust weekly benefits for workers who are supporting dependents.

In addition, the weekly benefit is limited to a state-determined maximum amount. The *maximum* weekly benefit is usually between 50 and 70 percent of the average weekly wage in the state. The 2004 maximum weekly payment ranged from $210 in Mississippi to $762 in Massachusetts (U.S. Department of Labor, Employment and Training Administration 2004). *Average* weekly payments in 2002 ranged from $167 in Alabama to $360 in Massachusetts. For the nation as a whole, the average weekly benefit payment in 2002 was 37 percent of the average weekly gross earnings of workers covered by the unemployment system. The gross replacement rate ranged from 27 percent in Arizona to 49 percent in Hawaii (Social Security Administration 2004).

Of course, average wage levels differ from state to state, and the kinds of workers who become unemployed also differ. These differences partly account for the wide variation in average benefit amounts and gross replacement rates between states with high and low average benefits. Most cross-state variability in benefit levels, however, is due to differences among states in the benefit formulas, including benefit maximums, used to calculate weekly payments.

States differ less in setting limits on potential benefit duration. Nearly all states limit the maximum duration of payments to 26 weeks. Montana allows some workers to collect benefits for up to 28 weeks, and Massachusetts and Washington permit benefit payments for up to 30 weeks. Although 26 weeks is usually the upper limit on benefit eligibility, most states calculate an individual claimant's potential benefit duration using his or her base-period earnings. A qualifying worker with low earnings in the one-year base period may qualify for fewer than 26 weeks of benefits.

After workers exhaust eligibility for regular unemployment benefits, they do not qualify for additional benefit payments until they have established eligibility by becoming reemployed and earning wages for two or more calendar quarters. Jobless workers who have exhausted their insurance eligibility can apply for means-tested benefits, such as food stamps and Temporary Assistance for Needy Families, but they will only qualify for such transfers if they meet the income and asset tests and other conditions of eligibility of the program. Experienced workers who have held a job that pays average or above-average wages for several years rarely qualify for means-tested assistance.

When the state or national unemployment rate is high, jobless workers sometimes qualify for unemployment compensation beyond the usual 26 weeks of benefits. The state-federal extended benefits program provides an additional 13 weeks of compensation payments for workers in states where the unemployment rate is higher than a threshold or "trigger" rate.[3] Half the cost is paid out of a federal government unemployment trust fund, and half is paid by states where the program triggers on.

In the past two decades, the program has rarely if ever triggered on in most states, even when the national unemployment rate is high. In June 2003, when the U.S. civilian unemployment reached a peak after the 2001 recession, extended benefits were available in only 3 of 50 states—Alaska, Oregon, and Washington. While the local unemployment rate was exceptionally high in those states, it exceeded 6.7 percent in six other states, including California, Michigan, and Texas. The Michigan extended benefits program triggered on (for five months) beginning in August 2003, but in no other state did extended benefits become available during or after the 2001 recession. Extended benefits were last available in California in July 1983. The state's unemployment rate has exceeded 8 percent in 45 of the 266 months since then. In none of those months were California's unemployed eligible for compensation under its extended benefits program.

On both humanitarian and economic grounds, it makes sense to provide longer-duration benefits to laid-off workers when the unemployment rate is high. Because unemployed workers usually need more time to find work in weak job markets, there is a compelling equity argument for offering insurance over longer spells of job search. In addition, the countercyclical effectiveness of unemployment compensation is reduced when a large percentage of laid-off workers is dropped from the rolls as a result of benefit exhaustion. For obvious reasons, workers are more likely to exhaust their regular unemployment benefits when the jobless rate is high (see figure 9.2). If no extensions of unemployment compensation were available, the percentage of unemployed who collect benefits would shrink as the length of a recession extends beyond the maximum eligibility period.

The logic of benefit extensions in recessions is apparent to most presidents and members of Congress. In every recession since the late 1950s, Congress has enacted a federally funded extension of unemploy-

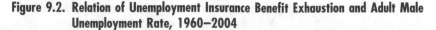

Figure 9.2. Relation of Unemployment Insurance Benefit Exhaustion and Adult Male Unemployment Rate, 1960–2004

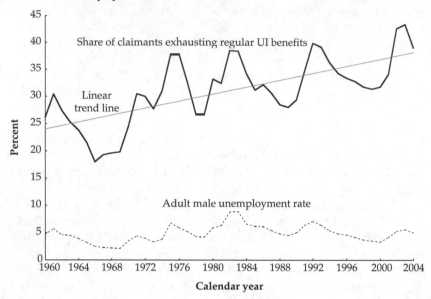

Sources: Adult male unemployment rate estimates from http://data.bls.gov; UI benefit exhaustion data from http://workforcesecurity.doleta.gov/unemploy/finance.asp.

ment benefits in addition to whatever extension might be available under the federal-state extended benefits program. The extension in 1975–77 was particularly generous, providing unemployment claimants who had exhausted both regular and extended benefits up to 26 additional weeks of compensation (for a total benefit duration that could last up to 65 weeks). The special benefit extensions in 1982–85, 1991–94, and 2002–04 were less generous but still provided extra federally financed benefits that could extend a worker's total eligibility period by up to six months. Special programs to extend the duration of unemployment benefits have been in effect during all or part of 14 of the past 31 years.[4] Depending on a worker's state of residence and the details of the federal supplemental program in effect, a worker might qualify for 6 to 39 weeks of additional unemployment compensation beyond the 26 weeks available under the regular state insurance program.

In most years, however, unemployment compensation is limited to the first 26 weeks after a worker is laid off. This eligibility period is one of the shortest in the industrialized world. Figure 9.3 shows the potential duration of standard unemployment benefits in 20 rich countries. Countries are arranged in the same order as in figure 9.1—that is, from highest to lowest initial replacement rate. The United States,

Figure 9.3. Duration of Unemployment Benefits in 20 OECD Countries, in months, 2004

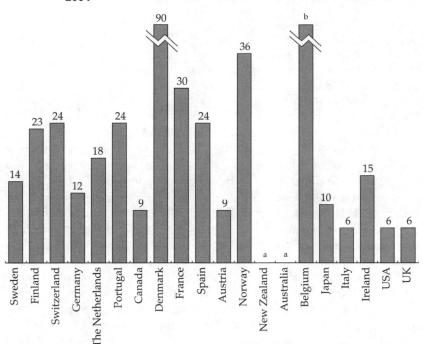

Source: OECD (2004).

[a] Australia and New Zealand offer only means-tested benefits. If the eligibility test continues to be met, unemployment benefits can last indefinitely.

[b] Belgium essentially provides unemployment benefits of indefinite duration.

Italy, and the United Kingdom now offer benefits for the shortest duration, six months. Unemployment benefits in Australia and New Zealand are means-tested, but these can last indefinitely for jobless workers who meet the income test and other eligibility conditions. Unemployed workers in 12 other countries can receive standard benefits that last a year or longer.

One clear implication of figures 9.1 and 9.3 is that workers who experience very long unemployment spells receive considerably less income protection in the United States than they would obtain in most other industrial countries. Average-wage workers who are unemployed for five successive years would typically receive unemployment benefits that replace 40 to 50 percent of their lost net earnings in the other 19 countries. In the United States, unemployment benefits replace just 5 or 6 percent of lost earnings. Even after adding the social assistance benefits available to jobless workers in a long unemployment spell, the replacement rate in the United States falls substantially below the average rate in the other 19 countries (OECD 2004).

Incentives

While most people accept unemployment insurance as an essential component of income protection, many would also acknowledge the program creates adverse incentives for recipients. Because an unemployment insurance payment replaces a sizeable percentage of the earnings a worker loses as a result of unemployment, it reduces the pressure on workers to accept a job. This can be an advantage both to the worker and the wider economy if it improves a worker's capacity to reject bad job offers and find better ones. By improving the matches between workers and job openings, the program improves the average productivity of the workforce. This function of unemployment insurance is much more important in advanced industrialized countries than it is in less-developed labor markets, where workers have less human capital and fewer specialized skills.

But unemployment insurance also creates important incentive problems (Fredriksson and Holmlund 2003). It allows workers to postpone serious search for a new job, and it encourages some of the unemployed to reject good job offers. In both these cases, taxpayers are obliged to pay for additional unemployment benefits to a worker even though the worker is not productively engaged in finding a job. A cynic might say the weekly payment subsidizes a vacation for the unemployed worker rather than purposeful search for new employment.

The policymakers who established U.S. unemployment insurance were aware of these incentive problems. To reduce their adverse impact, legislators limited benefits to a carefully restricted population, provided payments that replace two-thirds or less of workers' lost earnings, required workers to show evidence of job search, and limited benefits to just six months after a layoff. Whether these program features produce an optimal trade-off between good income protection and sound incentives is an open question.

Clearly, the United States has struck a balance between income protection and job-finding incentives that differs significantly from the one adopted in most other rich countries. By providing smaller and shorter-lasting benefits, the U.S. system encourages unemployed workers to find jobs quickly. There is some evidence the incentives are effective. Figure 9.4 shows the percentage of labor force participants who have been unemployed for one year or longer in 20 rich countries. Long unemployment spells are rare in the United States and some other countries that provide limited benefits to their unemployed. Long spells are more common in several countries where lengthy unemploy-

Figure 9.4. Unemployed Who Have Been Jobless for One Year or More as a Percentage of the Labor Force in 20 OECD Countries, 2004

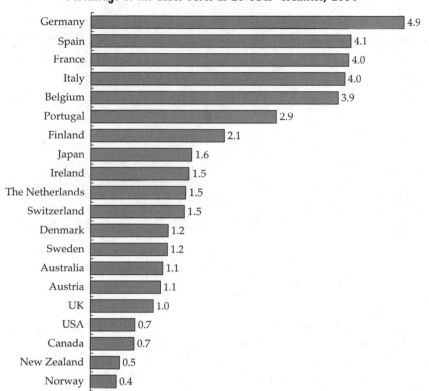

Germany 4.9
Spain 4.1
France 4.0
Italy 4.0
Belgium 3.9
Portugal 2.9
Finland 2.1
Japan 1.6
Ireland 1.5
The Netherlands 1.5
Switzerland 1.5
Denmark 1.2
Sweden 1.2
Australia 1.1
Austria 1.1
UK 1.0
USA 0.7
Canada 0.7
New Zealand 0.5
Norway 0.4

Source: Author's calculations based on OECD (2004), 237 and 258.

ment is generously compensated, particularly Germany, France, and Belgium. Note, however, that Norway has the lowest rate of long-term unemployment, even though it provides generous and long-lasting insurance, while Italy has high long-term joblessness even though its benefits are not much more generous than those in the United States.

Trends

Although the unemployment insurance system remains a vital part of the nation's social safety net, its importance has declined over time, both as a source of protection against income loss during unemployment and as a countercyclical stimulus when joblessness rises. Figure 9.5 shows the relationship between the adult unemployment rate and spending on unemployment benefits. The adult unemployment rate is measured using the civilian unemployment rate of men age 20 and older. Spend-

Figure 9.5. Relation of Unemployment Rate and Spending on Unemployment Compensation, Fiscal Years 1960–2004

Source: Author's calculations based on unemployment estimates from http://data.bls.gov, unemployment insurance outlays from OMB (2006), and data on U.S. wage and salary income from U.S. Department of Commerce NIPA estimates.

ing on unemployment benefits is measured as the ratio of state and federal outlays on all types of unemployment compensation compared with total wage disbursements in the public and private sectors. The chart shows the strong cyclical sensitivity of unemployment spending. Outlays on unemployment compensation more than doubled between fiscal years 1969 and 1971 and then fell almost 30 percent in the next two years. Spending nearly tripled between 1974 and 1976 and then fell about two-thirds by 1979. Note, however, that the surge in unemployment spending was smaller in more recent recessions, even though the peak unemployment rate reached levels comparable to or higher than the level attained in the 1975–77 recession.

The fall-off in unemployment protection is greater than implied by figure 9.5. Unemployment insurance spending is measured as the flow of gross benefits in relation to the money wages earned by U.S. workers. The calculation ignores the changing tax status of unemployment compensation. Before 1979, unemployment benefits were treated as tax-free income in the federal income tax code. Starting in 1979, however, some or all benefits became taxable for middle- and high-income households. In 1987, all compensation payments were made taxable as ordinary income. An analysis by the House Ways and Means Committee in 1998 shows that the federal income tax on compensation nets tax revenues that offset about 18 percent of the cost of benefit payments (U.S. House Committee 1998, table 4-4).

Since most states with income tax systems follow the lead of the federal government in defining taxable income, unemployment compensation has also become taxable in state tax systems, further reducing the net value of compensation payments. The inclusion of unemployment insurance benefits in the income tax base would not have affected income replacement rates if state legislators had increased weekly benefit amounts by roughly 20 percent when benefits first became taxable. But legislators did not increase benefits. The average weekly benefit amount is about 35 percent of the average gross wage in covered employment, and this ratio has remained essentially unchanged for the past 45 years.

Money wages have also declined in relation to total worker compensation. Fringes such as health and retirement benefits have become an increasingly important part of most employers' pay package. In the 1960s, money wages represented 91 percent of total worker compensation. By 2004, money wages accounted for just 81 percent of compensation. Figure 9.5 shows the percentage of money wages represented by unemployment insurance benefits, but the portion of total compensation that is replaced by insurance benefits has fallen even faster.

Several analysts have examined the reasons behind the decline in income protection provided under unemployment insurance (Blank and Card 1991; Burtless 1983; Corson and Nicholson 1988; Vroman 1991). Two reasons for the decline should be obvious from the previous discussion. The unemployment programs that protect workers who suffer unemployment spells longer than six months are less generous than they were in the 1970s. In addition, unemployment compensation payments have become taxable as ordinary income. The percentage of job losers claiming unemployment benefits also dropped after 1979. Figure 9.6 shows the share of unemployment weeks that was compensated under all unemployment programs, including the regular and extended benefits programs and all supplemental and emergency programs. The lower line, which provides estimates from 1960 to 2004, measures compensated weeks in relation to the estimated total weeks U.S. workers spent in involuntary unemployment. In the 20-year period through 1979, the average share of unemployment weeks compensated was 39 percent. In the 25-year period starting in 1980, it was less than 35 percent, a decline in insurance coverage of about one-eighth.

Many unemployed workers, however, are ineligible for benefits. New entrants and most re-entrants to the workforce are ineligible because they have not had recent employment in a covered job. Unemployed workers who quit their most recent jobs are probably ineligible for benefits or may be eligible only after a lengthy waiting period.

The unemployed who are most likely to collect benefits are job losers, workers who were permanently or temporarily laid off from their last

Figure 9.6. Weeks of Unemployment Compensated by U.S. Unemployment Insurance, 1960–2004

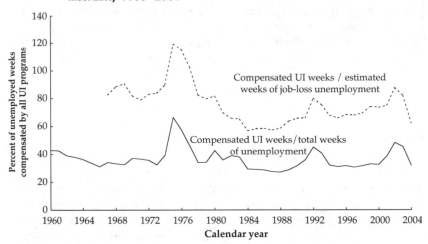

Source: Author's calculations based on unemployment estimates from http://data.bls.gov, UI finance data from http://workforcesecurity.doleta.gov/unemploy/finance.asp, and data on federal supplemental UI claims in *Economic Indicators* (various issues).

job. The top line in figure 9.6, which covers the 1967–2004 period, measures compensated weeks in relation to the estimated number of weeks of unemployment experienced by job losers. This measure shows a more dramatic decline in unemployment insurance coverage after 1979. Between 1967 and 1979, slightly more than 90 percent of job losers' unemployment weeks were compensated under the unemployment insurance system. Since 1980, less than 70 percent of losers' unemployment weeks have been compensated, a drop in coverage of about one-quarter. Even if we disregard the exceptional coverage rates in 1975–77, unemployment insurance coverage fell off by 18 percent starting around 1980.

Changes in the composition of the unemployed have contributed to lower unemployment insurance coverage ratios. A larger percentage of workers (and of the unemployed) consists of women, and women have historically had lower rates of participation in unemployment insurance than men. Part-time employment is also more common than was the case before 1980. The qualifying conditions for unemployment compensation require workers to have a minimum level of earnings to become entitled to benefits, so laid-off part-time workers are less likely to receive unemployment benefits than workers laid off from full-time jobs. These qualification requirements also reduce the percentage of low-income single mothers who collect unemployment insurance after they become unemployed (Acs, Holzer, and Nichols 2005). In addition, as unionization rates have fallen, the unemployed are less likely to receive help from a labor union in learning about unemployment benefits or where to apply for them.

Another reason for the fall in unemployment insurance coverage among the unemployed is the steady increase in the proportion of jobless workers who have been unemployed for six months or longer (figure 9.7). Although the average duration of unemployment spells in progress increases in every recession and declines (with a lag) after the job market starts to improve, unemployment spells have tended to grow longer in successive business cycles. Average spell duration has increased 1.3 weeks each decade since 1960. Compared with unemployed workers 40 years ago, the unemployed today have been jobless an additional month or more.

The growth in the duration of unemployment spells has increased the percentage of unemployed who are in spells of six months or longer. The increase is about 7.2 percentage points over the past four decades. This evidence, based on household interview responses collected in the Current Population Survey, is consistent with administrative data from the unemployment insurance system. Administrative records show that the percentage of unemployment insurance claims that end with benefit exhaustion—usually after 26 weeks of eligibility for regular unemployment benefits—has increased significantly since the 1960s and 1970s (top line in figure 9.2).

Figure 9.7. Indicators of Long-Term U.S. Unemployment, 1960–2004

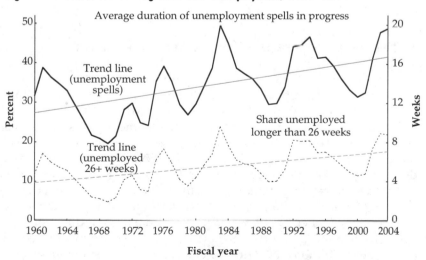

Source: Author's tabulations of Current Population Survey data from http://data.bls.gov.

Thus, both survey findings and administrative data indicate an increase in unemployment spells that last six months or longer. Few long-term unemployed qualify for jobless benefits under regular state unemployment programs. They are only eligible for benefits if an extended compensation program is in effect and if, earlier in their unemployment spells, they qualified for benefits under the regular unemployment program.

Why are unemployment spells longer today than they were in the past? One reason is the declining importance of temporary layoff unemployment in the U.S. economy (Vroman 2005). Industries, such as steel and autos, that historically placed workers on temporary (and hence short-term) unemployment are now smaller than they were in the past. Some companies are now more inclined to discharge workers permanently rather than temporarily.

One remedy for the problem of poor income protection is a boost in the maximum duration of unemployment benefits. But if such an increase were made permanent, the average duration of unemployment spells would almost certainly rise. A longer eligibility period for benefits will worsen the adverse employment incentives created by the program. In a recent survey of the empirical literature on the relation between extended unemployment benefits and worker welfare, Walter Nicholson and Karen Needels conclude, "Extended benefits programs do appear to have significant incentive effects. A median estimate is that each extra week of benefits is associated with an extra 0.2 weeks of unemployment" (Nicholson and Needels 2004, 22). Thus, a reform that adds 10 weeks to the current benefit maximum might add about 2 weeks to the average completed spell of unemployment.

ECONOMIC LOSSES FROM WORKER DISPLACEMENT

Even though long-term unemployment is more common today, it remains a smaller problem in the United States than it is in most other rich countries (see figure 9.4). One reason is that the United States is much less generous in insuring long unemployment spells than other rich countries. The evidence summarized above also suggests the level of U.S. protection is lower than it was in the 1970s. Despite the poor and deteriorating protection available to America's long-term unemployed, the average duration of unemployment spells has climbed steadily.

Unemployment insurance protects workers against the loss of money wages suffered when people are dismissed from a job. It does not offer compensation for loss of fringe benefits, such as health insurance and pension contributions. Nor does it compensate workers who become reemployed in a job that pays lower wages or provides worse fringe benefits than the lost job. Evidence on these losses suggests they are sizeable (Farber 2005; Helwig 2004; Jacobsen, LaLonde, and Sullivan 1993a, 1993b).

Unemployment insurance conspicuously fails to compensate many workers for the most important component of their economic loss: the drop in earnings they suffer when they take a new job. Louis Jacobsen and his colleagues found that when experienced workers are displaced from long-tenure jobs, their eventual earnings losses, including earnings lost while unemployed, can amount to as much as one-quarter of previous pay (Jacobsen et al. 1993b). Most losses occur *after* workers become reemployed and result from the drop in weekly earnings on the postdisplacement job. Younger workers, workers with less job tenure, and workers in low-wage industries (such as apparel or retail trade) seldom experience big weekly wage losses, mainly because their predisplacement wages do not have as far to fall. On the other hand, displaced workers who earn average or above-average pay often suffer greater economic loss as a result of earning smaller weekly paychecks than they do as a result of experiencing unemployment for weeks or months after they are displaced.

One source of information about workers' experiences after suffering permanent job loss is the Bureau of Labor Statistics' Displaced Worker Survey, a periodic supplement to the Current Population Survey that has been administered every other year since 1984. Henry Farber recently analyzed responses from all the surveys to estimate the economic losses that workers experience after suffering permanent job loss (Farber 2005). The rate of job displacement is strongly cyclical, with sharply higher displacement rates during and immediately after recessions and lower rates during the later stages of an economic expansion. Surprisingly, the reported displacement rate was nearly as high in the early 1990s and in 1999–2003 as it was in the recession of the early 1980s, when the peak unemployment rate was considerably higher.

To measure earnings losses suffered by reemployed workers, Farber examined the pre- and postdisplacement weekly earnings of displaced, full-time workers who became reemployed in full-time jobs. This calculation excludes the earnings losses of workers forced to accept part-time positions, and it ignores the earnings loss experienced while workers were jobless. Figure 9.8 shows the results of his tabulations. Reemployed workers who lost their jobs during and immediately after a recession suffered the biggest drop in weekly earnings, with average losses ranging between 11 and 14 percent of workers' predisplacement wage. Workers who lost jobs toward the end of an economic expansion fared much better (Farber 2005). Bear in mind that these represent *average* wage losses suffered by displaced workers. Many reemployed workers suffer much bigger percentage cuts in pay.

Figure 9.8. Average Wage Losses of Displaced, Full-Time Workers Who Become Reemployed in Full-Time Jobs, 1981–2003

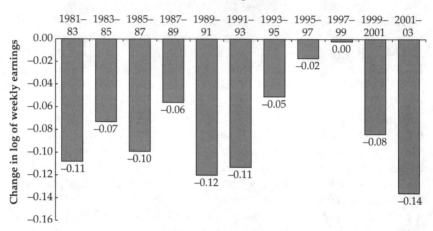

Source: Farber (2005), appendix table 10-11.
Note: The workers in the tabulation were employed in a full-time predisplacement job, suffered job loss in the three-year window indicated along the x-axis, and were reemployed in a full-time position by the time of the Displaced Worker Survey in the following calendar year.

Loss of Health Insurance

The Displaced Worker Survey can also be used to examine the loss of health insurance benefits connected with a job. Unlike governments in other industrialized countries, the U.S. government does not provide, or require employers to provide, health insurance to workers or their dependents. In 2004, nearly 46 million Americans—more than one in seven—were not covered by a public or private health insurance plan during the year (DeNavas-Walt, Proctor, and Lee 2005). Most of the uninsured were workers and workers' dependents, though many unemployed were also uninsured, and a large fraction of the unemployed lost their health coverage when they lost their most recent jobs.

Uninsured Americans usually have some access to low-cost or free emergency medical care through public hospitals, charity care in private hospitals, or public health clinics. The lack of health insurance coverage nonetheless limits Americans' choice of doctors and hospitals and discourages them from receiving beneficial care. Even though employers who provide insurance are now required to offer their laid-off employees continued coverage under their plan (almost always with a much higher premium), many unemployed workers cannot afford to pay the required premiums.[5] About three-quarters of long-tenure workers who reported becoming displaced between 1999 and 2000 were covered by an employer-sponsored health plan in their pre-displacement jobs (Helwig 2004). One-fifth of these workers lost health insurance coverage following their displacement.

Among workers who were reemployed by the date of the Displaced Worker Survey, nearly 85 percent retained health insurance coverage. About a quarter of the once-insured displaced workers had not found a new job, however, and a large proportion of these workers were not covered by a public or private health insurance plan. Among displaced workers who were still jobless and actively seeking work, less than half were covered by an insurance plan.

Trend in Worker Displacement

Because the first Displaced Worker Survey was not conducted until 1984, soon after the nation's deepest post-war recession, it is unclear whether displacement has been more or less common in the past two decades than it was in the first four decades after World War II. The percentage of long-tenure workers who suffer displacement each year is surprisingly high. A BLS analysis of the responses from the 1984–2002 surveys shows that American workers who have three or more years of job tenure with their current employer have about a 3 percent chance of permanent job loss each year. Even among workers with job tenures of 10 years or longer, the probability of involuntary job loss is 2.3 percent a year (Helwig 2004).

Workers' average tenure in a job depends on their willingness to remain in the job as well as employers' job separation policies. If workers' propensity to stay in jobs has remained unchanged, then an increase in employers' job separation rate should eventually be reflected in falling average job tenure. This is exactly the pattern uncovered by BLS worker tenure surveys (BLS 2004). Since 1983, male job tenures have fallen at all ages (figure 9.9), while the median tenure of women workers has remained roughly constant.

Given the shift in women's job market behavior, it is not surprising that men's and women's job tenure patterns should look more similar in 2004 than was the case two decades ago. Women are nowadays more likely to remain steadily in the workforce than was the case before 1983. What is surprising is that male and female tenure patterns have converged because average male tenure has *declined* while female tenure has remained virtually unchanged. Part of the fall in men's job tenures is almost certainly due to an increase in involuntary separation rates—that is, a long-term rise in the male permanent job displacement rate.

Figure 9.9. Median Years of Tenure with Current Employer among Male Wage and Salary Workers, by Age, 1983–2004

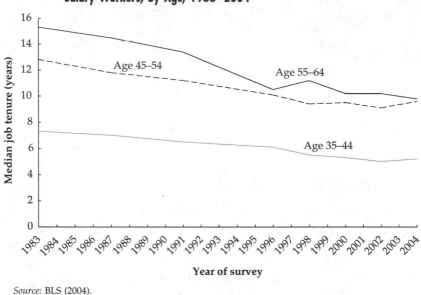

Source: BLS (2004).

HEALTH INSURANCE AS PART OF WORKER COMPENSATION

Health insurance is not only a problem for the unemployed, many of whom lose insurance coverage when they lose their jobs. It is also a problem for people who are steadily employed. Though statistics on health insurance coverage are subject to measurement error, the Census Bureau's annual survey on coverage shows a two-decade trend toward lower private insurance coverage among working-age adults (figure 9.10). Declines in coverage rates occurred mainly in 1990–92 and 2001–04 when the job market was weak. Between 1987 and 2004, coverage under private health plans, mainly provided by employers, declined 5 to 10 percentage points depending on the age group. Adults between 25 and 44 years old saw the biggest drops in coverage. People age 45 and older experienced smaller declines.

It is unclear whether employers are less likely to offer health plans than they were in the past, but some surveys show that a smaller proportion of adults is participating in plans offered by employers. About 80 percent of workers are employed by an employer that offers a health plan, though only 71 percent of employees are entitled to enroll. Others are short-term or part-time workers who are not included in the group covered by the employer's plan. About 85 percent of employees who are eligible to enroll in an employer plan choose to do so. According to tabulations of the Survey of Income and Program

Figure 9.10. Percent of Working-Age Adults Insured under Private Health Insurance Plans by Age Group, 1987–2004

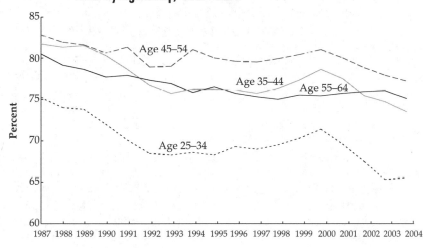

Source: U.S. Census Bureau, Housing and Household Economic Statistics Division, http://www.census.gov/hhes/www/hlthins/historic/hihistt7.html.

Participation, 60 percent of wage and salary employees participate in their employer's group health plan (Fronstin 2005). Some workers may be deterred from participating in a plan or enrolling their dependents in the plan because of the high price of participation or weaknesses in the plan's design. Other workers may be eligible for coverage as a dependent under another family member's group plan.

Sticker shock may explain some of the recent decline in employee participation. A survey of employer-sponsored plans shows that employees' premium contributions increased 9 to 10 percent a year between 2002 and 2005 (Kaiser Family Foundation 2002, 2005). Employers' premium contributions also rose steeply in those years because increases in health care usage and rising prices for medical care, drugs, and instruments drove up the cost of insurance. In 2005, the combined employee and employer premium for a family health plan was nearly $10,900, of which one-quarter is usually paid by the employee (Kaiser Family Foundation 2005).[6] For comparison, the average annual wage earnings among Americans with earnings was $34,200 in 2004.[7] The combined premium for a family insurance plan is therefore about one-third of the average U.S. wage. The annual premium exceeds the year-round earnings of a full-time worker who earns the minimum wage. Even if employees are only asked to contribute one-quarter the cost of the plan, some may decline coverage and gamble on remaining healthy.

The gamble appears attractive to a sizeable fraction of workers because they do not expect to incur large medical expenses over the course of a year. Annual health spending varies widely, even in a population of apparently similar people. Figure 9.11 shows the distribution of health spending among 25- to 64-year-old adults who were enrolled in a private health insurance plan in 2002. All spending for drugs and medical services is taken into account, regardless of the source of payment for the spending.[8] This population is divided into 13 groups depending on each individual's annual spending amount. The lowest spending group contains adults who consumed less than $500 of medical services over the year. This group contains 36 percent of the adult population enrolled in a private health plan. (Its population share is indicated by the bar.) The spending of this group accounted for 2 percent of total medical expenditures for the population examined. (The expenditure share is indicated by the line.) By contrast, the highest spending group consumed at least $30,000 in medical services during 2002. Adults in this group make up just 1 percent of all 25–64-year-olds insured by a private plan, but they consumed 20 percent of all

Figure 9.11. Distribution of Annual Health Spending among Working-Age Adults Covered by a Private Insurance Plan, 2002

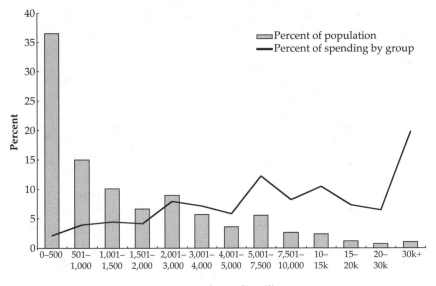

Annual spending ($)

Source: Author's tabulations of Agency for Healthcare Research and Quality, *2002 Full Year Consolidated Data File* (HC-070), released December 2004, Medical Expenditure Panel Survey (MEPS) Household Component Data.

Note: The tabulations were performed on all persons age 25–64 in the MEPS sample who were insured under a private health insurance plan in 2002.

medical services purchased by this population. The bottom spending group contains 36 times as many adults as the top spending group, yet its total consumption of medical services was just one-tenth the total consumption of the top spending group.

The tabulations in figure 9.11 offer a plausible picture of the risks faced by working-age adults who refrain from enrolling in a health plan or who lose their insurance when dismissed from a job. More than half of 25–64-year-olds received medical services that cost less than $1,000 in 2002. On the other hand, 3 percent of adults in this age group received medical services that cost at least $15,000. On average, each adult in the top 3 percent of medical spenders consumed $31,600 in medical services over the course of the year. Workers who refrain from enrolling in an employer health plan probably believe they will not face medical bills of $15,000 or $30,000 a year. Few of them will. But the small fraction unlucky enough to confront a costly medical emergency will face a painful decision: find good uninsured care and accept the big bills that come with that choice, or defer medical care and accept the attendant risk to future health and life.

The numbers displayed in figure 9.11 contain another lesson for workers considering the risks of becoming unemployed. The estimates in the figure are based on expenditure patterns among adults enrolled in a private health insurance plan, usually a plan sponsored by an employer. Workers who lose their jobs will immediately lose the employer's subsidy for the cost of the plan. If displaced workers were to drop their coverage under the plan, they would face the risk of bearing the entire cost of a medical emergency that could consume $10,000 a year or more. (For adults between 55 and 64 years old, the risk that annual medical spending would exceed $10,000 was 10 percent in 2002.) One reason that older workers leave their jobs is that their health is too poor to permit continued work. In this case, a costly medical condition may be the cause of job loss. Unless workers' health problems are so severe they qualify for Social Security Disability Insurance and Medicare, they face the prospect of paying for health insurance or health care out of household income that has shrunk as a result of job loss.

Much of the person-to-person variation in medical spending is unpredictable, but some of it is highly predictable. People with chronic conditions requiring costly drugs or therapy will run up big bills every year. Healthy 25-year-olds only rarely need care. Table 9.1 shows statistics on the distribution of health spending, by age group, among working-age adults insured under a private health insurance plan. The top section shows distributional statistics on total health spending. Medical expenditures rise steeply with age. Median spending is more than 3½ times greater for 55–64-year-olds than it is for 25–34-year-olds. Average

Table 9.1. Distribution of Annual Medical Expenditures and Sources of Payment of Working-Age Adults, 2002

	Annual medical spending ($)		Percent of persons with more than $3,000 in spending	Mean spending if spending is more than 3,000 ($)
	Median	Mean		
Total health spending (excluding premiums)				
All adults, 25–64	937	2,781	23	9,425
25–34	520	1,763	15	8,185
35–44	723	2,079	18	8,394
45–54	1,195	3,101	25	9,466
55–64	1,959	4,731	37	10,779
Spending paid out-of-pocket (excluding permiums)				
All adults, 25–64	240	573	3	5,151
25–34	135	368	1	5,216
35–44	164	450	2	5,849
45–54	330	645	3	4,907
55–64	511	926	6	4,997
Spending reimbursed by private health insurance				
All adults, 25–64	471	1,936	15	9,713
25–34	254	1,256	10	8,372
35–44	368	1,463	11	8,883
45–54	631	2,193	16	9,793
55–64	1,030	3,184	23	11,024

Source: Author's tabulations based on Agency for Healthcare Research and Quality, *2002 Full Year Consolidated Data File* (HC-070), released December 2004, Medical Expenditure Panel Survey (MEPS) Household Component Data.

Note: The tabulations were performed on all persons under age 65 who were insured under a private health insurance plan in the 2002 MEPS sample.

spending is more than 2½ times larger for the older age group. As people grow older, they are much more likely to face big medical bills. Compared with 25–34-year-olds, people age 55 to 64 are more than twice as likely to incur annual medical expenses that exceed $3,000.

The middle and bottom sections of table 9.1 show information on two major sources of payment for medical spending—out-of-pocket spending by the person or other family member and payments from private health insurers. Spending from these two sources does not add up to total health spending. Medical expenditures are also financed through public insurance programs, including Medicare, Medicaid, and workers compensation, as well as other sources. But out-of-pocket spending and reimbursement from private health insurance are the two most important sources of payment. Out-of-pocket spending pays for 20 percent of health care consumption, and private insurers pay for about 70 percent of consumption. Interestingly, these proportions do not vary much with age.

One implication of this reimbursement pattern is that private insurers must pay for predictably larger health outlays as workers grow older, a point also made in chapter 8, which considers the reasons employers may avoid hiring older workers or keeping them on their payrolls. Nearly all spending by private health insurers for working-age adults is derived from employer premium contributions to employee health plans. The results displayed in table 9.1 imply that employers can expect to contribute 2½ times more to a health plan for an employee over age 55 than for an employee under age 35. The difference in annual premium contributions is almost $2,000 for a single worker and $4,000 for a married worker with a dependent spouse. This translates into a pay difference of $1 an hour for a single worker and $2 an hour for a married worker with a dependent spouse. The difference narrows if the younger worker supports child dependents in addition to a spouse. Nonetheless, employer contributions heavily tilt the compensation package in favor of older workers.

An alternative view is that workers become increasingly costly to employers as they grow older, even with no seniority pay premium. In 2002, the average earnings of a production worker on private payrolls was slightly less than $15 an hour. The average employer contribution to worker health plans was $1.58 an hour, or about 10 percent of the average production worker's wage (BLS 2003). If employer contributions to different age groups varied according to the pattern shown in table 9.1, compensation to 55–64-year-old workers would have exceeded compensation to the youngest age group by $1.60 an hour, even if the hourly pay rates of the two groups were identical. The difference in compensation amounts to more than 10 percent of the hourly money wage of an average production worker. Unless the employer believes the productivity advantage of an older worker justifies this pay difference, it should tend to favor younger workers when filling job vacancies.

Antidiscrimination laws prevent employers from paying older workers lower hourly wages to offset the higher cost of financing their health care benefits. Discrimination in hiring is much harder to detect and prosecute than violation of the equal pay laws, so it is likely that cost differences in insuring young and old workers lead some employers to discriminate against older job applicants. Many voters and policymakers are aware of the health risks posed by lack of health insurance coverage. They are probably less familiar with the distortion that employer-sponsored insurance creates in the job market.

Employers are not obliged to offer a health plan, of course. About one in five wage and salary workers is employed by a firm that does not offer insurance. This poses other risks for both young and old workers. If the worker is the only family member with a job, the family may find it hard to find affordable health insurance unless its members are categorically eligible for means-tested public insurance. The cost of private health insurance obtained outside an employer-sponsored plan may be high or the medical condition of a family member may make insurance difficult to obtain.

REMEDIES

The two major risks highlighted in this chapter are worker displacement and loss of health insurance protection. These risks appear to have grown worse for working-age adults. While it is unclear whether worker displacement is any more common today than it was in the 1960s or 1970s there is considerable evidence the welfare losses suffered by displaced workers have grown larger. The average duration of unemployment spells has lengthened. The percentage of earnings loss replaced by unemployment insurance has shrunk. The components of employee compensation that are *not* insured by unemployment benefits have grown in importance. Employers devote a larger percentage of compensation to providing workers with health insurance and retirement benefits. When workers lose their jobs, they lose these benefits, too. Traditional unemployment compensation does not insure workers against this loss.

Even workers who manage to avoid job separations pay a heavy price for the nation's misbegotten health insurance system. A crucial problem is the link the system creates between access to affordable health insurance and employment at favored workplaces. Most employers offer health insurance to most of their workers, and the great majority of Americans under age 65 obtain insurance through an employer-sponsored plan. But 20 percent of workers are employed in a workplace without any health benefits, and another 10 percent are employed in a workplace with a group health plan that does not cover them.

The employment-based insurance system creates strong incentives for health-conscious workers to find and keep jobs where good health insurance is provided. It creates equally powerful incentives for employers offering health insurance to discourage enrollment in their plans by high-cost participants, including the elderly, the disabled, and people in chronic poor health. One way for employers to achieve this result is to structure health insurance benefits and other conditions of employment so they appeal to healthy, low-risk populations rather than people who may run up big medical bills.

A humane society would ensure that high-risk populations are provided with affordable and decent care, regardless of ability to pay and current employment status. Our employment-based insurance system provides no such guarantee. It offers good employers perverse incentives to discriminate against high-medical-cost populations when deciding who should be hired, who should be promoted, and who should be fired. From a social standpoint, the nation ought to welcome the labor contributions of willing and able workers, regardless of the possible burden they may impose on a particular company's health plan. The employer incentives created by our employment-based insurance system instead discourage employers from offering work to job applicants who are willing and able to work but who do not have perfect health.

An appropriate remedy for the shortcomings of the health insurance system is not hard to imagine, but it is very hard to achieve. The link between employment and health insurance coverage should be severed. When Americans lose their jobs, they should not also lose access to affordable insurance and appropriate health care. When business managers decide whom to hire and whom to dismiss, they should be unconscious of the impact of their decision on the experience rating of the company health insurance pool. Most other industrial countries have managed to establish insurance systems that provide insurance to all or nearly all their citizens. Some, including France, Sweden, and Japan, have even managed to combine universal coverage with a very high standard of care and reasonable cost. It is true that no universal system has proven immune to criticism, and none has achieved an ideal balance of efficiency, equitable access, and humane care. But none has achieved the astonishing combination of high cost, low coverage, and poor health outcomes that the U.S. system has managed to achieve.

The employer-based health insurance system has a couple of advantages. It permits efficiencies in purchasing and administering insurance that are hard to duplicate in an insurance system based on sales of insurance policies to individuals and families. The average health status of an employer's workers and their dependents may be more or less random, allowing insurance companies to form insurable groups of customers without severe problems connected with adverse selection. It is difficult to duplicate these advantages in an insurance system where there are many private insurers and insurance coverage is not employment-based. If there were only a single health insurer, the adverse selection problem would be greatly reduced and enormous efficiencies could be obtained in administration. Many Americans, however, oppose the kind of single-insurer system that works well in France and Japan.

If voters continue to reject this kind of system, it still may be possible to move the U.S. system in a direction that improves the equity and efficiency of health insurance for working-age Americans and their dependents. One step that would help young breadwinners is to provide universal health insurance to children and young adults through the existing Medicare system. Americans under age 22 could be provided Medicare insurance for free or for a modest monthly premium that is linked to family income. This will obviously require higher income or payroll taxes to finance the expanded coverage, but earnings could rise because employers and workers will not have to make such large payments for private health insurance coverage. Starting in July 2006, the state of Illinois offered low-cost insurance for uninsured youngsters in low- and middle-income families under its KidsCare program. This initiative makes affordable child health insurance available, and it thus represents a worthwhile step, but it will not ensure the enrollment of all youngsters in a basic health insurance plan.

To protect laid-off workers and their dependents against the loss of health insurance, the unemployment insurance system could subsidize health insurance premium payments during the first 18 to 24 months after a layoff. An obvious source of financing to pay for this extension of unemployment protection is taxation of employer premiums for employee health insurance plans. The current unemployment tax only applies to money wage payments. By broadening the tax base to include company health insurance contributions, the burden of the new tax would fall on employers whose workers face the greatest risk of lost health insurance when they lose their jobs.

The Massachusetts legislature has enacted a plan that should reduce the percentage of state residents who are uninsured, regardless of their employment status. A law passed in 2006 requires all Bay State residents to purchase a health insurance policy. It also obligates all employers with 11 or more employees to provide affordable insurance to their workers. Massachusetts residents who do not purchase insurance will be assessed a penalty payment, and companies who do not offer a qualifying insurance plan to their workers will be assessed penalty payments in proportion to the number of employees on their payroll. At the same time, the law tries to assure that low-cost insurance will be available for state residents who have incomes below three times the poverty level. As long as other states do not have similar laws, however, many unemployed and moderate-income working-age Americans will find themselves priced out of the health insurance market.

Unemployment durations have also grown longer over time. An obvious approach to the problem of lengthening unemployment spells is to extend the maximum duration of regular unemployment benefits beyond 26 weeks. This reform would also alleviate some of the increased hardship resulting from worker displacement. As noted above, however, workers receiving unemployment compensation already have an incentive to delay finding a job, sometimes until their eligibility for benefits is exhausted. The longer they delay finding a job, the more unemployment checks they receive.

Lengthening the potential duration of insured unemployment spells would exacerbate the adverse incentives in the current system. When workers delay job acceptance in response to longer benefit duration, they subtly undermine their chances of landing a good job. Employers tend to discount the qualifications of a job applicant the longer an unemployment spell lasts. By providing additional weeks of benefit eligibility at the end of regular unemployment compensation, a benefit extension would worsen the adverse incentives already present in unemployment insurance. This reform would slow rather than speed up worker adjustment. Another problem with a longer benefit entitlement is that it fails to compensate displaced workers for one of the most important components of their economic loss, the drop in earnings that many suffer when they take a new job. Many of the losses suffered by displaced workers occur after workers become reemployed.

Researchers at the Brookings Institution have long advocated supplementing traditional unemployment benefits with a new kind of compensation payment—time-limited earnings insurance (Baily, Burtless, and Litan 1993; Burtless and Schäfer 2002; Burtless et al. 1998; Kletzer and Litan 2001). Earnings insurance would provide displaced workers monthly or quarterly earnings supplements to compensate them for a percentage of the wage losses they suffer as a result of displacement. If the program insured workers for 50 percent of their earnings loss, for example, a displaced worker whose previous wage was $3,000 a month would receive a monthly check of $500 if forced to accept a new job that paid only $2,000 a month. The replacement or compensation ratio could be the same for all eligible workers. Alternatively, it could vary with a worker's age or previous job tenure.

There is a strong case on equity grounds for providing better insurance to older workers. These workers often find it harder than younger workers to land a new job. Evidence suggests they are also more likely to be forced to accept a large and permanent cut in their hourly wage. However, eligibility for earnings insurance should only be available to workers who have a minimum job tenure (say, two or three years) with their current employers. There is little economic or equity justification for providing compensation payments to employees who suffer displacement after working only briefly with an employer.

The total amount of compensation provided in any year to a worker should be capped at a ceiling amount, say, $10,000. This would avoid situations in which highly compensated workers receive extraordinary insurance payments. Highly paid workers can be presumed to have more savings to draw on than average- and below-average-wage workers. If the compensation ratio were set at 50 percent, a worker who previously earned $120,000 but was paid just $60,000 in her new job would be compensated at the ceiling amount (say, $10,000), assuming the ceiling amount is lower than the $30,000 that is otherwise due.

Some provision must also be made for displaced full-time workers who are reemployed in part-time jobs. The purpose of earnings insurance is to compensate workers for part of the wage loss they suffer as a result of job displacement. It is not to subsidize a reduction in workers' weekly hours of employment. One approach is to restrict compensation payments to workers in full-time jobs, that is, in jobs with regular hours of at least 35 hours a week. Another approach is to offer sharply lower compensation rates to workers who accept part-time positions.

A crucial element of the plan is that earnings supplements would not be payable until a worker becomes reemployed, and supplements would cease within a specified period after displacement occurs (say, after 18 or 24 months). Workers who find new jobs early in this eligibility period would be eligible for larger total payments than workers who delay accepting a new job.[9] This provides workers with a strong incentive to search energetically for a new job and to accept one promptly. It also encourages workers to face the consequences of permanent job loss immediately after displacement occurs. One of the main reasons that dislocated workers delay serious job search is their failure to accept the fact that the job loss is permanent. By encouraging workers to accept this fact right away, earnings insurance would induce workers to take constructive action to become reemployed as soon as possible.[10]

Earnings insurance is not a panacea for displaced workers' woes, nor would it solve the problem of lengthening unemployment spells in the United States or any other industrialized country. Although wage insurance can help improve incentives for workers who earned average and above-average wages before they were displaced, a different approach is needed to improve work incentives for displaced workers who earned low wages.

For displaced workers who earned average or above-average wages, earnings insurance holds the promise of encouraging jobless workers to look energetically for jobs. The sizeable incentive for early job finding may spur some workers to accept jobs they would have rejected without the earnings supplement. A powerful argument in favor of this policy approach is that it can boost the job-finding success and net incomes of participating workers without causing a sizeable reduction in their own self-support. Compared with other methods of improving the incomes of displaced workers, earnings insurance offers a strong incentive for beneficiaries to find work, positively affects the earned incomes of people who participate, and offers sensible compensation to a group suffering major hardship as a result of economic change.

NOTES

1. In three states, employees are also required to pay a small payroll tax for the program.

2. See OECD (2004). The 20 countries in this comparison include the 15 largest Western European nations plus Japan, Australia, New Zealand, Canada, and the United States. Australia, New Zealand, and the United Kingdom usually offer lower initial replacement rates than the United States.

3. Details of the trigger mechanism can be found in U.S. House Committee (2000), section 4.

4. Details about the federal laws that authorized supplemental unemployment compensation benefits are spelled out in U.S. House Committee (1998), section 4, and Congressional Budget Office (2004), 5–8.

5. Employers must offer continued coverage for at least 18 months after the worker's termination, although they may charge laid-off workers up to 102 percent of the full cost of providing benefits. Small employers are not obliged to offer continued (unsubsidized) coverage to their laid-off employees. The requirement only applies to employers with 20 or more workers.

6. An average health plan that covers a single employee requires combined employee and employer contributions of $4,000 a year. Fifteen percent of the premium is typically paid by employees (Kaiser Family Foundation 2005).

7. See Social Security Administration, Office of the Chief Actuary, "Average Wage Index, Updated October 14, 2005," http://ssa.gov/OACT/COLA/awidevelop.html.

8. Interviewers obtained information on all drugs and medical services consumed by an individual over the course of a year and on the charges for the drugs and services consumed. The tabulations refer to consumption and charges at the individual level. Spending in behalf of other family members, including dependents, is imputed to those family members. For details about the survey, see Cohen (1997).

9. Wage insurance would be paid only while a worker remains employed. If a displaced worker obtained a new job but then quit or was laid off, the insurance payments would cease. Payments would only resume when the worker became reemployed, and they would still be limited to the initially defined eligibility period (say, two years after the original layoff date).

10. Lori Kletzer and Robert Litan have estimated the cost of a variety of earnings insurance plans (Kletzer and Litan 2001). Their basic plan would replace 50 percent of lost wages for up to two years after job loss, with an annual benefit cap of $10,000. Only workers reemployed in full-time jobs would qualify for payments, and benefits would be restricted to workers who held their predisplacement jobs for at least two years. The annual cost of their plan was $3.0 billion in 1997, when the overall U.S. unemployment rate was 4.9 percent. The spending total was about 15 percent of the unemployment benefits paid out in that year. A more generous plan, which replaces 70 percent of lost earnings, would have cost $3.6 billion in the same year.

REFERENCES

Acs, Gregory, Harry J. Holzer, and Austin Nichols. 2005. "How Have Households with Children Fared in the Job Market Downturn?" *Assessing the New Federalism* Policy Brief A-67. Washington, DC: The Urban Institute.

Baily, Martin N., Gary Burtless, and Robert Litan. 1993. *Growth with Equity: Economic Policymaking for the Next Century.* Washington, DC: Brookings Institution Press.

Blank, Rebecca, and David Card. 1991. "Recent Trends in Insured and Uninsured Unemployment: Is There an Explanation?" *Quarterly Journal of Economics* 106(4): 1157–89.

BLS. See U.S. Bureau of Labor Statistics.

Burtless, Gary. 1983. "Why Is Insured Unemployment So Low?" *Brookings Papers on Economic Activity* (Spring): 225–49.

Burtless, Gary, and Holger Schäfer. 2002. "Earnings Insurance for Germany." Policy Brief 104. Washington, DC: The Brookings Institution.

Burtless, Gary, Robert Z. Lawrence, Robert Shapiro, and Robert Litan. 1998. *Globaphobia: Confronting Fears about Open Trade.* Washington, DC: Brookings Institution Press.

Cohen, J. 1997. *Design and Methods of the Medical Expenditure Panel Survey Household Component.* MEPS Methodology Report No. 1. AHCPR Pub. No. 97-0026. Rockville, MD: U.S. Department of Health and Human Services, Agency for Health Care Policy and Research.

Congressional Budget Office. 2004. *Family Income of Unemployment Insurance Recipients.* Washington, DC: Congressional Budget Office.

Corson, Walter, and Walter Nicholson. 1988. *An Examination of Declining UI Claims during the 1980s.* Unemployment Insurance Occasional Paper 88–3. Washington, DC: U.S. Department of Labor.

DeNavas-Walt, Carmen, Bernadette D. Proctor, and Cheryl Hill Lee. 2005. *Income, Poverty, and Health Insurance Coverage in the United States: 2004.* Current Population Report P-60-229. Washington, DC: U.S. Government Printing Office.

Farber, Henry S. 2005. "What Do We Know about Job Loss in the United States? Evidence from the Displaced Workers Survey, 1984–2004." Working Paper 498. Princeton, NJ: Industrial Relations Section, Princeton University.

Fredriksson, Peter, and Bertil Holmlund. 2003. "Improving Incentives in Unemployment Insurance: A Review of Recent Research." Department of Economics Working Paper No. 2003:10. Uppsala, Sweden: Uppsala University.

Fronstin, Paul. 2005. *Employment-Based Health Benefits: Trends in Access and Coverage.* Washington, DC: Employee Benefit Research Institute.

Helwig, Ryan. 2004. "Worker Displacement in 1999–2000." *Monthly Labor Review* 127(6): 54–68.

Jacobsen, Louis, Robert LaLonde, and Daniel Sullivan. 1993a. *The Costs of Worker Dislocation.* Kalamazoo, MI: W.E. Upjohn Institute for Employment Research.

———. 1993b. "Earnings Losses of Displaced Workers. *American Economic Review* 83(4): 685–709.

Kaiser Family Foundation. 2002. *Employer Health Benefits: 2002 Annual Survey.* Washington, DC: Henry J. Kaiser Family Foundation.

———. 2005. *Employer Health Benefits: 2005 Annual Survey.* Washington, DC: Henry J. Kaiser Family Foundation.

Kletzer, Lori, and Robert Litan. 2001. "A Prescription for Worker Anxiety." Policy Brief 73. Washington, DC: The Brookings Institution.

Nicholson, Walter, and Karen Needels. 2004. "Extended Unemployment Benefits: A Review of the Literature." Working paper. Amherst, MA: Department of Economics, Amherst College.

OMB. See U.S. Office of Management and Budget.

Organisation for Economic Co-operation and Development (OECD). 2004. *Benefits and Wages: OECD Indicators 2004.* Paris: OECD.

Social Security Administration. 2004. *Annual Statistical Supplement to the Social Security Bulletin, 2003.* Washington, DC: Social Security Administration.

U.S. Bureau of Labor Statistics. 2003. "Employer Costs for Employee Compensation—December 2002." News release USDL 03-130. Washington, DC: U.S. Department of Labor, Bureau of Labor Statistics.

———. 2004. "Employee Tenure in 2004." News release USDL 04-1829. Washington, DC: U.S. Department of Labor, Bureau of Labor Statistics.

———. 2005. "Employer Costs for Employee Compensation—March 2005." News release USDL 05-1056. Washington, DC: U.S. Department of Labor, Bureau of Labor Statistics.

U.S. Congress. House. Committee on Ways and Means. 1998. *The 1998 Green Book: Background Material and Data on Programs within the Jurisdiction of the Committee on Ways and Means.* Washington, DC: U.S. Government Printing Office.

———. 2000. *The 2000 Green Book: Background Material and Data on Programs within the Jurisdiction of the Committee on Ways and Means.* Washington, DC: U.S. Government Printing Office.

U.S. Department of Labor. Employment and Training Administration. 2004. "Significant Provisions of State Unemployment Insurance Laws, July 2004." Washington, DC: U.S. Department of Labor.

U.S. Office of Management and Budget. 2006. *Budget of the United States Government, Fiscal Year 2006: Historical Tables.* Washington, DC: U.S. Government Printing Office.

Vroman, Wayne. 1991. *The Decline in Unemployment Insurance Claims Activities in the 1980s.* Unemployment Insurance Occasional Paper 91–2. Washington, DC: U.S. Department of Labor.

———. 2005. "The Recession of 2001 and Unemployment Insurance Financing." Working paper. Washington, DC: The Urban Institute.

10

WORK–FAMILY POLICIES

Jane Waldfogel

Despite tremendous changes in the structure of the American family, the basic model for policies to support families in meeting work and family responsibilities has not changed. The United States continues to rely primarily on employers to provide, in addition to wages, essential benefits such as leave time and health insurance coverage. This model fit well with a male breadwinner family structure, in which husbands were the primary earners and wives did not work in the labor market or worked only as secondary earners while taking primary responsibility for family duties (child care in particular). But it is a poor fit today, with an increasing share of children living in single-parent families and an increasing share of mothers working in both two-parent and single-parent families.

As recently as 25 years ago, two-thirds of children could count on having a parent home full-time, but today only one-third can (Waldfogel 2006b). At the same time, more workers cannot count on having a stay-at-home spouse but rather have sole or at least partial responsibility for taking care of children themselves. As a result, both men and women are increasingly looking for policies to help them take care of their children while also holding down their jobs.

Remarkably, despite these dramatic changes in demographics and the labor force, the structure of employer-provided benefits has hardly changed. Child care, which would not have been an issue for most families under the male breadwinner model, is a pressing need for many now, but few employers provide any assistance. Indeed, as we shall see, the share of employees receiving tangible help with child care—in the form of funding or access to on- or near-site child care—remains in the single digits.

Public policies have been more responsive. Subsidies for child care expenses have expanded steadily for working parents, with a particularly large increase in the 1990s in conjunction with welfare reform. And the passage of the federal Family and Medical Leave Act in 1993 was a much-heralded advance in the area of parental leave policy. Yet, public work–family policies still tend to be meager in comparison to those provided in other developed countries and are limited relative to what families need.

Looking ahead to the next decade and beyond, the challenges posed by these demographic changes will become even more acute as the baby boomers age. If the labor supply of parents is to increase to meet the demand for skilled young labor, then the need for more comprehensive work–family policies will become even more pressing.

If more parents are to be drawn into the labor market or encouraged to work more hours, we must think creatively about how to meet the needs of children when parents work. Among the options we might consider are public provision, social insurance models, tax credits to workers or families, tax credits to employers, mandates on employers, or efforts to influence employers through technical assistance and the dissemination of best practices. These options will have different impacts in terms of efficiency and equity, and we will want to take both into account.

A good starting point is to understand the status quo. What policies are currently in place to support families in balancing work and family responsibilities? Which families are covered, and which are not? To what extent have employers responded to meet the needs of families and children and, where employers have not responded with adequate policies, what barriers have prevented that response? From that starting point, we can explore options such as those listed above to expand coverage to better meet the needs of children when parents work, taking into account their implications for both efficiency and equity.

THE STATUS QUO

Employers in the United States are a potentially important source of work-family benefits in the areas of parental leave, other leave time, flexible work hours, and help with child care. Yet benefits remain limited and are very unequally distributed, with the lowest-wage workers and part-time workers least likely to have access (Bernstein and Kornbluh 2005; Heymann 2000; Shipler 2004).

The next four sections review what employers and public policies currently offer in the areas of parental leave, other leave time, flexible work hours, and help with child care. These reviews summarize overall coverage rates and highlight disparities between low- and higher-paid workers and part-time and full-time workers.[1]

Parental Leave

Parental leave policies provide new parents with the right to job-protected leave around the time of the birth or adoption of a child. The first parental leave policies (maternity leave policies) covered mothers only, but now most policies also provide leave to fathers. A wealth of evidence shows these policies have important benefits for child health and development, as well as maternal health (Waldfogel 2006b). Most recently, Tanaka (2005) finds that when countries extend their period of paid parental leave, infant mortality rates decline. Unpaid leave extensions, however, do not have the same protective effect.

The federal Family and Medical Leave Act (FMLA), which provides the right to a job-protected parental leave for qualifying workers, did not come into effect until August 1993 and is limited compared with parental leave policies in other industrialized nations. First, the law is limited in its reach, applying only to firms with 50 employees or more and to employees who have worked at least 1,250 hours in the prior year. As a result, only about half the private-sector workforce is covered and eligible under FMLA's terms. Second, the law guarantees only unpaid leave and makes no provision for replacement pay during the leave (although it does require that employers who make contributions toward health insurance plans continue to do so during the leave). Third, the law provides only a very short period of leave—12 weeks— far less than is the norm elsewhere: our peer nations in the Organisation for Economic Co-operation and Development now provide an average of 18 months of job-protected parental leave after a birth (Waldfogel 2006a).

Some states have enacted more generous coverage. Particularly notable is California, which since 2003 has offered paid parental leave (for up to six weeks), with the funds coming from contributions made by employees to a social insurance fund. In designing and implementing its paid parental leave program, California built on its already existing Temporary Disability Insurance (TDI) program, which provides payments to workers who cannot work due to disability, with funds coming from employer and employee contributions. Since the federal

Pregnancy Discrimination Act was passed in 1978, TDI programs, which exist in five states (California, Hawaii, New Jersey, New York, and Rhode Island), have covered maternity as they would any other period of disability. Thus, a woman giving birth in a TDI state is typically eligible for six to eight weeks of disability payments through the TDI program. In enacting its paid parental leave program, California simply extended this benefit to all new parents; thus, fathers and adoptive parents are also covered.

In addition to the five states with TDI laws, 20 states enacted state parental leave laws before 1993, providing a period of job-protected (but unpaid) leave to at least some employees (Han and Waldfogel 2003).[2] Thus, pre-FMLA, half the states had some form of leave for new parents. But the leave provided was very brief, and many employees were not eligible for any leave under state laws. The major determinant of what type of parental leave an employee was eligible for was employer policy, whether set voluntarily by employers or negotiated with unions, and parental leave coverage was far from universal. In 1991, only 37 percent of full-time workers in medium- and large-sized firms (those with 50 or more employees) had access to maternity leave, and only 26 percent had access to paternity leave; coverage of part-time workers in medium and large firms and full-time workers in small firms was even lower, ranging from 8 to 19 percent (Waldfogel 2001a).

To some extent, the FMLA has equalized coverage. Most notably, coverage for men has increased dramatically, with the share of full-time workers in medium and large firms with access to paternity leave rising from 26 percent in 1991—two years before FMLA—to 93 percent in 1997—four years after FMLA (Waldfogel 1999). Even groups not covered by FMLA have gained access to coverage; about half of part-time workers in medium and large firms and full-time workers in small firms had access to paternity leave by 1999.

But because the FMLA only covers medium and large firms, and workers who have worked the requisite number of hours in the past year, coverage disparities remain. For instance, coverage is strongly correlated with education level, with the share of workers covered and eligible rising from only 44 percent of high school dropouts to 74 percent of those with graduate degrees (table 10.1). Access to family leave (whether through the FMLA or other provisions) is higher among full-time workers, with 94 percent now having access to some form of family leave compared with 71 percent of part-time workers (Bureau of Labor Statistics [BLS] 2005). Most family leave, however, is unpaid: only 9 percent of full-time workers and 3 percent of part-time workers have paid family leave. Although many workers are able to use paid vacation time or other paid leave time, about a third of all employees who take leave for family reasons receive no pay at all during their

Table 10.1. Workers Covered and Eligible under FMLA, by Education Level (percent)

	Covered and eligible
Less than high school education	44
High school graduate	57
Some college	62
College graduate	65
Graduate school	74

Source: Cantor et al. (2001), table A2-3.4.

leave (Waldfogel 2001b). In addition, the share of workers who receive no pay during family or medical leave is much higher among low-income workers than among those with higher incomes (table 10.2).

These figures underscore that even those who are covered and eligible under FMLA do not necessarily have access to *paid* parental leave. Surveys of employees post-FMLA have consistently found some who are covered and who say they need leave but who have not taken it because they cannot afford to miss a paycheck, while others have taken unpaid leave and turned to public assistance or borrowed money to cover the costs (Waldfogel 2001b). Indeed, the lack of paid leave has been a major criticism of the FMLA and one that the Clinton administration tried to address with an executive order allowing states to fund paid parental leave through their unemployment insurance programs. Although many states considered it, none actually put such a program into place, and the executive order permitting such programs has since been rescinded by the Bush administration. Thus, providing paid parental leave through the unemployment insurance program does not seem to be on the horizon at this point.

Other Leave

Other leave time, which may be paid or unpaid, includes sick leave, vacation leave, and personal leave, as well as more specialized forms

Table 10.2. Workers Who Receive No Pay during Their Longest Leave for Family or Medical Reasons, by Annual Family Income (percent)

	No pay
< $20,000	74
$20,000–< $30,000	38
$30,000–< $50,000	32
$50,000–< $75,000	24
$75,000–< $100,000	19
≥ $100,000	21

Source: Cantor et al. (2001), table A2-4.1.

of leave such as leave for jury duty or bereavement. The medical literature suggests that sick children recover more quickly, and are more likely to follow doctor recommendations for treatment and follow-up, if a parent stays home with them (Heymann 2000). The health and well-being effects of other types of leave have been little studied.

The FMLA, although often thought of as a parental leave or family leave law, also covers medical leave (for qualifying and eligible employees) if needed for an employee's own serious illness or the serious illness of a close family member. There is no provision under state or federal law, however, for employees to receive pay during such leave (unless they qualify through a disability program), nor is there any provision requiring employers to offer leave for less than a serious illness or leave for vacation or personal time. With the exception of medical leave for serious illness under the FMLA, whether employers offer sick leave, vacation leave, or personal leave, for how long, and at what rate of pay (if any) is up to the discretion of the employer.

Paid leave is the single most common employee benefit in the private sector, with 77 percent of all workers receiving some paid leave (BLS 2005), but there is a good deal of disparity in coverage. A recent study by the Urban Institute compared access to paid leave among workers with incomes below the federal poverty level (FPL), at 100 to 200 percent of FPL, and above 200 percent of FPL (Ross Phillips 2004); the study found that the share of workers with paid leave rises dramatically as incomes rise (table 10.3). Among workers with incomes below the poverty level, more than half have no paid leave at all, compared with one-sixth of those with incomes above 200 percent of FPL.

The amount of paid leave also rises with income, with three-quarters of workers with incomes above 200 percent of FPL having more than a week of paid leave, compared with under a third of workers with incomes below the poverty level. A similar pattern can be seen in BLS data for white-collar workers compared with blue-collar or service workers (table 10.4). The BLS data also highlight the gap in paid leave coverage between part-time and full-time employees.

The lack of paid leave, and the disparity in coverage, is particularly striking when it comes to paid sick leave. Over 40 percent of employees have no paid leave that they can take for their own or a family member's

Table 10.3. Availability of Paid Leave, by Annual Family Income (percent)

	No leave	≤ 1 week	> 1 week
Below poverty level	54	16	30
100%–200% of poverty level	39	18	43
> 200% of poverty level	16	8	76

Source: Ross Phillips (2004).

Table 10.4. Availability of Paid Holidays and Sick Leave, by Type of Occupation and Work Hours (percent)

	Paid Holidays			Paid Sick Leave
	None	*≤ 1 week*	*> 1 week*	*None*
Service occupation	51	12	37	64
Blue-collar occupation	19	9	72	54
White-collar occupation	15	4	81	26
Part-time workers	63	9	28	77
Full-time workers	11	6	83	31

Sources: BLS (2005), table 18, and author's calculations based on tables 18 and 19.

illness; again, the share without leave is higher among lower-paid workers and part-time workers (table 10.4). Even when workers have some paid sick leave, there may be limits on whether that leave can be used to care for a sick child. Roughly two-thirds of lower-income workers have no paid leave that can be used to care for a sick child, compared with a third of higher-income workers (table 10.5).

Flexible Work Hours

A third type of policy that employers may offer to help employees manage their work and family responsibilities is flexible work hours, or flextime. Offering more control over working hours and, in particular, starting and ending times is a high priority if highly skilled young men and women are going to be kept in productive jobs during their childrearing years. Large majorities of young men and women say it is very important to them to work for an organization with flexible work policies and programs, to have control over their schedule, and to have control over how they accomplish tasks (Stork et al. 2005). Of particular interest to parents is the opportunity to reduce their working hours without sacrificing job satisfaction and quality. Firms that are

Table 10.5. Availability of Paid Leave to Take Care of a Sick Child, by Family Income (percent)

	No paid leave to take care of a sick child
< $28,000	64
$28,000–$72,000	52
> $72,000	34

Source: Galinsky and Bond (2000).

able to offer high-quality flextime and part-time jobs—that are well-compensated and offer benefits—will be at a huge competitive advantage in recruiting and retaining skilled young workers (Christensen 2005).

No public policies in the United States require employers to offer flexible hours, but employers are increasingly likely to do so. The share of wage and salary workers with access to traditional flextime (which allows a worker to change his or her schedule permanently) increased from 29 percent in 1992 to 43 percent in 2002, while the share with access to daily flextime (which allows a worker to change his or her schedule daily) increased from 18 percent to 23 percent (Galinsky, Bond, and Hill 2004).

As in the other areas discussed, however, access to flexible work hours is uneven. Data from a survey of parents indicate that both types of flextime are more commonly available to higher-income employees, 62 percent of whom have access to traditional flextime and 47 percent of whom have access to daily flextime. Only 31 percent of lower-income employees have access to traditional flextime, and 13 percent have access to daily flextime (table 10.6).

Child Care

The fourth major area of work–family policy is assistance with child care, whether for preschool- or school-age children. Large literatures have examined both preschool and after-school child care, and they have shown that the quality of care, as well as the type of care, can substantially affect child health and development (Blau and Currie 2006; Smolensky and Gootman 2003; Waldfogel 2006b). It is also clear that parents' selection of care is influenced by its cost, as well as other factors including proximity, availability of alternative resources, and values (Meyers et al. 2004).

The federal government and the states have been fairly active in the child care area: developing and funding subsidy programs to help offset the costs of child care for low-income families, particularly those

Table 10.6. Parents with Access to Traditional or Daily Flextime, by Income Group (percent)

	Traditional flextime	Daily flextime
< $28,000	31	13
$28,000–$72,000	41	22
> $72,000	62	47

Source: Galinksy and Bond (2000).

moving from welfare to work; developing programs to offset the costs of child care for middle-income working families; and directly funding some compensatory education or early education programs (such as Head Start and, more recently, prekindergarten). These programs are described in detail elsewhere so they are only summarized here.[3]

Child care subsidies targeted to low-income working parents have expanded markedly (and changed name and form several times) in the past 10 to 15 years. Subsidies now make up the largest federal child care program, with $5.3 billion in Child Care and Development Fund expenditures in 2000 plus another $1.4 billion in Temporary Assistance for Needy Families expenditures, supplemented by $1.9 billion in state funding (Meyers et al. 2004). The main purpose of child care subsidies is to offset the costs of child care for low-income parents who are working (or engaging in activities to prepare for employment). Parents who are eligible and granted a subsidy can choose their own child care provider or program (so long as it meets all relevant reporting and licensing requirements) and then receive help paying a portion of the costs of that care. The exact amount that parents pay, and that the subsidy pays, is determined state by state; typically, parents pay around 30 percent of the costs and the subsidy covers the rest, with the share that parents pay rising as their income rises.

Funding for child care subsidies was greatly expanded in the 1990s in the wake of federal welfare reform, but subsidies do not reach all eligible families. The most recent estimates suggest that only about 15 percent of families who are eligible actually receive subsidies. Some others are on waiting lists; others have declined to participate because their preferred provider would not meet the requirements or would not agree to participate, or because families themselves were unwilling to go through the hassle and paperwork. Others do not know about the program or do not realize they are eligible.

Tax credits that offset the costs of care for middle-income working parents are the second major type of child care program. The federal child and dependent care tax credit (CDCTC) provides tax relief for working parents with a child under the age of 13 and with no other parent in the home or with a spouse who is also working or in school full-time. Families can claim a portion of their child care expenses, up to a specified maximum; as of 2003, the maximum credit a family could claim was $1,050 for one child and $2,100 for two or more children. Because the credit is nonrefundable, it does not benefit families with incomes too low to owe taxes. The federal government spent $2.7 billion on the CDCTC in 2000 (Meyers et al. 2004). About half the states also offer a state child care tax credit, usually set as a percentage of the federal credit.

Another option available to families with incomes high enough to owe taxes is a dependent care assistance program, or DCAP (families may use the CDCTC or DCAP, but not both). Under the DCAP, parents can ask employers to set aside a portion of their salary, up to $5,000, to pay for child care or other dependent care expenses. This program provides a tax savings because it allows workers to pay for child care expenses using pretax dollars. Like the CDCTC, however, the DCAP does not benefit families with incomes too low to owe taxes.

Dependent care assistance programs are somewhat restrictive because funds must be set aside in advance and are lost if not used as planned. And, depending on the family situation, taxpayers may bene- fit more from the CDCTC than from a DCAP. But, as we shall see below, the DCAP has proved fairly popular among employers, as it allows them to say they are offering a child care benefit without incur- ring costs (other than the costs of administering the DCAP)—"a cheap and easy way to signal responsiveness to the needs of working parents" (Kelly 2003, 609). The federal government spent just under $1 billion on DCAPs in 1999 (Meyers et al. 2004).

The other large category of federal and state child care programs is compensatory or early education programs, most notably Head Start and state prekindergarten programs that are typically provided free of charge to qualifying children. These early education programs are often only part-time or part-year and thus may not provide full-time child care for working parents, but they nevertheless can be used by children of working parents for at least a portion of their care. Head Start was funded with $5.3 billion in federal dollars and $0.2 billion in state dollars in 2000, and prekindergarten programs cost states just under $2 billion dollars in 2001 and 2002 (Meyers et al. 2004). Although early studies questioned Head Start's effectiveness, more recent evi- dence, including a random assignment study, is positive (Puma et al. 2005; see also Currie 2001). The evidence on state prekindergarten programs is also positive, showing them as or more effective than other preschool programs in boosting school readiness, with particularly large effects for disadvantaged children (Gormley and Gayer 2005; Gormley et al. 2005; Magnuson, Ruhm, and Waldfogel forthcoming; Magnuson et al. 2004).

State and federal policies have also provided some incentives for employers to help employees with child care costs or information. Most notably, a federal tax credit in place since 2003 allows employers to claim a credit for up to 25 percent of the costs of establishing and maintaining a child care center (up to $150,000 a year) as well as 10 percent of the costs of providing child care information and referral services for employees (Kelly 2003).

Yet, employer involvement in child care is essentially voluntary: there is no mandate on employers to offer particular types of assistance. Thus, employer policies in this area are determined by employers, either voluntarily or as negotiated through union agreements. Reports in the popular press and in company case studies suggest a lot of interest on the part of employers in setting up child care programs for their employees, whether in the form of information and referral (I&R) services that help connect employees to child care providers, on- or near-site child care centers that offer care for employee (and sometimes community) children, or funds to offset the costs of care for employees. Still, national survey data indicate that such programs are rare.

In 2005, only 14 percent of employees had access to any form of child care assistance through their employers (BLS 2005). I&R services represent the lion's share of programs. Only 3 percent of workers in 2005 had access to employer-provided funding help, while 5 percent had access to on-site or off-site child care (BLS 2005).[4] Again, low-paid workers and part-time workers are the least likely to have access to these benefits (table 10.7). Although across all groups the share with any child care help (and particularly funding help) is low, the share among higher-paid and full-time workers is generally twice or more the share among lower-paid and part-time workers.

As mentioned earlier, DCAPs are another way employers may help employees with child care. Indeed, they are more commonly provided than other types of child care assistance, with nearly a third of employees (29 percent) having access to DCAPs (BLS 2005). But again, access is skewed by occupation and working hours; only 12 percent of service workers and 14 percent of part-time workers have access to DCAPs, compared with 39 percent of white-collar workers and 33 percent of full-time workers (table 10.8).

OPTIONS TO EXPAND COVERAGE

Although each of the four work–family areas considered is a separate domain, with different policies and coverage rates and patterns in

Table 10.7. Workers with Access to Employer Assistance with Child Care, by Occupation and Hours (percent)

	Any help	Funding	On/ off-site	Information and referral
Service occupation	9	2	4	5
Blue-collar	8	2	2	6
White-collar	19	5	7	14
Part-time workers	8	1	3	5
Full-time workers	16	4	6	11

Source: BLS (2005), table 22.

Note: Total with any help is less than the sum of the three types because employers may offer more than one type of help.

Table 10.8. Workers with Access to Dependent Care Assistance Plans, by Occupation and Hours (percent)

	Access to dependent care assistance plans
Service occupation	12
Blue-collar	22
White-collar	39
Part-time workers	14
Full-time workers	33

Source: BLS (2005), table 23.

place, some cross-cutting issues should be taken into account in thinking about options to expand coverage. In particular, it is important to understand what barriers currently exist to more universal, and more equitable, coverage.

Economic theory suggests that if work–family benefits are valued by employees, then firms should be offering them as part of their compensation packages and should be able to shift at least some of the costs to employees by reducing wages to offset the costs (Holzer 2005). Thus, if employers are not offering these benefits, either employees do not value them or some market failure gets in the way. Several types of market failure might be operating in this context (Holzer 2005; Mitchell 1990; Ruhm 1997; Waldfogel 2001b). If employees do not realize the value of work–family benefits, or if there are gains to society that extend beyond the individual employee, then such benefits will be provided at a less than socially optimal level. It is also plausible that employers may worry about adverse selection (e.g., attracting employees who will take a lot of time off if employers offer more generous leave benefits). Information problems may also prevent employers offering what would be valued benefits (e.g., if employers do not know how many employees would choose flexible schedules).

There are also some common reasons for the inequities in benefit coverage. For instance, benefits are more often provided in large firms than in small firms. One reason is coordination problems in small firms. Having an employee take several months off, work a four-day week, or come in late when he or she has a child care emergency is easier to manage in a large firm than in a small shop. Whatever policies are implemented to expand work–family benefit coverage will have to take this reality into account.

But a more fundamental reason for the inequities in benefit coverage is the fact that benefits are closely tied to wages. Across a host of work–family benefits, higher-earning workers are more likely to be covered and to have more generous coverage. This makes sense: firms wishing to attract highly skilled labor pay top wages and offer first-rate benefits, while those hiring the least-skilled can attract them with lower wages and minimal or no benefits.[5] Thus, without government intervention, there will always be a problem of low benefits (alongside low wages) at the bottom of the labor market. On the wage side, the federal government sets a floor with minimum wages and supplements low earnings for families with children through tax and benefit programs such as the EITC and food stamps. But nothing comparable in the work–family arena sets a floor or provides a supplement, except perhaps child care subsidies and tax credits, as well as TDI payments for maternity in the five states with such programs.

With this context in mind, the following sections briefly consider some options for expanding work–family benefit coverage. The options considered include public provision, social insurance models, tax credits for workers or families, tax credits for employers, mandates on employers, and technical assistance or dissemination of best practices for employers. The discussions highlight the most promising options in each policy domain.

Parental Leave

There are two main ways to extend parental leave coverage: employer mandates or social insurance programs. Although both options have costs and benefits, the net benefits of a social insurance program would outweigh those of a mandated benefit program (Waldfogel 2006b).

The main shortcoming of a mandated benefit program is that it imposes costs on employers. Unless employers are altruistic (in which case they would go out of business in a competitive economy), they will pass on these costs to someone else. If employees value the benefit, then at least some of the cost will be passed on to them in the form of lower wages (Summers 1989).[6] If the costs of the policy cannot be shifted to workers, then employers will reduce their hiring instead. This outcome would be viewed by economists as inefficient; it also is undesirable on equity grounds. If employers are able to pass the cost of the mandate on to affected employees by reducing their wages, then a mandated benefit yields what economists would view as a more efficient outcome, but one that is still problematic in terms of equity (particularly since the affected group in this case is primarily women).

Social insurance programs also have costs. Assuming that a public paid parental leave program would be funded through payroll taxes, both employers and employees would bear some costs. But the evidence from California's new paid leave program indicates that such costs may be surprisingly low. California's program provides six weeks of paid leave to parents with newborns (or to employees with an ill family member), at a projected cost of about $22 a year in additional payroll taxes per employee in the state. If the cost of a program that provided 52 weeks of leave to new parents were proportional to the cost of this program, then it could cost $191 a year per employee. However, take-up of a program that offers 52 weeks of leave is likely to be lower than take-up of a program that offers six weeks, since many parents would not take the full year. So, the costs of a program that offered a year of paid parental leave are likely to be considerably lower than $191 a year, probably more on the order of $100 to $150 a year, or roughly $2 to $3 a week.[7] If another state followed California's lead, these costs would be paid by employees, not employers.[8]

Other Leave

It is worrisome that so few American employees have the right to take paid time off from work when a child is sick, and it is clearly inequitable that low-income workers are the least likely to have such rights. This is one area where the United States could learn from other countries, many of which require employers to offer at least some paid leave each year that parents can use for their own illness or to meet urgent family responsibilities. The cost of the leave can be paid for by employers or through a social insurance fund. As a target, the United States could guarantee all workers the right to take at least two weeks off work each year with pay and specifically guarantee the right of parents to take that time to meet important family needs including the need to care for a sick child.

Flexible Work Hours

Surveys of parents indicate their interest in having the option to work flexible hours or part-time. But employers have been slow to respond. Here the United States could learn from the European Union's model. Under the part-time directive adopted by the European Union in 1997, European countries now encourage employers to grant requests from employees with young children who want to work part-time (Gornick and Meyers 2003). Employers are required to give consideration to such requests and to grant them if feasible; if it would be unduly costly to the firm, an employer can say no. Similar policies could be created in the area of flextime, as has been done in the United Kingdom.

We do not know how many parents in the United States would take advantage of a right to request part-time or flextime hours. It is very difficult to gauge parents' preferences until the policy options are actually in place. When the United Kingdom implemented the right for parents (with a child under age 6 or a disabled child) to request part-time or flexible hours in April 2003, no one could have predicted that a million parents—a quarter of those eligible—would make such requests in the first year alone. The response in the United Kingdom suggests a large unmet demand for flextime of which employers were probably not even aware.

U.S. workplaces may prove more resistant to change. Some workplaces actively discourage employees from taking time off, penalizing those who have used too much leave or who have reduced their work hours when it comes to promotions or pay increases. Men in particular report that they are reluctant to use the benefits available to them because they feel that their supervisors would disapprove or because it might harm their careers (Kmec 1999; Waldfogel 2001b).[9] These aspects of workplace culture are hard to change, but changing benefits policies, and making sure they include antidiscrimination provisions, are sound first steps.[10]

Of course, there are both good and bad part-time jobs (Blank 1990; Ferber and Waldfogel 1998; Tilly 1996). What is lacking for parents with family responsibilities are good part-time jobs, as well as good flextime jobs (Christensen 2005). What are the prospects for those? Innovations in job-sharing have already paved the way in many firms for employers to see that part-time employees can be every bit as productive as full-timers (Galinsky et al. 2004). Again, the experience of the United Kingdom may be instructive. In the first year of its part-time and flexible working policy, employers granted 80 percent of requests made to them and were able to compromise with employees on a further 10 percent. Indeed, one of the employers' largest complaints was that the policy was too narrow and should on equity grounds be broadened to other employees with family responsibilities, not just those with young or disabled children (Waldfogel 2006b).

Child Care

When employees are asked about their child care needs, most of the discussion revolves around how to find, arrange, and pay for care when the parents need to be at work and the children are not in school. Young children may not be in school because they are preschoolers. Older children also spend time out of school during after-school hours, school vacations, and the long summer holiday, or when they are ill or schools are closed for snow days, teacher training, and so on.

An obvious option to help with caring for children while parents work is to expand the role of the schools by getting schools more involved in preschool and out-of-school care. Indeed, many schools are moving in this direction (Waldfogel 2006b). In terms of preschool provision, one in six American 4-year-olds now attends a prekindergarten program, whether at a public school or funded and supervised by the local school department. And such programs are expanding rapidly as states increase their investment and more states move to offer universal programs. States are also increasingly expanding their programs to serve 3-year-olds.

Several large urban school districts are experimenting with longer school days and years, while many districts in both rural and urban areas are expanding their involvement in out-of-school programming. More than half of kindergartners now attend full-day (instead of part-day) kindergarten. Half of schools host some after-school or before-school activities, up from only one-sixth in 1988.

But schools are not the only, or even the main, provider of preschool and out-of-school care. Most preschool and out-of-school programs continue to be delivered in community-based settings. Federal and state funding for such programs has grown rapidly, and business leaders have joined parents in calling for further expansions. So, expanded public provision or support for child care—with schools playing a larger role—seems an option whose time has come.

Even a large expansion of public provision, however, will not meet all the child care needs of employees, particularly for very young children or for emergency or back-up care. If the goal of policy is to support low- and moderate-income parents with child care costs, then expanding the existing subsidy and tax credit programs seems the most direct way of accomplishing that goal. Asking employers to subsidize costs would only duplicate existing programs and would pose a problem when employees changed jobs or were laid off.

What then should be employers' role in child care? Certainly, if employers can offer on- or near-site child care programs or contract with programs in their area, this should be encouraged and supported, through technical assistance and best practices dissemination, as well as through the existing employer tax credit. But many employers will not be in a position to offer care.[11] For those employers, a more sensible approach is to expand access to child care information and referral services.

CONCLUSIONS

The changing demographics of the American family and the labor force mean that employers and policymakers will have to think creatively about expanding work–family policies to support parents' employment and meet the needs of children when parents work. The current system, where benefits are tied to wages, results in less than socially optimal levels of benefits and in unequally distributed benefits across the four main areas of work–family policy: parental leave, other types of leave, flexible work hours, and child care.

What can be done to better support parents' employment and better meet the needs of children when parents work? In the area of parental leave, the United States should explore establishing a social insurance program, along the lines of California's new program, to provide some paid parental leave to all new parents. A social insurance program could also fund a minimal amount of paid sick leave or vacation leave for all employees. In the area of child care, many good federal, state, and employer programs already exist. Building on existing programs, policymakers should particularly emphasize expanding the role of the schools in providing preschool and after-school care, and expanding the role of employers in providing information and referral services and supporting on- or near-site child care programs where feasible.

One theme that emerges clearly is the importance of access to high-quality flextime and part-time time jobs. These are "benefits" that parents value highly and that are not costly to employers. So why don't more firms offer them? Perhaps employers have simply not realized how much parents would value flexible hours, or perhaps parents' desires for flexibility have only recently increased as more parents have found themselves managing as single parents or as part of dual-earner couples. But in any case, employers looking to attract and retain skilled young workers should target flextime and part-time benefits for expansion.

NOTES

The author gratefully acknowledges funding support from NICHD, the William T. Grant Foundation, Russell Sage Foundation, and John D. and Catherine T. MacArthur Foundation. She also thanks Kathleen Christenson, Nada Eissa, Isabel Sawhill, and the volume editors for helpful comments.

1. Health insurance and earnings supplements, while also very relevant to meeting the needs of children, are not covered because they are included elsewhere in this volume (see chapter 9). Elder care is not included because the focus here is on policies that help parents manage work and care for children.

2. In 8 states, the laws cover only public employees; in the other 12, they cover private-sector employees, but typically small firms are excluded. Like the FMLA, many state laws limit coverage to those who have worked a requisite number of hours in the prior year.

3. For more detail on child care programs, see Meyers et al. (2004) and Smolensky and Gootman (2003).

4. Comparable figures for the 1990s are unavailable due to changes in how child care assistance was measured (BLS did not collect data on I&R services until 2000), but it appears the share of employees receiving tangible help with funding or on- or near-site child care has not increased over time. In the 1990s,

the share of full-time employees receiving help with funding or on or near-site child care was 1–2 percent in small firms and 8–10 percent in medium- and large-sized firms.

5. For a more nuanced discussion of how employers decide what benefits to offer and to which workers, see Holzer (2005).

6. See Gruber and Krueger (1991) and Gruber (1992, 1994) for useful discussions and applications to workers compensation and health insurance coverage for maternity.

7. Any time the government sets up a social program funded by payroll taxes, some amount of deadweight loss will be associated with that tax. Given that the overall size of the program would be fairly small, the size of that deadweight loss is likely to be small as well.

8. Another option is to fund such programs through general revenues, as New Zealand does (Levin-Epstein 2004).

9. See also Crittenden (2001) and Williams (2000) on what employers expect of the ideal worker and how that conflicts with taking care of family responsibilities.

10. Some authors call for more fundamental reforms, such as reducing the length of the standard workweek; see, for instance, Gornick and Meyers (2003) and Jacobs and Gerson (2004).

11. See Kelly (2003) for a discussion of the factors that promote, or inhibit, establishment of employer-supported child care centers.

REFERENCES

Bernstein, Jared, and Karen Kornbluh. 2005. "Running Faster to Stay in Place: The Growth of Family Work Hours and Incomes." Washington, DC: New America Foundation.

Blank, Rebecca. 1990. "Are Part-Time Jobs Bad Jobs?" In *A Future of Lousy Jobs?* edited by Gary Burtless (123–55). Washington, DC: Brookings Institution Press.

Blau, David, and Janet Currie. 2006. "Pre-School, Day Care, and After-School Care: Who's Minding the Kids?" In *Handbook on the Economics of Education*, edited by Eric Hanushek and Finis Welsh (1164–278). Amsterdam: North-Holland.

BLS. See U.S. Bureau of Labor Statistics.

Cantor, David, Jane Waldfogel, Jeffrey Kerwin, Mareena McKinley Wright, Kerry Levin, John Rauch, Tracey Hagerty, and Martha Stapleton Kudela. 2001. *Balancing the Needs of Families and Employers: Family and Medical Leave Surveys*. Rockville, MD: Westat.

Christensen, Kathleen. 2005. "Achieving Work-Life Balance: Strategies for Dual Earner Families." In *Being Together, Working Apart*, edited by Barbara Schneider and Linda Waite. Cambridge: Cambridge University Press.

Crittenden, Ann. 2001. *The Price of Motherhood: Why the Most Important Job in the World Is Still the Least Valued*. New York: Metropolitan Books.

Currie, Janet. 2001. "Early Childhood Intervention Programs: What Do We Know?" *Journal of Economic Perspectives* 15(2): 213–38.

Ferber, Marianne, and Jane Waldfogel. 1998. "The Long-Term Consequences of Nontraditional Employment." *Monthly Labor Review* 121(5): 3–12.

Galinsky, Ellen, and James T. Bond. 2000. "Supporting Families as Primary Caregivers: The Role of the Workplace." In *Infants and Toddlers in Out-of-Home Care*, edited by Debby Cryer and Thelma Harms (chapter 11). Baltimore, MD: Paul Brookes Publishing.

Galinsky, Ellen, James T. Bond, and E. Jeffrey Hill. 2004. *When Work Works: A Status Report on Workplace Flexibility*. New York: Families and Work Institute.

Gormley, William, and Ted Gayer. 2005. "Promoting School Readiness in Oklahoma: An Evaluation of Tulsa's Pre-K Program." *Journal of Human Resources* 40(3): 533–58.

Gormley, William, Ted Gayer, Deborah Phillips, and Brittany Dawson. 2005. "The Effects of Universal Pre-K on Cognitive Development." *Developmental Psychology* 41(6): 872–84.

Gornick, Janet C., and Marcia K. Meyers. 2003. *Families That Work: Policies for Reconciling Parenthood and Employment*. New York: Russell Sage Foundation.

Gruber, Jonathan. 1992. "The Efficiency of a Group-Specific Mandated Benefit: Evidence from Health Insurance Benefits for Maternity." Working Paper 4,157. Cambridge, MA: National Bureau of Economic Research.

———. 1994. "The Incidence of Mandated Maternity Benefits." *American Economic Review* 84(3): 622–41.

Gruber, Jonathan, and Alan Krueger. 1991. "The Incidence of Mandated Employer-Provided Insurance: Lessons from Workers' Compensation Insurance." In *Tax Policy and the Economy*, vol. 5, edited by David Bradford. Cambridge, MA: MIT Press.

Han, Wen-Jui, and Jane Waldfogel. 2003. "Parental Leave: The Impact of Recent Legislation on Parents' Leave-Taking." *Demography* 40(1): 191–200.

Heymann, Jody. 2000. *The Widening Gap: Why America's Working Families Are in Jeopardy and What Can Be Done about It*. New York: Basic Books.

Holzer, Harry. 2005. "Work and Family Life: The Perspective of Employers." In *Work, Family, Health, and Well-Being*, edited by Suzanne Bianchi, Lynne Casper, and Rosalind Berkowitz King (83–96). Mahwah, NJ: Lawrence Erlbaum.

Jacobs, Jerry A., and Kathleen Gerson. 2004. *The Time Divide: Work, Family, and Gender Inequality*. Cambridge, MA: Harvard University Press.

Kelly, Erin L. 2003. "The Strange History of Employer-Sponsored Child Care: Interested Actors, Uncertainty, and the Transformation of Law in Organizational Fields." *American Journal of Sociology* 109(3): 606–49.

Kmec, Julie A. 1999. "Multiple Aspects of Work-Family Conflict." *Sociological Forces* 32(3): 265–85.

Levin-Epstein, Jody. 2004. "Taking the Next Step: What Can the U.S. Learn about Parental Leave from New Zealand?" Washington, DC: Center for Law and Social Policy.

Magnuson, Katherine, Christopher Ruhm, and Jane Waldfogel. Forthcoming. "Does Prekindergarten Improve School Preparation and Performance?" *Economics of Education Review*.

Magnuson, Katherine, Marcia Meyers, Christopher Ruhm, and Jane Waldfogel. 2004. "Inequality in Preschool Education and School Readiness." *American Educational Research Journal* 41(1): 115–57.

Meyers, Marcia, Dan Rosenbaum, Christopher Ruhm, and Jane Waldfogel. 2004. "Inequality in Early Childhood Education and Care: What Do We

Know?" In *Social Inequality*, edited by Kathy Neckerman (223–70). New York: Russell Sage Foundation.

Mitchell, Olivia. 1990. "The Effects of Mandating Benefits Packages." *Research in Labor Economics* 11: 297–320.

Puma, Michael, Stephen Bell, Ronna Cook, Camilla Heid, and Michael Lopez. 2005. "Head Start Impact Study: First Year Findings." Washington, DC: U.S. Department of Health and Human Services, Administration for Children and Families.

Ross Phillips, Katherin. 2004. "Getting Time Off: Access to Leave among Working Parents." *Assessing the New Federalism* Policy Brief B-57. Washington, DC: The Urban Institute.

Ruhm, Christopher. 1997. "Policy Watch: The Family and Medical Leave Act." *Journal of Economic Perspectives* 11(3): 175–86.

Shipler, David. 2004. *The Working Poor: Invisible in America*. New York: Alfred A. Knopf.

Smolensky, Eugene, and Jennifer Gootman, eds. 2003. *Working Families and Growing Kids: Caring for Children and Adolescents*. Washington, DC: National Academy Press.

Stork, Diana, Fiona Wilson, Andrea Wicks Bowles, Jenny Sproull, and Jennifer Bena. 2005. "The New Workforce Reality: Insights for Today, Implications for Tomorrow." Boston, MA: Simmons School of Management and Bright Horizons Family Solutions.

Summers, Lawrence. 1989. "Some Simple Economics of Mandated Benefits." *American Economic Review* 79(2): 177–83.

Tanaka, Sakiko. 2005. "Parental Leave and Child Health across OECD Countries." *The Economic Journal* 115(501): F7–F28.

Tilly, Chris. 1996. *Half a Job: Bad and Good Part-Time Jobs in a Changing Labor Market*. Philadelphia, PA: Temple University Press.

U.S. Bureau of Labor Statistics. 2005. *National Compensation Survey: Employee Benefits in Private Industry in the United States, March 2005*. Washington, DC: U.S. Department of Labor, Bureau of Labor Statistics.

Waldfogel, Jane. 1999. "Family Leave Coverage in the 1990s." *Monthly Labor Review* 122(10): 13–21.

———. 2001a. "Family-Friendly Policies for Families with Young Children." *Employee Rights and Employment Policy Journal* 5(1): 273–96.

———. 2001b. "Family and Medical Leave: Evidence from the 2000 Surveys." *Monthly Labor Review* 124(9): 17–23.

———. 2006a. "Early Childhood Policy: A Comparative Perspective." In *The Blackwell Handbook of Early Childhood Development*, edited by Kathleen McCartney and Deborah Phillips (576–94). Malden, MA: Blackwell Publishing, Inc.

———. 2006b. *What Children Need*. Cambridge, MA: Harvard University Press.

Williams, Joan. 2000. *Unbending Gender: Why Family and Work Conflict and What to Do about It*. Oxford: Oxford University Press.

ABOUT THE EDITORS

Harry J. Holzer is a professor of public policy at Georgetown University and a visiting fellow at the Urban Institute in Washington, D.C. He has served as associate dean of public policy at Georgetown (2004–06) and as acting dean in fall 2006. He is a former chief economist for the U.S. Department of Labor and a former professor of economics at Michigan State University. Dr. Holzer's research focuses primarily on the labor market problems of low-wage workers and other disadvantaged groups. His books include *The Black Youth Employment Crisis* (edited with Richard Freeman, University of Chicago Press, 1986); *What Employers Want: Job Prospects for Less-Educated Workers* (Russell Sage Foundation, 1996); *Employers and Welfare Recipients: The Effects of Welfare Reform in the Workplace* (with Michael Stoll, Public Policy Institute of California, 2001); *The Economics of Affirmative Action* (edited with David Neumark, Edward Elgar, 2004); *Moving Up or Moving On: Who Advances in the Low-Wage Labor Market?* (with Fredrik Andersson and Julia Lane, Russell Sage Foundation, 2005); and *Reconnecting Disadvantaged Young Men* (with Peter Edelman and Paul Offner, Urban Institute Press, 2006).

Demetra Smith Nightingale is on the faculty of the Institute for Policy Studies at Johns Hopkins University, where she is a principal research scientist. Much of her research involves evaluating policies and programs, especially those related to workforce development and welfare. Another stream of her research focuses on the functioning of the labor market, particularly changes in the structure of the nation's economy, the shift in employment opportunities for persons with limited education and skills, career ladders, nontraditional jobs for women, employment of maturing and older workers, and lifelong learning options for workers at all levels. Her books include *The Work Alternative: Welfare Reform and the Realities of the Job Market* (edited with Robert H. Haveman, Urban Institute Press, 1995), and *The Low-Wage Labor Market: Challenges and Opportunities* (edited with Kelleen Kaye, Urban Institute Press, 2000). Before joining Johns Hopkins, Dr. Nightingale spent over 25 years at the Urban Institute, most recently as a principal research associate and program director in the Labor and Social Policy Center. She is a senior affiliate of the National Poverty Center at the University of Michigan.

ABOUT THE CONTRIBUTORS

Burt S. Barnow is associate director for research and a principal research scientist at the Institute for Policy Studies at Johns Hopkins University. Dr. Barnow has over 25 years experience as an economist and manager of research projects in program evaluation, performance analysis, labor economics, welfare, poverty, child support, fatherhood, marriage, and employment. Before joining the Institute for Policy Studies in 1992, Dr. Barnow spent eight years at the Lewin Group and nearly nine years in the U.S. Department of Labor. He has published widely in the fields of labor economics and evaluation, including *Improving the Odds: Publicly Funded Training in a Changing Labor Market* (edited with Christopher T. King, Urban Institute Press, 2000) and *Evaluating Comprehensive State Welfare Reform: The Wisconsin Works Program* (edited with Thomas Kaplan and Robert Moffitt, Rockefeller Institute Press, 2000).

Gary Burtless holds the John C. and Nancy D. Whitehead Chair in Economic Studies at the Brookings Institution in Washington, D.C., where he has been a scholar since 1981. He researches issues associated with public finance, aging, saving, labor markets, income distribution, social insurance, and the behavioral effects of government tax and transfer policy. Burtless is coauthor of *Globaphobia: Confronting Fears about Open Trade* (1998); *Five Years After: The Long Term Effects of Welfare-to-Work Programs* (1995), *Growth with Equity: Economic Policymaking for the Next Century* (1993), and *Can America Afford to Grow Old? Paying for Social Security* (1989). He also edited and contributed to *Aging*

Societies: The Global Dimension (1998), and *Does Money Matter? The Effect of School Resources on Student Achievement and Adult Success* (1996), among other works.

Dan Bloom is director of the welfare and barriers to employment policy area at MDRC. He has directed three large-scale evaluations of state welfare reform waiver projects, and he is currently helping manage both the multisite Employment Retention and Advancement evaluation and the Enhanced Services for the Hard-to-Employ project. He has written more than 20 research reports, as well as a book—*After AFDC: Welfare-to-Work Choices and Challenges for States* (MDRC, 1997)—summarizing lessons learned from studies of welfare-to-work programs. He was a member of the team that developed the Parents' Fair Share Demonstration, and he managed MDRC's evaluation of Ohio's Learning, Earnings and Parenting (LEAP) program. He previously worked for America Works and for the Center on Budget and Policy Priorities.

George J. Borjas is the Robert W. Scrivner Professor of Economics and Social Policy at the John F. Kennedy School of Government, Harvard University. He is also a research associate at the National Bureau of Economic Research. Professor Borjas's books include *Wage Policy in the Federal Bureaucracy* (American Enterprise Institute, 1980); three editions of *Labor Economics* (McGraw-Hill, 1996, 2000, 2005), and *Heaven's Door: Immigration Policy and the American Economy* (Princeton University Press, 1999). He has published more than 100 articles in books and scholarly journals, including the *American Economic Review*, the *Journal of Political Economy*, and the *Quarterly Journal of Economics*. His articles and editorials also appear regularly in major magazines and newspapers, including *The Atlantic Monthly*, *National Review*, *The New York Times*, *The Wall Street Journal*, and *Le Monde*.

David Butler is a vice president of MDRC and director of the welfare and barriers to employment policy area. He directs the development and implementation of MDRC demonstration projects and leads the organization's technical assistance work. He currently manages the launch of a major new initiative, Enhanced Services for the Hard-to-Employ. With a special interest in transitional employment programs, Butler has directed operations of major projects, including the Jobs-Plus Community Revitalization Initiative for Public Housing Residents, the project on Devolution and Urban Change, the National Evaluation of Welfare-to-Work Strategies, and the Employment Retention and Advancement project. Before joining MDRC, Butler served as deputy commissioner for planning for New York City's Human Resource Administration.

Richard B. Freeman is a professor in economics at Harvard University, Labor Studies Program Director at NBER, and a senior research fellow at the Centre for Economic Performance, London School of Economics. His research interests include the job market for scientists and engineers; the growth and decline of unions; employee involvement programs; international labor markets; restructuring European welfare states; income distribution and equity in the marketplace; the effects of immigration and trade on inequality; international labor standards; Chinese labor markets; transitional economies; and the effects of the Internet on labor markets, social behavior, and the economy.

Robert I. Lerman, a senior fellow at the Urban Institute and professor of economics at American University, has conducted research and policy analyses on a wide range of issues involving employment, family structure, income support, and youth development, especially as they affect low-income populations. In the 1970s, he worked on reforming national income maintenance programs and on youth employment policies as staff economist for both the Congressional Joint Economic Committee and the U.S. Department of Labor. Dr. Lerman was one of the first scholars to examine the patterns and economic determinants of unwed fatherhood and to propose a youth apprenticeship strategy in the United States. His currently researches the interactions between men's marital status and labor market outcomes and the impact of public and private initiatives to strengthen marriage.

Alicia H. Munnell is the Peter Drucker Professor of Management Sciences at the Carroll School of Management and the director of the Center for Retirement Research at Boston College. Professor Munnell spent most of her professional career at the Federal Reserve Bank of Boston, where she became senior vice president and director of research in 1984. During the 1990s, she served on the President's Council of Economic Advisers and was assistant secretary of the Treasury for economic policy. Professor Munnell was co-founder and first president of the National Academy of Social Insurance and is a member of the American Academy of Arts and Sciences, the Institute of Medicine, the National Academy of Public Administration, and the Pension Research Council at Wharton.

Paul Osterman is the Nanyang Professor of Human Resources at the Sloan School of Management and the Department of Urban Planning, Massachusetts Institute of Technology. He is also deputy dean of the Sloan School. Dr. Osterman has written four books, including *Gathering Power: The Future of Progressive Politics in America* (Beacon

Press, 2003) and *Securing Prosperity: How the American Labor Market Has Changed and What to Do about It* (Princeton University Press, 1999). He has also cowritten and edited several volumes, including *Working in America: A Blueprint for the New Labor Market* and *Internal Labor Markets*. In addition, Dr. Osterman has written numerous academic journal articles and policy issue papers on such topics as the organization of work within firms, labor market policy, and economic development.

S arah Turner is an associate professor of education and economics at the University of Virginia. She is also a research affiliate of the Population Studies Center at the University of Michigan. Dr. Turner specializes in research on the economics of education in the United States. She has written extensively on the economics of higher education, including the behavioral effects of financial aid policies and the entry of new providers. She is currently collaborating with John Bound on a Russell Sage Foundation–supported project analyzing mobility of college-educated workers using U.S. census data.

J ane Waldfogel is a professor of social work and public affairs at Columbia University School of Social Work and a research associate at the Centre for Analysis of Social Exclusion, London School of Economics. She currently studies family leave, inequality in early childhood care and education, and child abuse and neglect. Dr. Waldfogel is a member of the (U.K.) Advisory Committee for the National Evaluation of Sure Start and was a member of the (U.S.) National Academy of Science's Committee on Family and Work Policies. Her books include *What Children Need* (Harvard University Press, 2006), *The Future of Child Protection: How to Break the Cycle of Abuse and Neglect* (Harvard University Press, 1998), and *Securing the Future: Investing in Children from Birth to Adulthood* (edited with Sheldon Danziger, Russell Sage Foundation, 2000).

INDEX

lower-income workers and families
  access to employer-provided child
    care programs, 283
  access to higher education, xxvii,
    96–101, 112*n*
  economic mobility and, 120
  funding for training and educa-
    tion of, xxvii
  Project QUEST and, 136–37
  representation at most selective
    colleges, 99–100
  training and education of, xxvii,
    119–20, 126, 127, 142–43
  WIRE-net and, 137

MacKenzie, Doris L., 170
Mane, Ferran, 64
Manpower Development and Training Act of 1962, 26, 148
Manufacturing Extension Partnership, 138–39
manufacturing sector
  apprenticeships in, 48
  decline of jobs in, xii
  public-private partnership for
    workforce development in,
    85*n*
Marcotte, David, 67
Massachusetts
  health care plan in, xxvi, 266
  job training programs in, 135
  unemployment insurance benefits
    in, 244
  Workforce Training Fund, 138
mathematical skills
  demand for, 15–19
  types needed for jobs, 74, 85*n*
Mathematica Policy Research on
  impact of Job Corps, 70
Medicare, xiv, xxiv, xxx*n*, 261, 266
  older workers and, 227
  Part B premiums, 204
mental retardation, 158, 167
merit aid programs, xx, 108, 109,
  110–11
Mexico, immigration from, 184–85
Michigan
  academic standards in, 74
  job training programs in, 129–30
  unemployment insurance benefits
    in, 245
Mikelson, Kelly, 55

Milwaukee and job placement assistance, 123, 130
minimum wage, xxix, 124
minorities. *See also* immigration
  black-white gap in high school
    graduation and GED certifi-
    cation rates, 59
  ex-prisoners and employment
    issues, 169
  increase in higher education of, 12
  projections for workforce popula-
    tion, xii, 7
  Social Security benefits and, 227
  temporary employment and,
    122–23
Mississippi's unemployment insurance benefits, 244
Mt. Hood Community College, 138
Munnell, Alicia H., xv, xxiii–xxiv,
  201–29
Murnane, Richard, 42

NAFTA debate in U.S., 11
National Assessment of Vocational
  Education (NAVE) on effec-
  tiveness of vocational courses,
  63
National Association of Manufactur-
  ers (NAM) on coming labor
  shortage, 4
National Center for Educational Sta-
  tistics
  on high school diploma and GED
    certification status of youth,
    59
  on projection of highly educated
    workers in U.S., 12
National Compensation Survey of
  Occupational Wages, 149*n*
National Evaluation of Welfare to
  Work Strategies, 129
National Governors Association
  (NGA) study on job training
  programs, 31, 74, 75
National Guard Youth ChalleNGe
  program, xix, 81, 83
National Household Education Sur-
  vey (NHES) Program
  on apprenticeship participation,
    54–55
  on job training, 124
National Income and Product
  Accounts, 206–7

The smash
#1 *New York Times* bestseller

"*Yes Please* delivers what it should: life lessons and vicarious thrills. . . . The book is largely a portrait of confidence. Reading it, some of it rubs off on us." —*The New Yorker*

"*Yes Please* is a great story . . . because it is self-damning and hopeful at the same time." —*LA Times*

"Pure charm." —*People*

"Poehler is very funny, so the jokes are very good. . . . Poehler is very wise, so her advice is on point." —Slate

"Delightful. *Yes Please* is less a book and more a compendium, in which a memoir, advice column, essay collection, faded photographs and ripped diary pages intersect. Poehler is frank and funny throughout the book, as is her nature, but her writing unearths a wise narrator who's seen some of the worst of life and come out the other side unscathed. . . . Can we get more from Amy Poehler? Yes, seriously, please." —*Newsweek*

"Demonstrates the skill of this excellent comic actress, a funny woman who roots hilarity in specifics." —*Washington Post*

"Required reading for all young women." —Huffington Post

"[*Yes Please*] is honest words of wisdom within a joyous story structure." —*Philadelphia Inquirer*

"*Yes Please* veers between reminiscing and philosophizing. Poehler had developed some principles over the years and shares them in usually funny fashion." —*Chicago Sun-Times*

"The path of comedic genius doesn't have to be dark and stormy, as Amy Poehler demonstrates in her bristlingly intelligent, guffaw-out-loud memoir, *Yes Please*. . . . But don't take Poehler for a blonde with no bite; she shares plenty of tales of mischief, mayhem, and even remorse. . . . *Yes Please* isn't a scan of the comedic brain so much as it is something far better—the full exposure of Poehler's funny and very magnanimous heart." —*Elle*